Praise for *The Big Bloody Book of Violence*

"In this sequel to the *Little Black Book of Violence*, Kane and Wilder go both deeper and broader into the thorny subject of violence. It's been six years since the LBBV hit bookstores, six years to learn, six years to grow. If you enjoyed the little black book and have matured over the last six years, you just might be ready for this one." **Rory Miller**, bestselling author of 17 books, including *Facing Violence* and *Meditations on Violence*

"I am a university professor and know Lawrence on a professional level through industry associations we both belong to. While I knew that Lawrence was a popular author and self-defense expert, martial arts really aren't my thing… Quite honestly, *The Big Bloody Book of Violence* would never have been on my radar screen to purchase or read, but when Lawrence asked me as a fellow author to review his manuscript as a favor I agreed. What I quickly realized in the first few pages is just how much someone like me SHOULD be reading this book.

"First, the authors do a fabulous job of putting violence in perspective. I was fascinated to learn about the types of criminals and their behavior patterns. But most importantly, I was glad to read the awesome tips that will help me be more consciously aware in the future. Will I become a martial arts expert after reading this book? No, of course not. Will I take a martial arts class? Likely not. But I WILL apply many of the practical tips that the authors recommend herein, actions which ANYONE can implement to help keep themselves safe.

"Thank you Lawrence and Kris for making me more aware and better prepared! Kudos for bringing such an important and often unspoken topic to the forefront. It enables simple 'sheep' like me to understand that I really do need to be responsible for my own safety, to be more aware of what's going on. I may not win if I find myself facing a big bad guy, but I certainly have a better chance than I did before reading this book. And, I now know how to avoid doing really stupid things. I'm very glad I read it." **Kate Vitasek**, Faculty, Graduate and Executive Education, University of Tennessee

---

"From the first pages of this book it is refreshingly apparent that Kane and Wilder are not suggesting ways or means to kick, punch, or shoot yourself out of a bad situation. The authors have taken a much needed and wholly accurate down-to-earth approach that addresses the realities of being able to identify, act, survive, and prepare for the aftermath of being engaged in a life-threatening event. This account will stop us from smiling with blinders on and allow us to take in our environment and its dangers while educating us in a smart response on how to survive in a perilous world. Highly recommended reading!" **David A. Davies**, security consultant and author

---

"Comprehensive and thorough, this big book lasers right in on its subject without ego or other distractions. Threats defined and methods recommended to avoid or to counter falling prey to violence are numerous and realistic. Implementing even a fraction of this book's suggestions will substantially increase your overall safety. I just wish the title was less provocative; I wouldn't want *The Big Bloody Book of Violence* discovered on my bookshelf and misinterpreted if, Heaven forbid, I'm ever investigated after using force in self-defense." **Gila Hayes**, Armed Citizens' Legal Defense Network

---

"Kane and Wilder do an excellent job of pointing out that the sexes are not equal. In a self-defense book it is vital that REALITY is the focus and they do this well. As much as the media would like you to believe that men and women are the same—in the world of violence, nothing could be further from the truth. The authors give great advice for the average woman when it comes to what they need to do if they are concerned about being responsible for their own safety. Kudos to the authors for avoiding the all too common Political Correctness crap and telling it like it is." **Tracy A. Getty**, Washington State Certified Handgun and Shotgun Instructor

---

"Fewer things alarm people more than the thought that they, or even worse their loved ones, could be the victim of crime. Particularly violent crime. It's a fear that oftentimes exists far out of proportion to the probability of it actually occurring. Still, being a victim of a violent crime is unfortunately not a rare occurrence, even while violent crime rates continue to fall. So it is incumbent upon you, the individual, to take responsibility for your own safety. No one is more invested in your safety than you are. As the saying goes, 'when seconds count, the police are minutes away.' I say that as the police. We will bust our ass to get there and risk our lives for you when we arrive, but you have to make it to that point. The heavy lifting is on you.

"Lawrence Kane and Kris Wilder have written a great preparatory book to aid you in beginning your education in self-defense. It is refreshingly light on actual physical techniques. Instead it spends the majority of its time where it's most needed—the mental aspects of self-defense, awareness and avoidance. This is where the bulk of self-protection lies, and where very few books spend any time. It also deals heavily with legal aspects, which is another aspect almost universally ignored in most purported self-defense books. Teaching people self-defense without also teaching self-defense law is like teaching someone to drive without teaching them traffic law. You can be the most proficient steering wheel turner the world has ever seen, can work the clutch like a pro, whatever, but if you don't know what side of the road to drive on, or to stop at a red light, your driving experience will not be a successful one.

"This is a very broad work, although due to the extensive nature of the subject, it only lightly touches each component of the totality of self-defense. A thorough book on the subject would be the size and weight where it could be used defensively… in self-defense situation. No, think of this is an 'Intro to Self Defense' class if you will. It will give you the solid basics you need. Once you have those down, then you'll know where you need to spend more time in advanced studies for you and your family's safety and peace of mind." **Montie Guthrie**, 25-year law enforcement veteran and Federal Air Marshal

---

"The authors of *The Big Bloody Book of Violence* used anecdotes, case histories, and their personal expertise to create what they call 'The Smart Persons' Guide for Surviving Dangerous Times.' This is a must read for anyone who plans to venture outside their home without a bodyguard." **William C. Dietz**, *New York Times* bestselling author of more than 40 novels

---

"Many 'self-defense' books contain little more than variations of how to strike, kick, grapple and related physical techniques. These books often neglect the fact that self-defense is not just a narrow set of fighting skills, but rather a lifestyle choice. Kane and Wilder don't just understand this; they've set out to convince you of this fact. In a recent conversation with Lawrence Kane about this book and related topics, we both acknowledged that if a situation goes physical, something was already done wrong. We spent considerable time discussing the broad spectrum that 'self-defense' covers. I am glad he and Wilder wrote another book addressing such matters.

"This book doesn't set out to turn readers into macho ass kickers. Instead, it provides valuable information on not only how to avoid and prevent violence, but how to respond with informed, thoughtful reason. This might be walking away, and it may be killing an attacker before he kills you. But if it is the latter, it's not because of a flippant 'I rather be tried by 12 than carried by 6' attitude, but rather because you are prepared and there was no other choice to save your or someone else's life.

"*The Big Bloody Book of Violence* a continuation of their excellent book, *The Little Black Book of Violence*, provides practical and realistic advice on self-defense and surviving dangerous situations. It will have you thinking about aspects of violence that you may never have considered before, and once you do think about what they discuss in this text, you'll better understand why self-defense isn't just about fighting, and why lifestyle choices that keep you from fighting should be your first line of defense. The smart choices they provide in this book just might save your life. If you listen to them that is, and if you implement the choices in your daily life…

"Both books, *The Little Black Book of Violence* and *The Big Bloody Book of Violence* should be read by anyone wanting to better understand violence, and more importantly, survive the violence we face in these dangerous times." **Alain Burrese**, J.D., former U.S. Army sniper, safety/self-defense instructor, and author of *Hard-Won Wisdom From The School of Hard Knocks*

––––––––––––––––––

"As a former police officer and journalist who observed violence and wrote about it for more than 25 years, I can honestly say Lawrence and Kris have pulled together the kind of advice and tips you won't find outside the police academy. This is an insider's bible to violence, what it is, how to spot it and how to avoid it. It's filled with case studies, real people, real stories and advice that works. If you read one book on self-protection, this is it." **Becky Blanton**, TED Global speaker

––––––––––––––––––

"This book is the perfect follow up to *The Little Black Book of Violence*. Kane and Wilder use real world examples to clarify their points. They share much more than the situational awareness to avoid incidents and the physical techniques to deal with an incident; they cover the after action legal quagmire that is often forgotten. Kane and Wilder are prime examples of mentors. They have acquired applicable and relevant information that they readily share with others. This book will be added to my collection of 'required reading' for myself and my family." **Frank Getty**, former USMC 5811 (Military Police)

––––––––––––––––––

"*The Big Bloody Book of Violence* is an outstanding companion volume to Lawrence Kane and Kris Wilder's book, *The Little Black Book of Violence*. In this opus the authors take a strategic, 30,000 foot view of violence and how everyday people can protect themselves from it. Furthermore in each chapter the authors use case studies to descend to the tactical ground level view in order to show how theory can be put into practice. I recommend this book for security pros and complete novices; everyone will get something valuable from reading this tome. If the average person practices a fraction of what is covered in this book they will be more aware and less of a target. After having read their first book about violence I was not sure if the authors could top themselves... They have." **Captain Jay Matzko**, USN, US Navy pilot and martial artist

––––––––––––––––––

The Big Bloody Book of Violence

The Big Bloody Book of Violence

THE SMART PERSON'S GUIDE FOR SURVIVING DANGEROUS TIMES

WHAT EVERYONE MUST KNOW ABOUT SELF-DEFENSE

Lawrence Kane & Kris Wilder

Stickman Publications, Inc.
Burien, WA 98146
www.westseattlekarate.com

Book Layout ©2013 BookDesignTemplates.com

Cover art and interior design by Kami Miller

Illustrations by MSB Design, Seattle (mike@msbdesign.net)

Photos by Lawrence A. Kane and Kris Wilder, except as otherwise noted

The Big Bloody Book of Violence/ Wilder, Kris; Kane, Lawrence. —1st ed.

ISBN-13 978-0692503447

ISBN-10 0692503447

Disclaimer

While self-defense is legal, fighting is illegal. If you don't know the difference you'll go to jail because you aren't defending yourself, you are fighting—or worse. Readers are encouraged to be aware of all appropriate local and national laws relating to self-defense, reasonable force, and the use of weaponry, and to act in accordance with all applicable laws at all times. Understand that while legal definitions and interpretations are generally uniform, there are small—but very important—differences from state to state and even city to city. To stay out of jail, you need to know these differences. Neither the authors nor the publisher assumes any responsibility for the use or misuse of information contained in this book.

Information in this book is distributed "As Is," without warranty. Nothing in this document constitutes a legal opinion nor should any of its contents be treated as such. While the authors believe that everything herein is accurate, any questions regarding specific self-defense situations, legal liability, and/or interpretation of federal, state, or local laws should always be addressed by an attorney at law.

*When it comes to martial arts, self-defense, and related topics, no text, no matter how well written, can substitute for professional, hands-on instruction. These materials should be used **for academic study only**.*

DEDICATION

"To flee vice is the beginning of virtue, and to have got rid of folly is the beginning of wisdom."

– Horace

For Max Kane. While Max was dealing with Stage 4 cancer, his wife Ginger's medical condition became more acute than his own. A devoted husband, he postponed getting needed chemotherapy for himself so that he would be well enough to care for her and to transport her regularly to the emergency room for the blood transfusions she often needed. A stand-up guy who always did the right thing, he worked for 38 years as a court reporter which gave him ample insight into those who did not. His walk through life led him along a higher path of humanity and compassion, an example we would all do well to follow.

TABLE OF CONTENTS

ACKNOWLEDGEMENTS

Thanks to Clint Overland for sharing his unique insight into criminality and professional violence, to Martin Cooper for sharing his wisdom and experience about how cops around the world think and act, and to Lisa A. Christensen who provided brilliant insight into what it takes to make women's self-defense effective. Rory Miller, Zach Zinn, and retired Portland PD officer Anthony Marshall graciously allowed us to use their photos. Early readers Lisa A. Christensen, Andrew Crain, Emily Crain, Syriana Crain, David A. Davies, Montie Guthrie, Marc MacYoung, and Rory Miller kept us honest and provided discerning feedback. We owe a special debt of gratitude to Brandon Canonica, Michael Canonica, Sean Canonica, Grayson Collins, Mary Collins, Jon Crain, Lori Crain, Edward Glenn, James Howard, Joey Kane, Joseph Lamp, Chris Mort, Peter Mort, Chris Nunez, Andy Orose, Randy Staula, Christopher Webb, Colin Wiggins, and Jackson Wilder who modeled for our pictures.

FOREWORD

"The superior man, when resting in safety, does not forget that danger may come. When in a state of security he does not forget the possibility of ruin. When all is orderly, he does not forget that disorder may come. Thus his person is not endangered, and his States and all their clans are preserved." – Confucius

Loren Christensen began his martial arts training in 1965, earning 11 black belts over the years, 8 in karate, 2 in jujitsu, and 1 in arnis. He is a retired police officer with 29 years of experience in military and civilian law enforcement, where he specialized in street gangs, defensive tactics, and dignitary protection. A martial arts Masters Hall of Fame inductee, he is the author of more than 50 books, fiction and nonfiction. His nonfiction work includes books on the martial arts, self-defense, law enforcement, nutrition, prostitution, meditation, and post-traumatic stress disorder. His book *On Combat*, which he co-authored with Lt .Col. Dave Grossman, is mandatory reading at the United States War College in Washington, DC. Loren's web site is www.lwcbooks.com.

From the late 1980s into the early 1990s, several new street self-defense writers—men who had been there and done that—arrived on the scene and, while they didn't turn the world of self-defense completely upside down, they for sure got it thinking. These writers—Marc MacYoung, Peyton Quinn, and <ahem> me, and a few others—offered fresh insight into violence and personal safety, along with a new way for martial artists to look at their training.

Martial artists were suddenly asking themselves, "Will my classical style work in the mean streets?" "Will my sports-oriented system work against someone hell bent on rearranging my facial features?" "Will my sure-fire-point-winning technique stop a guy coming at me armed with a tire iron?" Non-martial artists were asking smart questions too, and rethinking what they had so firmly believed were truths about personal safety for themselves and their loved ones.

Some people scorned us, but happily not many. Most were excited about this new way of looking at violence. Non-martial artists quickly went about fixing, altering, or completely revamping their thinking about their safety, and martial artists began to examine ways to make their training more street applicable.

I like to think those martial artists willing to change were students and teachers not encumbered by ego. Instead, they were people open minded enough to accept this new insight—one based on worldly experience, not theory—because they sought more functional self-defense for themselves and, as responsible teachers, they wanted the best for students, i.e., applicable information and training to face an enormously cruel world.

As I write this, the bloody headlines in the newspaper and all over the Internet are about Baltimore, Maryland where on a recent weekend there were 32 reported shootings, leaving 26 wounded and nine killed. I'm betting the numbers were higher because having been a cop for 25 years I know not all shootings are reported. There were likely more that occurred in houses and back alleys where it was quickly decided to not involve the police; keep it in house, so to speak. I would also argue there was more violence than just gunfire. Emergency rooms no doubt were crowded with stabbing victims, people beaten with heavy objects, whipped with chains, and with the winners and losers of empty-hand fighting.

Such occurrences are commonplace in big cities; less so in small towns, but stuff still happens in them too. Spend a weekend evening in any big city hospital ER or ride with a police officer and your eyes will be filled with "wonders" you aren't likely to soon forget. For sure it will give you pause to think about what efforts you're making to ensure your personal safety and of those closest to you.

There is much you can do to give you and your family an edge during these dark times; others are doing it now. Martial arts classes are full, an increasing number of people are carrying concealed gun permits, and more and more people are talking safety (the exceptions being the profoundly naïve and those happy to remain in their denial) than any time in recent years. New books on personal safety are published regularly, and magazines offer articles on everything from prepping for the apocalypse to surviving a home invasion.

This is a good thing, though many of them fall short of one key element.

"What is the most important weapon, master," the novice asks the wizened kung fu teacher. "Is it my fists? My kicks? My sword?"

The master snaps his hand out and smacks the beginner's forehead. "It is in there. Your mind. That is your greatest weapon."

Lawrence Kane and Kris Wilder are masters of our greatest weapon, the mind, and it shows not only in this current work *The Big Bloody Book of Violence*, but in their previous books, blogs, and interviews. In short, they aren't just experts at punching, kicking, and slamming people to the mat; they also possess a deep knowledge of the profoundly important issue we're all concerned about: crime, violence, survival, and a legal system with all its strengths and weaknesses.

Too many people think they understand violence—doctors, lawyers, politicians and, sadly, quite a few martial arts teachers. Unfortunately, many are so convinced that what they "know" is gospel, they can't be told otherwise. For example, see Chapter 2, "The People in Charge Don't Understand Violence" in *The Big Bloody Book of Violence* for an all-too-typical exchange with such a person. This time coauthor Lawrence Kane tried to get a doctor friend to understand why the police don't shoot at the bad guys' legs. Although the doctor had never treated a gunshot wound and never fired a gun this didn't prevent her from having an unchangeable opinion on the matter.

Well, your authors understand violence through their personal experiences, training, and in depth research and interviews. Fortunately for us, they are also expert at communicating their research and hard-earned knowledge so the open-minded reader (as opposed to the close-minded doctor) not only understands the critical issue but acquires practical information to put into place a plan of action for themselves, their family and their loved ones.

Whether you're a hard training martial artist, jogger, camper, bank teller, store clerk, parent, student, or any other person concerned about what is going on the mean streets of our cities, understand that Lawrence Kane and Kris Wilder are powerful voices on the broad topic of self-defense for this new millennium. This is reflected in their past works and now in *The Big Bloody Book of Violence*. They are indeed a welcome treasure for these troubling times.

You did a wise thing picking up this fine book. Now get to it because doing nothing won't keep you safe.

Only knowledge and action will.

INTRODUCTION

"Violence isn't always evil. What's evil is the infatuation with violence."

– Jim Morrison

Due to a recent spate of burglaries in the neighborhood and robberies in her office building, Helen Weathers kept a loaded gun in her desk drawer whenever she worked nights or weekends. Usually it was the heirloom .357 caliber revolver she had inherited from a beloved relative, but that gun had malfunctioned when she had practiced with it at the range earlier so that night she had brought along a larger .44 magnum instead.

At 8:00 PM on New Year's Eve, Helen slipped the heavy pistol into her shoulder bag, gathered up her papers, locked her office door, and stepped out into the temperate Miami evening. As she adjusted the stack of magazines she was carrying under her arm and set off toward the lot where she had parked, she noticed that the streets were unusually quiet. Normal early-evening pedestrian traffic had been drawn to a parade a dozen blocks away.

She was passing a hedgerow that abutted the parking lot when a voice cried out, "Hey girl! Look over here!" A bare-chested, six foot tall man emerged from the bushes. He was carrying a newspaper in his right hand which he pulled aside to reveal a small semi-automatic pistol underneath. He pointed the gun at her head while grabbing her elbow.

"I'll give you money," Helen said quickly.

"Shut up and keep walking!" the stranger replied.

Clearly this wasn't a robbery. He half-led, half-dragged her deeper into the darkened parking lot, actions blocked from any passersby by the hedgerow he had hidden in moments earlier. As her captor looked nervously over his shoulder for witnesses, Helen used the distraction to slip her left hand into her shoulder bag, awkwardly grasping a hold of the pistol hidden inside.

As her captor dragged her deeper in the parking lot, he did another witness check giving her the opportunity to slip the gun out, hide it alongside her leg, and pull back the hammer. When he furtively looked around a third time she managed to break free from his grasp, swinging the big revolver up toward his stomach. Spying her movement, her assailant brought his own gun into play, the crack of his .25 caliber semiautomatic coming an instant before the boom of her .44 magnum.

As she felt impact against her left arm she pulled the trigger a second time. Moments later he was on the ground lying in a growing pool of blood while she landed in a sitting position next to him. She quickly scrambled back to her feet to look for help... When officers responded she was still dazed and confused, but uninjured. It turned out that the impact she'd perceived was the bone-jarring recoil from the big .44 magnum, something she'd never felt with her weak hand before, not the other guy's bullet as she had feared.

Her prospective rapist wasn't so lucky. He had instinctively brought his arm down into her line of fire where it was hit twice. His radius and ulna were broken, skin along his forearm peeled back like a banana, tendons destroyed, elbow and wrist shattered. He would never be able to use that arm properly again, but surprisingly enough despite the massive blood loss he was still alive and eventually faced trial.

Unfortunately he was acquitted.

In an interview after the case Helen reported, "It didn't help when the suspect's lawyer said, 'Why did you have such a gigantic gun if you didn't want to shoot somebody?' and I got mad and answered, 'Look, the way things are going in Miami lately, my next purchase is going to be a *tank*.'"

While Helen was never charged with any crime, she wasn't treated like a hero despite her bravery either. Inconsistencies in her initial story brought on by fear and shock, compounded by the "he said/she said" nature of the case (no witnesses came forward to testify) led the jury to let her assailant go.

If this was a fairy tale it would be old school Grimm, not modern Disney. The heroine escaped without injury, but the villain is still out there somewhere, perhaps plotting to strike again. Or maybe he learned his lesson and gave up his life of crime…

Violent encounters are rarely what you'd think. Oftentimes they last seconds yet have consequences that last for years or even lifetimes. The best ones are those you can avoid, of course, but as Helen Weathers and countless others have discovered the hard way **knowledge, preparation, and training can get you through those times when you must fight for your life and failure is not an option.** Who knows exactly what the assailant would have done had Helen

Weathers not been armed, but whatever it was it doesn't take much imagination to presume that it would have left her scarred for life… assuming she survived.

To be clear, in many ways Helen got lucky. She hadn't trained with her offhand at the range, thus had problems using the heavy revolver left-handed. The other guy caught sight of her gun and fired first, yet had she considered pulling the trigger while the weapon was still in her handbag he wouldn't have seen it coming. She would have been able to dispatch the threat without the risk of getting shot in the first place.[1] And, sadly she fell for "dirty lawyer tricks" which kept her testimony from leading to a conviction. Nevertheless, in the greater scheme of things all's well that ends well. **We can all learn something from her tenacity and fearlessness**.

According to the Bureau of Justice Statistics firearms are used in more than 80% of justifiable homicide cases, whereas in non-justifiable cases guns are used about 65% of the time. In 60% of justifiable homicides the deceased is a stranger, whereas in 75% of non-justifiable cases victims know their killers.

Speaking of lessons, our massive, 370-page tome *The Little Black Book of Violence* was a great starting point for those interested defending themselves. It armed readers with the knowledge and good sense to make informed decisions when facing dangerous situations like the one that Helen Weathers survived. But, in all honesty, it barely scratched the surface when it comes to this vitally important subject. Violence is a very extensive topic, which is why we felt compelled to write more.

In this book we delve deeper.

Our goal is to pick up where the previous book left off, helping you understand the larger picture and arming you with more holistic understanding of the subject matter. There is very little overlap between books since we assume that folks will read them in order, yet we do reinforce some critical concepts from the original throughout the text or summarize it in the appendices just in case this volume is where you begin.

Lt. Col. David Grossman popularized the theory that there are three kinds of people in the world: (1) sheep, (2) wolves, and (3) sheepdogs, a concept that was used to great effect in the movie *American Sniper*. Sheep are regular, productive, law abiding citizens with little or no capacity for violence. For the most part, they would rather not even know that such dangers exist. Paradoxically some even get violent about their beliefs (such as riots at peace rallies, death threats against law enforcement officers, and assaults on soldiers). Wolves are, of course, the dregs of society who prey upon the ignorant sheep. They are scam artists, robbers, rapists, murderers, muggers, and such. If you are a sheep who does not believe that wolves constitute a threat the odds

---

1   This is not uncommon; psychologically few folks—both good guys and bad guys—consider shooting through objects to hit their target, even obvious ones like cloth handbags or closed car windows that are unlikely to block or deflect a bullet.

are good that sooner or later a wolf will get you.

Sheepdogs protect the other sheep as well as themselves from the wolves. They are prepared to use countervailing force as necessary to defend themselves and others. They would rather not have to resort to violence, of course, but clearly feel a need to know how and when it is appropriate to do so. Since there is not a police officer on every corner, you must proactively **take responsibility for your own safety**. Be a sheepdog rather than a sheep. Once you begin to take possible threats seriously, you can begin do something about them. Acknowledgement is the first step. The next is action…

You'll find a common theme throughout this book, our challenge that you become responsible and accountable for your own safety and that of your loved ones. We throw down the gauntlet but also provide enough information and insight for you to pick it up with assuredness. By the time you finish reading we will have helped you know what you're fighting for, and against, as well as how to do so effectively. This information will **increase your odds of survival** on "that day" should it ever arrive.

CHAPTER 1

THERE'S NO SUCH THING AS SENSELESS VIOLENCE

"In a closed society where everybody's guilty, the only crime is getting caught. In a world of thieves, the only final sin is stupidity."

– Hunter S. Thompson

One day a scorpion approached the edge of a stream and wanted to cross. A rabbit came along and asked the scorpion what it was doing. The scorpion replied that he wanted to get to the other side, but could not swim. He wondered aloud if he could ride on the hare's back, serving as a set of eyes to help guide the two of them while the rabbit swam across.

Now the rabbit, he was no dummy. He was afraid that the scorpion would sting him if he let it onto his back yet the scorpion promised that he would never do such a thing because they would both drown. The rabbit accepting this promise let the scorpion climb onto his back and they began their journey. Halfway across the stream the scorpion raised his stinger and plunged it into the back of the rabbit injecting him with a fatal poison.

The rabbit screamed, "You promised you would not sting me. Now we are both going to die."

The scorpion replied, "I am a scorpion, this is what I do."

The preceding fable was written sometime around 600 BC. It has stood the test of time not only because of its powerful message but also because it makes intuitive sense. Scorpions, driven by instinct, strike out at other animals with their poisonous stingers. Unthinking animals, it is conceivable that they would perform such behaviors even at risk of their own lives. After all, honeybees die after using their stingers, but that doesn't keep them from doing it. What about people? We are more evolved, use higher reasoning. How much does that change things? Surprisingly not as much as you might think…

Social violence, the old "what are you looking at" sort of stuff used to protect turf, establish hierarchies, and attract members of the opposite sex runs contrary to common sense yet it happens all the time. Ever been to a nightclub frequented by hormone-addled young men and college coeds? How about a party around 2:00 AM as it starts to wind down and stragglers become desperate to hook up? You can see dysfunctional behaviors in certain settings virtually all the time. The good news is that those who can rise above their animal instincts **need not fear dangers from social violence** most of the time, as they have the wherewithal to swallow their pride, give the other guy a face-saving way out, and leave.

But, there are other kinds of violence, deeper, darker, and more dangerous kinds. Asocial or predatory violence is complex, disturbing, and, thankfully, far less common than social violence in most societies. But, far more often than not, if you are caught in its grasp **you cannot just walk away**. You'll need to fight your way free and may very well be maimed or killed in the process. It's important to know what you're facing because actions that can de-escalate social violence such as backing down and apologizing make you look like a compliant victim, hence can spark predatory violence.

We discussed these two types of violence in depth in the previous book, and summarize them here in Appendix A, but here's a quick overview to refresh your memory:

- The intent of **social violence** is to **affect your environment**. In other words, you want to establish dominance, educate somebody, get him or her out of your territory, or whatever. There are virtually always witnesses, because you are seeking status from the outcome much like the schoolyard brawls many of us got into as kids.
- **Predatory violence** is aimed at **illicitly acquiring resources or taking advantage of others**. Witnesses are avoided unless they are accomplices. For example, while a pickpocket might operate in a crowd he (or she) uses sleight of hand and misdirection to disguise his actions. Muggers, serial killers, rapists, home invaders, arsonists, and other predators seek privacy so that they won't get caught.

We read about horrific acts of seemingly random violence in the headlines all the time, an innocent woman lured by a Craig's List add for baby clothes who has her unborn child cut from her womb, a predator who brings gullible young men into his home, chops them up, and eats them, or a guy who calmly walks into a crowded theatre and opens fire. To ordinary citizens acts like this make absolutely no sense whatsoever, but to the criminals who commit them every act has a reason. Most of these predators are the good guys in their own minds. Or, potentially, they're out of their minds, exercising flawed thinking due to psychological abnormalities or physiological damage.

Let's talk a bit about motivation. What makes a predator tick? What motivates them, at least at a high level? In an effort to keep things practical we won't delve into too much detail of the psychology, but it is important to have a broad understanding of what's going on in order to respond appropriately. It's not often that 40-year-old lessons from school still apply, but here's one that does:

> As a bored junior in high school, the warm room made paying attention to my teacher hard. Nothing new, everybody has experienced that sensation. That day's Current World Problems class was going to be a redefining moment in my life, but I was unaware of what was going to happen. My teacher was from the Vietnam War generation. He grew up with the very real possibility of getting his name pulled in a lottery called the draft and having his life redefined in the jungles of some small, foreign country. The war was against communism. Some would argue otherwise, that it was about greed or whatever, but our Current World Problems class was studying communism and the Vietnam War had ended only a few years past so it made for a good example.

A little context before continuing to retell what happened that day... The story of communism is the story of mass murder on an epic scale, far greater in fact than the Holocaust perpetrated by the Nazis during World War II. Stephane Courtois, Director of Research at the Centre National de la Recherche Scientifique (CNRS) in Paris, in the introduction to *The Black Book of Communism*, offers the this breakdown of the numbers of people murdered for the communist ideology:

- **China** – 65,000,000 dead.
- **USSR** – 20,000,000 dead.
- **North Korea** – 2,000,000 dead.
- **Cambodia** – 2,000,000 dead.

- **Africa** – 1,700,000 dead.
- **Afghanistan** – 1,500,000 dead.
- **Vietnam** – 1,000,000 dead.
- **Eastern Europe** – 1,000,000 dead.
- **Latin America** – 150,000 dead.

These horrific numbers are hard to wrap your brain around. Most of us can conceive one homicide, even a handful, but millions? We need to step behind the numbers and look to the motivation. These mass murders were seen as a necessity of social change. People who posed a threat to the ideology had to be removed. It was as simple as that.

> After hearing about atrocities like those enumerated above, the logical question arose from one of my classmates, "**Why on earth would anybody choose to be a communist?**"
> Our teacher replied, "**Because when you have a hungry family it doesn't make any difference if it is a capitalist or a communist filling your rice bowl.**"

That was the epiphany. People who are starving, people in desperation, they will do whatever is needed to meet their basic needs. If communism meets those basic needs, we suppose that we would be communists too. What does it really matter to us? What matters is survival, and for that you need food. Yea, communism! Sign us up. And, thanks for the rice! It all makes perfect sense.

Scary isn't it?

Similarly, violence toward a group that might strip us of our basic needs, well that can quickly make sense too. **Countries or criminals, the reasons are much the same**. Let's put these needs into a bit broader context. One of the best explanations comes from psychologist Abraham Maslow (1908 – 1970) who developed a theory of mental health based on fulfilling human needs in a hierarchical sequence, building on lesser necessities toward higher ones. This is generally depicted as a pyramid that describes basic needs, psychological needs, and self-fulfillment needs, each in order, which has become known as "Maslow's Hierarchy of Needs." Items at the bottom of the pyramid are necessary for those above them to exist, so if you find yourself at risk of starvation resolving that situation will become your sole priority. These levels, from top to bottom, follow:

- **Self-Actualization**: Achieving one's full potential, including creative activities.
- **Purpose needs**: Purpose, meaning.
- **Esteem needs**: Prestige and feelings of accomplishment.

- **Belongingness and love needs**: Love, intimate relationships, friends.
- **Safety needs**: Security, safety.
- **Physiological needs**: Food, water, warmth, rest, and clothing.

As you move from the bottom to the top of the triangle, the way one's basic needs are met is described. In other words, if you don't have food, water, clothing, and shelter, that's going to become your first priority. Nothing else truly matters. From there, if you have a warm place to sleep where your physical safety and security is assured then you can begin to think about higher things like love, relationships, or creative outlet. In other words, your fundamental physiological and safety needs are paramount.

Maslow believed that people are complex, a combination of aspects of this hierarchy. Because he believed that people who fall into the normal range of human existence have coherence in their life, Maslow was a proponent of what he called self-actualization. Here's how he explained this concept:

> "Self-actualization is the intrinsic growth of what is already in the organism, or more accurately, of what the organism is. It refers to the desire for self-fulfillment, namely, to the tendency for him to become actualized in what he is potentially. This tendency might be phrased as the desire to become more and more what one is, to become everything that one is capable of becoming."

Some of the other aspects of Maslow's work are for a deeper study, and as such are not covered in this book. What matters here are the characteristics of self-actualizing people; they are realistic about how they see the world. Acceptance is another aspect of those at the top of the pyramid. These people accept themselves, acknowledge regrets, and are not inhibited while keeping social norms in mind. Thirdly, these people are individuals and see themselves as such. They are interested in personal development and take actions to move in the direction of growth on a continual basis.

Most self-actualized people are devoted to something larger than themselves, although there are exceptions that turn their talents toward antisocial or criminal endeavors. In large part, however, people operating at the top of Maslow's hierarchy have a beneficial mission, a calling, and an imperative in life that they feel they must pursue. Another attribute is their need for privacy. They are often alone, but not lonely. Self-actualized people have a self-referring aspect to their make-up. In other words, external acknowledgment is nice to these folks, but not necessary. These characteristics extend to a sense of, and an appreciation for, the big things in life as well as the small.

It is obvious that the behaviors Maslow is speaking of here are actions that are far up the pyramid that constitutes his hierarchy of needs. The poor Vietnamese man trying his best to feed his family in a war-torn country had great difficulty moving his plane of existence up from the lower two rungs. He was stuck there because **physiological needs and physical safety were paramount**. He simply could not make the move because for him that movement likely equaled death. All his time and resources were consumed with finding sustenance and security for himself and his family.

It's not too different when dealing with drug addicts. Base needs are all that matters, the next fix, and how to get it, oftentimes become the totality of their world. When seen through the eyes of the criminal, striving for a higher self is as foreign to them as landing on Mars for a short vacation would be to most of the rest of us. With the right level of desperation there is no longer a moral question. **You have something and they want it**. Criminals take what they want using the method that works best at the time, or by relying on what has historically achieved results with low risk. Threats are based on one of three factors, (1) what you have, (2) who you are, and (3) where you happen to be.

In his *Logic of Violence* seminar Rory Miller put it this way (we paraphrase): **What would you do if your family was starving?** If you knew beyond any shadow of doubt that your child who you love with all your heart would be dead tomorrow morning if you didn't acquire something for him or her to eat? **Would you lie? Cheat? Rob? Steal? Would you kill?** It's hard for most of us to imagine that level of desperation, but **operating on the first rung or two of Maslow's hierarchy is where contemplating horrific things becomes far more ordinary and acceptable**.

It's not just folks working at the lower end of the pyramid who contemplate horrific things though. Some folks actually find esteem and meaning through dreadful acts. It may not make sense to us, but it absolutely does to them. Lieutenant Colonial David Grossman describes this well in his book *On Killing*:

> "The thing to understand here is that gang rapes and gang or cult killings in times of peace and war are not 'senseless violence.' They are instead powerful acts of group bonding and criminal enabling that, quite often, have a hidden purpose of promoting the wealth, power, or vanity of a specific leader or cause... at the expense of the innocent."

Here's an example that comes from La Crosse County Wisconsin. La Crosse is French for "The Cross," the most sacred symbol in Christianity; however Ed Gein (1906 – 1984), a resident of that city, made it anything but sacred. Ed Gein was insane. He died in a mental institution, but his depravity lives on. You may not recognize his name, but Ed Gein was the inspiration for Norman Bates from the movie *Psycho*, Buffalo Bob from *Silence of the Lambs*, and Leather Face from *The Texas Chainsaw Massacre*. Yes, **all three characters are loosely based on Ed Gein. He was that horrific**, that terrifying.

When Gein's mother suffered a stroke, he became her caretaker. A second stroke caused her to deteriorate quickly before she died. This left Gein with no friends and the only woman who had been in his life was now gone. Shortly thereafter Gein sealed off the rooms his mother had used by boarding them up. Nevertheless, he continued to live in the farmhouse where he had grown up, in a small room off of the kitchen, slipping further and further from sanity.

Ed Gein was a process predator. His would dig up graves at the local cemetery and steal the bodies, fashioning items for his home from their remains. Some of these items included **bowls made of human skulls and a human-skin corset that covered him from shoulder to waist. Gein also fashioned masks from skinned faces and human-skin leggings to complete his macabre outfit**, as well as many other grisly accouterments. The small parts of the house that he continued to inhabit after boarding up the rest quickly became squalid, packed with body parts from his incessant grave-robbing. **When that wasn't enough he moved on to living victims whom he murdered**, including Bernice Worden, a hardware store owner, and Mary Hogan, a tavern owner.

Some of the world's most infamous female murderers include Elizabeth Bathory (a Hungarian countess who killed 600 women, allegedly bathing in virgin's blood to maintain her youth), Genene Jones (who poisoned 46 infants while working as a pediatric nurse), Mary Ann Cotton (who poisoned 20 people with arsenic), Karla Homolka (who raped and murdered two teenage girls on videotape), and Lizzie Borden (who was actually acquitted of axe-murder).

Gein could be confused with a resource predator in that he was gaining satisfaction from the items that he fashioned from the body parts, but those things weren't kept for any material value. They were trophies the he brought home. Trophy-keeping is a trait that most serial killers have in common. The prizes are exactly that, trophies. They are kept in much the same way as a little league baseball player will put a league championship trophy above the mantelpiece in his or her living room or on a bedroom windowsill to remember the event and the victory that he or she was a part of.

When we, the normal, functioning people in society and look at the atrocities that Gein committed we have no way of making sense of the events and actions, yet to the insane process predator such acts make perfect sense, just like pouring milk on our morning cereal. Their actions satisfy a deep psychological need. We are not here to make an assessment of the whys and wherefores of these actions beyond saying that they made perfect sense… to him. **Grave robbing, murder, and vivisection were what he *needed* to do**. To try and make sense of Gein's actions is tantamount to being at the top of Maslow's hierarchy of needs and then reasoning from that position. His actions make no sense to the balanced and socially adjusted person. Nevertheless, his actions were deadly. Ed Gein and the scorpion of the fable that began this chapter are very much the same. Ed Gein very likely knew in the back of his mind that what he was doing was wrong, that it would eventually lead to his demise, **but he did it anyway**.

It is unlikely that Gein was raised to rob graves, that is was a sanctioned and as such considered a normal activity discussed at the family dinner table with his mother. Gein chose to rob the graves at night and not in the light of day, indicating that he knew if he was caught that others would stop him. He may have known that killing hardware store owner Bernice Worden was wrong too, as he waited until she was alone in her shop to shoot her in the head. Nevertheless, the point is that he did kill, just like the proverbial scorpion killed the rabbit.

Let's contrast Ed Gein with notorious bank robber William Francis "Willie" Sutton, Jr. (1901 – 1980), a different kind of criminal. Sutton was a resource predator, someone who stole an estimated $2,000,000 during his forty-year criminal career. He spent more than half of his adult life in prison and escaped three times. He wore disguises during many of his robberies, gaining the nicknames, "Willie the Actor" and "Slick Willie," and pulled off robberies that made for high profile headlines on a regular basis. Willie Sutton, who carried an unloaded Thompson machinegun because "somebody might get hurt," was perceived as dangerous by the public. Ed Gein, on the other hand, was considered simple; odd, not totally present, and not a real threat. Until he got caught.

Sutton was armed, but he was not dangerous. In fact Sutton was so not dangerous that he not only carried an unloaded weapon but also talked about prison reform and consulted with banks on techniques they could use to lower their risk of robbery after getting caught. In later years, he even did a television commercial for a bank. Further, Sutton now has a rule of medicine, "Suttons Law," named after him. Similar to "Occam's Razor," Sutton's Law states that doctors should consider and test for the most likely causes of their patients' diseases rather than leaping to outlandish and outlying possible reasons for them.

Sutton appeared threatening, but was not particularly hazardous. Gein, on the other hand, was incredibly dangerous, but appeared harmless. An insane psycho killer, he was institutionalized for the rest of his life after getting caught, never again to become a free man before dying of lung cancer.

Two different criminals; two distinct behaviors.

Resource predators tend to follow explicit rules—codes of conduct that help them avoid getting caught. Process predators do not, at least not in the same way. This lack of limits makes the process predators deadly.

Another example of this is Gary Ridgeway, the infamous "Green River Killer." He chose prostitutes as his victims because of ease of access and lack of general interest by society in their welfare. The bodies of the women he murdered were dumped, scattered across rural King County (in Washington State), but enough of them were found near the Green River to create his moniker in the press. Ridgeway would then revisit these shallow graves, oftentimes taking trophies. In at least one documented case, Ridgeway returned to the body of one of his victims in order to have sexual intercourse with the corpse. In contrast Ed Gein stated that he never had sex with the bodies of his victims because, "They smelled too bad."

Willie Sutton never returned to a bank he had robbed in order to relive the experience. He was done. Goal gained, he would move on—pure resource behavior. **Resource predators typically leave the scene of the crime taking their spoils with them**, while **process predators bring their victims to the crime scene**… and, oftentimes, a piece of them back home afterwards.

Oversimplified yes, but simple rules are easy to execute in high stress situations. Resource predators make a certain amount of sense in that tab "A" fits slot "B" logical way. It's easy to see people operating at the low end of Maslow's hierarchy behaving this way. A needed or desired resource is identified, your money, car, phone, or whatever, along with the action, "Give it to me now and you won't get hurt." Follow the directions and harm is unlikely.

Process predators frequently enter into the dance in similar ways as their resource counterparts in that an intended quarry is selected, isolated, and then the victimization begins. Two indicators that things are about to get ugly—not always but often—is an intent to move the victim to a secondary location along with an effort to keep them from escaping such as handcuffing or tying them up. This allows for the time and privacy needed to complete their malevolent efforts.

"Let's get out of here [the bar, the club, whatever] and go to my place," or "Now get in the trunk." **Both are attempts to relocate you**; one more subtle and perhaps less nefarious than the other, yet both must be evaluated in context of the situation to ascertain the danger. Similarly the phrase, "I'm *just* going to tie you up so you can't call the police" might be taken at face value, but it is more than likely the beginning of an execution-style murder. There are many layers and variations of this, of course, but one more element to highlight is the home invasion robbery which, in essence, makes your home a secondary crime scene. That's part of the reason such acts are so dangerous (a topic we'll discuss in depth in Chapter 29).

Once you have identified what they truly are by their behaviors, you cannot afford to believe anything that predators say. Threats, explanations, or flattery aside, a new location or a binding are not to happen. **It's time to fight.** Having said that, however, we are obliged to point out that there are no hard and fast rules in self-defense. While general principles apply, every situation is unique. For example, Kris knows a woman and her husband who, in the middle of an armed home-invasion robbery, allowed themselves to be tied up. They both survived. Their choice worked that one time, yet neither of the authors would have taken that path, in part because such things rarely end well.

The challenge when facing violence is that **you only have to get it wrong once for tragic results**.

Understanding the criminal mind and recognizing the goals by their actions allows you to see the violence from their perspective, because seeing it from any other perspective is a denial of what is actually happening. That ends badly. You must deal with what is going on, not freeze in place struggling to figure things out until it's too late. Don't worry about the perpetrator's tortured childhood, their unfair treatment by society, or their impelling need, **worry about how you are going to escape** their clutches and achieve safety.

If the bad guy just wants your stuff, fine. Give it to him. Fighting back more often than not has a higher risk than compliance. **If the predator wants you**, on the other hand, **all bets are off**. It's go time! If you learn the two simple rules of recognition (the differences between resource and process predators), then predatory violence no longer remains senseless, it begins to make perfect (albeit twisted) sense.

Legend states that Willie Sutton told the press, "I rob banks because that is where the money is." Sutton claims the quote was made up by an ambitious reporter, yet whether or not he uttered the words they provide terrific insight into the criminal mind. You might not rob banks, but you can certainly understand the motivation. If you are driven to acquire stuff, lawfully or illicitly, you go where the stuff is.

Sutton was a nonstop-talking, chain-smoking bank robber who spent half of his life behind bars. When it comes to crime he had many lessons to teach. Sutton was not opposed to using the threat of violence to get what he needed. As mentioned earlier, his weapon of choice was the famous Thompson submachine. A Thompson could fire so many rounds so quickly that the wooden fore-grip needed to be separated from the barrel by a spacer so that it wouldn't char or burst into flames from the heat. However, Sutton's was never used because it was only the threat he was after.

"This is a stick-up! Nobody move and nobody gets hurt." Clear rules expressed succinctly. **Resource crime has clear rules and an expectation of following those rules**. If you don't follow them, things can get very sideways very fast. Take a look at the classic Patrick Swayze movie, *Point Break*. The plot is based around surfers who rob banks to support their lifestyle. In a bank robbery one of the surfers got shot, because somebody didn't follow the rules. That was a movie, but even in real life resource predation is dangerous, potentially deadly when the rules aren't followed.

The Vietnamese pauper trying to feed his family goes to where the resource is. This man needs his belly filled, in this case by the communist benefactor who told him that things can and will get better if he just follows the rules. For those of you who can't see the crime here, communism has been responsible for more deaths than any other ideology in the world. So, therein lies the resource cry of communism. It's not that different at a geopolitical scale than it is interpersonally.

Whether stealing resources as Sutton did, or parsing them out as communism does, it is all about resources.

Two types of criminals, two distinct behaviors.

In his paper *Men Who Kill Policemen* Dr. Michael Stone studied 66 cases in the United States in which officers were deliberately murdered while on duty. While the sample size is relatively small, the results are enlightening. Among other things he found that 75 percent of the killers were 18 to 37 years old, the age range that sees the rise, peak, and beginning decline of testosterone concentration in men (there were no female cop killers during the study period). This is also the same age range as most male murderers. And, it also coincides with the age range for both genders where key areas of the brain related to inhibitory control and social decision-making are not fully developed. Dr. Stone wrote:

> "This helps account for the comparative impulsivity, recklessness, and daring-do of adolescents. Unlike many other murderers, killers of police tend not to plan their slayings but act impulsively on the spur of the moment, somehow imagining they can get away with it, even though it is common knowledge that police will hunt to the ends of the earth to apprehend those who kill one of their own."

Circumstances of these killings included traffic stops, arrest attempts, domestic violence interventions, armed robberies, attempted prison breaks, and wrestling over a gun while in court. Only about one in eight of these cop killers studied had some sort of psychiatric disorder that could explain his actions. In fact, cop killers are only half as likely to suffer from schizophrenia, paranoia, or some other type psychoses as mass murderers. It's possible that traumatic brain injuries may have played a role as well, as that often drives personality changes such as impulsivity, poor decision-making, and lack of emotional control, but he was unable to determine that from the study group.

While this particular study isn't comprehensive, it dovetails with other information found in Bureau of Justice Statistics, Federal Bureau of Investigation, and similar reliable sources. The most important point to remember is that while younger men may be statistically more dangerous than women or older individuals, **it is the specific behaviors, situations, and actions that should be concerning not the age or gender of the individual**(s) you encounter. As we elaborate more in Appendix A (Types of Violence Refresher), a key to social violence is the presence of witnesses. Asocial or predatory violence requires privacy to isolate the intended victim and commit the crime without getting caught. Resource predators include pickpockets, robbers, burglars, and the like. Process predators include rapists, murderers, and such. Here is a quick top line of how to tell the difference between them:

Resource predator:

- **Direct orders**: "Give me your wallet!"
- **Verbal shock**: Add whatever expletive you want, they're common enough that you're likely to hear one.
- **Lack of modifiers in command**: Few if any adjectives or adverbs, just straight up directions. In fact the use of modifiers is often disturbing.
- **Instructions about beginning, middle, and end of crime**: "Get down, nobody move, and don't get up for five minutes. We are watching you."
- **Physical shock**: Sudden, unexpected ambush designed to take advantage of vulnerability and obtain your property.
- **Primary crime scene**: Events take place where you encounter the criminal.
- **You are provided an exit**: The criminal separates from you. They leave, or make you leave, rather than trying to take you with them.

Process predator:

- **Subtle requests**: "What are you doing tonight?" "Are you here alone?"
- **Verbal Shock**: Often lacking. Many process predators (such as Ted Bundy) are quite charming, and use their charisma to nefarious intent.
- **Instructions with promise or excuses**: "Be quiet and I'll let you live." "I'm only tying you up for your own protection…" "Now look what you did; don't make me hit you again."
- **Physical Shock**: While subtlety often plays a role, a sudden, unexpected ambush with the intent to capture, render unconscious, or kill can also take place.
- **Secondary crime scene**: Attempting to bring you or trick you to another location where the predator will have the time and privacy to perform his acts without disruption.
- **There is no exit**: You are abandoned once the deed is done or left for dead.

Human predators do horrific things, oftentimes things that ordinary people cannot understand, yet there truly is no such thing as senseless violence. The best analogy is hunting, be it a human stalking a deer in the forest or a big cat, alligator, or shark hunting their prey in the wild. They don't square up and compare dick sizes with their victims, they don't puff up or pontificate, but rather stalk them, cut them from the herd, and harvest them for their dinner. To the predator their prey is nothing more than a juicy, hunk of nutritious meat. To certain human predators, you are nothing more than a hunk of meat. For others you're a walking ATM machine.

"Hello, my name is Inigo Montoya. You killed my father. Prepare to die!"
– Mandy Patinkin

In the iconic quote from the movie *The Princess Bride* above, the character's motivation is clear and unambiguous. More often than not in real life, however, events are far less certain. Motivation matters… but not in the moment, not when you are under immediate threat. What matters during a critical incident is how you are best able to keep yourself safe. **If the target appears to be your stuff** (e.g., money, jewelry, other valuables) **cooperation can be a good idea. If the target appears to be you**, on the other hand, **fighting back is the only reasonable option**. Worry about figuring out why it happened or what you may have done differently to prevent it later on after you are safe.

photo courtesy of Zach Zinn

CHAPTER 2

THE PEOPLE IN CHARGE
DON'T UNDERSTAND VIOLENCE

"I am, as I've said, merely competent. But in an age of incompetence, that makes me extraordinary."
– Billy Joel

On April 26, 2015 after the funeral of Freddie Gray, an African American man who died while in police custody under suspicious circumstances, Baltimore Mayor Stephanie Rawlings-Blake held a press conference. She made the following public statement:

> "I've made it very clear that I work with the police and instructed them to do everything that they could to make sure that the protesters were able to exercise their right to free speech. It's a very delicate balancing act, because, while we tried to make sure that they were protected from the cars and the other things that were going on, **we also gave those who wished to destroy space to do that** as well. And we worked very hard to keep that balance and to put ourselves in the best position to de-escalate, and that's what you saw."

While she and members of her administration attempted to walk her comments back a few days later, her initial remarks were followed by city-wide rioting, looting, and arson. The mayhem was sparked in part by high school students who used social media to launch a coordinated purge, a term taken from a movie denoting a night of uninhibited lawlessness. Bottles, rocks, and chunks of concrete were thrown at officers who responded with tear gas and pepper spray. Cars and buildings were torched, fire hoses slashed so that firefighters could not put out the blaze, and widespread chaos ensued. In one night more than a dozen police officers were injured, over 200 arrests were made, and the National Guard had to be called out to restore order.

After postponing their contest twice due to the rioting, the Orioles and Chicago White Sox baseball game was eventually played at Camden Yards in what is believed to be the first game without fans in major league baseball's 145-season history. Additionally, Baltimore's Friday-to-Sunday series against Tampa Bay was shifted from their home field to St. Petersburg, Florida. "All of the decisions in Baltimore were driven first by the desire to insure the safety of fans, players, umpires and stadium workers," Commissioner Rob Manfred told reporters. "Only after we were comfortable that those concerns had been addressed did we consider competitive issues and the integrity of the schedule." Orioles' manager Buck Showalter echoed that sentiment, saying, "It's all about what's best for the city and the safety of our people. The last thing you want to do is put the fans in harm's way. You have to err on the side of safety."

———————————————

Jim and I sat at a McDonalds in Seattle, Washington having a cup of coffee. We had run into each other by happenstance and decided to catch up a bit. I had first met Jim on the judo mat, a pleasant man, quiet and with a wild set of grappling skills. He was the king of zigging when you zagged, a lot of fun to work with. He was also a police officer. As we sat and chatted, the conversation moved into violence, specifically the violence that would be coming when the imminent earthquake hit Seattle.

On February 28, 2001 at 10:54 AM, the Nisqually earthquake shook the Pacific Northwest. Measuring 6.8 on the Richter scale, that earthquake caused roughly $2 billion in damage, one death, and left 400 people injured. The pros tell us another earthquake is coming… and it will be much bigger.

Jim casually looked across the table as I laid out my vision of what I thought the world would look like when it occurred to me that I was going all Road Warrior.

He paused after I had finished and calmly replied, "You own a gun?"

"Yup," I replied.

"Good because there in nothing we can do for you when it happens."

———————————————

What Jim was saying was that safety is a case of personal responsibility. In such a situation, a catastrophic earthquake, tornado, hurricane, or whatever, the system that he was part of as a law enforcement officer would not be able to assist a fraction of the population let alone address the mayhem that loomed. This isn't speculation; in the aftermath of most natural disasters there are those who take advantage of the chaos to enrich themselves by criminal means, looting, or worse. There are many parts of the discussion about crime, criminals, forms of violence, causes and reasons for its existence, and so on. It's a big topic. And, sadly, the folks in charge really don't understand it. Oftentimes it feels like they don't even want to try.

Yes, those in charge don't understand violence. We know we're talking in broad terms, so don't email us with the "I know somebody who has a friend who does taekwondo who is a City Council member in Chugwater Wyoming." Simply put the exception does not discount the rule. And, that is part of the problem… not focusing on the big issue. Like a small child turning our heads to the parent with the jingly keys, we are completely culpable in this process. Yes, you the reader and us the authors. After all, we are responsible for who gets elected into office. **We're the ones who vote them there**.

Consequently we need to have laser-like focus when it comes to addressing—well all of the issues that face us—but in this instance, violence. We point to an example of laser-like focus demonstrated by the University of Alabama football fan whose first question to the new Alabama coach at his introduction was, "How are you going to beat Auburn?" The question addressed defeating an archrival school, not a question about, "How do you feel about obtaining this job." So, in that vein, let's get down to business.

Predatory crime (e.g., rape, sometimes murder) and resource crime (e.g., money embezzled, accounts hacked, cars stolen) is not going away despite all the public policies and law enforcement and community resources set against it. And, the people in charge don't know why. They don't even have to know why. They don't get it because we let them not get it. Kris used to be a political consultant, one who managed local as well as national campaigns… but he got better. In all seriousness, as an insider he knows with certainty that politicians want to get elected so **they will say and do whatever it takes to place them in office**. Know this about politicians; they are one-trick ponies. Every elected official will have a bag of one or two tricks they know will work, and they will double-down on their go-to tricks whenever needed. Further, politicians don't often learn quickly as there is no incentive in doing so. The wheels of bureaucracy work slowly and so do those who run things.

People who have advanced degrees are held in high esteem, and they should be. They work hard and must demonstrate intelligence, insight, and diligence to obtain their masters or doctorates. However, having initials after your name or wearing the "magic" lab coat is not an automatic path to superior intelligence on all fronts of human existence. Further, it is not always the person who is wearing the lab coat or Senatorial pin that is making the assumption of intelligence, that they are smarter than you. Frequently we say, "Well, they must know what they are doing." Or we may ask for reassurance and validation from the person in the lab coat that what we are thinking or saying is correct. We are not suggesting that every moment with a specialist or a superior is an opportunity for confrontation, but we are suggesting that thinking, "They must know…" is an abdication of our personal responsibility.

Just because you have an advanced degree, hold elected office, or are a ranking corporate official doesn't mean that you automatically know everything. It seems kind of obvious that you can't know everything about everything. You can't even know a little about everything. So why should violence be any different? **Most folks are only experts in a narrow discipline**. For example, you take your car to the mechanic because he or she is trained and skilled in what must be done to keep it running properly, right? You hire an electrician if you have a wiring problem in your house because he or she knows how to fix it without inadvertently burning the place down. You go to a comedy club to laugh because the comedians are professionals and know who to make you laugh. And you go to a doctor because he or she is educated and practices daily in the art of healing.

Kris was over at Lawrence's house, it was a football game and several people were packed in the living room. We were all snacking and watching the game when a recent police shooting in which the suspect died became the topic of discussion. One of the guests, a doctor, said, "I don't see why they didn't just shoot him in the leg."

In addition to physical injuries and/or financial losses, crime victims often experience lasting emotional distress, relationship challenges, and issues at school or work as a result of the crime. Violence is more distressing for survivors when the offender is an intimate partner (87%) than if the victim is assaulted by a stranger (77%).

Kris sat still because he knew a mini-lecture on the fallacies of leg shootings (which we subsequently jotted down and printed here in Chapter 17) was coming. Lawrence was strident, fact-laden, and confident in his conversation. She (the doctor) in turn was as confident, and full of opinion slathered in no real-world understanding. The conversation ended with her still holding on to her, "Shoot them in the legs," position even after acknowledging she has never fired a round from any firearm, nor studied when or how to use one. And, as a pediatrician, she had never treated or even seen a gunshot wound.

Lifelong friends who have known each other since the age of five, Lawrence and the doctor still maintain a cordial relationship, but it was strained by that conversation about guns. The reason for this is simple: **his facts did not match up with her self-image of intelligence**. How could she be wrong in regards to a deeply held belief? She is smart, educated, and people trust her… with their children's lives!

Just because a person has an advanced degree, or several advanced degrees, and is very good at their job does not mean they understand violence, unless their job is in the violence field (which, depending how you count represents less than five to eight percent of the nation's population). Consequently, when the folks in charge legislate solutions to things they know very little about you can bet your bottom dollar that at best they're going to **treat symptoms rather than underlying causes**. Oftentimes they **create unintended consequences** that are **more harmful than the problem they were trying to solve**. Ultimately, they're going to make you feel good, perhaps, but they're not going to keep you safe.

This is why you must be responsible and accountable for your own safety. You can abdicate that responsibility to the folks in charge, but that turns you into a sheep, an animal to be herded, not a person. Don't be a sheep.

Marc "Animal" MacYoung was a bad man at one time who turned good and went on to help a lot of people. He spent many years in and around the criminal scene in Los Angeles, California. Eventually he got out of the life and has been writing books, lecturing, and working as a consultant and expert witness ever since. When Marc was working with a corporate client where he explained criminal motivation and tactics in a conference room full of middle- and upper-management executives, one guy could not comprehend Marc's point of view. This guy had gone from an occasional look of disagreement to asking for clarification in a less than truly inquisitive manner. Finally, the dam broke and the guy outright challenged the validity of what Marc was saying. Marc had a very interesting response to this executive's challenge:

> "I have an idea. Why don't you [the businessman] take a vacation, let's say a week. During that time, I will come in and take over, you know cover for you. Would you like that?"
>
> "No, because you can't do my job."
>
> "I'm pretty sure I could, I'm a smart guy," Marc replied.
>
> "Maybe so, but you don't understand my job," the businessman said.
>
> "Precisely! That is why you should listen to me. My job used to be violence."

Marc's point is clearly a valid one. The businessman is good at his job, but that job isn't dealing with predators. Marc is just as good at his job, which is not running a corporate business. Here's another example. In February of 2013, Vice President of the United States Joe Biden revealed that he had told his wife Jill that if an intruder was near their home when he is away that she should fire warning shots off their balcony with a shotgun. Here's an excerpt of what Biden told the press:

> "If there's ever a problem, just walk out on the balcony here—walk out, put that double barrel shotgun and fire two blasts outside the house—I promise

you whoever is coming in will run away... You don't need an AR-15, it's harder to aim, it's harder to use... Buy a shotgun! Buy a shotgun!"

Um, yeah... Riiiiight.

Let's work through this stupidity from big to small, starting with the gun. The icon of a double-barreled shotgun was invented about twenty years before America became a country. Yes, the idea is that old. It is from the era of the flintlock and the blunderbuss. In fact it was originally called a "fowler" because it was used to hunt birds. The double-barreled shotgun was introduced to give a person two shots in rapid succession as opposed to one round and then spending time to break open the action to remove the spent round and reload (which took even longer in the old black powder days than it does with modern shot shells and extractor/ejector systems).

We talk about home invasions in later in the book (in Chapter 29). Rather than skipping ahead, for the moment suffice it to say that they're incredibly dangerous, oftentimes requiring an armed response to save your life or that of your loved ones. Following the Vice President's advice to the letter rather than arming yourself, retreating to a safe place, and calling the authorities for help, you've emptied your shotgun into the air, which has four serious complications:

1. You've left the safety of your home, gone outside, and **exposed yourself to the threat**(s).
2. You now hold **an empty weapon** and need to reload.
3. Chances are good that the bad guy knows your gun is empty and **can take action before you do**.
4. What goes up must come down and **whatever it hits is your responsibility**.

To go a step farther, let's say you don't scare the bad guy(s) off and suddenly find yourself in a gunfight. And, you have time to reload before dying. The double-barrel shotgun requires practice and skill to accurately bring it back on target after the first round has been fired as recoil ("kick") tends to move the weapon off target. This is why it is very hard to find double-barrel, side-by-side shotguns in gun stores in the United States. Pump action, semi-automatic, and over/under models are used far more often for hunting and skeet, let alone for self-defense. Kind of like the two-bit dictators who have every medal you could possibly think of pinned to their uniforms, the double-barrel shotgun **is more of an icon than a useful tool**. This ignorant statement by the Vice President places symbolism over effectiveness. The double-barrel shotgun looks good, but **it's not the best choice for the job**.

But, that's just the weapon. There's another factor to consider. An all-important factor... the law.

We are not going to get too lawyerly here and cite all the specific laws as they vary by jurisdiction, but Biden's advice to his wife is clearly in violation of several statutes, some of which are misdemeanors while others are felonies. Yes, go-directly-to-prison, do-not-pass-go type crimes. For example, going outside violates the principle of preclusion, making you (in many jurisdictions) partially culpable, hence unable to legitimately claim self-defense if you don't scare off the intruders and end up having to shoot someone. To make matters worse, Biden is a member of the Delaware Bar Association, hence should have at least some modicum of sense of the laws in the state in which he is allowed to practice as an attorney.

Alright, we said we would not go all lawyerly here, but we can't help ourselves... Here are just two laws the Vice President of the United States of America suggested that his wife break (and these two are merely misdemeanors):

- Discharge of a firearm within 15 yards of a road (7 Del.C. § 719)
- Violation of the residential dwelling safety zone as set forth in (7 Del.C. § 723)

So, when we say the people in charge don't understand violence, this is an example from the man who is second in line to the Presidency of the United States of America, arguably the second most powerful position in the most powerful country on earth. And, as a policy it makes no difference if you use a shotgun, pistol, rifle, or what have you, the bottom line is that **warning shots are, in almost every instance, illegal**. Even where they're not, they are generally **a very, very bad idea**. We categorically **do not recommend them**, but if you truly must fire in warning, at least aim at the ground where you can control what you hit rather than randomly into the air where an inadvertent tragedy might occur.

In July of 2013, a short six months after the Vice President's proclamation, a Vancouver, Washington man followed the politician's advice and fired warning shots into the air. **He was promptly arrested**. He claimed he was only doing what the Vice President had told him to do. Shockingly, **that defense did not hold up in court**.

At this point you probably are saying to yourself, "What nutlog would go out and fire warning rounds in the air." But, what you should be saying is, "The people in charge don't understand violence, proper gun usage… or the law."

To reinforce this point, Gordon Van Gilder, a 72-year-old retired English teacher faces 10 years in prison for owning a 250-year-old flintlock pistol. Seriously! After buying the Queen Anne pistol in November of 2014, he wrapped his purchase in a piece of cloth and put it in the glove box of his car before driving home. Unfortunately he was pulled over for a routine traffic stop in Cumberland County, New Jersey, where the officer discovered the antique. Even though the flintlock pistol was unloaded (and had not been fired since before this nation was founded), Van Gilder could easily lose his pension and is likely to spend a minimum of three-and-a-half years in prison for owning it. Why? Because New Jersey gun laws don't differentiate between modern firearms and antiques. He is being charged with a felony.

> "I called the prosecutor to see what we could do on this, and the prosecutor told me that they were waiting for ballistics," reported Van Gilder's attorney Evan Nappen. "And I'm thinking, 'What? Ballistics on a flintlock?'"

Waiting for a ballistics test?! Seriously? While that is standard procedure for confiscated firearms, what criminal could possibly have used the antique to commit a crime? For those unfamiliar, flintlock pistols like the one Van Gilder purchased are real-life *Pirates of the Caribbean* stuff. They work a lot like cannons in that you pour in a black powder charge, shove a lead ball down the barrel, tamp it down, put another charge in the pan, and hope it actually works when you pull the trigger and the chunk of flint creates a spark. Even if they do go off when you shoot, they aren't very accurate since there is a slight delay between trigger pull and ignition. Further, even if your hands are steady enough to keep the muzzle directly on line with the target until the ball leaves the barrel most flintlock pistols do not have rifling to stabilize the bullet (which isn't horribly aerodynamic to begin with). And, they're heavy, awkward, and can take several minutes to load and fire.

All in all, an antique black powder pistol is not something gangbangers with any lick of common sense would ever carry around for drive-by shootings. Nevertheless, **in New Jersey flintlocks are apparently considered on par with semiautomatic AR-15 rifles** (the dreaded "assault rifle" that the vice president and many in the press rail against). Clearly it's not just firearms that the folks in charge don't understand, it's also common sense!

So, what can you do about it? Here are a few suggestions:

- **Get smart**. Acknowledge that no one knows everything when it comes to violence and (if you study or teach martial arts) avail yourself and members of your school or club of resources that can help. For example, if your weakness in understanding is gang violence then go out and find some information, vet it with at least three reputable sources, digest it, and pass it on to others in your group. Everybody will be better for it. A terrific (and free) place to start regarding researching voids in understanding of violence is Marc "Animal" MacYoung's website (www.nononsenseselfdefense.com). Bookmark it, read it, and plan on going back often and for long periods of time.
- **Encourage others to get smart too**. If somebody in your martial arts school is hungry for information and skill, stoke that furnace! Give them the most and best you can give.

If you don't know, find out. Or have others do the legwork and bring it back for the benefit of all. Read books, attend seminars, search the web, and truly educate yourself on the problems and solutions you can control. There's so much information out there the challenge isn't in finding it, but rather in separating the good stuff from the bad. This takes longer, but it is well worth it.

- **Apply what you learn**. Instead of focusing on the borders, working around the edges, take action that makes a difference right here, starting right now, by applying what you've learned. Practice, practice, and practice some more. What gets trained gets done. And, for those of you already way down the road on this, good on you. Good on you for being out in front.

- **Educate others**. If you're an expert, make your voice heard. The press needs informed sources. City councils hold hearings. Community activists write petitions. Get involved. Be the voice of understanding and reason that just might steer things in a positive direction. We cannot eliminate all violence from society, but we just might be able to help assure that rules and regulations put in place help ameliorate the problem rather than exacerbating it.

If a proposed solution, a piece of legislation only treats the symptoms then it's political. Its aim isn't to solve the problem but rather to make folks feel that the folks in charge understand their pain and are taking action, any action, even if it's ineffectual. As for trying to understand why somebody is committing crimes or performing acts of violence that threaten us… we truly don't care. Individual motivations don't matter. What we care passionately about how it is going to hurt us, our families, and community and what actions we must take in order to keep ourselves safe.

Those in charge don't understand violence, a fact which **elevates the need for ordinary citizens to become experts in their own self-protection**. Don't get overly caught up in underlying causes, worry about what's going on right here, right now. Don't deny what's happening. Don't point fingers or look for someone else to blame. Take personal responsibility, be accountable for your safety, and learn to deal with it.

CHAPTER 3

ZERO TOLERANCE PUSSIFICATION

"Over the past 25 years, these policies have gained tremendous momentum while also inviting deep controversy… The theory underlying zero tolerance policies is that schools benefit in both ways when problem students are removed from the school setting. However, there is no research actually demonstrating this effect. No studies show that an increase in out-of-school suspension and expulsion reduces disruption in the classroom and some evidence suggests the opposite effect."

– Vera Institute of Youth Justice

What if every cancer was treated the same? That would be ineffective and unacceptable, right? Why, then, does it make sense to treat all violence the same way? To go a step farther, what if the doctor was treating you for cancer and then decided to force your spouse (or significant other) to take the same medications too, even though he or she wasn't afflicted? That makes no sense. Neither do these decisions:

- **Four-year-old suspended for G.I. Joe action figure**. On January 29, 2004 John Spence was suspended for bringing three, three-inch tall G.I. Joe action figures to school. The four-year-old had packed the toys in preparation for an overnight birthday party. When he got to school one of toys was sticking out of his pocket which, when spotted by his teacher, led to the disciplinary action. Despite public outcry, a spokesman for Bemiss Elementary School (in Spokane, Washington) said that the school stands by its zero-tolerance policy on weapons, which does not specify the type or size.

- **Seven-year-old suspended for biting pastry into the shape of a gun**. Park Elementary School student Josh Welch was suspended March 1, 2013 for two days after school officials accused him of shaping the pastry he was eating into the form of a gun. Attorney Robin Ficker, who represents the seven-year-old student, is seeking to have his record expunged, planning to appeal to Maryland's highest court if necessary. "It would be funny," he told the press, "If it wasn't so serious as it being on his permanent record."

- **Twelve-year-old suspended for defending himself**. On October 17, 2013 a seventh grade student at Ocean Bay Middle School was punished for defending himself against a bully. The 12-year-old was verbally assaulted, slapped, and knocked to the ground before he fought back. "There was a police officer at the school. He was there as well, and he said our son defended himself. It shows the other kid started it," the boy's father, Chris Hite, told reporters afterward. Nevertheless the boy was slapped with a two-and-a-half day suspension.

Sex offenses (e.g., child pornography, sex abuse, and illegal sex transportation) are the second fastest growing federal crime in the United States. The number of suspects arrested and booked for a sex offense doubled from 1994 to 1998, then doubled again from 1998 to 2004, with an annual average of 3% year-over-year increase through 2012.

When we read about school kids being suspended for bringing plastic action figures to school, biting a pastry into the rough shape of a firearm in class, or defending themselves on the playground it's pretty evident that something's gone wrong. This isn't just anecdotal. In fact, a rigorous study of students in Texas, published in 2011 by the Council of State Governments and the Public Policy Research Institute at Texas A&M University, proved that the culture of zero tolerance in schools has become so pervasive that **harsh punishments are meted out even when they are not strictly required**. Getting suspended for bullying other kids makes sense. But, suspending those who defend themselves too, **what message does that send?** And, **at what cost?**

Intentionally or unintentionally, society is teaching us from a very young age to outsource responsibility for our safety and security to authority figures, be they school administrators, law enforcement officers, or legislators. We've already established that the folks in charge don't understand violence. A further challenge is that these policies drive several nefarious, unintended consequences, such as:

1. Making predators more effective.
2. Degrading interpersonal coping and communication skills.
3. Giving rise to reverse-bullying.
4. Raising a whole generation of young adults who do not know how to lose gracefully, hence are more likely to act out in extreme ways.
5. Learning to fear the wrong things.

These are very serious issues, ones that can have lasting and pervasive impacts to society. Let's address each one in turn:

1. **Zero tolerance makes predators more effective**. When safety and security are not seen as our personal responsibility we lose the will to defend ourselves. Consider the feminist avocation that young women ought to be able to walk naked through a biker bar unmolested. Of course they *should* be able to, but seriously how likely is that to happen if someone tried it in real life? Taking stupid chances because of the way things should be, as opposed to how they are, is foolish. Nevertheless, many people out there don't even realize when they're taking risks. **Just because nothing bad happened yet doesn't mean it never will**. Those who take personal accountability for their actions tend to have better situational awareness[2] and common sense than those who do not. That's a huge deal since **predators thrive on willing victims**.

2. **Zero tolerance degrades interpersonal coping and communication skills**. Social media, online gaming, and other societal factors that keep people from interacting and solving problems face-to-face certainly play a role, but never being allowed to resolve disputes physically can be a very bad thing too. Hell, even dodge ball is banned from most schools, so **there is no safe outlet for pent up teenage angst and aggression**. If every time you get into a dispute growing up an authority figure (e.g., teacher, parent, or school administrator) steps in to resolve the issue you never really learn how to settle disagreements peaceably as an adult. Many folks, particularly Millennials, develop an undue sense of entitlement that left unrestrained can become deadly. Remember actress Nicole duFresne's famous last words (from an incident we described in detail in *The Little Black Book of Violence*), "What are you going to do, shoot us?" She died shortly thereafter in her fiancé's arms. Righteous indignation is dysfunctional. Everyone needs to learn how **to resolve disagreements with words or actions that both settle the issues *and* keep them safe**. Without considerable experience with face-to-face

---

2 We assume that you have already read about this in *The Little Black Book of Violence* where we covered the subject in-depth, but if you need a refresher refer to Appendix C at the end of this book.

communication, resolution, and negotiation skills that's virtually impossible.

3. **Zero tolerance gives rise to reverse-bullying**. As of this writing both authors are in our fifties. In our day grade school kids would never consider taunting upperclassmen, yet that kind of behavior is not at all uncommon today. Knowing they can hide behind "the rules," little kids punch, kick, pinch, and harass older ones, then go crying to school administrators if there's any retaliation (which is oftentimes what they seek). This dynamic is dysfunctional in so many ways it's hard to enumerate, but the bottom line is that **while this may work in school it's a recipe for disaster if you try it on the street**. Rules, laws, and regulations only work when people follow them. Bending or breaking those rules in hopes that "the system" will punish the other guy **only works so long as the other guy plays nice** too. It's unbelievable what some folks think they can get away with because they haven't tried it on the wrong person yet.

4. **Zero tolerance raises a whole generation of young adults who do not know how to lose gracefully**, hence more likely to act out in extreme ways. Back in our day (sheesh, we're sounding old and curmudgeonly now, aren't we?), playground fistfights were commonplace. Teachers and students stood around watching, but didn't intervene unless it looked like somebody was going to get seriously hurt because they realized that participants were trying to establish a pecking order, not maim or kill each other. **We learned how to take our lumps and move on**, often befriending the bullies who'd previously tormented us. We demonstrated our toughness while they acquired prestige or power. Nowadays, when folks never learn how to lose gracefully they oftentimes cannot see a way out from under their tormentors. This can lead to excessive retaliation, say bringing guns or bombs to school (or work), horrific acts that were far rarer a quarter century ago than they are today. The selfie-stick generation has enough problems with narcissism already; this dynamic only exacerbates it.

5. **Zero tolerance teaches us to fear the wrong things**. When Lawrence was in high school he gave a firearm safety lecture for a class project, and then took his fellow students out target shooting with a .22 caliber rifle on school grounds behind one of the portables. Not only did he have permission to do this, the principal and his speech teacher participated too. Imagine how that would go over nowadays when folks freak out over toaster pastry images of what might, possibly be interpreted as guns. While everyone is born with survival instincts **we need to learn how to listen to them**, refining our intuition to keep us safe. If we don't understand what's truly threatening and what is not that simply cannot be done. The focus needs to be on **danger management not on fear management**, but in order to do that we need to understand the difference.

Our survival instincts are being socialized away. For example, many folks would rather step into an elevator with a menacing stranger than risk offending anyone despite the chance of being assaulted, raped, or murdered... largely because **zero tolerance has robbed them of their ability to know the difference**. This is dangerous, dysfunctional, and stupid, yet all too common. Here's a real-life example:

> In the last couple years before retiring from the stadium where Lawrence worked as a security supervisor there was a vendor who became known by pretty much everyone at the facility as "Creepy Popcorn Guy." Everyone who ran across this dude got seriously weirded out by his demeanor, yet no one did anything about it, perhaps assuming that he'd passed the requisite background check and was strange but not unsafe. After hearing a variety of reports about Creepy Popcorn Guy's antics, such as lingering glances or touches bordering on inappropriate with younger football fans, Lawrence grew concerned enough to check things out. He discovered that this guy had somehow evaded the mandatory background check yet was employed by a concessions vendor anyway. When Creepy Popcorn Guy's management pulled the appropriate records they discovered, much to their chagrin, that he was a registered sex offender, one who was barred from contact with children. He was immediately fired and later returned to prison for multiple parole violations.

Bureaucracy has a tendency to remove personal responsibility and accountability. When judges, school officials and other folks "in charge" have the ability to review the facts and judge individual situations on their merits, more often than not they will make prudent decisions. But, they're humans so invariably they will get things wrong from time to time too. **Zero tolerance assures that anyone who violates a policy, even a stupid one, will be punished**. It means that un-empowered, unthinking administrators will blindly churn folks through "the system," rather than exercising good judgment and sound decision-making. Not only do they not have to think, they're not allowed to.

Zero tolerance policies may have laudable goals, but the unintended consequences are spectacularly dangerous. Because people cannot solve their differences through social violence (e.g., fistfight) they often resort to asocial violence (e.g., shootings), oftentimes without truly comprehending the magnitude of what they've done until afterward. In other words, **righteous indignation turns to impotent rage, then fury, and when the pent up frustration erupts things get ugly**. This dynamic is compounded by violent television shows, movies, and videogames that can desensitize folks to violence, a catalyst in the recipe for disaster. All-in-all, ordinary citizens become pussified while **predators are emboldened**. The longer these policies go on, the worse their ill-effects will be. But, there's still hope… Here are some things you can do about it:

- **Take responsibility for your personal safety**. Learn everything you can about threats, violence, and circumstances that might cause you harm. Exercise and refine your situational awareness, communication, negotiation, and coping skills. After all, self-defense is primarily about awareness, avoidance, and de-escalation, not fighting. In other words, if you take proactive measures to not be there when the other guy wants to fight, you won't get hurt.

- **Never operate on autopilot**. We all know that texting or talking on the phone while driving is just as dangerous as becoming impaired by drugs or alcohol when operating a vehicle, yet all too many folks out there do it anyway. The same thing applies to operating in public places. You may have read about the infamous case that occurred on September 23, 2013 when Nikhom Thephakayson, a passenger on a San Francisco light rail train, pulled out a gun and waved it around for several minutes yet no one noticed until he started shooting because they were all so absorbed in their smartphones (perhaps we should call them dumbphones). Text if you want to, but stop and look around frequently too. If you don't see it coming there's no way you can be safe.

- **Hone your interpersonal communication skills**. Most conflicts don't get violent, but even those that do are often preventable if you say or do the right things early enough in the process. And, of course, no matter what you do for a living you talk a hell of a lot more than you fight. There's no downside to being a good communicator. When Lawrence apprenticed as a knife-maker many years ago he worked in a shop that was frequented by outlaw bikers. These were dangerous, scary guys, real one-percenters with long rap-sheets, but he was in no danger because he was unfailingly polite, diplomatic, and knew how to act in their presence.

- **Become an agent of change**. Consider joining a parent-teacher association, running for a school board (commission) office, joining an affinity group at your workplace, or volunteering for groups that seek to change these policies. The more knowledgeable, informed people get involved, the better policies will become. It's easy to complain about zero-tolerance policies, but why not direct those energies into getting them changed instead. Or at least try.

Zero tolerance policies are society's way of turning you into a sheep, a passive creature that cannot fend for itself. It might make you a low maintenance, pliable little citizen, who does what he or she is supposed to do, but it doesn't keep you safe. We've said it more than once, but it's so fundamental that we'll repeat ourselves once again—don't abdicate your personal responsibility and accountability. Don't outsource your safety to others. In other words, be a man (or woman), not a sheep.

CHAPTER 4

DAMNED IF YOU DO; SCREWED IF YOU DON'T

"A bully is a person that attacks only those who cannot defend themselves."
— Burt Lancaster, *The Young Savages*

In November of 2013 transgender teenager Jewlyes Gutierrez got fed up with the bullying that had been laid out upon her by fellow students. She chose to fight back. The police were called, a report filed… and she was suspended from school. She was charged by Contra Costa County (California) with misdemeanor charges of assault and battery. This is pretty serious stuff for a schoolyard fight.

People often use the phrase "assault and battery" together, but assault and battery in the state of California (and in many jurisdictions) are actually two different crimes. California assault law, Penal Code 240, defines an assault as an attempt to use force or violence on someone else. Battery is the actual use of that force or violence. In other words, assault might be making a fist and threatening harm while battery is following through and beating the other guy into a bloody pulp.

Here are some of the potential fines and penalties for **Assault** (Pen. Code, §241), which is charged as a misdemeanor in the state of California:

A person who is convicted of simple assault (most often a charge that stems from a fistfight as opposed to the aggravated version of the crime that stems from using a weapon or other extenuating circumstances) faces the following possible penalties:

- Up to six months in jail
- A fine up to $1,000 and
- Probation up to six months

Here are some of the potential fines and penalties for **Battery**[3] (Pen. Code, §243(a)), which is charged as a misdemeanor in the state of California:

A person who is convicted of battery faces the following possible penalties:
- Up to six months in county jail
- Fine up to $2,000 and
- Probation up to six months

Dan Cabal, the Contra Costa County Senior Deputy Attorney, said he was not at liberty to comment on Jewlyes Gutierrez's case. Nevertheless, he did tell reporters, "Words are never enough to justify fists, that's the law." On the other side of the aisle, Public Defender Kaylie Simon said, "I don't understand quite why the district attorney's office would prosecute someone who's already been a victim of bullying. I think it's a further victimization of someone who's been a target."

The school administration did what it was required to do. By policy, when a fight occurs everybody involved gets suspended. There is little or no attempt to discern what happened, just blanket suspensions. **The principal is not empowered with the authority to make decisions on the merits of any individual case**. He or she has no choice. It's the policy. Failure to execute the policy as written could mean anything from an administrative sanction to termination for failure to perform the principal's duties. In other words, the principal's job is on the line so he or she is not going to stick his/her neck out to alter the policy.

The administration gets it. There is no subtlety in the policy. By not following the policy you make a personal sacrifice. To avoid this sacrifice, you do what you are supposed to do and step back behind the curtain of, "I did what I supposed to do according to school policy." Hmm, sounds a bit like infamous Nazi war criminal Adolf Eichmann who defended himself at Nuremburg by saying he was just following orders doesn't it?

It's. The. Policy. Okay, we all get it...

But, then the School Board President, Charles Ramsey, entered the equation. Ramsey stood outside of the policy a little bit and said, "If a crime happens, a crime happens, but I'd like to have a better understanding of the rationale and motivation behind it. I want to learn why this is or is not punishment enough, especially when a child expresses a position that she's been bullied."

As the letter of the law goes, when a fight takes place it is a crime. Police make an arrest, file a

---

3 If the victim is maimed, seriously injured, or requires hospitalization, higher level charges will often be applied.

report, and then prosecutors review the facts and choose how and in what manner to pursue a case (or not) based each unique situation. According to school policy, a fight means police are called and then there is an automatic suspension. So, in this instance we have a school that has a policy that must be followed that spells out clear repercussions for certain behavior and we have laws that follow that a very similar path.

And, just to put a bow on all this, Gutierrez claimed that she had reported the ongoing harassment to school officials previously, yet no action had been taken. Reporting the alleged bullying was obviously the correct choice, however, no school official, no camera on campus, is going to catch every instance of every moment of the day. Bullies know that their actions cannot be seen at every moment, so like jackals they choose their spots carefully and ambush their prey when they least expect it. Oftentimes they strike in packs or are otherwise supported by their friends, so they are not only hard to catch but also tend to have their alibis ready to go if they ever get called out for their actions.

This means that we have a potent cocktail of institutional policies, laws, and trained weakness. Trained weakness is the idea that you are not to take action on your own behalf, that there are others better suited to handle the situation at hand. In other words, the institutions that surround most citizens are designed to take individual responsibility out of the hands of the person and replace it with the promise that everything will be okay. All you need to do is abdicate your human rights to the state and become deliberately ignorant of what is going on. Sound familiar?

Jewlyes Gutierrez was appointed a public defender. That means that she comes under the threshold in her Miranda rights of, "If you cannot afford an attorney one will be appointed for you." And, as the case progressed it appears that the District Attorney saw an easy conviction… until the Transgender Law Center entered into the picture. Then the media got involved. From local news to the Huffington Post, the story got more and more press. Then, responding to public outcry, Change.org formed a petition to have the charges against Gutierrez dropped. **Suddenly the case took on a whole different trajectory**.

Contra Costa County Superior Court Judge Thomas M. Maddock accepted an agreement with the Gutierrez's public defender that allowed her to enter a restorative justice program. These programs are designed around an active involvement of the perpetrator to repair whatever harm he or she has done. It could involve publically apologizing, performing community service, or similar non-jail-related remediation. In other words, restorative justice makes a point that a crime has been committed against a person or a community rather than against the state. Consequently when Gutierrez successfully completes the program the charges will be dropped and her record expunged. She makes restitution and is off the hook. One thing that should not be overlooked, however, is that should Gutierrez fail to complete the restorative justice program to the court's satisfaction her case will result in a default conviction of the original crimes for which she was charged.

The breakdown of who filled what role in this dance of officiousness is:

- **The Defendant**: A double victim, bullied by peers, bullied by the system.
- **The Bullies**: A pack of girls who outnumbered and picked on one person who was different.
- **The School Administration**: Followed policy to the letter.
- **The School Board**: Questioned the school policy.
- **The Prosecuting Attorney**: Intended to get a slam dunk conviction… and failed.
- **The Public Defender**: Actively involved in the victim/defendant's defense, both in the courtroom and with the media.
- **The Media**: Shone an antiseptic light on the situation.
- **The Law**: A tool used to bludgeon the defendant.

The end result of Gutierrez's willingness to stand up for herself and fight back was largely a good one, but it cost her time, resources, pain, and public humiliation. And, she still had to make up for lost schoolwork.

Jonathan Kirby broke into a home wanting to steal whatever he could; maybe something to pawn, but cash money would be great if he could find it. Kirby had burglarized before and this house was plush, well to do. Kirby had made a great, fat, juicy, choice, or so he thought… Living a life of crime, Kirby had a Texas conviction for voluntary manslaughter (committing a homicide with no premeditated intent to kill another human being) in 1988. Kirby had a couple of other convictions in Los Angeles such as auto theft, first-degree burglary, and petty theft under his belt as well.

In other words, despite being in and out of trouble for much of his life, Kirby was pretty good at his job. He got away with a lot, was only got convicted a handful of times. He was in his element… until he met the homeowner, well the owner's fist anyway. By the time the confrontation was over and the police arrived **Kirby had a broken nose, a broken jaw, and broken ribs**. You see, the home Kirby chose to burglarize belonged LL Cool J. The famous rapper/actor is in very good shape; he stands 6 foot 3 inches tall and weighs 214 pounds. Further, Cool J had a well-documented, rather rough childhood and teen years. You might remember LL Cool J's first hit, titled "*Momma Said Knock You Out.*"

Yeah, we think it's kind of funny.

No charges were brought against Cool J. Kirby, on the other hand, faces the "Three Strikes and You're Out," law when he goes to trial. He may very well spend the rest of his life behind bars due to this event. So, our theme of damned if you do and screwed if you don't actually applies both ways, for the victim and sometimes painfully for the criminal too.

A Pennsylvania boy woke up every morning with Attention Deficit Hyperactivity Disorder (ADHD) along with a comprehension-delay impediment that caused a lag in how long it took him to understand speech or ideas. He also had an anxiety disorder. To add to the daily challenges this 15-year-old faced, he looked down the barrel of every school day knowing that he was going to be tormented and bullied. This situation was not unknown to the school, the boy's mother had complained about the bullying some four months earlier.

One day he had enough and decided to take action. This South Fayette High School student was determined to take on the bullies, but not physically... He was going to catch them in the act. To get the proof of what they were doing, **he recorded a seven-minute video on his iPad that showed the other kids bullying him**. There were threats of pulling his pants down as well as a loud noise that was intended to scare the teenager. There was even a recording of one of the tormentor's voices saying, "I was just trying to scare him."

Principal Scott Milburn, upon learning of the recording, called the police. But not for the reasons you might think. No, he was not turning in this poor 15-year-old's tormenters. Milburn's position was that **there had been a "wiretapping incident."** When the police arrived they told the young man to dispose of the recording and charged him with disorderly conduct. In the Commonwealth of Pennsylvania, the bullied boy was facing a lower level crime called a "summary offense," one that could stay on his juvenile record. To make a long story shorter, at the end of the day he was fined $25.00 and ordered to pay court costs.

It appears from our research that nothing was done by the school to arrest the bullying. However, we can only assume that something was said to the bullies post facto to close the loop and leave a trail of "we did something" to cover the administration's collective butts. We would submit that the system in this instance, as it does in so many others, failed the weak, the poor handicapped victim of the bullies. And, the system failed to answer the challenge, made by the 38th Vice President and United States Hubert H. Humphrey who wrote:

> "It was once said that the moral test of government is how that government treats those who are in the dawn of life, the children; those who are in the twilight of life, the elderly; and those who are in the shadows of life, the sick, the needy and the handicapped."

Sad isn't it?

———————————

We made a pretty extensive introduction to this chapter to prove a point: **Laws bring resolution.** In many instances **that is not the same thing as justice**. The laws and criminal justice system are built by the people, through our elected officials, to make sure the bad guys are prosecuted, convicted if guilty, and punished. If you are innocent, the system is designed to make sure you are not prosecuted, convicted, and punished. Most of the time… Don't get us wrong, we are not going to place the American system of justice, as imperfect as it is, second to any other form of jurisprudence on the face of the planet. However, that doesn't mean that you should throw the rights and responsibilities that you have to the wind. You need to be aware of what is the law in your area, what the boundary conditions are, because oftentimes they are not what you'd think.

Seriously, **who would have thought that a bullied 15-year-old who chose to "fight back" with a video camera would be the one who got prosecuted**? And, for wiretapping of all things?! Certainly not us…

Incidents like this might make you wonder how many criminal statutes there are in the United States. That's a good question, but unfortunately one that is virtually impossible to answer. Let's take the Federal laws, and then all the State laws, then county, and municipal, and you can see that the number of laws seemingly borders on infinite. In fact, in 1985 (just that one year alone) there were more laws passed in the State of California than there had been in the entire history of the Soviet Union. That's outrageous, isn't it?

So, for our purposes we will try and make it manageable and just look at federal law. The place to start counting is The Statutes at Large, a collection of all the federal laws passed by the United States Congress. This includes new laws, amendments to existing laws, and some laws that have been repealed, but it is incomplete in that it doesn't contain regulatory provisions that have the force of law. Those are somewhere else. You get the picture, right? Laws everywhere and in every place.

To illustrate our point: If you drive too fast, you risk getting a ticket for speeding. If you drive too slowly, you risk getting a ticket for impeding the flow of traffic. There is a ticket, a citation, a charge for almost every act. Now don't think we are advocating anarchy, we are simply pointing out that as a society we have passed an awful lot of laws and no one person could possibly be aware of all of them, unless that's their full time job. Unfortunately ignorance of the law is no excuse for not following it. **This is why attorneys exist. And, why you should know one or two**… In fact, if you are a martial artist or concealed weapons permit holder you'd be remiss to not only know a good attorney but also to have his or her number on speed dial in your smartphone just in case you need it with short notice.

So… **get an attorney!**

Public defenders should be avoided if at all possible. If you can't pay for an attorney, there is no choice but to go with a court-appointed public defender, but otherwise facing the criminal justice system (or even a lawsuit) is not a time to be cheap. Seeing it as a cost of doing business, professional criminals invest in legal defense funds. You should too. We want to make it clear that we are not anti-public defenders either; they have a very important role to fill in our justice system. What we are saying, however, is they are well-meaning people who are overworked and underpaid. Further, public defenders have to deal with multiple languages, translators, often unappreciative clients, personality issues, and much, much more. Public defenders are pulled in many directions and those directions are often not your direction. A private attorney on retainer works only for you (and a handful of select clients).

Hopefully you've got someone on retainer but will never need to use him or her. Nevertheless, it's good to preemptively spend some time getting to know the laws in your local jurisdiction (where you live, work, and travel most frequently). If there is something that you don't understand, have your attorney explain it to you as many times as it takes to get it. Really get it. This is a new world with its own language and rules you don't understand, but need to. So, go do it. If you're ever charged with a crime it's paramount that you have topnotch representation.

Before we go off on a tirade about how horrible the justice system is in America, or what might sound like a tirade, we want to be clear that if given a choice we would, without exception, choose to be tried in a court in the United States than in any other place in the world. Now having said that there are some things you should know, especially attitude-wise, if you ever wind up in court:

> **Give up on the notion of "justice."** It will make your time in front of a judge go better. Know that what you are seeking is a **reasonable resolution**. While justice is usually off the table, with good counsel reasonable resolution is achievable.

Take the case of the two high school students we used in our examples. It does not seem fair what happened to them. One wound up on double-secret probation and counseling, while the other was fined and ordered to pay court costs. But let's look at the resolution: Both of these kids had been working inside the system to get the bullying to stop. **Neither was successful until they stepped out of the shadows of inept authority and into the light of personal responsibility**. We think it's a safe bet that neither kid is going to face bullying again for several reasons:

- **Bullies don't like the daylight**. They flee from it. In these instances, consider the press "daylight." The press is often a double-edged sword, one that could just as easily cause harm as help, but a good attorney can help you navigate the perils and leverage publicity toward favorable outcome.

- **Systems of authority do not like being held accountable**. Neither school is pleased with the attention, but they both know that they will face a lawsuit if anything happens to these kids again. The documentation is in the courts and with the press, so it's virtually impossible for administrators to do nothing or look the other way.
- **They demonstrated a willingness and ability to fight back**. Bullies want meek, compliant victims. Fighting back with fists, or even a video camera, demonstrates that you're not going to go along quietly. Oftentimes that's all that's needed to get the bullies to find someone else to pick on. Criminals prefer compliant victims as well, passing over those who appear to be tough, prepared targets for easier prey.

So now both kids have resolution. Is it just or fair that they got fined? Not in our book. But, is it the cost of doing business? Yes. That's oftentimes the best we can expect from the justice system, **a resolution that may be unfair yet one that we can live with**. Professional representation is required to get there, but at least you have an opportunity to prevail. Some additional things to keep in mind if you find yourself before a judge as a defendant in either a civil or criminal case:

- **You are not special**. The judge has seen this same case hundreds of times before. Don't expect special treatment or deference.
- **Dress well**. Showing respect for the court never hurts. Yes put on a suit and tie, or a professional businesswoman's attire. A clean shave and a conservative haircut may not be your preferred style, but even though it's not fair you will be judged in part by your appearance. Consider this if you have visible tattoos or piercings too, they may be commonplace for Millennials, but for older generations who make up most juries they can create negative perceptions.
- **Shut-up**. Seriously. You have nothing to say; your attorney does all the talking. If there's a speaking role for you, your counselor will let you know exactly what it is and help you prepare to get it "right." This will likely include extensive coaching and practice.
- **Be early**. Never be late for a court date. Even being on time can be problematic as security lines, parking, and the like can be far more time consuming than planned. The judge and jury won't wait for you and you really don't need a contempt-of-court citation on top of your other troubles.

It's not just the court that you need to worry about, it's also the press. Sometimes it's a godsend, such as in the bullying case we described above, but other times its hell on earth. Seriously! Consider what happened to Officer Darren Wilson in the aftermath of the shooting in Ferguson,

Missouri. Despite the fact that **"hands up don't shoot" never happened**, that he was **exonerated by a grand jury as well as by the US Justice Department after thorough investigations**, Wilson had to resign from his law enforcement career due to **pressure from protest groups fueled by negative press**. His integrity and reputation in tatters, his life has been forever changed by what was misreported in the media. This example is far from a one-off. Consider the *Rolling Stone* magazine fraternity rape expose which **turned out to be completely false yet ruined the victims' lives** and nothing happened to the false accusers or the reporters who made hay from these bogus accusations.[4] The same thing happened with the Duke Lacrosse rape story and countless others as well.

People are often cruel, especially when they have anonymity. Just go to any comment on a controversial YouTube video, national news article, or local message board. Know that if your case makes it to the press you are going to be judged in the public arena. Chances are good that reactions to the story will be cruel, mean, hurtful, and designed to crush you. Here are a few examples:

> "You deserve to be fucked up the ass with a broomstick until death!"
>
> "How can you clueless teabaggers manage to get EVERYTHING so very BACKWARDS? Fucking MORON!"
>
> "I hope you try that semantic bullshit on St. Peter when you get to the Pearly Gates. Lake o' fire any?"
>
> "If they would not have racially profiled him, and never stopped him he would not have been entrapped into shooting them."
>
> "Just put two bullets in this guy and save the taxpayers. What's wrong with this country?"
>
> "I hope you get AIDS and die!"
>
> "Just disband the police and let these animals kill each other and burn the town down."
>
> "The only deal you should get is fried until extra crispy. The death penalty was invented for reprobates like you!"

The preceding **are real comments from public posts**, and there are thousands more like them... Not fair, not pleasant, but the way the world works. Yes, if you end up in the wrong spotlight you will not only have to experience the act, whatever it is, and then go through the

---

4 To clarify, Associate Dean Nicole Eramo from the University of Virginia filed a $7.5M defamation lawsuit against *Rolling Stone* and more civil litigation may follow from the fraternity whose reputation was impugned, yet no one was fired from the magazine and no charges were brought against the false accuser.

courts, but will have the dubious pleasure of being publicly excoriated too. That's one of many reasons to do everything you can to avoid confrontations where possible. And, why fighting is not the same thing as self-defense, even though you may be called upon to defend yourself physically from time to time.

To be clear, you have a fundamental right to defend yourself. You have a personal responsibility to defend yourself too; few others will do it for you. However, if you defend yourself on the street, be it from bullies, burglars, or thugs of most any flavor or variety, in all likelihood you'll get hit three times, by the assailant, by the legal system, and by the press.[5] You'll truly be **damned if you do** (defend yourself) **and screwed** (or possibly even dead) **if you don't**. Understand that the damning can come from unexpected places; places you thought were designed to protect you for instance. Understand that you may well have not done anything other than be who you are yet the confluence of the system, individual weakness, expediency, and flat out moral distortion will likely be headed your way.

This is the way of things. A tangle of laws, policies, and competing interests creates a gauntlet for you to run if or when you find yourself in the unenviable position of having to physically tangle with a bad guy in order to defend yourself or others. **Your job is to find a path to a resolution**, one that is unlikely to be perfect, but that will get you the most important parts of what you need.

Never let fear of consequences keep you from acting in defense of yourself or others, but **know that there will be a cost for taking or not taking action and be prepared for it**. Here are some specific things you can do:

- **Pay attention**. Build solid situational awareness and interpersonal communication skills to help stave off violence. We know that this is repetitious, but it's imperative hence worth repeating. After all, if you never have to fight you can't be screwed over by the system for fighting.
- **Think like a criminal**. Understand how predators think and act, then continuously scan your environment as if you were a criminal to better predict areas and situations that may become problematic. There is a certain "logic" to violence that makes most acts predictable, hence avoidable. Think like a wolf, not a sheep.
- **Make good decisions**. Know what's worth fighting for and develop the confidence and self-discipline to walk away from trouble whenever you're able (a subject that was covered extensively in our previous work, *The Little Black Book of Violence*). The tougher you are the less you should feel a need to prove it. Sure, fighting is always an option, but it's virtually always the *last* option.

---

5   And, depending on the severity of the event, you risk facing serious repercussions from your school or employer (such as being expelled or fired) as well as from your friends and family (such as being isolated or ostracized).

- **Find good representation**. Find a good attorney and have him/her on retainer so that you'll know he's available if needed. Even experienced attorneys do not represent themselves in court; you need a professional to help you navigate the system. If you're a martial artist or concealed weapons permit holder you're remiss if you don't proactively set aside funds for your legal defense in case they are ever needed. Be sure to purchase a personal liability (umbrella) policy of a least $1,000,000 too.

- **Know the law**. Develop a working-level understanding of the laws as they relate to self-defense and personal protection (we covered this in depth in the previous book and provide a brief summary in Appendix B here, which you can reference for more information). You'll likely never know all the laws, but major topics like when countervailing force is justified, where you can carry weapons, and how to communicate with responding officers (a topic which is discussed in Chapter 22) are essential.

- **Be prudent**. Understand what levels of force may be appropriate for any given situation. This includes everything from doing nothing skillfully (presence) to talking your way out (voice) to holding the other guy down (empty-hand restraint) to fighting your way free (less lethal force) all the way up to killing someone (lethal force). *Scaling Force* (both book and DVD) by Rory Miller and Lawrence Kane is an excellent resource to help with this. Keeping your temper and ego in check makes reasoned decision-making much, much easier too.

- **Practice, practice, and then practice some more**. Practice applying techniques in the training hall so that you will be prepared if you ever need to use them on the street. The more realistic and holistic your training experience the less likely you are to encounter a situation for which you have no response on the street. In this manner you can react to what you face without freezing or over-thinking. Even if you already practice martial arts it is important to get perspective from multiple instructors too; seminars and symposiums are a great way to do that. No one knows everything, but diverse perspectives can help build a holistic appraisal.

- **Keep your mouth shut**. If you are involved in a violent altercation, don't convict yourself. We'll talk about this more in Chapter 22, but expect to be arrested, even if you are completely innocent. Responding officers need to control the situation first and foremost; they can sort out exactly what happened and decide whether or not to press charges later on. A confrontational attitude will do you no good. In the United States you have a right to remain silent; in most cases it is best to use silence until you are represented by counsel. That goes both for speaking to officers at the scene and the press afterward. Your attorney can preemptively prepare you ahead of time so that you will know what to say or not say immediately after a critical incident, and then coach you through all stages of the legal process if you ever find yourself in need of advocacy.

- **Be able to justify what you did**. If you need countervailing force to defend yourself or others, simply claiming that you were in fear for your life won't cut it. You will need to be able to explain *exactly* what the other guy did that warranted your actions (with coaching from your attorney, of course). Even where there are witnesses or video, that is often not enough. Cameras can't catch everything and subtleties that may have been missed could prove vital to your case. How you explain your actions can determine your fate—whether or not your case will wind up in court as well as the outcome of any trail.

Self-defense is a lot like the tale of *Goldilocks and the Three Bears*. Like the porridge, beds, and such, you want it to be just right. **Too much force and you wind up in jail, whereas too little and you may not survive**. The challenge is not only in getting it right during the encounter, something that realistic, well-rounded martial arts training can help with, but also in navigating the aftermath as perfectly as possible too. That's where **education, training, and a good attorney are worth their weight in gold**.

CHAPTER 5

Know What You're Fighting For

"Be a craftsman in speech that thou mayest be strong, for the strength of one is the tongue, and speech is mightier than all fighting."

– Ptahhotep

On October 16, 2012, Italian soccer star Leonardo Bonucci was leaving a Ferrari dealership in Turin with his wife and baby when he was confronted by a mugger. The man pointed a gun at Bonucci's head and demanded that he hand over his watch. According to news reports the athlete held perfectly still and let the gunman grab his wrist, and then when he spotted an opening he punched the mugger with his free-hand. The thief then ran toward an accomplice who was waiting on a nearby moped, hopped on board, and sped away. Although Bonucci chased after the pair for a short distance, they escaped.

———————

Was it wise for Bonucci to physically defend his property, possibly endangering his wife and child in the process? We'll never know if the incident described above was a case of an athlete's rage getting the best of his common sense, or if he recognized and reacted to some danger that wasn't reported in the news. Heck, we don't even know if the bad guy's illicit weapon was even loaded. What we do know is that the soccer star chased off a bad guy without injury or unforeseen consequence. But, it could easily have ended differently. He or someone in his family **could easily have been shot while chasing after the gunman who** by all accounts was retreating and **no longer posed a threat**.

Most of us won't get mugged in front of a Ferrari dealership, since most of us cannot afford their vehicles. Nevertheless, it would be interesting to know how an armed threat managed to hang out in front of a Ferrari dealership in a place where guns are illegal for long enough to confront the soccer star without getting caught. Regardless, that's probably not a place where you'd expect much danger. In fact, statistically-speaking it's in **fringe areas adjacent to heavily traveled public places where the majority of violent crimes occur**. This includes areas such as parking lots, bathrooms, stairwells, ATM kiosks, and the like, especially at night. In order to initiate an attack, however, the threat or threats must close distance and/or control your movement so that they can get into range to strike. Or the bad guy must lay in wait somewhere along your route. Spotting potential ambush sites and pre-attack indicators such as closing, cornering, herding, or surrounding gives you time and options to formulate a proper response.

You already know that with good situational awareness and communication skills most, but not all, physical confrontations can be avoided. Sometimes you can make the decision to fight, but if you're the good guy then more often than not the choice will be made for you by your adversary. Consequently one of the most important decisions you must make in a violent encounter is why. **Why are you fighting? What is your goal?** Are you trying to control a situation? Are you trying to escape from a threat? Everything hinges on this.

The strategy of escape verses control, for example, will drive the tactics necessary for success:

- **If your goal is escape**: It is very hard to capture someone who is bound and determined to get away, even when confronted by multiple assailants. If that is your goal, simply running away may be enough, particularly if you have a few steps lead and are able to move first. If in attempting to escape you let yourself be drawn into a fight however, it becomes self-defeating. Knocking an adversary aside so that you can run is better than squaring up to him. After all, your goal is to escape, not to beat down the other guy, win the fight, control the adversary until authorities arrive, or whatever else you can think of.

- **If your goal is control**: It is very hard to restrain another person who is capable of fighting back. Consequently in order to hold him securely you will have to push him against a solid object, most often the ground, and place him into a lock or hold of some kind. For best effect, the adversary should be pinned face-down so that he has less leverage with which to fight back. The challenge is that if you're grappling on the ground with someone it is virtually impossible to get back up again flee quickly if your tactic turned out to be ill advised, such as if he's stronger, more skilled, or has friends nearby.

As you can see by these two examples above, keeping the goal firmly in mind is critical. Strikers like to move and hit, while grapplers like to roll around. Neither tactic is correct for every situation. **Knowing exactly what you're fighting for can keep you from doing dysfunctional things that training or habits might indicate**, but that ultimately prevents your success. Striking may not help you capture somebody whereas grappling is unlikely to help you escape. Hitting the other guy to set up a takedown which you subsequently turn into a pin, on the other hand, could conceivably work pretty well if your goal was to sit on the threat until law enforcement arrives.

Consider the aftermath too. How will you explain the other guy's intent, means, and opportunity, how you knew that you had to go physical in order to keep yourself safe? Unless you're a law enforcement or security professional with a duty to act, you will need to be able to explain preclusion too. Why couldn't you simply withdraw or walk away and avoid the fight altogether? These factors are very important when determining your goals during a conflict.

According to the Bureau of Justice Statistics, while the overall number of hate crime victimizations has remained stable over the last eight years, the percentage of hate crimes motivated by religious bias more than doubled (from 10% to 21%), while the percentage motivated by racial bias has dropped slightly (from 63% to 54%).

As mentioned previously many altercations these days are captured on video, be it from surveillance systems, cell-phone cameras, dash-cams, or some other source, at least when they occur in major populations centers across the United States. Even where video is not in the picture, bystanders may witness the event. **If your actions don't match your statements you will be in serious trouble** when you get to court, particularly when it comes to the matter of preclusion. If you escalated things or participated in letting events escalate in any way then claiming self-defense may be off the table.

Know your goal and make tactical decisions that support it. Sounds easy, but in the heat of battle this is a very, very common mistake. If you're ambushed and attacked you don't get a vote, of course, but sometimes getting involved is your first decision. With good situational awareness it could always be your first decision. **The first question to ask yourself**, therefore, **is should you intervene?** An additional complication arises whenever you come across a fight in progress and are not certain who the good and bad guys are. Clearly you wouldn't want to play for the wrong side, but even highly trained uniformed officers sometimes kill their plainclothes counterparts, tragedies brought on by mistaken identity. Physically breaking up a fight is tricky, best handled by professionals whenever possible. Thankfully, getting physical isn't the only way to go.

Once you've decided (or been forced to) get involved, **the next choice is how**. Do you have to get physical or are there other options? Can you talk your way out? Using verbal de-escalation, flattery, trickery, or even shouting for help are all solid options right up until fists begin to fly.

And, if it's others who are fighting then verbal or non-verbal interventions is still an option for you. Shouting something along the lines of, "Hey someone just called the cops" has broken up an awful lot of fights. It's a great, non-violent tactic. In fact, in certain situations the mere presence of a witness is enough to stop the assault; you don't even need to do anything beyond being seen. Sometimes pulling out your smartphone and filming the altercation works but be cautious if you go that route as it can bring unwanted attention your way. And, some folks are stupid enough to *want* their fight recorded on video. Sometimes, such as when weapons are in play or the combatants are wearing distinctive clothing or gang symbols, you are far better off not being there. That doesn't mean that you cannot get involved, however, just that you need to **do it from a safe distance**. Withdrawing to a more secure location and calling 911 is a very viable and valuable tactic. It lets you do your civic duty and allows professionals to intervene, all while keeping yourself safe.

This brings up a very important determination, **are you protecting yourself and/or protecting others?** If you need to defend someone smaller, slower, weaker, or disabled, fleeing might not be an option even if it's otherwise prudent. Let's say you have a toddler in a stroller. This means, among other things, that you cannot run away and abandon your child or even stray too far away during the fight because your adversary or adversaries might get a hold of the kid and injure, kill, or use him/her as a hostage against you. The dynamic of fighting around a stroller is wholly different than that of working on the open floor of a *dojo* (training hall) or gymnasium.

As you can see, escape is not always an option and stopping the threat in certain circumstances can get complicated. Nevertheless, keeping the end game in mind helps you make good decisions. In the stroller example your movements are restricted but not your moves. In fact, peril to your child arguably justifies a higher level of force, so you may choose to do horrific damage to the other guy(s) in an attempt to end the threat as quickly as possible—damage you wouldn't normally consider in other situations.

Restraining a threat adds different complications. Oftentimes it's illegal unless you're a sworn officer, security professional, or otherwise have a duty to act. Nevertheless, if it's your drunken uncle, out-of-control fraternity brother, drug-addled roommate, or whatever, it's often better to sit on him (or her) until he calms down even if that's technically unlawful restraint (kidnapping). Chances are good that he's not going to press charges anyway. He might even thank you in the morning…

All this is well and good, and essential to think about ahead of time, because there is a massive complication that comes into play whenever you find yourself in a serious confrontation in real life: Adrenaline.

Adrenaline is, in many ways, the equivalent of the Incredible Hulk… or insuperable Mr. Hyde, were they to step out of the comic books and take over your body. **When adrenalized, you can be stabbed, shot, or beat to hell and still persevere**, at least until you come down from the adrenal cocktail and the pain kicks in... or you bleed out. On the positive side you become stronger, tougher, and more resilient yet simultaneously **you will have degraded motor skills**, experience tunnel vision, and, depending on the severity of the incident, likely suffer temporary hearing or memory loss too. This is where gender differences can make a substantial impact. When men are confronted with extreme emotional or violent situations, their adrenaline surges near instantly and then dissipates rapidly afterward, whereas women have a much slower, longer-lasting adrenaline surge. This means that women have more time to think, but must often defend themselves before becoming adrenalized, whereas men get the advantages and disadvantages of adrenaline without the clear-headed ability to plan at the beginning of the violent encounter.

Your ability to think and act rationally is significantly reduced once adrenaline kicks in,[6] driving you toward instinctive responses, a reason why thinking things through ahead of time is so important. And having comprehensive, realistic training, of course. While precise movements are extraordinarily tough, even imprecise ones like grabbing a wrist or hooking a leg can be problematic if you haven't trained regularly under pressure. Gross motor movements, especially those that target vital areas of the adversary's body, can work pretty well. Conditioned responses, "combat breathing" and other techniques can help you counteract, or at least work through, the effects of adrenaline.

In addition to countering the adverse effects of adrenaline to some degree, scenario training and pre-planning can help you avoid freezing in indecision rather than immediately responding to whatever situation you find yourself in. Your instinctive reaction can be fight, flight, or freeze, any of which may be a good choice, so long as it's a conscious choice and not an unthinking reaction. Sometimes it is good to freeze in place, such as taking cover during a gunfight, but oftentimes the adrenaline cocktail renders you unable to make decisions in the heat of the moment.

Perception under extreme stress is altered. Your senses and your perception of time are both affected, such as when things begin moving in slow motion. That doesn't always mean that you are moving or thinking faster; in fact oftentimes it means that you're caught in your brain and not making decisions at all. There are complex reasons for this, but the bottom line is that **if you believe you should be doing something and you are not doing it, you are frozen**. And that's a bad thing. Once you recognize it, acknowledge it immediately. Saying "I'm frozen" out loud can help break the freeze simply because it subconsciously reminds you that you can affect the world around you. It might sound weird to the other guy(s), but that's irrelevant if it kicks you into fight

---

6   Adrenaline may affect the other guy(s) as well, but not always. Like law enforcement officers, military personnel, and security professionals, the more seasoned the criminal the lower the chances of him/her having to struggle through the adverse effects of adrenaline along with his intended victim.

or flight mode, whichever is tactically better for whatever situation you face. It is easy to say stuff in your head and not do it, so speaking aloud is best. Tell yourself to do something, anything, in order to break the freeze. **Say it and do it**. Then tell yourself to do something again and do it. In other words, if you discover that you are frozen make yourself do something and keep it up until you are acting in a manner that helps you achieve your goal.

As the situation unfolds don't forget that the bad guys tend to cheat, oftentimes using weapons, striking from ambush, or merely using their words to obfuscate their intent until it's too late for you to react. **Fight with your mouth too**. It's not just speaking aloud to break the freeze. Yelling for help is an incredibly valuable yet underappreciated defensive tactic. First off, it gets bystanders attention and can create witnesses (a topic we cover in Chapter 14) who will be favorably disposed to your cause if you find yourself in court afterward. You can use your voice to startle, confuse, or trick the other guy too.

In summary:

- **Know what you're fighting for**. Are you trying to get away, keep the other guy from getting away, or something else like protecting a loved one, breaking up a fight, etc.? Have a clear goal before the fists start to fly so that in the heat of the moment you can stay on plan.
- **Implement a strategy that supports that goal**. Keep the end game in mind at all times. If every tactic supports your strategy the odds of a successful outcome increase exponentially.
- **Account for adrenaline**. Keep tactics simple, direct, and in line with your goal. And, if you find yourself frozen tell yourself aloud what you feel you must do. It helps to subconsciously remind yourself that you can affect the world and then begin to do so.
- **Stay on plan**. Assure that the tactical situation doesn't distract or deter you from focusing on the end game and losing focus on your goal. Tactical decisions often need a certain amount of fluidity as fights are dynamic, so be flexible, but stay on point.

If everything you do supports your goal you will markedly increase your odds of survival. And, you'll have a leg up in the aftermath as well since **you'll be able to paint a clear picture of why you had to do whatever you did as well as why it was necessary**. It's valuable to think this stuff through ahead of time, practice scenarios, and get a little experience under your belt since it's very hard to think logically during the heat of battle.

CHAPTER 6

"GUN FREE" EQUALS "TARGET RICH"

"Lawbreakers, by their very definition, break the law—they've literally made it their job description. Only the most childish naiveté could lead an honest person to believe someone who would break the most stringent laws somehow wouldn't break a much less important one with a far less serious penalty."

– Massad Ayoob

Before he killed 20 children and six adults at Sandy Hook Elementary School in Newtown, Connecticut on December 14, 2012, 20-year-old Adam Lanza committed about half a dozen felonies. Among other things, he stole his 52-year-old mother's gun and shot her in the head four times. He then drove a stolen car to the school, marched right passed a "gun free zone" sign, shot his way through a glass panel next to the locked entrance doors, and proceeded to a first grade classroom where he opened fire on his helpless victims. Horrified administrators and students heard the initial shots over the school intercom system which was being used for morning announcements at the time. Approximately four and a half minutes after receiving a frantic 911 call, the Connecticut State Police arrived. Realizing that he now faced armed resistance, Lanza committed suicide by shooting himself in the head.

A few months earlier, on July 20, 2012, James Holmes dressed in an outfit reminiscent of the DC Comics villain, The Joker, opened fire on innocent citizens who were watching the newly released Batman movie, *The Dark Knight Rises*, killing 12 and injuring 70. This atrocity took place at the Cinemark Century Theater in Aurora, Colorado. The killer passed up seven other theaters that were closer to his apartment, including ones that held larger audiences, to select the one venue that had posted signs prohibiting guns outside their entrance. Writing about the incident shortly afterward Professor John Lott related, "Why would a mass shooter pick a place that bans guns? The answer should be obvious, though it apparently isn't clear to the media: disarming law-abiding citizens leaves them sitting ducks."

The first legislative response to keep the public safer from mass shootings and other horrific acts of violence is invariably a ban of some kind. Legislation prohibiting the sale and manufacture of certain types of weapons, magazines, and ammunition, or restricting where and how guns can be carried are quite common, oftentimes augmented by proposals for waiting periods, universal background-check systems, and the like. While such actions might make the voters feel good, they are based on the flawed logic that if there's only a rule, a sign, a piece of legislation, prospective bad guys will follow it.

Reality check people: Rules and regulations absolutely can prevent *some* crime, threat of punishment is a significant motivator to certain individuals, yet simply writing things down does not necessarily affect everyone's behavior. **Bad guys don't follow the law!** In fact, when it comes to criminals, breaking the law is pretty much their job description. Some examples:

- **Murder is already illegal, yet people do it anyway**. Even though overall crime rates have been declining for over a decade, homicides occur about 15,000 times a year in the United States (according to the Unified Crime Reporting database).
- **Forcible rape is outlawed, but not uncommon**. This disgusting crime happens about 90,000 times a year… that's reported. Anecdotal evidence suggests that the true number is significantly higher in the United States, though we'll obviously never know for certain.
- **Aggravated assaults, they're illegal and commonplace**. Aggravated assaults are those that either involve weapons and/or cause serious injuries to the victim, the kind that generally require two or more days of hospitalization. Despite being against the law, citizens are assaulted roughly 800,000 times a year in the United States.

As the quote at the beginning of this chapter states so eloquently, it's downright silly to believe that bad guys will stop being bad simply because society tells them to. And, it's dangerous to think that way. Nevertheless, it is all too common. And, it's been going on for a long time. For example, after a shooting at the Empire State Building in which one person was killed in 1997, then New

York mayor Rudy Giuliani called for national gun licensing laws, a perspective that has since turned into a national movement led by fellow former-mayor Michael Bloomberg among others. Their ultimate goal? Taking guns away from law-abiding citizens under the false assumption that such actions will make everyone safer.

Laws restricting access to guns or ammunition are often justified as producing a "cooling off period" to prevent domestic violence, spree shootings and the like that ostensibly are caused by fits of rage. While some crimes really do take place in the heat of the moment, when guns aren't available knives, vehicles, bludgeons, and a whole host of impromptu weapons take their place. The Rwandan genocide that wiped out one-seventh of the entire population of the country was perpetrated primarily through the use of machetes and clubs.

Banning guns not only doesn't stop crime, **the unintended consequences actually make things worse!**

Consider the battered wife whose homicidal husband ignores the restraining order, another piece of paper intended to keep folks safe, and comes after her with a vengeance. **How does a smaller, weaker person ward off violence without an equalizer?** Let's face it, criminals know how to obtain contraband weapons, not only handguns but also explosives, fully automatic weapons (that are either banned outright or require special permits in every state in the US) and a host of banned substances that ordinary citizens would never dream of owning let alone know how to acquire.

Let's be perfectly clear, **the only way to stop homicidal violence is with homicidal violence.** Period. We might not like it, but that's the way it is. That is also why politicians, celebrities, business moguls, and the like have armed bodyguards. That's why there's a fence around the White House and Secret Service agents guarding the president and his family 24 hours a day, 365 days a year.

Elites might have the position, power, or resources to afford such protections, but what about the rest of us? There are not enough cops in the country, let alone the world, to defend everyone at every time in every location. Even if it's only for a few minutes before help arrives, when it comes to self-protection we're on our own. An awful lot of bad things can happen in a few minutes… For instance, most people can empty a gun in seconds, reload, and do it again. And again. Unarmed citizens are at a tremendous disadvantage when confronted by armed thugs, terrorists, or spree shooters, a disadvantage that rarely ends well for the prospective victims.

In a groundbreaking 1999 study, *Multiple Victim Public Shootings, Bombings, and Right-to-Carry Concealed Handgun Laws*, Professors John R. Lott and William M. Landes of the University of Chicago Law School found a common theme in mass shootings: **They occur in places where guns are banned.** In a shocking fit of common sense, spree killers have figured out that they will have a far greater chance of success in places such as shopping malls and schools where their prospective victims are unarmed than they will in other areas where folks can shoot back. Conversely, concealed handgun permits and "shall issue" laws that allow responsible individuals to carry handguns for self-defense reduce the number of multiple victim public shootings. Not only are potential attackers deterred, but also the number of people injured or killed per attack is greatly reduced. The study also demonstrated that:

- **Guns save lives**. Despite the fact that most incidents never make the news, ordinary citizens use guns defensively against criminal attacks somewhere between 760,000 and 3,500,000 times per year in the US.
- **Guns keep women safe**. The risk of serious injury from a criminal attack is 2.5 times greater for women offering no resistance than for women resisting with a gun.
- **Gun ownership reduces crime**. Laws permitting individuals to carry concealed weapons reduce murder rates by about ten percent, with similar declines in other violent crimes.
- **Legal gun owners are almost always the good guys**. Contrary to a popular misconception, concealed handguns by permit holders are virtually never involved in the commission of any crime, let alone murder.

About 90% of homicide victims are killed with a weapon in the US. Although the likelihood of sustaining some type of injury is the same for victims facing armed and unarmed assailants (26%), serious injuries are more than three times more likely to result from armed offenders. For nonfatal violent crimes, assailants are more likely to have a firearm than a knife or club.

It's not just the government that has failed to learn this commonsense lesson, major corporations and small businesses fall for this flawed logic all too often as well. A sad fact is that **well intended, goodhearted people have a very difficult time understanding that not everyone thinks or acts like them**. If the worst thing you've ever faced is harsh language, it's extremely hard to contemplate what a homicidal assault looks like, let alone why anyone would want to commit one. If you obey the law, why wouldn't everyone else do so as well? And that's the rub, good guys do good things. They follow rules. Bad guys don't.

We know a woman—let's call her Susan—who works for a large company that has major distribution warehouses located in several regions across the United States. Despite local firearms laws that allow concealed carry at most of their locations, the company also prohibits weapons of any kind on their premises. Susan was in charge of the night shift at one of their warehouses. Everybody comes in, goes to work picking orders, loading trucks, and moving merchandise around with heavy equipment while she oversees and directs the work.

One employee didn't make it through his probation period and was let go. Apparently he couldn't get along well with others, wasn't a team player. Now that is not unusual, it happens all the time. People get dismissed during their probationary period all the time, not only at Susan's company but at virtually every company around the world. That's why such policies exist; it's a test drive, so to speak, to assure a good fit. However, this was a somewhat rarer case… The ex-employee was angry about his dismissal and told friends that he was going to buy a gun, come back, and shoot the place up. His friends believed him and they called the company to warn them about what might be coming.

After getting wind of this incident, management took serious note of this guy's threats. They talked with people who knew him and were able to confirm that he had, in fact, recently purchased a hunting rifle. Armed with that information, management shifted into a defensive posture. Now we are not going to get into a lot to of the details because we want to focus on one single issue in this instance, the policy that was created to respond to the ex-employee's threat. All managers were called into a special attention meeting. The topic was implementation of a new policy that would be enforced should a shooting take place on the premises. Their attorneys outlined the policy:

> In the event of a shooting, the floor managers (like Susan) were to gather the employees, all 250 of them. Then the managers were to quickly move the employees into a room at the end of the warehouse and lock the large industrial door shut behind them.

After hearing and understanding the policy, Susan began to ask logical questions:

"How am I supposed to get 250 people to listen to me when they are being shot at?"

"Use the intercom system," replied the attorney.

"You do realize that the area you want us all to get into is going to turn into a killing room, right?"

"We don't believe so," came back the attorney. "It is a concrete-walled room."

Susan responded, "You know the guy who threatened us used to drive a forklift. Anybody can use one of the forklifts we store in this warehouse to take out a wall or the door. And, he bought a hunting rifle. Rifle bullets will go right through it."

After some more exchange, Susan's immediate superior interrupted, "Susan, what's your point?"

"My point is that your policy is bad. It is dangerous and unworkable."

The reply came back, "I suppose you have a better idea?"

"Yes, yes I do."

"Let's hear it."

"Scatter. That's what people want to do anyway. It is what nature does, and what we should do too. We shouldn't cluster up in one confined space, a place with a single entrance and no doors or windows to escape from, making ourselves an easy target."

"That is your idea, scatter?" The attorney sneered.

"Yup," Susan said calmly.

Her manager chimed in, "Susan you are on the second floor. You will have to run down the stairs and across part of the shop floor to get to a door. That means running past the shooter. It doesn't make any sense."

"No I won't," Susan replied. "I will be going out my window."

"The windows don't open. They are sealed."

"My office chair is my key to the window. I will break it easily enough in an emergency."

"And jumping two stories?" somebody said in an incredulous tone.

"Yup, right onto the sloping grass below. It's actually a bit less than two stories. If I hang from the window and let go I can do that easily. So can anyone else on that side of the second floor."

"With your policy how are we supposed to account for everybody? We need to get a headcount."

Susan, holding her ground, had thought about this too. "How about everybody calls into the front office phone system with their name and status using their personal cell phone? Everybody carries one nowadays."

The tit-for-tat questions and answers followed this line for a while longer. Susan never backed down from her policy of scattering; something she knew in her heart was safer and far more practical than trying to herd fearful employees in to a killing zone.

The meeting started to wind down when the attorney who had helped develop the policy finally called Susan out, "You're not a team player.[7]"

Susan kept her mouth shut, but wanted to say, "Yeah, and I don't play on stupid teams." But instead chose to remain gainfully employed instead.

Look at the preceding conversation with the eyes of a member of the United States military, especially those who fought in the horrific 82-day battle of Okinawa in 1945. Or those who

---

7 This tact was unsurprising. Anyone who is unwilling to admit that he or she is incorrect or has made an error will eventually take the argument down to a personal level. At this point the conversation is no longer about the mistake; it has become a battle of egos.

participated in Afghan cave battles of recent years. **A cave is a great hiding place… until it is discovered. Then a cave becomes a grave.** Similarly, a tip-up concrete room is a great hiding place until it is discovered. Then that room becomes a tomb.

While Susan stopped arguing, she never did agree with the misguided policy. The policy that the company's attorneys put into place had not been reviewed by security experts, hence was poorly thought out and unworkable. It may have given the company legal cover if something bad had occurred, but it did nothing to actually keep employees safe. Thankfully the disgruntled former employee never did follow through with his threat, yet the policy remains in place today.

What if you find yourself in a similar situation? What do you do about it? Are you going to be a lemming and follow the policy or **are you going to take personal responsibility for your own safety?** If someone threatens to bring a gun to work, what will you do? Think about it. Such incidents happen all the time. Will you take a few weeks off work, hoping not to be there when something bad happens? Is that even practical? Will you carry a gun of your own, even if it violates the company's policy?

What about the rest of your day? Your nights? Your weekends?

Violence can happen anywhere, even in a place of worship such as a church, synagogue, mandir, or mosque… Compare the June 17, 2015 shooting rampage instigated by 21-year-old white supremacist Dylann Roof at the Emanuel African Methodist Episcopal Church in Charleston, South Carolina with a similar attack by 29-year-old hardened criminal Kiarron Parker at the New Destiny Christian Center in Aurora, Colorado on April 22, 2012. Roof killed nine unarmed people at a bible study meeting before fleeing the church, a gun free zone. Emanuel's pastor, one of the victims, had publicly spoken against lawful concealed carry. In South Carolina a firearm can only be carried legally in a house of worship with approval by church authorities, so the only person with a gun at that venue was a racist asshole who hoped to spark a civil war by committing mass murder. New Destiny, on the other hand, had a different policy. Consequently, Parker was able to murder the pastor's mother, 67-year-old Josephine Echols, but before he could harm any of the other 30 innocents in the building he was shot and killed by the victim's nephew, off-duty police officer Antonio Milow, who religiously carried his sidearm to church along with his bible.

After the horror in Charleston acclaimed martial artist and actor Chuck Norris reinforced this point when he wrote in an editorial:

> "Imagine once again, if just one of those Christians who held a bible in their hand at that AME church also packed a pistol via a legal concealed weapons permit. Souls could have been saved. That is why I have a challenge for pastors and church leaders. With all due respect, it's about time that they woke up to the idea that providing for and protecting God's flock means increasing church

security, from children's classes to main sanctuaries and fellowship halls. Faith is not an excuse to bypass self-defense. That's not my original idea or position. It's found in the Good Book.[8]"

So, what about you? **Will you be armed or unarmed?**

Gun ownership drives lots of decisions, everything from how you dress (to facilitate concealment yet still allow rapid deployment under duress), where you shop (we won't spend money at business that advertise themselves as "gun-free" zones), how you travel (without universal reciprocity, the hodgepodge of carry laws can make moving around the country problematic if you don't carefully plan ahead of time), where you work (certain companies won't allow their employees to be armed, even those who are legally licensed to carry), who you tell about your weapon (this brings up a whole other can of worms), and so on... Think these things through carefully before you act. Some additional actions you can take:

- **Know yourself.** No matter how concerned you are about personal protection, guns aren't for everyone (nor are knives, bludgeons, or other weapons either). If you don't have the right mindset, training, and ability, you can easily put yourself in more risk with a firearm than you will be without one. Begin with self-assessment. **Are you capable of taking a life? Under what circumstances?** Spend some serious think time determining whether or not you could be a killer under the gravest extreme. If the answer isn't an emphatic yes, **do not purchase or carry a weapon.**
- **Study gun laws.** If you do decide to purchase a firearm (or any other weapon for that matter), it is imperative that you know the law, understanding where and under what conditions you can carry and use it. Ignorance is no excuse. We see foolish gun owners do incredibly stupid things regularly, stuff that winds up on the nightly news and fuels the anti-gun efforts. **Don't be part of the problem.** A multi-state concealed pistol license should probably be in your future too, if you haven't gone that route already.
- **Be responsible.** This not only means using the weapon prudently, but also keeping proper control of your gun at all times. It should either be strapped to your waist (or wherever you choose to carry it) or secured in a manner appropriate for your situation (e.g., whether or not you have kids or roommates) such as locked up in a quick-release safe where it's ready for an emergency but only you can access it. **Don't let your weapon get into the wrong hands.** Further, when moving around in public it is important to

---

8   A couple of examples: "But we prayed to our God and posted a guard day and night to meet this threat" (Nehemiah 4:9), and "If you don't have a sword, sell your cloak and buy one" (Luke 22:36).

be cognizant of the folks around you, subtly positioning your arms to avoid anyone coming in contact with your weapon (either making a grab or just bumping up against it).

- **Know your weapon**. Keep it in prime condition and practice with it regularly. All too many gun owners spend thousands of dollars on their weapon yet virtually nothing on their training. This is an investment in your safety; **you need to be able to access and deploy the firearm under virtually any sort of duress and still hit your target**. Practice until you can, and then practice some more. What you can do on the range and what you will be capable of in extreme conditions when you are adrenalized is not necessarily the same thing. Maintain your firearm properly, be cautious that any accessories you buy are as fault-tolerant as the weapon, and keep it cleaned and properly lubricated at all times.

- **Know your holster**. Using a high quality holster that covers your trigger goes a long way toward eliminating the possibility of having a negligent discharge. And, it helps assure that your weapon will be exactly where you expect it to be when you need it. Consider the tradeoffs between Kydex®, leather, and other materials. A good holster (which we cover more in Chapter 15) should be resilient, durable, reliable, and just as easy to draw from as it is to re-holster without looking. A common challenge is that many folks either get cheap or don't think things through when they purchase one. Consider how your weapon retention system works with your preferred carry position (e.g., visible holsters require a higher retention level for safety/control), attire (e.g., business or casual), and lifestyle (e.g., do you need to take it on and off frequently) as well as where the barrel is pointing when you're wearing it. Bra and underwear holsters, for example, leave a loaded weapon aimed at yourself whereas the "Miami classic" shoulder holster keeps the weapon pointing behind you at all times, all of which may be asking for problems. You may need multiple holsters to support your lifestyle, so consider that as well.

- **Know your ammunition**. Because hollow point bullets tend to not over-penetrate, which means more stopping power with less risk of collateral damage to bystanders who may be behind or beyond the threat, they are very popular. They're also illegal in certain jurisdictions. Knowing your ammunition means not only understanding where and if you can use it, but also what types of bullets are most reliable in your gun (they aren't all the same) and how well they've fared in the field. It also means rotating your ammunition (semi-annually in most instances) so that it's fresh and there's no risk of oil or solvents seeping through the primer and inhibiting function if you need to fire in self-defense. Target ammunition is less expensive to practice with, but be sure to use whatever you carry regularly at the range from time to time too. It tends to be hotter, hence deliver more perceived recoil, among other things.

- **Get involved**. If you believe in gun ownership consider joining the National Rifle Association, Second Amendment Foundation, Citizen's Committee for the Right to Keep and Bear Arms, National Shooting Sports Foundation, or some other group that helps protect your rights. Despite the Second Amendment, the stroke of a pen can change everything overnight. If you don't believe in gun ownership, well there's a bunch of groups that advocate for the other side too… sigh.

- **Set a good example**. The decision to own and carry a firearm is a deeply personal one. If you make that choice you have also decided to do all the other things that come along with it. Gun ownership necessitates a much higher level of accountability, diligence, and conscientiousness. **Be the paragon of responsible gun ownership**. Do the right things, behave in the right ways, and (where appropriate) teach others to do the same.

While the only way to get out of certain dire circumstances is by using a gun, those situations are thankfully few and far between. Not everyone needs a gun nor should everyone own one. It's a determination that takes heavy thought and carries significant responsibility. **Whatever you decide, be sure it's a wise choice**.

CHAPTER 7

WHAT WORKS WITH WORKPLACE VIOLENCE

"Let the fear of danger be a spur to prevent it; he that fears not, gives advantage to the danger."

– Francis Quarles

Los Angeles jewelry store owner Lance Thomas is a law abiding citizen. As a small businessman who had a big Rolex sign outside his shop and sold expensive, easy to fence merchandise near a gang-infested neighborhood, he knew that he might become a target for violent criminals. As such, he was determined to take responsibility for his personal safety as well as that of his customers. He legally purchased several weapons, learned how to use them, and placed them strategically around his sales floor so that they would be in easy reach wherever he moved about in his small shop.

It's a very good thing that he did, because **that's why he is still alive today**.

Thomas' life story reads like a movie script, yet it is absolutely real. He has survived numerous violent robberies, including a well-coordinated assassination attempt. In fact, in four gun battles, he fired more than 40 rounds, thwarted 11 assailants, killed five men, and wounded another. The rest surrendered or fled. He has more experience under fire than most law enforcement officers.

Here's an example: On November 27, 1989 a five-man team rolled up on Thomas' shop. One thug stayed in the driver's seat of the getaway car while another perpetrator remained outside, pretending to be an unaffiliated passerby so he could provide covert support. The other three men burst into the shop and began firing without any warning whatsoever. One moment Thomas was serving customers and the next he was targeted by a furious storm of lead. Of the first eight shots, he was hit four times, three .25 caliber rounds striking his right shoulder and a fourth slamming into the side of his neck, mere millimeters from being a lethal strike.

Without missing a beat, the wounded shop owner grabbed his nearest pistol, a .357 magnum revolver. His first shot missed the gangbanger, yet his next five bullets slammed home, knocking the bad guy to the floor where he died on the spot. Dropping his now empty weapon, Thomas lunged for a .38 caliber revolver, snatched it up, and engaged the second perpetrator who was already shooting at him. Both combatants emptied their weapons but missed each other despite the close proximity, though the assailant figured he'd had enough and fled from the fight. Continuing to move, Thomas got a hold of another .357 and used it to target the third gunman. They exchanged fire and by the time Thomas's hammer fell on an empty chamber the bad guy had gone down for good.

It must have been quite a shock to the thugs outside, one moment they think they have the upper hand on an easy victim and the next there's an intense volley of gunfire. Then their friend stumbles out of the shop, unscathed but shaking with fear. The gangbangers still outside took the better part of valor and fled for their lives. The entire encounter couldn't have taken more than a than a minute or two. In that short time Thomas fired 19 rounds from a combination of three guns, all in self-defense.

> "Lance Thomas was totally justified in everything that he did," Detective Lee Kingsford, who investigated the case, told the press afterward. "All of the suspects had extensive criminal records. They knew what they were doing; they just didn't know who they were doing it against."

We love how Massad Ayoob summed things up, "Each and every one of them **died from a sudden and acute failure of the victim selection process**."

According to the National Institute for Occupational Safety and Health, 18,000 people a week are victimized by some sort of workplace violence in the United States. In fact, although industrial accidents abound, **homicide is actually the leading cause of death among female workers and the second leading cause of death for men**.

Does that statistic surprise you?

There is an average of 17 homicides in the workplace each and every week and countless aggravated assaults, rapes, and lesser acts of violence. We don't hear about most of them because the national media rarely reports on such things unless a Fortune 500® company, multiple fatalities, or high visibility victims are involved. Workplace violence is horrible, but victims aren't the only ones who suffer. Businesses are often crushed by such incidents too. Thomas, by way of example, eventually had to close his shop, moving to an online-only business model. Employers can face civil claims from victims, witnesses, *and* perpetrators for things such as negligent hiring, negligent retention, wrongful termination, or failure to warn. For publically traded companies, a 15 percent stock price hit is typical due to lost productivity, negative publicity, medical costs, and legal bills.

So, how do you protect yourself? Knowledge is the first step toward prevention. While dangers vary by industry, job type, and location, general factors that elevate the level of risk include:

- **Significant change or workplace disruption** (e.g., outsourcing, downsizing, restructuring).
- **Unstable or volatile clients** (e.g., health care, social services, law enforcement, bail bonds, or criminal justice).
- **Public contact or work in community-based settings** (e.g., social services, real estate agencies, or retail stores).
- **Mobile workplace or delivery of passengers, goods or services** (e.g., Uber, Lyft, taxicab, bus, pizza delivery drivers, or construction trades).
- **Isolated, late night or early morning work** (e.g., gas stations, convenience stores, or package deliveries).
- **Valuable possessions or property** (e.g., armored car, bank, or jewelry store).

3.3 million About 3,300,000 persons aged 18 or older are stalked every year in the US. Although both genders are equally likely to experience harassment, women are at greater risk of stalking than men. Most victims experience at least one unwanted contact per week, 25% are subjected to some form of cyber-stalking, and 11% of are stalked for 5 years or more.

Unfortunately those who draft violence prevention policies often do not have the requisite knowledge to assure their program's success. Simply put, **knee jerk reactions don't work**. They might make people feel better, but they rarely resolve anything or make anyone safer. Processes and procedures must be well thought out, comprehensive, fair, clearly communicated, and fully implemented. We've all heard stories of convenience store clerks who were fired for defending themselves against violent threats. Their employers' policies placed them in situations where they were forced to comply and die or be fired for legally defending their lives, a lose/lose proposition if ever there was one. Take the example of Nouria Energy Corporation who released the following statement in response to a 2013 incident:

"We do respect the constitutional right to bear arms. However, we believe the best way to keep our employees and customers safe is to prohibit weapons in the workplace."

Really?! Why?

Compliance with predatory violence may keep you safe, but not always. It depends on what the predator wants, you (e.g., Ed Gein), your stuff (e.g., Willie Sutton), or both. In cases where a criminal ties his victim up and/or transports them to a secondary location where he has the privacy and time necessary to commit whatever perversions he has in mind, things simply do not end well. Imagine the lawsuits and bad publicity that would result from a clerk being tied up, dragged into the walk-in refrigerator, raped, and then murdered at a company's facility. Oh wait, that was a lawsuit…

So, how do create a safer workplace? Well, **if you're an employer, why not start by actually trusting your employees?** You hired 'em right? That means they must have knowledge, skills, and abilities that create value. Likely they can exercise good judgment too. We have yet to see a weapon jump up and attack anyone without a person wielding it. Therefore, it's not the weapon in the workplace that's the issue but rather the person who uses it. **If you've hired good people they will usually make good decisions**. You're already betting the company's resources, reputation, and stock price (assuming it's a public company) that they will do smart things on your behalf. Besides, most workplaces are already packed with items that could be turned into weapons if someone had nefarious intent, things like fire extinguishers, vehicles, kitchen knives, construction tools, and pots of scalding hot coffee to name a few.

Consequently if an employee has passed all the requirements (e.g., background check, training) necessary to be issued a concealed weapons permit, shouldn't that mean **you could and should trust them *more* than someone who has not**? After all, the government has extensively researched the person for you. As a result of this background check you know beyond any shadow of doubt that they don't have a history of criminal activity, mental illness, domestic violence, outstanding warrants, or other red flags that you need to know about. As long as employees follow all applicable laws **there's really no legitimate reason to prohibit them from bringing weapons to work**.

So, **begin by trusting your employees**, especially the legally armed ones, but that's not enough. Bring experts in to help craft actionable policies that actually solve the problem and not just make folks feel better while remaining unsafe. And, have the employees weigh in too. They might not be self-defense experts but they do know the job, the environment, and many of the threats they have encountered or might face.

Well-thought-out procedures should be set in place to ensure a coordinated response if an attack occurs, addressing **employee safety, site security, emergency services, and medical triage** among other vital issues. If an incident occurs, site safety must be assessed, medical and law enforcement personnel must be contacted, incident areas must be secured to preserve evidence, and all employees must be accounted for once the dust settles. Provisions for medical and psychological follow-up, confidentiality, and payment of salary or benefits after the event must be in place where needed to prevent victims from suffering further losses as well. As a sidebar, virtually none of these things were covered in the plan that our friend Susan objected to at her company.

Measures an employer takes to prevent workplace violence are not only a good thing generally, but they may well limit potential liability should something bad happen too. So yeah, **it makes the lawyers happy… and it's the right thing to do**, a win-win. Some important steps include:

- **Have a plan**. Develop and implement a comprehensive risk mitigation plan, one that covers what must be done before, during, and after a critical incident. And, don't just write it once and throw it into a file drawer, go back and revalidate, update, and improve it on a regular basis (such as annually or bi-annually) as things change.
- **Educate the workforce**. Provide safety education for employees so that they will understand what conduct is acceptable as well as what to do during an emergency. Provide this training for all new hires and refresh it annually for all employees so that it will stay at the forefront of everyone's mind.
- **Carefully evaluate who you hire**. Conduct comprehensive background and reference checks for all potential new hires and use credit checks to verify job applicant information. Research prior criminal convictions of potential hires that might reasonably relate to job duties as permitted by law (e.g., registered sex offenders cannot legally work with or around children in most jurisdictions). Question any gaps in employment or suspicious items on applicants' resumes.
- **Implement physical security protocols**. Secure the workplace, limiting access by outsiders to sensitive areas via the use of identification badges, cipher locks, electronic keys, security personnel, and/or other reliable methods and use CCTV video where appropriate and legal (e.g., areas frequented by customers, areas where valuables are stored). Alarm systems, video, and other safety precautions not only provide a layer of security they can also stave off certain problems such as petty theft, hence have unforeseen collateral benefits too.
- **Make it easy to call for help**. Pre-program emergency numbers into employees' phones and cellular devices. Personnel who have not been trained how to react under stress will have degraded fine motor skills making it very difficult, if not impossible, to do something as simple as dialing 911. In locations where you need to dial 8 or 9 to reach an outside line (making an emergency call 9-911), the extra digits can be even more challenging to type as more conscious thought is required to do it correctly.
- **Screen regularly**. Conduct routine drug and alcohol testing where appropriate (this generally means that testing must be job related and consistent with business necessity as permitted by law). While medical privacy laws will likely keep you from finding out

about mental health issues suffered during employment, employee assistance and/or counseling programs can help prevent violence prophylactically.

- **Don't tempt the bad guys**. If employees work with large amounts of cash, provide safe drops to limit the amount of available cash on hand, especially during late evening and early morning hours. Where feasible incentivize customers to pay with credit cards, PayPal, or electronic funds transfers.

- **Have prudent policies**. Don't force employees to choose between your policy and their personal safety. Make sure you incentivize the right behaviors too. For example, if employees must make home visits establish specific policies and procedures regarding client contact, ensure the presence of others as appropriate, and establish the right of employees to use discretion in avoiding hazardous situations or places that "just don't feel right."

- **Provide the right equipment**. Ensure that any company vehicles are properly maintained and equip field staff with cellular phones or other communication devices that assure coverage throughout their routes. Where possible track employee's movements in the field via GPS so that you will always know where they are if an emergency occurs.

Okay, all the above is nice if you're in senior management or own a company, but what if you are "just" an employee and work for someone who isn't doing the right things? What then? **Start by alerting management of any safety or security concerns you may have** and be assertive to ensure that your fears are understood. That doesn't necessarily mean that things will change, but corporate policies often dictate that documented concerns must be addressed in some manner. If you can get to the right decision makers, pointing out the costs of inaction and benefits of prudent planning may prove useful. Education can go a long way toward enabling needed change.

Nothing can guarantee that an employee will never become a victim of workplace violence, yet there are precautions that anyone can take to become more secure regardless of whether or not their company has a comprehensive workplace violence prevention program. Start by learning how to recognize, avoid, or de-escalate potentially violent situations by attending employer-provided training where available or finding private courses to go to on your own. Rory Miller's book *Conflict Communication* is an outstanding resource for understanding conflict and talking your way out of tough situations. Additional suggestions include:

- **Know the rules**. Know your company's workplace violence procedures and emergency plans. In most instances you will want to follow them too.

- **Be professional**. Treat everyone you interact with on the job with dignity and respect. What you think is funny could incite rage in others, so be very careful about workplace humor, initiations, pranks, hazing, and the like. It can easily get you fired or worse.

- **Make yourself a low value target**. Carry only minimal money and required identification if you have to travel into community settings on the job. Avoid ostentatious jewelry and clothing too.
- **Be smart**. Hone your situational awareness and listen to your gut instincts. Avoid entering any location that you feel is unsafe, even if that risks means making someone else feel uncomfortable.
- **Inform management about any concerns you may have**. Report unusual co-worker or customer behaviors to management, focusing specifically on the behaviors and why they're suspicious. Differentiating between the person and their actions helps make it clear that this isn't a personal problem but rather something that merits investigation. There is virtually always a series of warning signs before somebody snaps.
- **Make sure they know where you are**. Use a "buddy system" so that someone else is prepared to act in concert with you should an incident occur at the job site and so that someone knows where you are at all times if you have to travel to other locations to perform your work.
- **Be aware**. Identify hazards, escape routes, alternate exits, and hiding places at your workplace as well as along any routes you must travel to, from, or on the job. Investigate unusual sounds, smells, or activities to determine whether or not they constitute threats to your wellbeing.
- **Have a fallback plan**. Identify areas of cover or concealment where you can hide from an attacker but also be aware that those same areas can also be used by perpetrators for ambushing their victims. If your primary escape route is blocked, know what alternates are available.
- **Protect yourself**. Be aware of improvised weapons such as hot coffee, fire extinguishers, chairs, tools, lumber, company vehicles, cutlery, flashlights, scissors, telephones, attaché cases, or car keys that you can easily access in an emergency. If you have a concealed weapons license, understand your company's policy regarding weapons in the workplace.

One more safety thing… **break the pattern**. Park in a different place, take a different route, choose a different seat at the conference table, or otherwise change up your routine regularly. Simple things like placing your smartphone in a different pocket than you usually carry it in forces you to move into your beta wavelength as opposed to being in your delta (which is effectively cruise control for your mind). **Varying your routine helps you pay more attention**, see what's really going on, hence tackle challenges in a more effective manner. And, if you're not doing the same thing in the same way every day you become a harder target as well. Not only can breaking the pattern keep you safer, it also helps you **think more creatively thus perform better at work too**.

Finally, if something bad does happen on the job, never assume that someone else has already reported the incident. Don't be a victim of the bystander effect,[9] call law enforcement personnel immediately upon reaching a safe location. Answer questions calmly and concisely, stay on the line, and follow the dispatcher's instructions.

---

9 The "bystander effect" is a sociological phenomenon where the more witnesses present the less likely it is that any individual person will intervene. The term was coined after the infamous murder of Catherine "Kitty" Genovese in 1964.

CHAPTER 8

THE FATAL FALLACY OF TALISMAN THINKING

"Falsehood is never in words; it is in things."

– Italo Calvino

During the Great Pestilence in 1347 if you contracted the bubonic plague on a Sunday afternoon you likely would not see the sun rise on Thursday morning. In roughly seventy-two hours your body would be dumped into one of the mass graves outside the city limits. Individual burial was a luxury that could not be afforded; cost, land-use issues, and expedient disposal of infected bodies was paramount. The bubonic plague was both merciful in its swiftness and horrifying in its ugliness as it killed.

The term bubonic is derived from the Greek word *bubo*, meaning "swollen gland." Unable to stave off the swift progression of the illness, the glands of the body swelled, with symptoms showing up in the lymph nodes which are located in the victim's neck, groin, and armpits. What followed close afterward was bleeding under the skin. The combination of swelling and internal bleeding choked off a victim's critical blood supply such that large areas of his or her flesh died or became gangrenous. The plague also attacked inner body tissues as well, often resulting in vomiting and coughing up blood. As we said, an ugly way to die…

Plague doctors were hired by cities to treat everybody who had the plague, rich and poor alike. These doctors wore heavy coats of oilcloth to serve as a barrier against the infectious disease. Further, they wore masks that had glass eyes, in effect goggles, and a respirator of sorts which was often shaped like the beak of a bird. This "beak" was filled with mint leaves, cloves, camphor, and other combinations of herbs and resins. These concoctions were believed to protect the plague doctors from contracting the deadly disease.

While it may have arisen with a certain degree of superstition, in actuality the reasoning behind these protections was sound. Oilcloth jackets, goggles, and bird-like masks full of herbs aren't all that different from what doctors in modern hospitals use for protection today. Their smocks are cleaned and changed regularly, clear visors are used during operations, and surgical masks are ubiquitous. Similarly, firefighters use special heat-resistant clothing and respirators that are designed for personal protection as they perform their work. So, how are these things different? Plague doctors relied on faux science and talisman thinking, whereas modern doctors and firefighters rely on scientifically proven methods of safety and disease prevention.

The plague doctors believed in miasmatic theory. This notion was based on the idea that disease was caused by bad air. The theory was even given its name based on the Greek word *miasma*, a term for air pollution. This theory made no distinction on the transference of the illness. Cholera is transferred from drinking contaminated water that carries the bacteria while chlamydia is a sexually transmitted disease, yet both cholera and chlamydia were both thought to be transmitted via miasma. The bubonic plague was treated no differently; they believed it was caused by bad air even though it was actually transmitted by fleas and small rodents.

We know today the miasmic theory contained some truth, that some diseases are in fact transferred via the air. A cough creates thousands of free-floating volatile that upon entering a victim's nose, lands in an opening in the nasal passages or even makes its way to the lungs and subsequently leads to the spread of infection. Since many victims became sick with pneumonia from *yersinia pestis* (pneumonic plague) too, hence spread the disease to each other by coughing and sneezing, the plague doctors' crude respirator masks likely had some success in forestalling the spread of infection. Similarly, their oil cloth jackets served to separate the doctors from inadvertent contact with contaminated bodily fluids, such as blood that victims coughed up. Further, the doctors also used a stick to move clothing or prod their patients, minimizing skin-to-skin contact with infected individuals.

Nevertheless, despite these precautions many plague doctors died while carrying out their duties. The deaths of these plague doctors comes as little surprise today; the unsanitary conditions, the magnitude of the infection, and the inability of the social structures to manage the corpses all contributed to exacerbate the problem. Wading through the thousands of dead and dying with the miasmatic theory and cutting-edge protection was well-meaning, but ill-founded, yet several case studies from that time served as positive proof points to reinforce the process.

One of these high profile successes was Pope Clement VI. During the plague Pope Clement retreated to the inner realms of the Vatican to avoid infection. Surrounded by incense, he applied a very similar methodology to the one that the plague doctors used. And, Pope Clement VI survived at a time when the population of Europe was devastated. Some sixty percent of the continent's inhabitants passed away from the plague.

How did Pop Clement VI survive? Was it the burning of frankincense and myrrh? Did the very spices and incense that the wise men brought to the crib side of the baby Jesus serve as a barrier to the evil that was The Great Pestilence? Was it the isolation? Did the time honored and historically proven method of quarantine work? Was this a case of divine intervention? Or, was it pure luck? The answer is most likely some combination of the above, but we will never know the true reason why he survived when so many of his compatriots died. Nevertheless, to those in the Vatican, those in service to the Pope and the Church, they believed that burning incense and chanting prayers prevented the plague.

The plague doctors plied their trade based on the science of the day, just as the Pope's people applied talisman thinking and unknowingly implemented a solid quarantine program that saved Clement VI's life.

The town of Reim in France is located a little over an hour from the modern day border of Germany. In 407 BC, the distinction of a border was flexible, just a line on a map, perhaps a treaty or two. The Vandals, an East Germanic tribe, thought very little about crossing over these mythical lines to crash the gates of cities they wished to plunder. Reim was in another sovereign country, yet Reim was solidly in their sights nonetheless. Bishop Nicasius is said to have prophesied the Vandal attack on Reim, but then again it probably didn't take any special insight to see smoke on the horizon where the invading army had camped.

When asked by the townspeople what to do he is reported to have advised that the people should abide in the mercy of God and pray for salvation from their enemies. So, pray they did. Sadly, it didn't end well…

Nicasius was cut down in the church by a Vandal warrior, some say at the altar, others by the door, not that it really matters all that much. Legend has it that he was reciting a psalm at the time he was struck dead. A lector and a deacon were also killed; they were standing by Nicasius' side when he was attacked. This left only Nicasius' sister Eutropia alive in the church. Eutropia had value, hence was spared from the initial slaughter. However, she turned and attacked the Vandals, kicking and scratching. The Vandals quickly had enough and ran her through as well, dumping her corpse with the others. Despite passionate prayers of the pious, the corporeal world walked up, kicked in the door of the ethereal world, and began hacking, slashing, and stabbing away.

Nicasius may have had a very real picture of the violence of which the Vandals were capable. He was an educated man for his time and the news of the barbarian's exploits, whether Vandal or Goth, must have made it to his ears. Nevertheless, he chose prayer, hymns, and psalms as a way to meet the enemy. All of these were, no doubt, comforting, but as a method of self-defense they were utterly useless.

Standing in the doorway of the church as the Vandals roared forward was a massive act of talisman thinking, belief that evil cannot occur in a church. Now, does this mean that the authors find prayer, hymns, and psalms foolish? No, not in the least. We are saying, however, is that violence has a momentum, a single-minded purpose. You must speak its language, or reach it in a manner that it can understand. In other words, meeting the sword with a hymn is unlikely to work. Meeting the enemy's sword with a sword of your own, on the other hand, is another matter entirely.

We would also like to point out that this piece of history is a glowing example of the people in charge not understanding, or refusing to acknowledge, violence. Sadly, the only way to stop homicidal violence is with homicidal violence. Words alone simply won't do it. As a result, an untold number of people in the town went to an untimely death.

There is a bad thing that can happen to law enforcement officers, one that is often called the "John Wayne Syndrome," named after the famous actor. Wayne took on man's-man roles, playing hard, tough and true men, men who were always on the side of justice and always won the day. Enrobed in the authority to act on the behalf of the laws made by a community, with a uniform, a badge, and a gun, it's easy for cops to begin to think of themselves as more than mortal, as symbols rather than men. This is exactly why police officers must guard against the John Wayne Syndrome, the sense that they are immune, that all of their equipment and authority makes them something more. Another term we've heard used is "hiding behind the badge." No matter what you call it, this is a form of talisman thinking.

Because they feel protected by their badges and authority, officers in uniform often take chances that civilians would never think of. Heck, these same folks when in civilian clothes often don't take the same risks they do in uniform, so subconsciously they must know when they're doing it.

Don't get us wrong, officers are paid to run toward danger while savvy civilians run away from it. That's part of the job description. The challenge is that many cops begin to feel comfortable and forget to exercise good situational awareness, body positioning, and other commonsense precautions. They leave openings that bad guys could take advantage of but often decide not to because of the badge. But, just because a momentary lapse doesn't lead to disaster one time, or even several times, doesn't mean that it never will. Lawrence, for instance, has seen dozens of altercations at the stadium where fans could have gotten a hold of an officer's duty weapon had they been so inclined, though fortunately only one person actually tried it during the 26 years he worked there.[10]

---

10 Going after a cop's gun is a horrifically bad idea, one that rarely ends well, which the lady in question discovered the hard way. She was charged and convicted of multiple felonies… after she got out of the hospital.

Unless you work as a security professional as Lawrence once did, it is difficult for civilians to see police in action, to watch an interaction or altercation from beginning to end. If you are not involved in the incident, you can expect to be asked to move along, to clear the area, and told that your presence is not needed or can only complicate matters (security guards hear that too from time to time). If you see a traffic stop, for instance, you generally only observe for a few seconds and then you have passed the incident. The same thing goes for an auto accident, a drug arrest, or a shooting—you are waved through, told to move along.

Prison tattoos have special significance to inmates as well as to associates they encounter back on the streets. Tattoos are commonly applied with homemade relay pistols, which prisoners build from transistor radio and mechanical pencil parts, using sharpened wire bristles as needles. A clock with no hands, most commonly inked on the upper arm, symbolizes doing time.

One way to see police in action is the television show *COPS*. The officers who are showcased there are presented in the best light possible. These lawmen and women are almost, without exception, devoid of talisman thinking. Part of their selection for the show is that the idea of talisman thinking is not within them. Not only are these seasoned police officers who know how to conduct themselves safely, but also they have a film crew capturing their efforts… and they know it. Consequently what we get to see is the best of the best, on their best behavior, something which bears only a superficial resemblance to what goes down on a daily basis on the streets and alleyways of most cities.

It's not just cops; civilians can easily fall for talisman thinking too. Black belts, concealed pistol license holders, and those who carry a knife for self-defense can easily fall for the John Wayne Syndrome, believing that their training or their weapon conveys some sense of superiority. **Talismans may instill confidence, but they do not keep you safe from harm**. Even the authors have done it from time to time, though we recognized the mindset and snapped out of it quickly too. Massad Ayoob sagely wrote:

> "The average citizen makes one, terrible, frightening mistake when he buys a gun for self-defense. He sees the weapon as a talisman that magically wards off evil. In fact, it is nothing of the kind."

This syndrome can be exacerbated by alcohol or other drugs. When the mind is distorted by depressants or stimulants the result can be a sense of invincibleness combined with bad decision-making, like yelling at the person on the other side of the door to, "Go ahead, just shoot!" after they have retreated to a bedroom when a party has gone sideways. The liquid talisman is nefarious, it undermines common sense. And, by the way, that was a real incident. As the drunk found out the hard way, hollow core doors are pretty easy to shoot through… he survived, and fully recovered, though the rehab was reportedly rather unpleasant.

Where does talisman thinking come from and, more importantly, how do you avoid it? History shows us that talismans have great power. It also shows us that that perceived power is one-sided. When the other side of the battle chooses to ignore the power of the talisman, things tend to go south quickly. While we personally believe in religion, prayer, and miracles, for example, neither of us is interested in pushing our religious beliefs on you. We do think it is important that you know we are religious people when we simultaneously say that we understand that we all live in a very physical world and that to deny it can result in our quick demise. So don't get hung up on our belief systems other than this one: The world has its rules. Know them, don't deny them. **Faith won't make those rules magically go away**.

One of the key elements of a talisman is the specialness that is imparted on the item. This is a subject that has been researched, written on, published, and deeply mined. Rather than boring you with all that, we are just going to give you the top-line, enough for you to come to a reasonable conclusion. Talisman thinking can be born of the culture. The culture has rituals. These rituals can be public, like a graduation ceremony where students receive their degrees from an institution of higher learning. Public rituals are for everybody's consumption, so the rites involved are designed as a community display for all to see and understand. Rituals may be private as well, such a small family funeral. While a funeral may be kept private, what happens at ceremony is accessible for anybody who really wants to know. You can go look up the deceased person's religion, peruse their funeral rites, and get the gist of what likely took place.

Other rituals, such as most fraternity and sorority initiations for example, are secret. These ceremonies have very limited attendance and what goes on is rarely if ever released publicly. In fact, closely held codes, obfuscation, lawsuits, and (sometimes) threats of bodily harm are all designed to keep outsiders in the dark about such things. For example, Phi Sigma Sigma Sorority filed suit against a former member in May of 2015 claiming that she had shared secret information about the group's rituals such as their secret handshake, knock, robe colors, and other practices on a social media website. In the civil lawsuit, attorney Karin Jones wrote:

> "The defendant knew that the information that she was posting had not been publicly disclosed and would damage the sorority. The defendant admitted in her posting that the confidential information she disclosed is never written down or recorded and that that the organization and its members consider the information sacred."

Rituals have rites, these rites can be religious, they can be ones of passage or allegiance, but they all have a sacrament of some type. For instance, gang initiations often involve "jumping in," where the new member is physically beaten by his or her peers. Regardless of the ritual, once completed the talisman is given to the initiate. The talisman may be a diploma from a university that carries their crest, logos, and Latin words, all promising a better life. Or, it may be gang colors, a special patch, or a tattoo. Or, it might be a secret sorority handshake and knock. Talismans take many forms, but they all promise something, and if you listen you will believe.

There are also personal talismans, ones that come from culture. In the West, a rabbit's foot is considered lucky.[11] If a Major League Baseball player carried a rabbit's foot for good luck, nobody would blink, however, a pickled frog in a jar... well, that would be considered weird. Even without a physical talisman, more than likely that baseball player performs some type of ritual before batting or pitching (you can see some amusing examples of that lampooned in the movie *Major League*). This sort of thing is extremely commonplace, yet these personal forms of talisman are based on experience that is rationalized via erroneous conclusions and spurious relationships much like Pope Clement VI and the plague.

Don't get us wrong, neither author is above this dance, as are most sports fans for that matter (remember the beer commercial... it's only weird if it doesn't work?). We've both been known to participate in the "Rally Cap" ritual where fans turn their baseball hats inside-out and then wear them in hopes that the Seattle Mariners will put together a comeback in the late innings. Doesn't often work, truth be told... and **that's the point of talisman thinking isn't it? It doesn't really work.** These are but a few origins and examples of how talisman thinking can take root in our minds.

Here's another, for those who practice martial arts: Have you earned a black belt or an equivalent rank? Would it be necessary to strap on your belt or sew on your patch prior to a fight to give you the power you need to prevail? No, not at all. In fact merely suggesting that is ludicrous. Yet, we go through the ritual of putting on specific clothing, patches, or belts when we get ready to train in our perception of combat or combative art. See the dangers? **Talisman thinking is complex, an intertwining of many levels of emotions, responsibilities, and beliefs.** Nevertheless, your job, to protect yourself and those you care about, is to understand this and **not engage in delusion**.

Speaking of delusions, let's talk wall hangers and peashooters for a moment. You don't need a lot of skills to use a sword or fire a gun, a monkey can do that. But, understanding that a cheap sword, what is condescendingly called a "wall hanger," may break when it hits... well, anything. That's different. And, that's important to understand if you pick one up as a drug-addled maniac crashes through your door. Although a gun is a great equalizer, being able to hit a target is important.

---

11 Although since the rabbit had to die in order for you to obtain its' foot that seems counter-intuitive; wouldn't it be the foot from the hare that got away that was actually lucky?

These two items cross over into the realm of talisman very quickly if you don't stay grounded in reality. The wall hanger looks good, but its faux golden hilt will snap at first contact. That cool-looking .44 magnum you bought, the one that looks like something Dirty Harry might own, can you actually carry it around with you? A gun that is too heavy to carry comfortably or too large to conceal is pretty much useless since you are unlikely to have it on you if you need it. Assuming it's there when the bad guy shows up and you need to use it, can you get on target with it? And, can you get back on target after you've touched off the first round should a second or third one be needed?

These two weapons border on useless, one breaking under stress and the other imparting more recoil, noise, and physical stress than most folks can handle.[12] One a poor tool, one a poor fit for the operator… God help us all when poor tool meets poor operator.

Do you carry a Knife? What kind?

Opening a new shipment of books, Kris leaned over the brown box wrapped in packing tape. "Lawrence, hand me your knife," he said holding out his hand without looking back. Lawrence always, when and where legal, has a knife. He tends to "MacYoung" his blades,[13] but he always has one and Kris knows it. He also knows that whichever one Lawrence has on him at any moment in time it will be legal in the city of Seattle, which means a short-bladed folder, so Kris also knows that live steel is not coming for his palm while he isn't looking.

Lawrence's knife is always carried discreetly and legally, and a fair amount of training in how to use it properly has taken place as well. If you carry a knife like he does, why? Kris carried one in his pocket to school back in the day. A lot of guys carried knives. They were tools; Kris and his classmates didn't see it any other way. However it is likely that one stabbing would not have occurred if the kid didn't have a knife with him that morning. It really shocked the other kids in the group that anyone would use their blade to stab a classmate; it didn't register in their eight-grade minds. Sadly, incidents like that take place all the time, particularly when younger men who's brains aren't fully developed make poor judgments without fully considering the consequences.

What is a knife really? Tool, talisman, four inches of the steel courage… or an instrument of rage? If you carry a knife as a tool like Lawrence or as farm kids did back in the day, the knife is a tool first. The knife can be a weapon just like it was that morning on the basketball court in eighth grade. However, if you reverse the thought process and the knife is no longer primarily a tool, it becomes a weapon that can be used as a tool. That's rarely a good thing. Check your mindset if you carry a blade (or any weapon for that matter).

---

12 As you may remember from the introduction to this book, Helen Weathers mistakenly thought she'd been shot when she touched off a .44 magnum with her off-hand; they kick like a son-of-a-bitch.

13 That means that he uses them as pry bars, chisels, digging instruments, and such, so at times they break and must be repaired or replaced. Consequently while Kris knows that Lawrence always has a blade, he's rarely sure which one he is carrying at any given point in time.

If you have a black belt that ties your karate uniform together, you have a tool. If your belt is deliberately distressed like a piece of fake antique furniture, it is a talisman. If you have a badge that shows what police department you work for and your badge number for people to easily communicate with your superiors, you have a tool. A badge that gives you a sense of superiority, yeah, not an attractive talisman…

The test is simple. If what you have is first and foremost a tool, and you know how to use it, you are okay. **If you see the object as a talisman first, then you are likely on the wrong path and you should audit your behavior**. If we ask this question about the plague doctors' cutting-edge gasmask full of spices, what answer would the doctor provide if the mask needed to be replaced? Would he be frightened or frustrated, or merely relieved to have new piece of equipment? Standing in the door of his place of worship Nicasius was wholly banking on his gigantic talisman, the church, to defend him and his people from the swords of Vandals. If Nicasius had been alive to witness the sacking of his church would he have felt inconvenienced or crushed?

What does the loss of a badge or a karate belt stir? Kris had his *gi* (uniform) and *kuroi-obi* (black belt) stolen out of his vehicle one night. He was pissed, who wouldn't be, but the next day he simply went out and bought a new one. To him the uniform doesn't make the man.

Here is a simple test, a rough audit and not perfect, yet a great first cut:

- If you feel sad about a lost object it may be a talisman, maybe. If you can't leave the object in a drawer untouched for a week before carrying it again you're likely seeing it as more than it truly is, exercising dangerous and flawed thinking.
- If you lost or broke the object and the emotion is based in frustration, not sadness, then the object is likely a tool. Despite any cost or inconvenience, if you could toss it aside or give it away and not dwell on your decision then you're on the right track.

Talisman thinking is dangerous and dysfunctional. It keeps you from observing and responding to the world as it truly is, which means that dangers will not only come from others but **also from yourself**. You cannot control everyone else, but you can regulate yourself. Some things you can do about it:

- **Be a realist**. It is vital to see the world as it truly is in order to keep yourself safe. Test your assumptions regularly, learning from a variety of reputable sources to hone in on the truth. And, importantly, be willing to change your thoughts or actions if you discover that you were wrong.
- **Your first and best defense is your mind**. Sharp wits, quick decisions, a flexible mind, and proficient verbal skills are far better protection than any trinket. Humility and a

decent sense of humor help too. Never rely on a talisman, but it an object or a mindset.

- **Keep your wits about you**. Pay attention to what's going on and use good situational awareness to anticipate and steer clear of danger. Unthinkingly falling into a routine makes you unnecessarily susceptible to harm.
- **Dump the talisman**. Don't hide behind a beak, a badge, a black belt, or any other trinket. As mentioned previously, if you cannot leave the object in a drawer untouched for at least a week before carrying it again you're likely seeing it as more than it truly is, exercising dangerous and flawed thinking.
- **Help others see the truth**. Silly superstitions such as the Rally Cap are fine if you know you're playing a game and guard against letting them disconnect you from reality. If others in your circle fall for flawed thinking gently point out to them what they are doing. Humor (such as the aforementioned beer commercial) can help you enlighten others in a non-threatening way.

CHAPTER 9

EVIL CANNOT BE NEGOTIATED WITH

"Politics is the womb in which war develops."

– Carl von Clausewitz

Arthur Neville Chamberlain (1869 – 1940) was the Prime Minister of the United Kingdom from 1937 to 1940. Before being elected to the highest office in England, Chamberlain had an extensive background in both business and government. Here's a brief summary of his accomplishments:

- 1916 – 1917: Director of National Service, responsible for military conscription policies and implementation.
- 1918: Elected to Parliament.
- 1923: Promoted to Minster of Health, a cabinet-level position responsible for running the country's Department of Health.
- 1931 – 1937: Chancellor of the Exchequer, the cabinet minister responsible for all economic and financial matters of the country.
- 1937 – 1940: Prime Minister of the United Kingdom.

Clearly Chamberlain had a solid résumé and seemed to be a good choice for running his country. Sadly he was not. Best known for his foreign policy of appeasement, history demonstrates that he was for too idealistic and trusting to navigate the dangerous times his country faced. For instance, he signed the Munich Agreement that gave the green light for Adolf Hitler to annex part of Czechoslovakia. Touting the deal in September of 1938, Chamberlain used the phrase, "Peace in our time" yet in less than a year Hitler would invade Poland and plunge Europe into World War II.

When evil sees weakness, it pounces.

On one side, we had a man that had been in business for some seventeen years before he entered into government service. Chamberlain had spent his life making contracts and handshake business deals. His word was good and he believed that the pledges of others would be trustworthy as well. This may have been naïve in retrospect, but at the time it was grounded in his experience. On the other side, you had an angry misfit who had gone to war and done jail time. In Hitler's world view the ends justified the means, even if it meant lying or breaking bargains so long as he thought he could get away with it. In other words, **evil saw weakness. Evil pounced**.

Chamberlain was succeeded by Winston Churchill who pulled his country from the brink of defeat to hard-fought victory. But, more than 60,000,000 people paid the price for World War II. Roughly three percent of the total population of the earth was wiped out. And, that's just the number who died. It doesn't tell the full tale of the injured on all sides, the millions of Jews, gypsies, homosexuals, and political prisoners who were rounded up and murdered by the Nazis and their Axis allies, as well as the untold millions of innocent civilians who were displaced from their homes, facing starvation, depravation, and suffering.

There are three immutable truths regarding evil:

1. **You cannot wish evil away**.
2. **You cannot rationalize it away**.
3. **You cannot negotiate with it**.

A sad truth is that **the only way to stop evil from committing violence is through violence**, be it administered by the state or by the individual. It sounds crass, but some people really do need killing. Nothing else will stop them, not even spending the rest of their lives in prison. For example, on March 20, 2015, warrants were issued for inmate Tylon King, Deidre Bingham, his cousin, and another suspect referred to as "Murdoc" for conspiring to commit murder, engaging in violent criminal gang activity, and bribery of a witness. Using prison visits and cell phone calls, the group allegedly arranged to bribe and later murder a key witness against King, all while he was behind bars.

Prison didn't stop Al Capone either. He spent the first two years of his incarceration for tax fraud in a federal prison in Atlanta, but after he was caught bribing guards he was sent to the notorious island prison Alcatraz in 1934 where his influence was diminished along with his ability to reach the outside world. In a more modern example, Heartless Felons is a gang that once existed only in Ohio prisons, but is now operating throughout the Akron, Canton, and Cleveland areas. Members are often armed and so dangerous that the US Marshal Service had to make public service announcements warning about their violent nature. In fact, criminologists who study these things have found that **prisons rarely alter criminal behavior, but rather promote criminality for many inmates**. To some, prisons can be considered crime schools.

Evil stands on its own. Any attempt to quantify evil works to strip it of its inhumanity. That is to say the larger the number of people killed, the less personal it becomes. Joseph Stalin was no paragon of virtue, but he was exactly right when he said, "**One death is a tragedy; one million is a statistic**." The less the killing has quality and the death personal meaning, the dead tend to become nothing more than a number, an almost inaccessible number.

Small evil in proximity to our home is jarring, particularly if we personally know the victim(s). Small evil is accessible because of its familiarity and its ease of understanding. Even if we don't know the parties involved, it remains comprehendible. The larger the number, the less accessible the evil becomes. Our brains simply can't wrap themselves around the size, the numbers, or the statistics. We can even become numb to photos or film of massacres; they feel like Hollywood film clips rather than scenes of dark reality. The bigger the atrocity the harder it becomes to comprehend.

This following is by no means a complete list of evil, but rather it is a small sampling that the authors wish to emphasize to reinforce our point. It is a partial listing, in no particular order, of despicable evil based not only on the number of people murdered by these men, but also the method and means they used to do it:

- **Talat Pasha**. Pasha was the Grand Vizier (Prime Minister) of the Ottoman Empire for one year (1917 to 1918), but before then, in 1915, he declared genocide on the Armenian people. Somewhere between 1,000,000 and 1,500,000 people died at his direction. Methods of death included whipping, death marches, bayoneting, clubbing, axing, hammering, shoveling, sawing, burning, drowning, poisoning, dismemberment, crucifixion, and mutilation. Pasha died in 1921, killed in revenge for his atrocities by an Armenian assassination squad.

- **Reinhard Heydrich**. A Nazi SS[14] officer, Heydrich was the chief of the Reich Main Security Office. Heydrich forced more than 60,000 Jews, homosexuals, and Gypsies to leave Germany and relocate to Poland. Considered the mastermind of "The Final Solution," he chaired the Wannsee Conference where he presented his plan to deport and work to death or outright murder 11,000,000 Jews. Heydrich also created the idea on which Germany invaded Poland, killing over 80,000 people and igniting World War II. Gravely wounded by an assassin's bomb in 1942, he died nine days later from his injuries.

---

14 SS refers to the Nazi's *Schutzstaffel*, or protective squad, known for its inhuman brutality during World War II.

- **Joseph Stalin**. A disciple and handpicked heir of Vladimir Lenin, Joseph (Iosif Vissarionovich) Stalin was the second leader of the Soviet Union. He solidified a centralized command economy which brought the USSR out of agrarian society to become a world-leading industrial power, yet simultaneously instituted a series of purges where his enemies were imprisoned, exiled, or executed. According to the book *Unnatural Deaths in the USSR*, the people of Russia and their satellite countries suffered somewhere between 34,000,000 and 49,000,000 deaths directly attributable to their leader. The majority were killed through famines, executions, deportations, and Gulags (Soviet work camps). Show trials designed to create some semblance of legitimacy preceded most capital punishments yet many were killed simply for being too educated… or for "thought crimes" such as expressing an unacceptable political opinion. Stalin died in 1952, likely assassinated with poison.

- **Mathieu Ngirumpatse**. The National Revolutionary Movement was a Hutu extremist crusade led by Ngirumpatse. He planned the extermination of the Tutsi population of Rwanda as well as the elimination of members of opposition parties, and was ultimately responsible for the deaths of some 800,000 people in his country. Most of these killings were conducted up close and personal, involving some of the most brutal methods imaginable, primarily through the use of bludgeons and machetes. Approximately one-seventh of the entire population of Rwanda was murdered during this reign of terror, with Tutsis accounting for 94 percent of the victims, and that doesn't even factor in those who were raped, tortured, or maimed but did not die. Ngirumpatse was sentenced to life in prison for genocide, crimes against humanity, and various war crimes including rape and sexual violence.

- **Caligula**. Born Gaius Julius Caesar Augustus Germanicus, Caligula[15] was a Roman emperor who proclaimed himself a god in 40 AD. In the grand scheme of things, Caligula didn't kill nearly the number of people that others on this list did, however he was pure bat-shit crazy, known for cruelty, sadism, extravagance, and sexual perversity. His murderous and brutal behaviors put him on the list just for that reason, and to also serve as proof that anybody can rise to power regardless of rectitude or lack thereof. He was assassinated in 41 AD by his own Praetorian Guard who stabbed him to death because of his depravations.

- **Mao Zedong**. A Chinese communist revolutionary and the founding father of the People's Republic of China, he governed as Chairman of the Communist Party from its establishment in 1949 until his death in 1976. Mao had a simple goal, make his nation a superpower and use communism to accomplish his aims. While he ultimately

---

15 Caligula means "little soldier's boot," a nickname earned by accompanying his father on campaigns as a youth.

turned his country in a modern-day super power, the result of his efforts was the largest famine and genocide ever known to man. Mao directly and indirectly, through edict and policy, killed some 60,000,000 to 70,000,000 people, eclipsing Stalin by snuffing out some 20,000,000 more lives. Yeah, twenty million! He died in 1976 from a heart attack.

- **Attila the Hun**. He was the most feared enemy of the Western and Eastern Roman empires. His birth date is unknown, his linage suspect, and nobody knows exactly what he looked like as no firsthand accounts exist. Despite his well-documented military exploits, true numbers are hard to come by. Nevertheless, insight to the Hun's violence circa 383 AD was brought to light when he captured St. Ursula's traveling party on their trip to Cologne. The Huns beheaded some 11,000 women and shot St. Ursula dead with an arrow. His army sacked numerous cities and razed Aquileia so completely that it was unrecognizable afterward. Attila died in 453, likely from internal bleeding. Historians theorize that his heavy drinking caused dilated veins in his esophagus to rupture which, in turn, caused him to bleed to death.

- **Genghis Khan**. He was the founder of the great Mongol Empire. When he defeated rival tribes he conscripted surviving warriors into his service. As his armies grew and conquered, Genghis Khan became responsible for the massacre of between 20,000,000 to 60,000,000 people. Projections of the number of people living during Khan's time indicate that he may very well have been responsible for exterminating 10 percent to maybe 30 percent of the entire world's population! At the time of his death, the Mongol Empire stretched from the Caspian Sea to the Sea of Japan. He died in 1227 after falling from a horse.

- **Ivan the Terrible**. While Ivan Vasilyevich, known as the Formidable or Terrible, was an accomplished diplomat, his legacy was one of fear and terror. Proclaimed Tsar of Russia, he conquered the Khanates of Kazan, Astrakhan, and Siberia, transforming Russia into a world power, yet paranoia, fits of rage, and mental instability marked his reign. In fact, he killed his eldest son (and carefully groomed heir) after losing his temper. To protect his power, he forced thousands of Russians from their homes, ordered exorbitant tributes in taxes and fees, and had his enemies strangled, burned, maimed in horrific ways, or impaled. In an interesting bit of irony, Joseph Stalin evoked Ivan's image in an effort to revive Russia nationalist pride during his own cruel reign. Ivan suffered a stroke and died in 1584.

- **Pol Pot**. During the late 1970's Pol Pot came rose to power as the leader of Cambodia's Khmer Rouge party. Pot's goal was to bring Cambodia back to its roots of agriculture. He organized some 150 execution centers across the country, one of which is S21

(Security Prison 21) which now displays the skulls of millions of innocent victims killed during Pot's reign. An estimated 3,000,000 people perished under his brutal regime. Most of executions were performed by means of clubbing to save on the cost of bullets. Disgraced, he died in 1998, likely from suicide.

You have probably noticed that we didn't include some obvious choices on the list, mass murderers, reprobates, and scumbags like Adolf Hitler, Idi Amin, Saddam Hussein, Jeffry Dahmer, Al Capone, Charles Manson, Ted Kaczynski, Tom Horn, Adam Lanza, Andrew Kehoe, John Wayne Gacy, Ted Bundy, Timothy McVeigh, Jim Jones, and many, many more. This book is only so big… The first three are too easy. As for the rest, **how does one truly compare a few homicides**, no matter how horrific, **to the guy who wiped out a quarter of the world's population**? There's no contest. Nevertheless, the aforementioned were all disgusting, horrible individuals, men who may or may not have had good intentions (in their own minds), but whose legacies can only be described as evil.

Yes, evil exists. Evil men, evil ideologies.

But, **good exists too!**

Andy McNab was a member of the Special Air Service (SAS). He is known for his work with Kevin Dutton, a research psychologist at the Department of Experimental Psychology at the University of Oxford. He appeared in Dutton's book, *The Wisdom of Psychopaths: What Saints, Spies, and Serial Killers Can Teach Us about Success*. Later on McNab collaborated with Dutton on, *The Good Psychopath's Guide to Success: How to Use Your Inner Psychopath to Get The Most out of Life*. Both of these books were published by Bantam Press.

Before entering a gentile life of writing, study, and book tours, McNab was elbows deep in counter-terrorism and drug operations across the world. He worked in South America and Central America as well as in the Middle East and Far East. His most public event took place in the Middle East arena. During the First Gulf War (1990 – 1991), McNab was in command of an eight-man SAS patrol. The patrol's job was to destroy the communication systems that linked Baghdad to other parts of Iraq, ruining the enemy's ability to move and fire missiles effectively. It was a critical mission, but one of stealth, not overwhelming force. Unfortunately the squad was compromised when they were discovered by a shepherd boy. They faced three options:

1. **Let the boy go**, knowing that he would give away the squad and compromise their mission.
2. **Drag the boy along**, which would slow the team to the point of ineffectiveness.
3. **Kill the boy and hide his body**.

They decided to let the boy go. Knowing that they could no longer complete their objective, they made tracks to friendly territory as fast as possible. The decision to not kill the boy was encapsulated by McNab's statement, "**We are the SAS, not the SS.**" Due to that decision, however, **three of the men in McNab's command were killed and the entire group was captured and held for a month-and-a-half** before being released. **Evil would have killed the boy.** Any of the men we listed above wouldn't have given that murder a second thought. The tactical and strategic issues at hand would have dictated their choice. Or, perhaps they simply would have enjoyed it… The mission was far more important than some unknown shepherd's kid. It would have been an easy kill as well; a small boy versus a team of soldiers, ones with special training no less.

It would have been no contest, yet McNab and his men made a different choice. **Doing the right thing cost them dearly.** Knowing that it likely would, they made the right choice nonetheless.

Despite technological advances in warfare, 19% of US soldiers deployed to Iraq and Afghanistan reported using hand-to-hand combat skills in at least one encounter during the war. This included grappling techniques (72.6%), striking techniques (5.5%), and combinations of grappling followed up by use of a weapon (such as a rifle-butt) to strike the person they were fighting (21.9%).

Let's talk about choices…

As Kris and his son Jackson rode the tour bus through the historic city of Boston, they passed the statue of Mary Dyer. Jackson had only a half second of interest in the statue, but as her story was told by the bus driver he became fascinated by the brutality and injustice of her execution. Yes, Dyer's death was an execution. What McNab and his squad faced was a killing, and there is a difference between a killing and an execution. Mary Dyer's death was sanctioned by the state, the community. The issue McNab faced was one of a non-combatant who posed no immediate threat but could, and did, compromise his mission.

Here's what happened: Mary Dyer (1611 – 1660) lived in Boston, Massachusetts. Dyer was originally a Puritan who converted to become a Quaker. The Quakers held that all believers were priests, hence actively avoided creeds and hierarchical structures, keeping to a very flat organization that wouldn't get between the people and their god. Puritans, on the other hand, created a religious and political environment, one where the two aspects of life were intertwined to such an extent to as become one.

The Puritans believed that the Quakers posed an existential threat to their organization, the viability of their social system, and their beliefs. By their very existence the Quakers tore at the fiber of everything the Puritans had fought, suffered, and endured soul-crushing hardships to achieve. As a result of their clear and present threat to the Puritans, the Quakers were banned from practicing their version of Christianity in Boston.

Any threat to their group would be met with state-sanctioned force. From the Puritan perspective, Mary Dyer was a heretic of the most serious kind. First she was imprisoned, released, and then banished. She returned but was banished for the second time with threat of death if she was ever found in Boston again. She returned once more and, in 1659, was sentenced to be hanged by the neck until dead, but she was given a reprieve while she stood with the rope around her throat. Dyer was told to get out of town, but she was stubborn and didn't listen so once again she was sentenced to death by hanging. In 1660, this time they withheld mercy. She was hanged and died.

The Puritans had warned her. They had given Dyer multiple chances and choices and now they were left no option. You see the Puritans were involved in a battle, a fight for their own eternal souls as well as the eternal souls of those in their charge. From their perspective Mary Dyer had to be stopped and the only way to stop her was to execute her. When Kris and his son rode past her statue in Boston, seated in a tour bus more than 300 years later, they could easily see the insanity, cruelty, and evil of what had happened so long before.

The Puritans were using groupthink, and groupthink is not designed for nuance. Groupthink is a term first used in 1972 by psychologist Irving L. Janis. It refers to a sociological phenomenon in which people strive so hard for consensus within a group that **they will set aside their own personal beliefs or adopt the opinions of others**. People who are opposed to the decisions or overriding opinion of the group as a whole frequently remain quiet, preferring to keep the peace rather than disrupt the uniformity of the crowd. They will kowtow to the group and conform, even if the group is dysfunctional or dangerous.

Need a more modern example? Think Nazi Germany. The Nazis justified their actions, their groupthink, to the bitter end. Otto Adolf Eichmann, a Lieutenant Colonel in the SS, was one of the key organizers of the Holocaust. In his defense while on trial for war crimes, Eichmann used what has become known as, "The Nuremberg Defense," named for the location of the war trials where his case was adjudicated. He said, "**I was just following orders**," in essence vacating all moral and basic human decency to be part of the groupthink. After all, under laws promulgated by the Nazi party everything he did was legal… Here are Eichmann's words after being found guilty of war crimes, crimes against humanity, and crimes against the Jewish people:

> "I cannot recognize the verdict of guilty… It was my misfortune to become entangled in these atrocities. But these misdeeds did not happen according to my wishes. It was not my wish to slay people… Once again I would stress that I am guilty of having been obedient, having subordinated myself to my official duties and the obligations of war service and my oath of allegiance and my oath

of office, and in addition, once the war started, there was also martial law… I did not persecute Jews with avidity and passion. That is what the government did… At that time obedience was demanded, just as in the future it will also be demanded of the subordinate."

Reading the statement above it is easy to see how Eichmann had justified his actions. In his mind these atrocities were not his own and, therefore, he could not be held responsible or accountable for the evil he had committed. **Evil that fails to recognize its own hand cannot be negotiated with**. The abject inability to see their actions for what they truly are is chilling. Eichmann in his closing words rejects the conviction brought down by the world court, as he was *only* following orders. But look at the very end of his statement, he goes on to give a warning to the world, "At that time obedience was demanded, just as in the future it will also be demanded of the subordinate." Eichmann in an attempt defend his actions tells us in an indirect way that we must be vigilant because **there are many more like him out there**. More followers ready, willing and, in today's world, quite able to commit heinous acts of evil because **they are eager to blindly follow orders**.

Groupthink has led to some horrific things. It was behind the mass suicide at Jonestown in 1978 too. At the People's Temple compound in Guyana, 912 people died from drinking poison, a concoction of grape Flavor-Aid,[16] cyanide, and valium. Sadly, 276 of the victims were children whose mothers used syringes to pour the toxic substance down their throats before committing suicide themselves. Cult leader Jim Jones died from a single gunshot wound to the head, but it is unclear whether or not he did that to himself.

About fifteen years ago Wilder sat in his Saturday-morning men's get together. There was a core of guys who regularly attended, but new members floated in and out from time to time. That morning a new guy sat down. After a little bit of time, it became apparent why he was there; his world was not what he had hoped for and he and his wife were facing a serious moral dilemma.

A little history to set the stage: During the Ceausescu regime in Romania, the communist dictator banned abortions and the result was a large number of unwanted children, kids whose parents could not afford to feed or clothe them. The government chose to deal with the issue by creating orphanages that took care of the abandoned children's basic needs. However the fundamental requirement of human interaction was lacking and the results are now well-known… and devastating.

The man, looking into his cup of coffee that morning, started to describe how his son, adopted from Eastern Europe, was now far more than he and his wife had anticipated. The couple had

---

16 While "Drinking the Kool-Aid" is a common rhetorical expression which stemmed from this event that refers to a person or group holding on to an unquestioned belief without critical examination, the poison wasn't actually administered via Kool-Aid.

decided to adopt this young boy into their existing family in hopes of plucking a child from a life of brutality to one of having all the opportunities middle-class America could provide. What a wonderful thing to do. How well-intentioned. Unfortunately that's where the fairy tale ended… To their horror they discovered that their adopted son was dangerous, **a hazard to himself and to others in the family**. Outbursts, both verbal and physical, were on the increase. A thunderclap during a rainstorm would send him into a wild rage, or something else unrelated might result in the same, violent eruption. For example, the man talked about having to go out to the front yard and pick up the young boy from the sidewalk stopping the distraught child from violently banging his head against the pavement repeatedly.

> "As the stories went on, we all fell silent. I swear you could see the chests of these men just cave in around their hearts. It was brutal and none of us had anything, nothing," Kris said afterward. "We all realized why he was there, that man needed justification to protect his family, and he was seeking it from other men in the group."

What this man in the story was running up against was **a damaged brain**. The adopted child had suffered deprivation in infancy and the results were catastrophic as he came of age. The boy had his basic needs met in the orphanage, food, drink, shelter. He was kept warm, but he was emotionally neglected and this resulted in a poorly developed brain. Professor Sir Michael Rutter of the Institute of Psychiatry, King's College London, is considered the leader on this issue. The findings of his work are that some regions of the subjects' brains are atrophied, such as the temporal lobes where we regulate sensations. Without this region of the brain functioning properly, **a person will have cognitive and emotional problems such as an inability to govern anger and fear**. Now this poor man's adopted son's situation was an extreme case, yet other forms of abuse or neglect can result is poor brain development too. And, it can happen anywhere in the world, not just at an orphanage in some remote part of Romania.

So, what we are saying is that there are people who can and do act in anti-social ways, even evil ways, because for all intents and purposes their brain is broken. And, **a broken brain is not something you can negotiate with**.

Was McNab's choice to be "not evil" a good choice? Good men died? Would anybody really have known about a dead shepherd boy? Would a true psychopath have cared one whit? What about the groupthink the Puritan's exhibited in dealing with Mary Dyer? Was Dyer culpable for her own death? What about Eichmann's complete lack of ability to own up to his deeds and his prediction that it will happen again? And what about a broken brain, a brain that can't control itself. What if that small, poorly treated child with an underdeveloped brain becomes another Genghis Khan, Ivan the Terrible, Caligula, or Dahmer?

Most importantly, **what can you do about it?**

There is a famous photograph from June 13, 1936 where August Landmesser, a dockyard worker, is one of the only people in a crowd of hundreds not to perform the Nazi salute. He tried to flee to Denmark shortly thereafter with his pregnant wife but was apprehended by the Gestapo and found guilty of "dishonoring the race." He appealed and the couple was acquitted in 1938 for lack of evidence, but with the warning that a repeat offense would result in a multi-year prison sentence.

Sometimes doing the right thing takes an act of heroism, risking your life like Landmesser or McNab. Other times it means getting involved, working within the system to make a difference that staves off the adverse impacts of groupthink. Occasionally it means using violence to save your life or that of those around you.

Here's the deal, while talking is better than fighting, **evil simply cannot be negotiated with, reasoned with, or wished away**. Now we're not suggesting that you go all vigilante here, but rather that you must understand viscerally and fundamentally that **the only way to stop an evil from committing horrific acts of violence** upon you and yours **is to act with countervailing violence**. If you are a good person who cares about doing the right things, you must be committed to resorting to your baser instincts if and when self-preservation dictates. It's **not about revenge, punishment, or vigilantism**, but rather about defending yourself or others when or if called upon to do so.

Every human being has a fundamental right to life, one that cannot be overridden by anyone save by the consequences of one's own actions or by one's own choosing. To state it in a manner that gets more directly to the heart of the issue, each and **every person on earth has the fundamental right not to be killed**. This right not to be killed is a human entitlement, a mark of any civilized society. Of course, there is also a paramount reciprocity factor. **It is possible to waive the right not to be killed by murdering or attempting to murder someone else**. In other words, you have the duty not to kill or harm others so long as others adhere to the same duty toward you. It is the breakdown of this reciprocal relationship that explains why aggressors fail to have the right not to be killed by their victims, and why **you possess the moral right to kill someone in self-defense if there is no other way to resolve a confrontation**.

If someone makes an unprovoked attack against you, your friends, or your family, the aggressor is morally at fault for the attack, and all consequences thereof. The defender is both morally and legally innocent so long as he or she acts within the true definition of self-defense, guarding him or herself against a real, imminent, and unavoidable threat of serious physical injury or death.

We're not making this stuff up; it's even found in the Bible, albeit commonly misunderstood. A common translation of Matthew 5:39 reads, "But I say unto you, that ye resist not evil: but whosoever shall smite thee on thy right cheek, turn to him the other also." A more accurate translation according to many biblical scholars would be, "But I say to you, **do not resist evil *with* evil** (or in a like manner)..."

There is a huge difference between a command to not resist evil and an admonishment to not resist with evil. Turning the other cheek is a metaphor for not seeking vengeance for or responding violently to insults. While very sound advice, it is not a literal requirement to stand there and let someone beat you down without offering even token resistance. **Evil must be resisted; evil impulses in yourself as well as evil actions from others**. As Edmund Burke famously wrote:

"All that is necessary for the triumph of evil is that good men do nothing."

Fighting is not nice. It's not glamorous. It isn't even heroic, truly, even though heroic acts are often performed on the battlefield. But, **from time to time violence is necessary**. That's the mark of the civilized man (or woman); willingness to do what's right even at great personal risk, even if you may not live through it, because **not doing so is unacceptable**. It makes you far less than who you are.

This mindset and understanding is vital. Evil exists. And, we must be prepared to face it. Rather than giving a specific list of additional things you can do here, we're using this chapter to set up the next one, in which you will find additional clarity and actionable advice about how to deal with criminals should you find yourself in their sights.

CHAPTER 10

BAD GUYS DO THIS FOR A LIVING...
SO DON'T GET COCKY

"Obviously crime pays, or there'd be no crime."
— G. Gordon Liddy

Habitual criminal statutes, sometimes known as "three-strikes and you're out" laws, are designed keep individuals that society is unable to rehabilitate off the streets. In 2006, Daimon Monroe (aka Daimon Hoyt) was tried in the state of Nevada under a habitual criminal statute after being convicted for more than 30 felony counts in three different jury trials. He had previously been convicted of 15 felony counts in a criminal case in 1992, two additional felony counts in 1993, and two more in 1996. While most of his convictions were for commercial burglaries, one was for being an ex-felon in possession of a firearm while another was for evading police during a car chase that resulted in a rollover crash.

According to court documents, after completing his second prison stint in 2001 Monroe returned to his life of crime almost immediately after being released, stealing more than $2,000,000 worth of cash and merchandise in several hundred burglaries before he was caught again in 2006. District Court Judge Stewart Bell sentenced Monroe to life in prison without the possibility of parole for his crimes. But, that's not the end of his story... After being locked away he was later tried and convicted for soliciting the murder of the judge along with a prosecutor and the police detective who had investigated him.

What do you do for a living? You might be an accountant, architect, lawyer, IT professional, or engineer, someone for whom a harsh words or a pink slip are the worst things you might expect on the job. Or, maybe you're a doctor, someone who's seen the impact of violence from time to time, but who hasn't really experienced homicidal violence directed against you up close and personal. Or, maybe you're in the "fighting" profession, say a martial arts instructor, Olympic judo practitioner, professional boxer, or MMA competitor or coach, but that's really more of a sport than the real thing isn't it? Or, maybe you actually are a violence-professional, say a soldier, law enforcement officer, bodyguard, or bouncer. In that case you've definitely got an inkling for what violence is all about, likely including firsthand experience, but then again your rules of engagement tend to drive far different constraints and outcomes than the guys who make a living by breaking the rules that polite society operates under.

Whoever you are, whatever you do, we think it's a safe bet that you don't operate outside the law. You go to school or hold a regular job, perhaps more than one. You go to work, pay your taxes, and except for the occasional speeding ticket or parking violation generally lead a forthright lifestyle. Certainly you don't commit felonies for a living. You are the good guy (or gal), and that's a good thing. But, if you find yourself tangling with someone who has a different worldview, someone who sees you as a resource to take or an obstacle to overcome, it is vital to understand that person isn't like you. They think differently, act differently, and operate in an entirely different manner.

To put it another way, **you might be a professional criminal if**:

- It's uncomfortable to tell the truth even when there's no reason not to.
- If someone gets up in your grill the first thing you do is a witness check.
- You've set aside $250,000 for your legal defense fund and consider it a cost of doing business.
- You think "regular" jobs are beneath you.
- You know what a teardrop tattoo really means and know people who have earned them.
- You've never been in a fair fight and don't understand why anyone would want to.
- The taxman has no idea how much money you make and never will.
- You can't remember the last time you were in a room (outside jail/prison) where everybody wasn't armed, especially those who aren't licensed to carry.
- You are only willing take on a regular job to set up a crime.
- Your lawyer is on speed dial because public defenders are for punks.
- You have a clock with no hands tattooed on your upper arm.

- You know where you can buy a gun at 2:00 AM.
- You have three dots arranged in a triangle tattooed on the web of your hand between the base of your thumb and forefinger.
- Drugs are for losers but you sell to them anyway.
- Your girlfriend with a regular job feeds you information to help set up your crimes.
- You know who not to cross because they'd feed you through a wood-chipper feet first… and you knew people who crossed them.
- A night in jail, even a stint in prison, is nothing more than a chance to catch up with some old friends and maybe learn a useful thing or two.
- You've attended multiple funerals… this year.
- 95 percent of your income stream comes from illegal activities.

The preceding isn't a complete list, of course, but it does give you a little flavor of a criminal mindset. These guys believe that regular workaday stiffs who follow the rules are suckers. **At best you're a nuisance, at worst a plaything**… and not in a good way. We're not talking about mental midgets with low impulse control, suicidal spree killers who've flipped their lid, or pedophiles who like to expose themselves in public here, but rather **professional criminals**. Professional, as in **they make their living by breaking the law**. Here's a little "day in the life" example:

> "A few weeks ago I was at my in-laws house with my wife for her birthday dinner. We had just finished and were getting ready to go when my text message went off. Brother of mine was asking about a local 1% wannabe motorcycle club, one that was wanting to move up into the big leagues. I asked if he was all right and he replied that he was about to get jumped. I grabbed the wife and we made the short trip, only about four or five blocks over, to the bar. I arrived at the front door as my brother's girlfriend was walking out seriously distraught. I told her stay with my wife and went in.
>
> "My brother was talking to the manager and tempers were beginning to flare. I approached and told him, 'Let's go.' He nodded and we begin to walk out. I noticed the club he was having problems with and saw their two enforcers walking the same way to follow us out. I turned, smiled, and told them if they followed us I would kill them right there. They stopped.
>
> "The club's President approached me. I repeated that we were leaving and a few other things, maybe something along the lines of two wheels aren't a great way of avoiding a claymore[17]. We agreed that it was best to let bygones be

---

17 An antipersonnel mine used by the US military. Its inventor, Norman MacLeod, named the mine after a Scottish medieval sword (the big two-handed one Mel Gibson used in *Braveheart*). Unlike ordinary landmines that detonate when stepped on, the claymore fires steel shrapnel in a 60-degree arc in front of the device.

bygones and then my brother and I left.

"My brother is a Special Force Vet in forced retirement who would have killed as many as he could before they got him. I spent the next hour talking him out of going back and blowing the bar up with everyone in it. Hell, I like to drink there. I find it odd that people want to get someone like him involved in their lives in a bad way.[18]"

How does this compare to your daily routine? Do you stare down outlaw bikers on a regular basis? We think not. In reading this account it is vital to understand that there was no posturing here, **no bluff or bluster**. Most criminals see right through that sort of thing so it backfires spectacularly. These bikers had no doubt that if they had followed Clint and his brother out of the bar **someone would have died**. You'll note that that there are no names mentioned beyond that of the narrator (see footnote). That is because right now they have a peace with the club involved and don't want it to break.

When you read about the professional criminals that Clint rubs elbows with your natural reaction might be disdain. Sure, it's probably not a lifestyle you'd choose, but never forget that just because someone else decides to operate outside the law does not necessarily mean that he or she is stupid, drug addled, or moronic. In fact, **many of these criminals are just as smart and hardworking as you are**. They channel their efforts differently, however… World class conman, brilliant thieves, and inspired muggers, to name a few, these folks make their living by doing bad things to good people. They are resource predators like. And, they're really good at it.

Whatever you do to earn a paycheck, you want to be the best right? You might take classes, obtain certifications, perform extra projects, put in overtime hours, whatever it takes… day after day, month after month, and year after year you perfect your craft with the hopes of rising toward the top of your chosen profession. Bad guys do exactly the same thing, not in the same way of course, but the same thing nevertheless. They hone and refine their craft, ever seeking better, faster, and easier ways of fleecing their victims. The only difference is that what they learn, practice, and do does not lead to fancy titles or a corner office. It does, however, lead to **more reward with less chances of getting caught**.

It's not just burglars like Daimon Monroe and confidence men like Bernie Madoff, somewhere out there is a superlative rapist and a first-rate murderer too. These process predators are even scarier than their brethren who merely rip you off because they don't care all that much about

---

18 Clint Overland spent 27 years as a bouncer, thug, and SOB for hire. Not someone you'd want hanging around your teenage sons as a role model. Reformed, he currently lives in West Texas with his beautiful wife and four children. He's trying to make up for some of the bad he has done by telling people the truth about training for real violence. He pastors an Outlaw Church where he spends a lot of his day ministering to those that have come out of the violence professions.

your stuff. They care about you… having power over you. These are the guys and gals who might rob you, but only after they've taken you to a secondary crime scene where they have the time and privacy to do some truly nasty things first. It's about getting their jollies through rape, torture, or murder, not about making a living.

Process predators are horrifically dangerous individuals who do some truly nasty stuff, but thankfully they tend to have shorter runs than resource predators because law enforcement tends to give higher priority to violent crimes like kidnapping, assault, and murder than they do to property crimes. Spokane, Washington was recently ranked as the city with the fourth highest car theft rate in the nation by the National Insurance Crime Bureau, for example, in part because such crimes are rarely prosecuted there. Murder and mayhem, on the other hand… authorities in the State of Washington are pretty tough on that. This doesn't mean that process predators never injure, maim, or kill people, just that most of the acts they do commit aren't law enforcement's first priority in many instances. The code they follow, to the extent that there is one, tends to be along the lines of:

> Some of the world's most infamous male murderers include Andrew Kehoe (who murdered 43 people at an elementary school in 1927), Adam Lanza (who killed 27 people at an elementary school in 2012), Al Capone (who mastermind of the St. Valentine's Day massacre), and Charles Manson (cult leader of the "Manson Family" who attempted to start a race war with his "Helter Skelter" murders).

"**Don't get caught**," and
"**Don't kill anyone unless you absolutely have to**."

Nevertheless, in certain criminal subcultures violence comes with the territory. For instance, as mentioned previously many gangs require that new members are "jumped in," going through a horrific beat down by way of initiation into the group. Others require initiates to randomly (or selectively) target non-members with violence to prove their loyalty. Rules and social norms of these groups are virtually always enforced with violence. To be clear, it's not just one-percenters or outlaws who do things like this. For instance, in certain parts of the country rape is a killing offense. The victim or her family will hunt you down, take you out, and feed you to the gators (or pigs or bears or whatever voracious wildlife happens to be handy) or dump you in a vat of acid. Your corpse is never found and your disappearance will never be questioned.

All this is our way of saying that **an awful lot of criminals get away with it**. Serial killers can go for decades without getting caught (such as Gary Ridgway, aka, "The Green River Killer") and some never are (such as "The Zodiac Killer," as of this writing). Similarly, process predators like pedophiles are sometimes able to groom their victims in such a way that they come to believe that the abhorrent behaviors they experience are normal, hence never reported even after they become adults. That's not saying these guys are never brought to justice, only that **it can take years for their crimes to catch up with them**. Certain burglars, conmen, identity thieves and the like are never caught or, if they are, it's for petty stuff that has them back on the street plying their trade again in short order.

Sadly, a criminal's career doesn't always end once he or she is caught. We've already stated that in many cases jail or prison time often leads to more effective criminals. In fact, recidivism rates amongst convicted felons are shockingly high. According to the Bureau of Justice Statistics, **67.8 percent of inmates are rearrested within three years of release and 76.6 percent within five years**. In part this may be because it can be challenging for convicted felons to find and keep legitimate work, but oftentimes it is nothing more than a lifestyle choice. Broken down by category, **recidivism rates** are:

- **71.3 percent** for violent offenders.
- **82.1 percent** for property offenders.
- **73.6 percent** for public order offenders.
- **76.9 percent** for drug offenders.

Clearly many of these folks see jail time as an acceptable cost of doing business, just like the rest of us see paperwork and bureaucracy as a necessary evil. While they don't mind doing a little time, they play the odds in order to stay in the game (especially where habitual offender rules that can lead to lifetime imprisonment apply). If the chances of succeeding aren't all that great, more often than not they'll move on to an easier victim. This means that before a criminal makes his or her move against you, they need to evaluate their odds of success in much the same way that a corporate executive does a business case, IRR, or ROI analysis.

This evaluation is often called an "interview." Unlike a job search, however, it is one examination that you do not want to pass. If you are not paying attention to your environment, have something of value, and appear to be an easy target, you are more likely than not to be selected as the bad guy's next victim. Even if you're flat broke, to a process predator your value is as a plaything; something he can deliver pain to, exert power over, and get his rocks off by breaking, so "something of value" is open to interpretation.

This interview may be conducted by a single individual or a group of thugs, though criminals often work alone. Groups of antisocial people can find challenges hanging out with each other for extended periods of time, especially when they realize that if caught everyone around them could throw them under the proverbial bus in exchange for a lighter sentence. Nevertheless, the interview may take place quickly (e.g., target of opportunity) or be drawn out over a period of time (e.g., stalking). Either way, your goal in such situations is to be both calm and resolute. Don't start anything you don't have to, but be prepared to finish whatever is necessary.

While most people look at someone's size and physique, experienced predators know how to recognize a threat from a person's posture, proxemics, or movement. **If you have martial arts training, carry a weapon, or a fair amount of brawling experience under your belt the other guy will likely know**. That means that if you're paying attention to your surroundings he is likely to either leave you alone in favor of easier prey… or take extreme measures to take you out before you can exercise countervailing force, so it's a bit of a good news/bad news scenario.

If you are confronted by a single individual, be wary of bystanders who may join in. Don't forget to glance behind you when prudent because he or she may have an accomplice(s). This may look like a witness check, helping deescalate a tense situation, though it can also ignite violence if done too furtively (which makes you look scared, hence less threatening). Exercise good situational awareness, continuously using sound, smell, reflective surfaces, and shadows to sense what is going on where you cannot look while simultaneously paying attention to escape routes and sources of concealment and cover along the way.

The less you look and act like a victim during the interview process, the safer you will be. Breathe low and slow, clear your spine, and be prepared to fight or flee at a moment's notice all while maintaining a relaxed posture. That sounds difficult, but for a seasoned martial artist it's natural (assuming you don't succumb to a premature adrenal dump). Be wary of the other guy's hands, particularly if you cannot see both of them because he or she may very well be armed and preparing to use his weapon(s) against you.

From time to time you may need to fight to escape, though there are numerous advantages to walking away if you're able to do so peaceably. First off, there's no paperwork (booking papers, depositions, adjudication, etc.). That's always a good thing. Further, your blood stays on the inside where it belongs and all the pain, trauma, and rehabilitation that follow most violent altercations is avoided. And, you don't have to worry about retaliation. Even if you successfully defend yourself against a lone predator, walk away unscathed and are never charged with any crime you may still face public outrage, trail by media, and personal or professional challenges. Tough as all that can be, it tends to get far worse if the other guy runs with a pack (e.g., outlaw biker, gangbanger, or organized crime member).

You may or may not be smarter or craftier than the other guy, but it's vital to remember that anyone who makes his living doing dirty deeds should not be taken lightly. If nothing else, **you're unlikely to be more dangerous, ruthless, or nasty than the criminal is**. Hesitation can cost you in a fight. But, it doesn't usually have to come to that. Something in the neighborhood of ninety percent of all interpersonal violence can be avoided. Much of the rest can be reasoned with. Consequently, fighting isn't self-defense; awareness, avoidance, and de-escalation are what keep you safe. **Fighting is what you do when you've screwed up your self-defense**.

The good news is that, with the exception of identity thieves, swindlers, and conmen who can get at you remotely, it's possible for those who eschew the outlaw lifestyle to avoid professional criminals. As with everything self-defense, start by exercising good situational awareness. Then, avoid high risk activities, relationships, and locations. Some additional strategies for staying safe:

- **Pay attention**. It makes no difference how tough you are or what kind of weapon you carry if you're not paying attention to what's going on around you. Darn near anyone can punch your ticket if you don't see them coming, so exercise good situational awareness whenever you travel in public or interact with others. We cover this subject more deeply in the next chapter.

- **Be polite**. It's amazing how often you can avoid trouble if you're not the person starting it. There are few legitimate reasons for being a jerk, and losing your temper isn't one of them. Popping off to the wrong people can easily get you beat down, maimed, or killed. If you make a faux pas, gracefully acknowledge the error and go on about your day. When others are at fault, giving the other guy a face-saving way out goes a long, long way toward keeping you safe. Save righteous indignation for afterward when the bad guy(s) isn't in close proximity (as in can no longer see or hear you).

- **Keep good company**. If friends or lovers have a way of sparking confrontation you're hanging with the wrong people. What falls on them can easily blow back on you... or drag you in. Besides, high achievers who surround themselves with positive, supportive people tend to have more success than those who don't. Background checks are your friend, especially on those who have access to your home and loved ones.

- **Protect your stuff**. Despite advances in technology, identity thieves and scam artists still have an amazing amount of luck doing things the old fashioned way. Don't fall for social engineering scams on the internet or in person. That multimillion dollar lottery you never entered but just got the e-mail that you've won, that's a scam. So is the bank account confirmation query, the Zambian prince who wants to send you his inheritance, and just about anything else that sounds suspicious or simply too good to be true. Religiously maintain your computer, keeping anti-virus and anti-malware software up to date, creating robust passwords, and changing them routinely. And, don't write the damn things down where others can find and use your passwords, memorize them.

- **Understand your priorities**. Don't be like Isaac Martinez, a narcissistic fool who after getting shot by rampage killer Ryan Elliot Giroux in Mesa Arizona on March 18, 2015, stopped to take selfies of his injuries and post them on Snapchat instead of heading directly to the hospital. Avoid violence whenever you can, fight to survive if that's your only option, and then manage the aftermath once the incident is over. This includes performing first aid on yourself or others, managing witnesses, interacting with law enforcement, finding a good attorney, navigating the legal system, dealing with the press, and coping with physiological or psychological trauma.

- **Know your neighborhood**. Understand what's "normal" where you live and work. This makes it much easier to spot anything that diverges from the customary, signaling the need to pay greater attention. Strange cars, people, sounds, smells, or situations, all warrant attention even if only to validate that they're not going to cause you trouble. If they are, being on your home turf gives you a leg up in evasion and escape or obtaining help.

- **Cover the basics**. Lock your doors and windows, use an alarm and/or video surveillance system where prudent, have adequate lighting, and maintain landscaping in ways that keep break-in artists from having excessive privacy or an easy way in. If you live in a problematic neighborhood consider moving… or buy a dog. Keep items of value in your trunk, under the seat, or otherwise out of plain sight whenever they must be stored in your vehicle and use a portable safe where appropriate. And, lock your car doors too.

If someone decides to target you, chances are good they've done it before and think they can win. Property can be replaced, but you must **take threats to your life and wellbeing seriously**. After all, bad guys do this for a living. They're good at their job, so never underestimate them. **Practicing martial arts in the *dojo* a few hours a week does not make you a seasoned street fighter**. Don't get cocky.

CHAPTER 11

RACIAL PROFILING IS STUPID; BEHAVIORAL PROFILING CAN SAVE YOUR LIFE

"We at El Al Airlines have used the hand/body search for so many years, but we did it only to suspicious passengers that were interviewed by us. We asked the questions and we were able to determine that there was something wrong with a passenger. Profiling is not that I am choosing that I want to interview them. We don't have discrimination. Every passenger, I don't care who he or she is, has to be interviewed by security. We have to be polite. We know how to ask questions. If you want to hide from us, we see the physical changes in your face, suddenly you raise your voice, suddenly your Adam's apple jumps up and down, you're nervous. Then we ask, 'Why are you nervous? I'm doing it for your safety sir or Ma'am.'"

– Isaac Yeffet

It should go without saying, but we'll do so anyway: Racial profiling is stupid. It's prejudicial, unjustified, and dysfunctional. Behavioral profiling, on the other hand, can save your life. For example, if you're a Caucasian and approach a group of African American males clustered at a street corner are you in danger? That's a trick question; there's no way to know... **Race has nothing to do with it**. In fact, chances are good that they are just a group of guys innocently waiting for the light to change so they can safely cross the street on the crosswalk. But, maybe not...

What if they're dripping color or sporting gang tattoos, does that change anything? Choice of clothing is a behavior, they're self-identifying with an anti-social group so it should be concerning, but there's no way to tell for sure without knowing more about the scenario. Needless to say if it was a bunch of white guys dressed as outlaw bikers it would be equally concerning; it's not the skin color but rather the distinctive clothing that matters. What if they begin to spread out to surround you, suspiciously reach under their jackets, or suddenly appear tense and angry as you approach? Coordinated flanking movements, fighting stances, intense focus (thousand-mile stare), posturing, and targeting glances all change the equation. These behaviors are, and should be, concerning regardless of the race, gender, sexual orientation, or ethnicity of the aggressors. Why? **Because they are pre-attack indicators**, signals that you're about to be in serious trouble.

Shifting to one-on-one encounters for a moment, as they are more common and somewhat harder to spot than group movements, pre-attack indicators can include a slight drop of the shoulder, a tensing of the neck, a flaring of the nostrils, rapid eye movements or blinking, or even a puckering of the lips. These subtle signs can be very difficult to spot, yet changes in a threat's energy are more easily seen. Amateurs and those engaging in social violence will try to send a message of domination, so they get big, red, and loud. They lock eyes so that you will know who beat (or is about to beat) you. A professional, on the other hand, tries to calm him- or herself (abdominal breathing, slow smooth movements) and not draw attention. He or she typically looks away just before the attack to check for witnesses. As you can see there are many variations to consider. Consequently, **it's not the specific action or reaction you're looking for, but rather the change in energy that might indicate peril**. Here is a list of danger signs that often precede an attack:

- **Motion**. A person who was standing still moves slightly. A weight shift is far subtler than a step, but this change is a possible preparation for attack.
- **Voice**. There is a change in the rate, tone, pitch, or volume of a person's voice. An overt example is when someone who is shouting becomes suddenly quiet or, conversely, one who has been quiet suddenly raises his voice.
- **Eye contact**. A person who was looking at you suddenly looks away or, conversely, a person who was looking away suddenly makes eye contact. Watch this one. As humans we focus on eyes/face to gauge attention, which we think is important, but often turning the head away, especially with an experienced fighter, loads and clears the shoulders for a strike. As the threat breaks eye contact many folks relax only to be sucker punched immediately afterward.[19]
- **Breathing**. There is a sudden change in the person's breathing. Untrained adversaries will begin to breathe shallow and fast in the upper chests as they psych themselves up for the fight while trained opponents will breathe slow and deep from their abdomens in preparation for combat.
- **Complexion**. A person develops a sudden pallor or flushing of his or her face (paling

---

19 Consequently this is a good time to not only increase your awareness, but also to move to a more advantageous position in case an attack is coming.

is adrenaline-induced vasoconstriction, reddening is vasodilation). This spike in adrenaline may be fear-induced or brought on by rage, but either way it foreshadows impending action on the other person's part.

- **Bearing**. There is a change in the person's posture. Untrained adversaries tend to "puff up," opening their chest and arching their spine, while trained opponents tend to close down their chest, straighten their spine, and lower their center of gravity. The untrained behavior is indicative of social violence, ingrained patterns that are used making themselves bigger, louder, and more intimidating. It's concerning to witness this behavior, but the actions of skilled adversaries are far more dangerous, hence ought to be frightening and spur you to action.

You get the point, right? **Skin color, gender, sexual orientation, religion, and the like are not on the above list. It's all about <u>behavior</u>.** Is the other guy or gal doing something you should be concerned about? That's all that matters.

Here's an example: Yeffet, quoted above, is a retired senior intelligence director for the Israeli Secret Service. During his tenure he was responsible for the security of all Israeli embassies, consulates and delegations around the world. Later as El Al airline's chief security officer, he formulated the company's safety measures, which by most objective accounts are the best in the industry. The heart of their approach is the passenger-profiling and screening programs that train their security personnel how to proactively spot and remediate threats.

Behavioral profiling is nothing new. In fact, the Behavioral Research and Instruction Unit (BRIU) was established at the FBI Academy in Quantico, Virginia in 1972. Since its inception, the BRIU has pioneered the development of tactics, techniques, and procedures subsequently **adopted as standards in behavior-based anti-crime programs** for academic, law enforcement, intelligence, and military communities. This behavioral science program focuses on helping industry professionals better understand lawbreakers—who they are, how they think, why they do what they do—as a means to help solve crimes and prevent unlawful activity. This isn't woo-woo pseudoscience; it's factual, accurate, and based in decades of research and study.

Working with federal, state, and local law enforcement personnel, Lawrence helped develop and test a revised stadium security plan at a Pac-12[20] facility after the 9/11 attacks on the US. A nightmare scenario they discussed included a suicide bomber in the seating area supplemented by a truck bomb in the parking lot outside. **It's impossible to control 70,000 panicked football**

---

20 The Pac-12 Conference sponsors championship competition in eleven men's and twelve women's National Collegiate Athletic Association (NCAA)-sanctioned sports. The twelve participating universities that lend the conference its name include Arizona, Arizona State, California, Colorado, Oregon, Oregon State, Stanford, UCLA, USC, Utah, Washington, and Washington State. Nicknamed the "Conference of Champions," the Pac-12 has won more NCAA National Team Championships than any other conference in history.

fans, so the only way to defend against such attacks is via preemption, spotting and acting on suspicious behaviors before the bad guys can put their nefarious plans into play. This may seem like a daunting task, but with the right awareness, training, and diligence it is absolutely possible. Behavioral signs that should raise suspicion hence warrant further investigation include:

- **Evasion**. Attempts to maintain distance from or otherwise avoid security personnel or eye contact with law enforcement where present.
- **Disguises**. Attempts to wear a disguise, carry fake identification, or blend into a crowd where the person does not seem to belong.
- **Excessive nervousness**. Repeated and nervous handling of fashion accessories or clothing or looking nervous, irritated, or sweating profusely (in excess of what might be expected due to environmental conditions).
- **Overt/covert surveillance**. Conducting reconnaissance in sensitive locations using a camera, cell phone cam, or video recorder. It is harder to spot covert surveillance, whereas overt reconnaissance seems innocent until it is observed and challenged by security or law enforcement personnel.
- **Overly intense focus**. Slow-paced movements with overly intense focus (thousand-yard stare) or nervous muttering, mumbling, or praying.
- **Unusual attire**. Unseasonable dress, particularly when conspicuously bulky. This includes any suspiciously protruding bulges or exposed wires under clothing, potentially seen through the sleeve.
- **Carrying suspicious objects or illicit weapons**. Bringing suspicious or dangerous items such as canisters, tanks, metal boxes, bottles, or illicit weapons into a restricted area. This includes carrying anything that releases a mist, gas, vapor, or has any unusual odor.
- **Planting a suspicious object**. Abandoning an item such as a backpack or briefcase and then leaving the area quickly or furtively.

The list above covers the people half of the equation, but what about the vehicles? Potential car or truck bombs can often be identified by mismatched or precariously hung license plates, an extra heavy load in the back, or attempts to park in an inappropriate spot. Whether an explosive device is worn or carried by an individual or packed into a vehicle, it can be extraordinarily dangerous and deadly. According to the FBI Bomb Data Center, six pounds of explosives (cigar box) has a fragmentation range of 832 feet. Forty pounds of explosives (briefcase) has a fragmentation range of 1,129 feet. One hundred and sixty pounds of explosives (suitcase) has a fragmentation range of 1,792 feet. Augment the explosive charge with ball bearings, nails, or other shrapnel and you have a deadly disaster waiting to happen. You can imagine how devastating a truck bomb twenty times that size could be… think Oklahoma City.

No matter how well trained a martial artist you are; **you cannot fight a bullet or a bomb with your hands and feet and expect to win**. As we've said many times, the best defense is awareness, becoming conscious of and avoiding dangerous situations before it is too late. And, of course, what often cues you to impending danger is the behaviors of those around you. While it may very well be the potential assailant who gives him or herself away, reactions of those around him or her play a vital role as well. So do unusual sights, sounds, or smells.

It's vital to understand what you're seeing too. There's a difference between fear management and danger management. **Fear tells you to pay attention, but it's the specific threat you need to address, not the fear itself**. In other words, pay attention to the danger signals you receive from others, identify the underlying behavior that set off your "Spidey senses," and then be prepared to act if necessary. It's unhealthy to walk around in a state of constant paranoia, yet you should take prudent precautions and avoid clearly dangerous situations. Awareness can be used to protect not only yourself, but to save others around you as well. In *The Gift of Fear*, Gavin DeBecker wrote:

> "Before the courageous FBI raid, before the arrest, long before the news conference, there is a regular American citizen who sees something that seems suspicious, listens to intuition, and has the character to risk being wrong or seeming foolish when making the call to authorities."

You've heard it before—"see something, say something." But first, you need to know what you're looking for. This concept includes two components: (1) awareness of your **environment** as well as (2) awareness of **timing**. Awareness of environment includes listening to your intuition and being aware of what is going on around you. Identify and report suspicious unattended vehicles, luggage, or packages in high traffic areas. Monitor irregular activity, such as when someone leaves a large package in a trashcan across from a government building or other strategic location and report anything suspicious to the proper authorities.

For example, on January 23, 2005 a young boy playing in the village of Barangay Malisbong, an Abu Sayyaf stronghold in the Philippines, discovered a powerful explosive device concealed in a two-liter plastic soy-sauce container packed with shrapnel and rigged to a timing device. He reported his discovery to the authorities who disarmed the weapon and subsequently arrested two terrorist suspects. Similar devices were retrieved unexploded from a packed public market in Midsayap and the Cotabato City Cathedral the next day.

Awareness of timing has to do with the time of day during which attacks are most likely to occur. Terrorists try to time attacks to inflict maximum casualties—typically during "rush hour." For example, the April 19, 1995, Oklahoma City bombing and the September 11, 2001 attacks all took place during the workday **when and where the highest number of potential victims congregated**. Similarly, the London subway and bus bombings on July 7, 2005 and the Madrid train bombings on March 11, 2004 also took place during peak traffic hours.

Obviously a crowded mall in daytime is much more likely to be hit than the same location late at night or just before closing. Conversely, a dance club is more likely to be hit late at night once a sizeable crowd has gathered than during the day. Awareness of timing in the United States can also include Department of Homeland Security threat level indicators that help predict likely attacks. The US State Department also issues travel restrictions and warnings when they sense hazardous conditions in other countries.

When environment and timing converge, **your level of alertness should be at its highest**.

A football game was played at the stadium where Lawrence worked a couple of weeks after the 9/11 attacks. Right before that game, stadium officials got word that a local TV station was trying to plant a fake bomb in an unattended backpack to test the security. They were, of course, hoping to catch stadium security unprepared and point out holes in their program. While security and law enforcement personnel had always swept the stadium before each game, including a pass with bomb-sniffing dogs, extra diligence was taken due to a combination of the recent terrorist attacks and word of this so-called test. No such backpack was planted nor found at that time, but the incident was considered a good training opportunity. This event led to drills in which suspicious packages were randomly left unattended to keep the event staff on our toes. Occasionally a timer would be set and left inside a package so that if it was not discovered expeditiously (that is, before the timer went off), it would simulate having already exploded. Similar drills can be duplicated in a *dojo* to help increase practitioners' levels of awareness.

While awareness can help you avoid all kinds of assaults, it can also help you thwart one before it can be pulled off successfully. **Because we are far better prepared than the average citizen to take action in these cases, martial artists should be prepared to intervene when necessary**. Prudent application of countervailing force can be very effective even when dealing with suicide bombers. For example, on March 8, 2002 a Palestinian youth in his 20s walked into the crowded Caffit coffee house in Jerusalem and asked for a glass of water. This was nothing unusual as that particular part of town was a popular hangout for Palestinian teenagers, many of whom frequented the café. What was unusual, however, was the fact that he was carrying a large black school bag, appeared nervous, and was sweating profusely. An astute waiter, Shlomi Harel, **became concerned by the youth's behavior, noticed a suspicious wire leading from the backpack, and took immediate action**. Pushing the youth outside, Harel and a security guard who also worked in the building snatched the bomb from the assailant's hands, yanked the wire from the detonator, wrestled him to the ground, and held him until police could arrive. Their quick action averted what Police Chief Mickey Levy said would have been, "a major disaster."

People acting suspiciously may not have something to hide yet it's prudent to pay attention to them anyway. For example, the disheveled guy talking to himself and gesticulating wildly might be clinically insane, or he might be having a fight with his girlfriend who he's talking to via a Bluetooth transmitter you cannot see under his hat or hair. **Just because something draws your attention does not necessarily mean that you will have to act**; only that you should be prepared to do so if the threat becomes real. And, acting might mean running toward or away from the danger, depending on the unique circumstances you face. Training and experience temper the reaction.

For example, as Lawrence approached his car after a doctor's appointment in the medical center parking lot around 2:00 in the afternoon he flicked his key open. They guy opening the door of his car in the next stall heard the click, mistook it for a switchblade or something, spun and drew his gun. Now Lawrence was armed and could have pulled his weapon too, but instead he shouted, "It's a car key, man. Just a car key." The other guy turned red, started shaking, mumbled something that might have been an apology, and quickly put his gun away. Chalk that up as an epic failure in behavioral profiling. Hopefully the other guy learned a lesson from it. A few tips for getting things right:

- **Learn to think like a bad guy**. Watch others as you go about your business. If you were a professional criminal, think about who you would attack and why. Consider locations and situations where you would be most able to get away with it. Then, pay extra attention in circumstances where the roles might be reversed.
- **Know what's normal**. Get a feel for what typically happens where you live, work, study, or play, and pay extra attention to any behaviors that stray from the expected routine. You may or may not need to act, but at least you'll be prepared.
- **Understand pre-attack indicators**. We listed several danger signs earlier in this chapter. Memorize them, but also realize that they can be incredibly hard to spot where you are not expecting a threat or during a confrontation in the heat of the moment when your attention is diverted by other things. Any change in energy on the other guy or gal's part should be concerning.
- **Watch how others react**. Oftentimes you can spot danger not by actions of the threat but rather by behaviors of those around him or her. This is particularly useful in crowds where you cannot see everyone directly, but even in small groups or intimate settings bystanders may notice things that you miss.
- **Plan Constantly**. As James Mattis (USMC) famously wrote, "Be polite, be professional, but have a plan to kill everybody you meet." Hopefully you'll never need to act, but

if you're constantly planning how to keep yourself safe on that rare occasion when nefarious intent comes your way you'll be ready.

It doesn't matter what the other guy looks like, it matters what he (or she) does. Paying close attention to the actions of others not only helps you respond appropriately if/when you are threatened but also makes it much easier to explain why you needed to do what you did to keep yourself safe. Platitudes like "I was in fear for my life" simply don't hold up in court, yet specific descriptions of events, actions, what they mean, and why will hold you in good stead. "He looked nervous, was wearing sweater and long pants on a 90-degree day, sweating profusely, and looking around furtively. This caught my attention. As I took a closer look I spotted an outline of the gun he had stuffed in his waistband where it printed through his sweater. When he reached back, grab a hold of the gun, and started to draw I took action..." This is why behavioral profiling can keep you safe both **before** *and* **after** a violent encounter occurs. It's a valuable tool in your self-preservation arsenal.

CHAPTER 12

WHEN THE ODDS ARE STACKED AGAINST YOU

"The physical context of self-defense is completely alien to most trained people's comprehension. Have you ever been hit, had your bell really rung? Maybe a good concussion? Start from there, but there is no pause after the hit, just more damage and you cannot see the guy because he is probably behind you and at least some of the damage is coming from your head bouncing off the wall or maybe it is the floor by now and maybe one of your arms will not work and you realize that you do not know who is hitting you or how many or with what and the blood in your eyes is starting to taste funny. This is where physical self-defense STARTS. This is where you begin."

– Rory Miller

For a horrific five years during the early- to mid-1980s the community of Garden Grove, California was terrorized by a masked man who committed dozens of burglaries and rapes, more often than not surprising a couple in their home, tying up the husband, stuffing him in a closet, and making him listen as he raped the wife. This guy, nicknamed "Ski Mask," was serious bad news... In fact, he was known to stab or shoot victims who resisted. He began his crime spree with a knife, but in addition to jewelry and cash, he had stolen several firearms which he then put to nefarious use. On Saturday, June 21, 1986 police Sergeant Steve Sanders and his partner Dave Kivler were on patrol looking for the masked horror when they spotted a silhouette lurking in the bushes near the Lawrence School parking lot. When he spotted the officers, the man fled toward a nearby cul-de-sac. After a short pursuit the officers caught sight of the shadowy figure squatting near a camper with what appeared to be a pistol in his hand.

"Police, freeze!" Sanders yelled.

"Freeze," the suspect shouted back, echoing the officer's command.

"Drop the gun," Sanders commanded, pulling back toward a brick wall where he could keep his eyes on the suspect while achieving some modicum of cover.

"Back off! Drop the fucking gun!" shouted the suspect, simultaneously moving to clear the cover and get a clean shot at the officers.

A mere five feet separated the camper at the suspect's back from the wall where Sanders and his partner were crouched when gunfire abruptly rang out. Sanders fired three times, but was hit in the arm by the suspect, the bad guy's bullet burrowing through his wrist and forearm before lodging in the officer's chest. Fortunately it was stopped by the ballistic vest he wore before doing any further damage. While he never felt the blow to his chest, the bullet separated his ulnar nerve, creating the most intense pain he'd ever experienced. He reported afterward that his wrist and forearm felt like they were being immolated by hellfire.

Knowing he'd been shot, but not how badly he was injured, time seemed to slow (from the tachypsychia effect which is quite common for those engaged in mortal combat). In the second or two Sanders had to process the situation, an image of his three-year-old son flashed through his head giving him the strength he needed to reengage, but by then the suspect was already sprinting away from him.

Sanders raised his gun, took a bead on the fleeing suspect, and pulled the trigger… but nothing happened. Thinking it had jammed, he cycled the slide and then attempted to fire again. Belatedly he realized that there was nothing wrong with his gun, it was his weakened hand that had failed to pull the trigger far enough to make the pistol go off. Afraid to switch hands in the middle of a gunfight, he redoubled his efforts. This time, thankfully, the gun went off. So did his partner's, as Kivler engaged the threat too, emptying his magazine at the fleeing bad guy.

The suspect who had been shooting back over his shoulder while running suddenly staggered and clutched at his lower back, but continued to run. After reloading the officers called for backup and then continued to cautiously follow in the direction in which the masked suspect had disappeared into the night. They could barely make out a blood trail in the darkness as they moved.

The officers didn't know it at the time, but the suspect, 35-year-old Barrie Hill, was dying from at least two fatal wounds yet still mobile when he escaped from the initial gun battle by the camper. After fleeing he broke into an empty house to hide, reload, and tend to his injuries as best he could. When he heard sirens approaching he slipped out another door, staggered another 50 yards or so, then slumped against a neighbor's tree where, in a final act of defiance, he placed his gun against his head and pulled the trigger a short time later.

An autopsy later showed that Hill had been hit five times by .45 caliber bullets before his final, self-inflicted gunshot wound. While he was still crouched down by the camper he had been struck alongside his head by a bullet that tore through his signature ski mask, traveled down through his shoulder, and lodged deep in his chest. The second bullet went through his left arm and entered his abdomen. The third shot struck his foot, injuring his big toe. The fourth bullet caught him in the right side of the back, seriously damaging his liver before continuing all the way through him. The fifth bullet fired by the officers struck him in his hip, shattering a pair of binoculars he had stashed in his pocket. The only damage from that final shot was from glass and shrapnel that distributed across his buttocks.

Consider the damage unleashed in few seconds during the lethal encounter described above. The burglar-rapist, Barry Hill, was fatally wounded yet continued to fight and run for quite some time. The heroic officer, Steve Sanders, was severely injured and, likely, saved by his ballistic vest. And, despite the close range, a mere five feet, most shots from all three combatants missed. Statistically this is not unusual, yet it can come as quite a shock to many, even martial artists who ostensibly train for self-defense.

The challenge with a lot of martial arts training is that it fails to consider the realities of a life-or-death struggle. If you're the good guy, you're often working your way out of a horrifically bad situation, injured, stunned, bleeding, even possibly dying, all **while trying to overcome an attacker who got the jump on you**. Psychologically it's valuable to always train for success, but scenarios must account for the fact that you are often not in good position at the beginning of the fight. Consequently you need to stave off further damage while stopping the bad guy from continuing his attack.

To reiterate our four simple rules of self-defense (which were described in depth in *The Little Black Book of Violence*) include:

- **Rule 1: Don't get hit.** That's primarily about using awareness, avoidance, and de-escalation to eliminate the need to fight in the first place. Where a physical confrontation is unavoidable, it's also about warding off the other guy's blows or avoiding his weapon(s) so that you can counterattack successfully. Oftentimes this must include regaining your balance or structure so that you can perform any kind of armed or unarmed technique successfully before you are able to strike back.
- **Rule 2: Stop him from continuing to attack you.** A purely defensive response is insufficient in a street fight as it can only keep you safe for a very short period of time. You must stop the assault that is in progress so that you can escape to safety or otherwise

remain safe until help arrives. Your goal is to be safe, not to kill your attacker, or teach him a lesson. Nevertheless, stopping the other guy typically means physiologically incapacitating him. As described above, Barrie Hill was shot five times yet still managed to flee before taking his own life several minutes later. Humans oftentimes (but not always) take a LOT of breaking to put them out of a fight.

- **Rule 3: Always have a Plan B.** No matter how good a fighter you are, whatever you try is not necessarily going to work. The other guy will be doing his damnedest to pound your face in, pulling out every dirty trick he can think of in an effort to mess you up. It is prudent, therefore, to have a Plan B, some alternative you can move to without missing a beat when things go awry. Proxemics and angles are particularly useful such that if your counterattack fails you've moved away from the other guy's angle of attack (out of immediate harm's way) and/or set yourself up to flee successfully. Regardless of how you implement it, always have a fallback plan.

- **Rule 4: Don't go to jail.** This is about judicious use of force, both knowing when it is appropriate to take action as well as knowing how much force to apply. The IMOP (Intent, Means, Opportunity, and Preclusion) principle (described in Appendix B) can hold you in good stead during conflict situations. One of the toughest elements of Rule 4 is learning how to stop. Oftentimes we're furious and flushed with adrenaline, continuing to counterattack even once the bad guy is no longer a threat, something that rarely ends well in court even when we are truly defending ourselves and had no culpability for the initial assault. Further, certain martial arts teach "finishing moves" that we may be trained to instinctively apply even when not warranted. That sort of thing does not play well to armchair quarterbacks on a jury either. Keep this in mind as you practice your martial art.

Since we're often out of position, injured, and/or under duress, and that's where things begin, **we need to train that way**. Maybe not all the time, but often... This means that drills must help us learn how to use proxemics, evasion, and blending to simultaneously defend and attack, hit hard enough to damage the other guy without the perfect posture that *kata* (forms) demands, and perform techniques to the point that they can become instinctual so that we can counterattack even when we're reeling in pain or cannot clearly see what we're doing.

Interestingly enough, case studies show again and again that **the mental game is more important than the physical one for your survival**. It's not that fighting skills aren't effective, but rather that **fights are more often lost by those who give up than by those who can no**

longer continue.[21] As the rapist/burglar described above demonstrated, humans usually take a lot of killing. Usually, but not always... We're pretty robust. Barring unusual slips and falls where your head hits the curb just right, sudden cardiac arrest, or some other freak incident we can shrug off a lot of damage when adrenalized and on the fight.

If you can do so many pushups that your arms give way causing you to fall on your face at the risk of giving yourself a bloody nose you've almost certainly got what it takes to persevere through most any physical confrontation, even if you're not a martial artist. The importance of the mental aspects of survival are so paramount that elite military operators such as Navy SEALS are pushed beyond their physical limits in training in part to show them what they're capable of. Boot camp is similar, but less strenuous. So is classical martial arts training, be it Okinawan, Japanese, or Chinese in origin, the rigors are much the same. Even many modern arts such as Brazilian Jujitsu and many forms of MMA do much the same thing.

In 2012 there were 414,065 people under some form of Federal correctional control (62% in confinement; 38% under supervision in the community) in the United States. Five federal judicial districts along the US-Mexico border accounted for 60% of federal arrests, 53% of suspects investigated, and 41% of offenders sentenced to prison.

Next comes strategy... **Fighting hard is nice, but fighting smart is much better**. For example, what's the bigger threat the gunman or the gun, the thug or his knife? Clearly it's not the weapon that's trying to kill you, it's the guy wielding it, yet all too many practitioners focus on the instrument, a dangerously suboptimal approach. **The best way to stop a bad guy with a knife is with a sniper. Or an airstrike**. Most of us don't have those options, but we can use distance and angles to our advantage, while working to kill or severely disable our assailant before he can do the same to us.

For example, an effective method of taking on a knifer empty-handed is to check/evade his strike, fire off a palm heel to his chin, step past while reaching around his head, twist your body, and drop to your knees while performing a neck-twist takedown (movements which Marc MacYoung creatively describes as tap/shave/drop/turn/pray). Done right you'll put the other guy out of commission, oftentimes permanently. Will you get cut in the process? Perhaps, but odds are good that **you're trading a cut for a kill** when you break his neck. That's a pretty good strategy for a horrifically bad situation.

Did you notice that there's no mention of grabbing or grappling for the knife in this example? **It's not the knife you're most worried about, but rather the guy wielding it**. The strategy is to avoid the initial strike (Rule 1 above), then immediately continue on to stop the threat (Rule 2).

---

21 Exceptions include instances such as where a combatant believes he is cornered and is about to die hence slips into a berserker frenzy, is unable to feel pain (e.g., under the influence of certain drugs or mental instabilities), or is enthralled by rage or ideology (e.g., suicide bomber).

If it doesn't work you're on the outside and stepping past the assailant, which leaves room for a variety of bailout options (Rule 3). And, it's a potentially deadly response to a lethal threat (Rule 4). It won't work without a bit of skill, timing, and (very possibly) luck, but oftentimes it does work.

Mental toughness and sound strategy, supported by effective techniques… That is a good way to fight. And, it's also a great way to escape too. Never forget that running is a viable option (yes we know we said that previously, but it bears repeating). Everyday civilians naturally run to safety, but oftentimes martial artists forget that they can do that too. **The goal is to be safe**, not to beat or beat down the other guy. Do whatever gets you to safety most efficiently and effectively. Obviously, figuring out what the optimal approach actually is can be a real challenge if you haven't had a chance to practice. This is why drills are so important. Well thought out scenario training can make a monumental impact on your ability to adapt and survive on the street. After all, **what gets trained gets done**… perhaps not as smoothly or well given the adverse effects of fear, adrenaline, blood, and whatnot, but it does get done nonetheless. Some strategies to help you prevail:

- **Use scenario training**. Reality-based scenario training, under appropriate supervision, can make monumental improvements in your ability to protect yourself. Incorporating "woofers," using racial slurs/ugly language and realistic scenarios gives you a tremendous leg up on learning when and how it is appropriate to talk, fight, or run. Taunting by the woofers is extremely uncomfortable, especially where/if it gets to race, religion, gender, sexual orientation, or other hot topics, but it helps move you past righteous anger, depersonalize, and focus on good decision-making under stress. Fighting angry usually means fighting stupid, which is never a good thing when your life is on the line.
- **Record and debrief training sessions**. For some reason martial artists rarely take advantage of technology like most other athletes do, yet it's a vital aspect of training. Free applications like Coaches' Eye (which was originally developed for football but works great for just about any sport) help you not only review and discuss actions you took (or didn't take) during the scenarios, but also helps your instructor(s) demonstrate angles, distance, proxemics, and other important factors on screen during the appraisal. Discussions that take place after practice can often be even more valuable than the training itself. After all, if you do tens of thousands of repetitions incorrectly or at cross-purposes with your goals you're working really hard while training to fail.
- **Perform posture drills**. Working on situations where you begin with compromised structure/body mechanics and have to respond appropriately. Variations on this theme can include trapped in the corner (e.g., elevator), start on the ground (with the other guy standing), bent over the car (using pads not a real vehicle), and pretzel (body

turned and twisted). Since you're often caught unawares on the street (otherwise, why did you have to fight in the first place), it's vital to know how to extricate yourself from bad situations, generate power with compromised structure, and counterattack adversaries you cannot clearly see.

- **Do proxemics drills**. These are variations of posture drills, save that they focus on positioning, angles, evasion, and blending more than anything else. Oftentimes you don't even utilize striking or grappling techniques, but rather rely on movement to keep you out of harm's way. In our experience variations that have proven especially valuable include zombie (moving through a crowd to extricate yourself without being captured and "eaten"), shadow dancing (mirroring the other guy's movements), and hood ornament (fighting in and around a mockup of a car).

- **Practice regain-the-count drills**. These are typically done in slow motion where your training partner starts first, you "honor" his/her technique (hence are in a compromised position and behind the count), and work to find ways to defend and counter simultaneously. Once proficient such things can be performed at speed, but you need to be careful to assure that it is angles, tactical movement, prudent tradeoffs, and solid techniques that let you retake momentum in the fight and not simply being faster (or more skilled) than your training partner. You cannot count on being the higher skilled combatant in a real fight. Performing these drills by count can help.

- **Fight blindfolded**. Oftentimes in real life you'll be forced to fight when you cannot see the threat you face, because you are ambushed from behind, facing multiple assailants, have blood in your eyes, had glasses or contact lenses broken or knocked loose, something thrown into or covering your face, or the like. Blindfold drills help you learn to overcome such challenges. These drills also refine your ability to use sounds, smells, and touch to best advantage. Clearly working blindfolded can become dangerous if not well monitored, but viscerally understanding how contact with one part of the other guy tells you where to aim is a critical aspect of prevailing in a real-life fight.

- **Perform goal drills**. Oftentimes we get so hung up on the drill that we forget why we're doing it. Having a goal in mind, say escape to safety, bodyguard a client, rescue a friend, or get to a weapon, provides needed context and focus. Sometimes the drills can be a little silly, something like picking the other guy's pocket while grappling or keeping your (fake) baby safe during a melee, yet this hones your ability for creative decision-making and problem-solving under duress. Rory Miller's *Drills: Training for Sudden Violence* is a valuable resource for that.

Another vital aspect of extricating yourself from hazardous situations is stopping the threat through physiological damage. Remember, you don't necessarily have to break the threat, but you do need to make him stop. It's hard to hit another person hard enough to do damage in optimal conditions let alone when you're behind the count and your structure is compromised. If you're the bad guy chances are good that you'll have the upper hand from the first moment of contact since you stack the odds in your favor by determining the location, timing, and opening movements of the altercation, which is why targeting is so crucial for the good guys. While opportunities to connect may be few and far between if you make the most of each of them you get you'll have a fighting chance.

Few things will stop a determined adversary, but in a life-or-death encounter forensic evidence demonstrates that solid blows to the head, eyes, throat, or cervical spine can put the threat out of commission. These could be administered by you, a weapon or tool that you happen to be carrying, or any solid object (e.g., car, curb, rock) around you. Done right, chokes, strangulations, and (assuming the other guy doesn't know how to fall correctly) even hurling him to the ground with impetus can also end the fight… but not always. Most other targets, even strikes to the groin or kidneys, can cause intense pain, but while pain might make him stop it could just as easily enrage the adversary, causing him or her to use even higher levels of violence against you. And, as we saw with the example at the beginning of this chapter, **even fatally wounded adversaries continue to be a threat until they are no longer able to move against you**. As the proverb states, "Dead tigers kill the most hunters." So, be aware that it's not over until it's over, the other guy is no longer a threat, and you have reached a place of safety.

To be clear, not all situations require extreme violence to successfully resolve. Remember that if you use too much force you will likely go to jail. On the other hand, if you use too little and you very well may not make it home. Scenario training can help you better understand what you face, hence use prudence in your response.

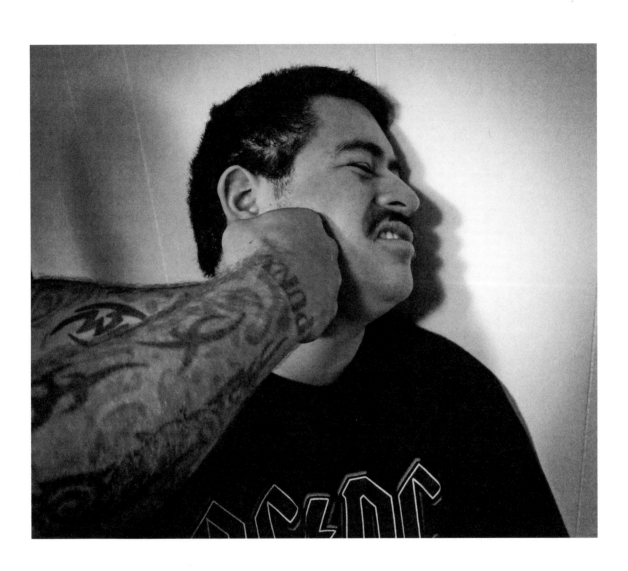

CHAPTER 13

STRIKE FIRST, STRIKE HARD

"Don't hit at all if it is honorably possible to avoid hitting; but never hit soft!"

– Theodore Roosevelt

Itosu "Anko" Yasutsune, a legendary karate master, traveled to the port city of Naha in the summer of 1856 to find relief from the heat and humidity of his home town of Shuri. He found a large rock there that provided some relief from the sun, settled down to enjoy the ocean breeze, and was about to doze off when he overheard several local villagers disparaging Shuri karate. Insulted by this banter, he decided to uphold the honor of his style through *kakidameshi* (dueling), an honored Okinawan tradition in those times.

Making his way to the challenge area, he made himself known to the crowd, quickly defeating three lesser practitioners in order to attract attention of the local champion, Naha-no-Tomoyose. When Tomoyose arrived on the scene to defend his city's honor, Itosu discovered that he faced a monster of a man, bigger, stronger, and far more powerfully built than himself. He realized that he would need to end the fight near instantly or risk becoming overwhelmed by his rival's superior size and strength.

As the fighters began to circle, sizing up each other, the crowd observed this physical disparity as well, wagering at odds of ten to one against the challenger from Shuri. Tomoyose threw the first blow, a mighty lunge punch, yet as the other Naha master's massive fist came screaming toward his head Itosu shifted aside and blocked with a sword-hand strike. The crowd heard a loud snap, like the breaking of a branch, and suddenly the fight was over... Tomoyose's arm had been snapped neatly in half. This victory solidified Itosu Yasutsune's reputation as one of the greatest karate masters in Okinawan history.

––––––––––––––

While dueling may have been an integral part of feudal Okinawan culture, it's not something one encounters all that much in modern times. Nowadays it's criminal thugs and bullies that we're most concerned about. Martial artists learn skills that can keep them safe from violence, yet one of the downfalls of such training is that oftentimes it limits a practitioner's thinking. For example, if you practice a martial sport, one that emphasizes competition, you will have certain "illegal" techniques (such as eye gouges, rabbit punches, or using a weapon) trained out of you. Things like this are obviously far too dangerous to do in the ring, yet they sometimes they are exactly what's needed on the street. Unfortunately, in the heat of the moment, you are extremely unlikely to consider doing them simply because they aren't part of your curriculum. Conversely, you may have certain deficiencies trained in as well. For example, grapplers are taught to instantly stop fighting when their opponent taps out. That's all well and good in the ring, but it leaves a Pavlovian reflex that can be exploited by a savvy street fighter who is willing to cheat in order to win. Tap, get a reflexive break in the action, and use it to tear the other guy's face off while his guard is down. Lawrence saw that exact scenario play out a few times at the stadium.

Another challenge with martial arts training often lies with misinterpretations of what has been taught. For instance, if you study a classical martial art you have likely been taught that what you learn must only be used defensively. Gichin Funakoshi, the founder of *Shotokan*, famously stated, "*Karate ni sente nashi.*" This translates as, "There is no first strike in karate." While this statement makes a whole lot of sense from a philosophical perspective, all too many practitioners take it too literally. They erroneously believe that they must wait until they have already been attacked before taking countervailing action. While that tactic may have worked for Master Itosu in 1865, for most folks nowadays **by the time the other guy throws a punch it is too late** to defend effectively.

To be clear, karate practitioners, like most martial artists, should be taught to avoid seeking conflict. Fighting is a participatory act, much like dueling, and it is illegal in most jurisdictions. Even where it's not prohibited, avoiding such behaviors is a good thing. We really don't want martial arts students running around picking fights outside the ring to stoke their egos or create senseless havoc. This mindset is so important, in fact, that it goes beyond mere words and is even reflected in the training methods and physical movements of many arts. For example, every *kata* in *Goju Ryu* karate begins with a defensive technique.

The challenge then becomes **learning how to make defensive movements work to our advantage**. What many practitioners don't realize is that defensive techniques when executed properly are designed to be just as fight stopping as offensive ones. Itosu broke Tomoyose's arm with a block, though to be accurate the term *uke* which is often translated as "block" in Japanese really means "receive," an entirely different connotation. Since these arts were developed before the advent of modern medicine, almost any injury suffered in battle could ultimately prove fatal through infection or other collateral impact. The ancient masters understood that if they were to only block an assailant's attack he would continue to strike until either they did something more effective to disable him, or they were beaten into a bloody pulp, or he decided to stop of his own volition. Consequently **all martial applications**, including the defensive ones, **were designed to end confrontations as quickly as possible**. Despite advancements in technology, the nature of hand-to-hand fighting remains much the same today as it was in ancient times.

That said, here's where the confusion lies: To many "no first strike" implies waiting for an adversary to attack and then trying to successfully counter when you are already injured or out of position from the force of your attacker's initial blow. After all, once you block the first strike another is inevitably already on its way so you are effectively behind the count before you begin, something which tends to end poorly unless you are stronger, faster, or more skilled than whoever attacked you. More often than not, that simply isn't the case. Bad guys are pretty good at choosing victims. If someone is attacking you he almost certainly plans to win and believes that he can prevail, likely from previous experience with other victims. If nothing else, this means he is likely going to be meaner (or madder or more drug addled or whatever) than you are.

What's true today was just as true in Funakoshi's time (or Itosu's for that matter). In order to decipher the true intent of Funakoshi's statement, therefore, we must understand the proper context. This can be deciphered from three Japanese terms: (1) *go no sen*, (2) *sen no sen*, and (3) *sen-sen no sen*:

- *Go no sen*. This means "late initiative," blocking and riposting after an adversary has already attacked. This is the method that new practitioners are initially taught. It means to receive or block a blow and then to strike back. It is a great learning method because it breaks advanced techniques down into small movements but it is not practical on the street where you are likely to become overwhelmed by a determined aggressor. This is elementary karate, abandoned quickly once any significant level of skill has been achieved.
- *Sen no sen*. This means "simultaneous initiative," intercepting the other guy's blow just after it begins. This is an intermediate form of karate, using quickness and power to simultaneously attack and defend, cutting off the opponent's strike before it makes contact. This is where we begin to find street-worthy application.
- *Sen-sen no sen*. This means "preemptive initiative," cutting off a blow before it even starts. Practitioners sense that an attack will be forthcoming and then cut it short before

the aggressor has the chance to transform the mental desire to attack into the physical movement necessary to execute that desire. This is the ultimate goal of martial training insofar as self-defense is concerned, advanced karate. It also takes thousands upon thousands of hours of experience to master, so while it is an admirable goal it is not readily achievable for many martial arts students.

Sen-sen no sen, cutting off an attack before it is fully in play, looks an awful lot like a first strike yet is still a defensive movement. This is what Funakoshi really meant. Striking to cut off an impending attack is okay, while instigating unwarranted violence on your own initiative is not. If you can walk away from a confrontation you absolutely should do so. It is not only morally the right thing to do but it also allows you to avoid serious legal, psychological, and/or medical repercussions as well. In modern society, most rational people would agree that picking fights is a bad idea. There's no honor in dueling. In fact, the more dangerous you really are the less you should feel a need to prove it. To clarify further, Funakoshi wrote:

> "When there are no avenues of escape or one is caught even before any attempt to escape can be made, then for the first time the use of self-defense techniques should be considered. Even at times like these, do not show any intention of attacking, but first let the attacker become careless. At that time attack him concentrating one's whole strength in one blow to a vital point and in the moment of surprise, escape and seek shelter and help."

Notice that he wrote, "At that time attack him" as opposed to "After he strikes launch your counterattack." *Sen-sen no sen* is fully consistent with this approach. And, justifiable in court if you are able to explain how and why you know the other guy was about to strike. This is where a solid understanding of pre-attack indicators described earlier not only helps keep you safe in a violent encounter but also helps you explain your way out of trouble afterward.

Sometime around 506 B.C. Sun Tzu wrote:

> "To win one hundred victories in one hundred battles is not the highest skill.
> To subdue an enemy without fighting is the highest skill."

There are many peaceful ways to settle a disagreement, any one of which is preferable to a physical confrontation in most instances. If you cannot escape from danger, however, that does not mean that you must stand around waiting to get hit before you can act in your own defense. This is especially important in multiple attacker and armed aggressor scenarios where hesitation will most likely get you mutilated or killed. Consider this:

136

- **You're not the other guy's first victim**. Whoever is attacking you has almost certainly assaulted someone before. The more times he (or she) gets away with it the more dangerous that person is likely to become.
- **By fighting you may be helping others too**. If you successfully defend yourself against an assailant you not only save your own life or wellbeing but likely that of the criminal's next victim as well. This is particularly true if he not only loses but also faces charges after the assault.
- **The best defense is often a good offense**. There truly is no first strike in karate (or any other martial art for that matter), at least there shouldn't be, because martial practitioners shouldn't run around starting fights. There should, however, be vigorous, proactive defense in situations that warrant it. Clearly that can be a challenge, but it's also what we train for.
- **Don't go overboard**. Your goal is to be safe, not to kill your attacker, humiliate him, or otherwise teach him a lesson. Break the other guy if you must, but only when necessary to keep you or your loved ones safe. As mentioned previously, beware of "finishing moves." These can easily be habituated in training and subsequently get you into serious trouble on the street if you operate on autopilot.

 There are seasonal trends to most violent crimes in the United States. Rape, sexual assault, aggravated assault, and violence involving weapons occurs more often in the summer than in the winter, spring, or fall. In comparison, simple assault rates are higher during the fall than during other seasons of the year. Robbery rates, however, do not exhibit seasonal variations.

Good people ignore insults and avoid seeking revenge yet that does not mean that they should be passive in the face of danger. If confronted with an unavoidable threat a vigorous response is necessary. Your intent, however, must be to stop the assault that is in progress so that you can escape to safety or otherwise remain safe until help arrives. This is the ultimate meaning of *karate ni sente nashi*. And, it's a valuable lesson in self-defense. But, here's the problem: **if you have the option of hitting first then more often than not you're the bad guy**. With good situational awareness and a little luck you can turn the tables on a would-be attacker, using *sen sen no sen*, but it takes a significant skill and training in order to do so. Most folks, even most trained martial artists, have serious trouble pulling that off in real life.

For instance, even though Lawrence is a black belt who has been in more than 300 violent altercations while working security, he was sucker-punched in the last fight he got into at the stadium before he retired. Why? Because it wasn't the threat he thought he was facing who attacked, but rather that guy's buddy who had been standing quietly by while Lawrence and his team separated a couple of fans who had gotten into an altercation and started to calm things down. Not only did Lawrence take an elbow to the side of the head, he also received his seventh concussion (that he knows about) even though in the last instant he caught movement and rolled with the blow to shed much of the impact. The point here isn't what happened to Lawrence, but rather that what happened to Lawrence in that particular fight is pretty typical of what most people will face if attacked on the street. If you're the good guy, the odds are good that **you're going to start off in trouble and have to fight your way to safety**. Unless, of course, you see it coming and manage to get in the first strike (via preemptive initiative) or have an unusually effective simultaneous response (such as breaking the other guy's arm with your block).

Hitting first where and when warranted is great, but unfortunately simply hitting first in and of itself isn't enough. You must hit hard enough and accurately enough to stop the threat too. Clearly your response must be proportional with the danger as well, since you will need to justify your actions later on, either to be able to look at yourself in the mirror afterward, to keep from being prosecuted or convicted, or both. Nonetheless, if you need to hit someone you need to know how to hit him (or her) hard enough to actually make an impact.

A good rule of thumb for identifying applications to use in real life is what we call the "Green Belt Rule." This means that if a 100-pound female greenbelt could make it work against a 300-pound male mugger, it's a street-worthy technique. In other words, **if someone who is in decent shape and has a fair amount of proficiency** (say a year or two of martial arts training), **but isn't excessively strong, fast, skilled, or experienced can pull it off, you can too**. Anything that requires a very high level of skill or a superior athletic ability **is not recommended**, because the odds of your being attacked by someone significantly smaller, slower, lighter, or less skilled than yourself are small. As mentioned previously, career criminals may be bad guys, but they're not stupid.

Here are some tips for doing that:

- **Use a tool**. If you truly need to break someone, it's very hard to do that with your fist or foot unless you are very highly trained. We all know that a shod foot can do more damage than a bare foot, especially with a steel toed boot. Fist-loads (such as a roll of quarters), fighting rings, and other strike enhancers can help, as can weapons such as batons, knives or guns where appropriate. Don't forget about things you don't carry around with you too. You may be able to turn some stray object (such as a rock, pool cue, or beer bottle) into an impromptu weapon or simply throw the other guy onto or knock him into something solid (such as a car, curb, or doorknob). The ground oftentimes hits harder than the fist. Our point is that if you're fighting for your life then you must take every advantage you can get. Usually this means using some sort of weapon.

- **Stay connected**. Body alignment, when you're able to utilize it, is the key to hitting hard empty handed. The more connected your striking appendage is to your body, the more energy is transferred into the target. That is why a straight punch that lands with the elbow down, shoulder relaxed, spine straight, and deltoid muscles locked down tight hurts more than an identical punch where the elbow is raised up a bit. Any disconnectedness breaks the "power chain," allowing energy to bleed off. Further, when using a firearm connectedness stabilizes your "shooting platform" making yourself more accurate too. We once brought an Okinawan karate master who had never even seen a gun before to a shooting range where, once he learned about sight picture through the translator, he managed to place every shot into the black at 25 feet simply due to exceptional body control.

- **Use your core**. Try this with a partner: Shake hands. Using your forearm, you will see that you only move his or her forearm. If you use your shoulder, however, you can move the other guy's whole arm. If you use your hip, so that your entire body is engaged, you can move his or her core. Tying this concept in with the previous principle, a connected power chain helps you put your entire bodyweight behind your blows so that you are hitting with everything you've got rather than just the strength of your arm. It works similarly with blunt instruments and even many edged weapons too. Putting your whole body behind each blow increases your power even when you are relying on mass and acceleration or a sharp cutting surface to cause damage to your adversary.

- **Accelerate**. If the speed of your blow remains constant, you are pushing the other guy. If, on the other hand, your fist or foot (or elbow or whatever) is moving faster than it started when it connects with the other guy, you're striking. Don't push, strike. For best results, relax until the moment your blow touches the other guy, then tense your whole body at that moment of impact while you drive through. Skilled martial artists don't even need to tense at all; as long as their structure is correct they can strike both faster and harder that way, but once again that takes significant training. Acceleration is vital when using many types of weapons too.

- **Contour.** The principle of contouring helps you identify the best target for any given technique, assuring that you do maximum damage to the adversary while minimizing the risk of injury to yourself. In general, that means that your hard parts strike soft targets and vice versa. For instance, punching another guy in the jaw with you knuckles tends to end badly, while a palm heel strike can knock him out without breaking your hand. It's not just about safety though, it's also about effectiveness. A single knuckle strike to the solar plexus can work because it fits the target area, whereas a fore fist punch covers too much area, hence is less successful. Target selection is critical with weapons too, though there are vital areas you can reach with a gun or knife that are simply not as accessible or effective empty handed (such as the subclavian artery located behind the collarbone).

This sort of goes without saying, but none of these principles will do you any good if you don't internalize them through repeated practice. While hands-on instruction is best, particularly tandem drills, solo training with a Body Opponent Bag (BOB) can be an extremely valuable supplement to what you learn from your instructor. The BOB is shaped like the torso and head of person, so it not only helps you build the fundamentals of hitting hard (staying connected, using your core, and accelerating), but also work on contouring simultaneously too.

CHAPTER 14

CREATING WITNESSES

"As frustrated as we get at what onlookers claim to have seen we have to keep in mind that people are always going to be, well, people. They perceive things based on a combination of what they see, what they think they see, what they want to see, and what they see through a mind filter of their life experiences up to that point."

– Loren Christensen

On June 18, 2015 a man in his 20s was shot dead just off Indian School Road near an Auto Title Loan store in Phoenix, Arizona. A witness said he heard what may have been an argument followed by four or five shots. When he went outside, he spotted the victim lying on the ground, unmoving, in a pool of blood. "It was very terrifying," he told reporters. "We were just here trying to get rid of a vehicle and next thing you know there's gunshots and somebody has potentially been murdered or whatever the case is—I don't want to jump to conclusions—but the fact that somebody was shot within 300, 400, 500 feet from us, is probably one of the most terrifying things you'll have to deal with."

Those of you who routinely watch professional or college sports such as football or basketball have, no doubt, seen instances wherein one player fouls another who subsequently retaliates. More often than not, it is the second player that the referee observes committing the infraction. Consequently, the victim is penalized rather than the person who started the confrontation. It works that way on the streets as well. Witnesses frequently see the retaliation rather than the person who initiated the fight. If they misinterpret what actually occurred that could be highly problematic, oftentimes leading to your arrest, prosecution, and conviction.

So how do people misinterpret events? The general **mindset and biases of each individual will color his or her perception**, filtering what is actually observed through the lens of previous experiences, beliefs, and expectations. These biases are part of the human make-up, both intellectually as well as emotionally. Influences on how people will interpret what they see include their previous experience with, and attitude about, the subject matter, what is urgent and important to them at the time, the mental models through which they make sense of the world, any previous experience they might have had (or may have heard about) with the subject, and any outside issues that may distract their attention. Another compounding factor is critical-incident amnesia. The **more traumatic the event is, the greater the chance of distorted perceptions among those who experience it**.

Even when a person carefully observes an entire incident from start to finish, his or her perception is bound to be at least a little biased, inaccurate, and/or incomplete. Memory is not like a digital recording. What we commonly think of as memory is actually constructed from available bits of information placed in long-term storage in your brain. Since even those paying careful attention rarely observe everything that happens in a sudden, violent encounter, **they unconsciously fill in any factual gaps with inferences**. Afterward all the elements are integrated into what makes sense as a whole, thus they become what we commonly think of as memory.

To delve a little deeper, memory has three major components, (1) encoding, (2) storage, and (3) retrieval. It is virtually impossible to encode every single element of a situation we observe, store, and later retrieve it with complete accuracy. **While you may remember what you ate for breakfast**, for example, **you will not remember the exact sensation of every bite, chew, and swallow**.

Furthermore, there are three distinct phases of memory—(1) sensory, (2) short-term, and (3) long-term. Sensory memory is transitory, retained for only a few seconds at best. Short-term memory or working memory lasts no longer than a few minutes. These stores have limited capacity and duration within your brain. Unless you're one of the unique individuals with eidetic memory (perfect recall), only select data is transferred into long-term memory, hence can be recalled days, months, or years after the event. Since everything we sense is not automatically stored nor retrievable, **certain gaps are inferred when we recall a memory**, potentially creating divergence between perception and reality. Most of the time that is not a big deal but on occasion it can be critical.

For example, Lawrence once took a psychology class taught by Professor Lee Roy Beach at the University of Washington which covered, among other things, eyewitness testimony. Dr. Beach related to the class that he used to perform an experiment whenever he taught his introductory psychology course. The class he described was held in a huge auditorium where he introduced the subject of psychology to between 700 and 800 freshmen and sophomore students. Here is how the experiment went:

> Dr. Beach began the first day of class in each session with an overview of the course curriculum. About halfway through this introduction he had an actor walk in late, approach the podium, and then instigate a shouting match with him. He "accidentally" left the microphone on but moved far enough away from it that the students could not hear every word that was said. The argument would be about grades from the previous quarter. After a minute or two, he would appear to calm the disaffected student down and the actor would leave the room.
>
> Ten or fifteen minutes later as the class was underway another actor who looked completely different from the one who started the argument would enter the room. While the first actor might be tall and blond, for example, the second actor would be short and brunette. Both actors were always the same gender (usually male), but not necessarily the same ethnicity. They would also wear completely different clothing; say a brown leather jacket and jeans for one while the other chose slacks and a sport coat. This second actor would take a few steps through the door, just far enough to be seen by the class, pull out a handgun, shoot the professor several times (with blanks), and then flee the room. As the stunned students watched, their teacher would crumple to the floor, apparently injured or dead.
>
> After a moment of chaos, Professor Beach would stand back up, brush himself off, and explain that everyone had just participated in a psychology experiment. He asked them to take out a piece of paper and write down what they saw, and then explained that they would be told more about the experiment and its results sometime later in class. This not only gave him data to use for his research but also ensured a high level of attendance for the duration of the class as everyone wanted to know what had transpired but did not know when it would be explained.[22]

What the students observed was, of course, not entirely logical. After all, the person who "shot" the teacher was not the one who had previously argued with him. Despite that fact, over

---

22 Pretty sneaky, huh? Gotta watch out for those psychologists... Incidentally, he eventually had to stop doing this when an off duty police officer pulled a real gun and almost returned fire on the actor. From that point on students watched a recording of the experiment on videotape.

90 percent of eyewitnesses reported that they had seen a student argue with the teacher about grades, leave visibly upset, and return later with a gun to settle the disagreement violently. Only one student in ten realized that the "murderer" was a completely different person than the actor with the grading dispute. Roughly, three quarters of the students got the perpetrator's description wrong as well, combining elements of both actors' appearance and/or clothing.

Most colleges and universities have dedicated law enforcement agencies with armed officers who address crime prevention, victim assistance, and drug and alcohol education. Nearly all campuses have a mass notification system that uses email, text messages, and other methods to alert and instruct students, faculty, and staff in emergency situations.

The point of the experiment, of course, was to **show the inherent fallibility of eyewitness accounts**. Real-life violent events happen suddenly and traumatically. Regardless of what actually occurred, our minds try to draw logical connections between events we observe that appear to be connected in some way. Consequently, the "argument" must have led to the "murder." That narrative makes complete sense even though it is not at all what was truly happening at the time.

Speaking of arguments and murders, did you jump to that conclusion when reading about the shooting in Phoenix that we described at the beginning of this chapter? The witness didn't see the incident, and may have heard some kind of wordplay before the gunshots, but even with those vagaries his report to the press could easily lead you to connect the dots. At this point we can only speculate on what actually took place…

Let's pretend for a moment that the witness actually observed the entire incident. Do you think he would have gotten everything right? By now you know that **memory is not always the same thing as truth**. To elaborate, in her book *Witness for the Defense*, Dr. Elizabeth Loftus (a colleague of Dr. Beach) wrote:

> "Eyewitness testimony, which relies on the accuracy of the human memory, has an enormous impact on the outcome of a trial. Aside from a smoking pistol, nothing carries as much weight with a jury as the testimony of an actual witness. The memory of a witness is crucial not only in criminal cases but in civil cases as well. Implicit in the acceptance of this testimony as solid evidence is the assumption that the human mind is a precise recorder and storer of events… But, in fact, the human memory is far from perfect or permanent, and forgetfulness is a fact of life.
>
> "The danger of eyewitness testimony is clear: Anyone in the world can be convicted of a crime he or she did not commit, or deprived of an award that

is due, based solely on the evidence of a witness who convinces a jury that his memory about what he saw is correct."

Some information is never transferred from short-term to long-term memory in the first place, hence inaccessible later on. Most people, for example do not remember details of their drive into work each day. They retain only unusual or interesting occurrences but not every detail. For information we do retain, we do not always get it right. Observations are not continuously complete or correct. Furthermore, **memory is fallible and corrodes with time**. Contradictory or interfering facts can distort a person's perception from reality, often without him or her even realizing it. As time goes by a person's memories can change, blending fact and fiction, until he is convinced that what he observed is something completely different from the actual truth.

According to the Innocence Project, of the 314 DNA exonerations that took place in the US since 1989, eyewitness misidentification led to 72 percent of the wrongful convictions. Recent changes in police procedure which have been adopted by 13 states and roughly 40 percent of police departments in the US, such as using sequential lineups rather than traditional lineups, appear to be leading to fewer false-identifications. As forensic science progresses this danger becomes partially ameliorated through DNA testing and other safeguards too, but eyewitness misidentification is still a very real danger if you are charged with a crime. Here's an example:

> David Wiggins was convicted of a sexually assaulting a 14-year-old girl in Texas in 1988. While prosecutors were unable produce any physical evidence at his trial, the victim picked his image out of a photo lineup and wrote "looks familiar" next to his name, which was enough to convince the jury to convict him. It turns out that both the witness and the prosecution were mistaken and an innocent man went to prison for the crime. After serving 24 years of a life sentence, Wiggins was exonerated based on DNA evidence in 2012. This case, sad as it is, is far from unique.

No matter how legal, moral, and ethical your behavior during a violent confrontation, if you wind up in the legal system **you will get judged not only by the court of law but also in the court of public opinion**, especially if your actions are recorded on video tape, described by reporters, or otherwise communicated by a news organization. Few reporters are naturally sympathetic to those who employ countervailing force, especially where a weapon was involved. Consequently, it is important to act in a manner that demonstrates to any who observe a violent encounter that you are the victim rather than the instigator of the attack.

Always act as if you are on video camera, even if no one else is around (that you know of). There are numerous instances of law enforcement officers' actions being recorded without their knowledge or consent, many of which have led to allegations of police brutality or institutionalized racism even when thorough investigations proved that wasn't actually the case. The same thing can happen to you. **Assume anything you do will be interpreted in the most derogatory manner possible and used against you in a court of law**. Never forget that most witnesses' only exposure to violence is through movies, books, or television shows. The common person really does not understand the reality of the situation you are in, hence is likely to judge you harshly because of his or her ignorance.

So how can you create a witness who is likely to interpret your just actions favorably?

Start by acting afraid, calling for help. This is something you are likely to want to do anyway on the chance that you can ward off your assailant or convince someone to intervene on your behalf. Shouting, "Oh my god, don't kill me with that knife!" is a pretty good indicator of peril. It clearly differentiates who the bad guy is and can help you justify countervailing force in a court of law. "Put down the weapon," "Please don't hurt me," "I don't want to fight you," and "Help, he's got a gun" all put you in a much better light than "Go ahead, make my day!" or "I'm going to tear your arm off and beat you to death with it motherfucker!" Think about various scenarios ahead of time so that you will have a better chance of articulating strategically.

It is pretty easy to shout something during a fight. The real challenge is finding words that put you in the best possible light and your assailant in the worst. In other words, **it is easy to shout but hard to verbalize so you need to practice**. What you say before, during, and after a confrontation holds a lot of weight in convincing witnesses about your intent. Incidentally, studies in eyewitness testimony have concluded that merely describing the presence of a weapon leads witnesses to report seeing one even where it didn't exist, so the power of suggestion can play a role too.

What you do has significant impact as well. Once you have evaded the initial attack and disarmed, disabled, or escaped your assailant, be wary of reengaging the threat. It is not only dangerous physically but also puts you on dangerous ground perceptually. If, for example, you have knocked your attacker to the ground then proceed to kick or pummel him, you will be seen as overreacting even in many instances where you are on sound tactical ground and merely being prudent. A far better tactic in this example would be to precede any further action with verbal commands such as, "stop fighting me," "drop the weapon," or whatever is most appropriate for the tactical situation you find yourself in.

Where you have the option, the use of open-hand strikes, throws, and certain grappling techniques looks less offensive than closed fists and is less likely to injure your hands (e.g., boxers fracture) too. Beware of chokes, however. While judoka, MMA fighters, and other grapplers understand that chokes are only truly dangerous if applied improperly, **they have a bad reputation in the news media and are frowned upon by many law enforcement personnel** (at least in the administration ranks, anyway). Remember the infamous Eric Garner "I can't breathe" incident in New York? You don't want to be responsible for something like that...

Everyone knows that blows to the head and face can be fatal. What you may not realize is that even minor wounds there can draw a lot of blood, something that looks really bad to the casual observer. Open-hand techniques are less likely to draw blood than closed-hand contact. Where sensible, you may be better off striking an ankle or a knee instead of aiming for the opponent's head or face too. While severely disabling, a knee strike is rarely considered excessively forceful and it sets you up to get away. If the other guy has a knife, gun, or bludgeon and you're forced to defend yourself empty-handed, however, targeting the head, eyes, or throat is not only on the table but highly recommended.

Even though it is prudent to consider how your actions may look to an independent observer, **never let the fear of prosecution keep you from surviving a violent encounter**. Do whatever it takes while doing your best to react in a manner that helps others realize you are the good guy. And, however you fight, be sure to fight with your mouth too. Yell, scream, and cause a commotion.

Here are some words you can use to alert others to your peril:

- Don't come any closer!
- Don't hurt me!!
- Don't touch me!
- Drop the weapon!
- Five feet!
- Get off me!
- Get the hell away from me!
- Help, he's got a gun!
- Help, he's got a knife!
- Hold it right there!
- I don't have any money, go away!
- I don't want any trouble!
- I don't want to fight!
- I said stand back!
- Leave me alone!
- Oh my god, don't cut me with that knife!
- Stand back!
- Stay away from me!
- Stop fighting me!
- That is far enough!
- You're getting too close to me!

Like anything else, it's extraordinarily difficult to put in play on the street what you haven't practiced in the training hall. Traditional martial artists use *kiai* (spirit shouts), but while that might startle an adversary or give you a little more energy in your technique it does nothing to create witnesses. Instead of just shouting, **practice articulating using words such as those above when you spar, perform *kata*, or otherwise practice your techniques**. It will seem strange at first, but will ultimately give you a leg up in putting this strategy into play during a critical incident.

CHAPTER 15

THE "SHOOT ME FIRST" VEST AND OTHER HAZARDS OF CONCEALED CARRY

"Forget about knives, bats and fists. Bring a gun. Preferably, bring at least two guns. Bring all of your friends who have guns. Bring four times the ammunition you think you could ever need."

– Joe B. Fricks, USMC

On July 7, 2003 Albuquerque Police Sergeant Carol Oleksak was confronted by an emotionally disturbed man named Duc Minh Pham. Their encounter quickly devolved into a struggle wherein Pham threw a powerful left hook to her head that knocked the officer unconscious. Then he went for her gun. Her .45 caliber pistol was holstered on her duty belt with a Level I holster, meaning that it had a safety strap which must be released before the weapon could be drawn. Pham didn't know that. In an effort to acquire her gun he pulled so vigorously on the weapon that he jerked her unconscious body upright and bounced her around so hard that witnesses to the encounter thought she was still awake and fighting with him. Eventually his efforts paid off, the thumb-break strap tore loose. He pulled the gun free, fumbled with it for a moment, and then fired a shot into the air. After determining that the pistol worked, he lowered the gun and fired three shots into the officer lying at his feet.

One shot missed, another hit her shoulder, but unfortunately the third tore into the left side of Oleksak's head, shattered her skull, and left a splatter of blood and brain matter on the sidewalk. Pham, brandishing the stolen weapon, fled the scene. He was confronted by more APD officers a few blocks away and was killed after pointing the pistol at them. Oleksak, on the other hand, survived. She recovered from severe brain damage, relearned how to speak, and still lives in New Mexico where she has become a champion for affecting change in how the mentally ill are treated in that state. Mentally ill defendants like her attacker are often deemed incompetent to stand trial and end up back in the community without proper assistance. "I don't think he had any control," she told reporters. "That's the reason I'm working very hard now to get some changes, some of the laws, to get help for these people."

And, she still owns the gun she was nearly murdered with.

Speaking about self-defense Marc "Animal" MacYoung once said, "You're not an ape, use a tool." That's awfully good advice in many circumstances. Unlike empty-hand martial arts which can take years to master, it doesn't take a whole lot of skill or special training to club, stab, or shoot someone at close distance. That's why lawbreakers victimize ordinary citizens with weapons about 1,800,000 times per year in the United States. In fact, more than 90 percent of all homicides, about half of all robberies, and a quarter of all assaults involve an armed assailant. Two thirds of murder victims die of acute lead poisoning, typically administered via a handgun.

There are an awful lot of weapons out there, many of which are in the hands of bad guys. For example, detectives recovered 14 guns, 107 knives, two hammers, two wrenches, and nine large flashlights in and around Harrah's casino after an April 27, 2002 fight between Hells Angels and Mongols motorcycle gang members in Laughlin, Nevada. Dozens of shots were fired in the crowded casino, several people were brutally beaten and stabbed, and when the dust cleared three bikers were dead. Fourteen members of both gangs were charged with more than 70 crimes from the melee. Assuming that those charged carried a majority of the confiscated weapons that is roughly **nine deadly objects per person**.

To confront this threat many citizens choose to travel armed as well. Handguns are a popular choice for self-defense purposes in large part because they are so portable. They're not all that great offensively-speaking, which is why wars are fought with rifles that make it possible to hit targets accurately at extreme distances. After all, if you can shoot the other guy before he sees you or from beyond his range you're in far less danger of counterassault. Nevertheless, despite their limitations semi-automatic pistols, revolvers, and the like are commonplace in the US. In other parts of the world knives, bludgeons and other devices are more ubiquitous, but even where firearms are illegal to own an awful lot of people carry guns anyway. Our focus here will be on handguns since most folks in the US don't carry rifles or shotguns around with them for defensive purposes even though they are oftentimes stored in homes where they can be used for self-defense during break-ins.

The challenge is that even where it's legal to carry a handgun or other weapon in the open, you tend to freak the mundanes whenever you do it (especially with guns which are scarier to civilians than most other implements which can be used for self-defense). For example, on March 5, 2015 a Michigan resident legally brought his handgun with him when he attended a play at Pioneer High School. Not realizing that while it is illegal for citizens with pistol licenses to carry concealed weapons on school grounds, license holders can carry openly under the law, the choir director immediately called the police. Even though the legality of the situation was quickly straightened out by responding officers and the man was allowed to stay at the event, another attendee, University of Michigan music professor Brian DiBlassio, photographed the man and excoriated him on Facebook, posting:

> "There's an idiot with a handgun with two magazines attending the Ann Arbor Pioneer Choral Cavalcade, sitting in the tenth row. Police came in droves, escorted him out to interview him in the hallway and could do nothing based on his permit. He's now back listening to 8th grade girls singing *Hey Jude*. My first experience witnessing this ridiculous show of… I don't know what. Who does this at an event with 100s of children ffs??? Who does this anywhere? 'Merica!"

Even where it's perfectly legal to do so, open carry is a bad idea in places where folks are likely to call the cops whenever they see you coming. An additional problem is that the bad guys will know that you are armed too. Tactically this means that they will either leave you alone… or ambush you with extreme violence such as what happened to Sergeant Oleksak. An axiom of concealed carry is that there's an inverse relationship between accessibility and concealability. In other words, the better your weapon is hidden the harder it is to access quickly. Conversely, if it's carried too openly you can grab your gun quickly but have also made yourself a bigger target.

Consequently, most armed citizens carried concealed. Bad guys do too, but for somewhat more nefarious reasons. They also do things like concealing the weapon behind an arm or leg, palming it, or covering it with an object such as a folded newspaper or jacket. These methods pretty much only work just prior to an attack, they're not something practical to do all day, but if not spotted fast enough they give a major advantage to the assailant because he can bring his gun or knife into play very quickly. Since action beats reaction, that's a very tough situation to extricate yourself from.

A challenge with concealed carry is that if you select the wrong attire or pick up the wrong habits everyone observant will know that you're armed. Let's start with the clothing… Most folks keep their gun somewhere around their waistline. For law-abiding citizens that's almost always in a holster of some kind whereas with criminals more often than not it's just shoved into their waistband. There are varieties of holsters that can be attached to one's belt either inside or outside of the pants. They cover the trigger guard, which minimizes the chances of shooting yourself or others due to a negligent discharge, and simultaneously affix the weapon to a specific spot so that you can always find it when you need to under stress.

Citizens use firearms to protect themselves against criminal assaults somewhere between 760,000 and 3,500,000 times every year in the United States. Laws permitting individuals to carry concealed weapons reduce murder rates by about 10%, with similar declines in other violent crimes. The risk of serious injury from a criminal attack is 2.5 times greater for women offering no resistance than for women who defend themselves with a gun.

Regardless of where and how you carry the gun, you'll need to cover it with something like a vest, jacket, or loose shirt (or if it's in an ankle holster, a pant leg). If your clothing isn't cut properly or doesn't hang right distinctive bulges will appear as you move around. This is commonly known as "printing," meaning that the weapon's outline is visible through your garments. It can be minimized with good posture, but you will need to pay close attention to that until it becomes habit. Regardless, some clothing can be a red flag whether people see bulges beneath it or not. For example, wearing a photographer's vest without carrying any camera equipment is a dead giveaway that you're carrying a gun—which is why we affectionately call them "shoot me first" vests (as in target the gravest threat first). Similarly, if you choose distinctive clothing such as the 5.11 Tactical line you'll look like an operator to those in the know. That is not necessarily a bad thing, but it does tip off those around you that more likely than not you're armed… and make you a prime target in certain circumstances.

Another possible way to tell whether or not you're armed is to look at your belt. For example, a businessman in a suit with an overly heavy belt, no matter how dressy, likely gives away the fact that he has a gun to those in the know. Some pistol belts are wider in the back and narrower in the front to disguise their girth, making them harder to detect. Savvy criminals know to look for a jacket worn in hot weather, a vest that covers the waistline (especially the hips/lower back), or a loose shirt that is buttoned high but not low since they tend to associate with people who are habitually armed.

In order to avoid detection you could always shove the gun into your pants or jacket pocket, assuming it's small enough, but that is not as reliable an option as using a holster since the gun will likely repositioned itself as you move about during the day so you'll have to fumble around for it if you need it. Not a good thing when you're under fire. Worse, if you carry anything else in the same pocket as the weapon, such as a set of keys, it's really easy to accidentally shoot yourself by entangling the exposed trigger. This danger can be diminished by using a pocket holster; they tend to help minimize printing too. Regardless, carrying a gun in a pocket or waistband un-holstered tends to build bad habits where you subconsciously touch yourself frequently to check and/or relocate the gun. New gun owners do that anyway, oftentimes, but bad ergonomics or equipment only exacerbates the problem.

Speaking of equipment, every type of concealed carry method has strengths as well as weaknesses. For example, some belt-attached holster systems make the weapon nearly impossible to draw while seated, especially if you are belted into your vehicle's restraint system. Ankle holsters that are easy to access when seated, on the other hand, require stooping and moving a pant leg before you can access the weapon while you are standing. If you spend most of your day sitting down (e.g., taxi driver, air marshal) you might make a different choice than if you spend most of your day standing up (e.g., construction worker, store clerk).

Shoulder holsters, which gained popularity on TV's Miami Vice, are a reasonably popular method of carrying guns, knives, and even tactical batons. Unlike most hip or small-of-the-back holsters, they have the benefit of ready access while sitting, yet require reaching across the body to retrieve the weapon. Not only may this extra reach take a certain amount of time to perform, but also an adversary could press against your arm while attacking to keep you from being able to retrieve your weapon and defend yourself with it, a challenge inherent to cross-draw holsters too.

Fanny pack and purse holsters offer excellent concealment as well as accessibility when seated but typically require both hands to free the weapon, something that not only takes time to perform but may also be stopped by an attentive adversary. Further, they can be harder to keep control of than other types of holsters. If someone in the know spots the tab sticking out between the zippers that's a dead giveaway that you're armed. It may have been a surprise for the audience when Tommy Lee Jones's character in *The Fugitive* whipped his backup pistol out of the man-bag strapped to his waist, but it was obvious to us what was inside the second we saw him wearing it.

Paddle-style holsters allow you to take them on and off easily should your lifestyle demand it, whereas traditional holsters require you to unbuckle and remove your belt first, another consideration. Here are a few strengths and weaknesses of some of the more common types of holsters that you might choose from if you decide to carry a handgun:

- **Ankle holster**. Holds the weapon at the base of the shin just above the ankle, covered by the pants leg. The weapon is frequently placed on the inside of the weak-side leg (e.g., left leg if right-handed). A challenge with this method is that if you're not sitting down it's cumbersome and slow to draw. Running with an ankle holster can be problematic too as it can work loose and fall off. And, it often chafes when you're walking around too.
- **Belly band holster**. Holds the weapon snug against the wearer's mid-section. It is typically covered by a loose fitting shirt to facilitate concealment and rapid access. Unfortunately can be a challenge to access quickly and are not horribly comfortable or easy to conceal for anyone who has much of a gut.

- **Belt slide holster**. Similar to a high-rise hip holster, another method of securing a weapon to your waist near the same location alongside your hip. It is typically covered by a loose shirt, sweater, or jacket. Oftentimes these holsters are augmented with a safety strap to keep the gun from falling out. They can become very uncomfortable to use when sitting for long periods of time as the handle of your handgun will jamb into your kidneys or ribcage.

- **Cross-draw holster**. Secured at the waist on the off-hand side, these holsters are easier to use while seated than most other varieties, though it can take longer to do so than something strapped to your strong side as you have to reach across your body to do it. Importantly, you cannot draw without panning 90-degrees of the room, including your own weak-side arm, so from a muzzle control perspective it's not a good choice.

- **Fanny pack holster**. A hip bag with two to three pockets that can be used to carry a wallet, keys, or other small items that can also conceal a firearm within. It is typically worn bag-forward on the front hip or below the stomach and looks much like a normal fanny pack save for a small loop, tab, or string between the zippers that facilitates rapid deployment of the weapon. Unfortunately this tab is a giveaway to those who know to look for it, and it takes two hands safely open the bag and draw the weapon making it easier to stop you from doing so than other choices that can be done with one hand.

- **High-rise hip holster**. Worn on a heavy belt, this type of holster conceals the weapon firmly against the wearer's kidneys, just above the hip. It is typically covered by a loose shirt, sweater, or jacket to facilitate concealment and rapid access. A properly made leather or Kydex® holster is not only easy to draw from but also easy to re-holster without looking (with proper training of course). They can become very uncomfortable to use when sitting for long periods of time as the handle of your handgun will jamb into your kidneys or ribcage.

- **Inside-the-pants holster**. Similar to a hip holster save that it is worn under the pants with only the pistol grip and securing strap/snap visible around the belt. Offers slightly better concealment than a high-rise hip holster but also requires looser trousers (or a relatively small gun) in order to fit properly. It is typically covered by a loose shirt, sweater, vest, or jacket to facilitate concealment and rapid access. With many full sized firearms you'll have to buy pants that are one size larger than normal in order to use this type of holster comfortably.

- **Pocket holster**. Typically rectangular in shape, they disguise the shape and cover the trigger of small "pocket pistols" making much safer to carry a gun in your pocket. They are smooth on the inside and rough on the outside to increase the odds that when you draw your gun the holster won't come out with it, but are not as reliable as a hip or belt slide, especially for re-holstering which is pretty much impossible to do without first taking the holster out of your pocket.

- **Purse holster.** Similar to a fanny pack holster, a secret pocket, typically in the center of the bag, holds a weapon. A snap is usually released to free the weapon, though in most instances it takes two hands to remove and deploy the weapon. Another challenge with purse holsters is that if you set them down you've relinquished control of your weapon, a major no-no in the safe weapons-handling department.

- **Shoulder holster.** There are two major varieties of shoulder holsters, vertical and horizontal. Either way, the weapon is held snug against the side of the chest and concealed beneath a loose-fitting shirt, or jacket. Unlike a hip holster, the concealing garment must be moved relatively far in order to free the weapon unless it splits down the middle so buttoned shirts, vests, or zippered jackets are the most common type of cover. It's also easier for someone to stop you from drawing from this type of holster than from something strapped to your waist. Additionally there's a higher skill set needed to draw quickly from these rigs because you need to squeeze with your carry-side arm just enough to hold the holster in place but not so much that you can't draw it (or wind up accidentally throwing your gun when it clears leather).

- **Small-of-the-back holster.** Holds the weapon near your tailbone. A benefit is that it more easily can be drawn with either hand than any type of hip holster, though if you are tackled or slammed onto the ground a gun in this position can damage your spine. It's also somewhat harder to use your arms to keep folks from bumping up against the pistol if when you're moving through a crowd. And, it's generally uncomfortably to wear when sitting for any length of time.

- **Underwear holster.** Specially made briefs, bras, and undershirts have holsters built in. While these methods can allow for deep concealment, they tend to be more difficult to draw from than other methods and make it especially challenging to re-holster the weapon as the pouch is not held rigidly open when not in use. Further, some models tend to leave your handgun pointing at your private parts, something that makes many people uncomfortable. And, they tend to chafe too.

Whatever type of holster you choose it's imperative to practice with it so that you can draw and deploy your weapon under stress. In other words, go to a range that allows you to draw and fire and then practice doing it under appropriate supervision, working slowly up to speed until the movements become smooth and natural. If you only practice after the weapon has been drawn (as required by many ranges), you may not be able to clear your holster quickly enough to do you any good since you will not have practiced doing it.

If you do need to draw your weapon in self-defense the upward or sideways motion is pretty evident to those looking for it. Oftentimes this means that you will need to clear space within which to operate. A really solid technique for those who prefer one of the hip carry methods that allows you to draw one-handed is to slap your upper chest with your off hand while simultaneously twisting to the strong side and reaching back for your gun. **You only need to get a little distance between you and the threat in order to draw** and this technique simultaneously helps keep your weapon away from the bad guy until it has cleared leather. If the threat is too close, you're likely to deliver an elbow strike with your offhand too, something which might knock him or backward or off balance, giving your further advantage. And, your off hand is out of the way so you're less likely to shoot yourself in the heat of combat.

Carrying a gun in public is a serious responsibility. Make sure your weapon is in prime operating condition, your ammunition is fresh, the trigger is covered, and (where applicable) the safety is engaged (some weapons such as most revolvers have no external safety; pull the trigger and the gun goes off, don't pull the trigger and the gun doesn't go off). You will also need to keep your weapon out of sight, assure it is secure, know where it's pointed at all times, and be ready to use it with virtually no notice if necessary.

With the right setup, once you've carried your handgun for a while you should be able to move around comfortably and easily with few clues to others that you're armed. Nevertheless, **don't get too comfortable with it. Tragedies occur if you get sloppy**. Here are a couple of examples:

- On February 19, 2015 Christina Bond, a 55-year-old Michigan woman, died after accidentally shooting herself in the head. She was adjusting her bra holster when the gun went off. St. Joseph Public Safety Department Director Mark Clapp told reporters that, "She was having trouble adjusting her bra holster and could not get it to fit the way she wanted it to and was looking down before accidentally firing the weapon." She was taken to Lakeland Hospital and then airlifted to Bronson Methodist the next day before she died. Bond spent two years in the US Navy after high school, later working as an administrator at a local church and ministering at a jail.
- on January 5, 2015 Officer Darryl Jouett, a 25-year veteran of the Erlanger Police Department, was in an elevator in the Mercer Commons parking garage just after 8:30 p.m. when he went to adjust the weapon in his holster and his gun went off. The .40-caliber bullet ricocheted off the walls of the elevator and struck Jouett in the stomach. He was taken to the University of Cincinnati Medical Center with a non-life threatening injury.

Guns are dangerous, but **they don't shoot people without human intervention**. In fact, unlike "Saturday Night Specials" of the bad old days, modern handguns are perfectly safe when used properly. In most cases you can even drop or slam them against a hard surface without accidentally discharging a bullet, though that's not something you'll want to bet your life on as a Gluck salesman once did at a demonstration that Lawrence attended back when that brand first hit the American markets. The sales guy put a live 9mm round in the chamber, grabbed a hold of the barrel, aimed the weapon at his own stomach, and smacked the countertop several times with the handle. It viscerally made the point that despite not having an external safety the gun (a first generation G17) wouldn't negligently discharge easily, but a manufacturing flaw discovered several years later demonstrated that it actually was possible to make the gun inadvertently go off that way. And, that brings us to the all-important caveat: you must **follow the safety rules at all times**. You're betting your life (and others) on them. That guy may have sold a lot of guns, including the one that Lawrence bought, but he was a moron for doing it in that way.

Gun legend Jeff Cooper (1920 – 2006), promulgated the following four rules which are extraordinarily good advice:

- **All guns are always loaded.**
- **Never let the muzzle cover anything you are not willing to destroy.**
- **Keep your finger off the trigger until your sights are on the target.**
- **Always be sure of your target (and what's beyond it).**

In addition to carrying properly and operating safely, there's another important rule. Don't get jumpy. **Never draw on anyone unless there's a real threat <u>and</u> you're willing to pull the trigger**. Morons with guns not only ruin their own lives, but also cause significant damage to those around them even if only by becoming the "example" that "proves" that gun owners cannot be trusted. **Don't be *that* guy** (or gal).

CHAPTER 16

THE LUNACY OF DISARMS

"Insanity is just what we call stupidity when it doesn't make sense."

– Josh Lieb

On November 12, 2006, Ambioris Antonio Peña-Duran, a 35-year-old grocery store worker, was fatally shot while trying to wrestle a gun away from a robber. The incident took place just after 8:00 p.m. at Cesar's Grocery Store in South Camden, NY. Reports state that Peña-Duran grabbed the robber from behind after the man pointed a gun at his 42-year-old female co-worker and demanded money. The robber broke free, twisted, and subsequently shot the would-be hero to death. The co-worker, who was not identified, was able to escape during the struggle.

On May 28, 2012, a Burlington, NC, man Wesley Long was approached by two males wearing jeans and dark, hooded sweatshirts. When one of the men pointed a handgun at him and demanded money, Long reportedly attempted to disarm him but was shot in the hand. He was rushed to the hospital in Greensboro with non-life-threatening injuries. The suspects, who got away, faced charges of assault with a deadly weapon, inflicting serious injury, and attempted armed robbery.

On July 9, 2012, an off duty police officer, 41-year-old Ian Dibell, was murdered as he tried to wrestle an illegal revolver away from 64-year-old Peter Reeve. The incident occurred in the quiet, seaside town of Clacton, Essex. Reeve reportedly had an altercation with the officer's neighbor,

Trevor Marshall and Marshall's girlfriend, when the Dibell intervened. He was shot in the right hand and upper chest as he attempted to disarm the older man. The following day Reeve, who fled the scene and hid from police, was found dead after shooting himself once through the forehead in All Saints churchyard.

Since so many people own or carry guns in the United States (according to one survey there are more guns than people here), martial artists frequently practice under the assumption that they might wind up on the wrong side of one of them. That's probably a good thing. The challenge with most commonly taught gun disarms we have seen, however, is that they totally ignore context. Do a YouTube search and you will find that most of what is posted online starts from the "disarm position" (sometimes called the "surrender position"), that is with the threat standing in front of you pointing a weapon at your chest or head, with no regard to how you got there in the first place.

That's the life-or-death question... literally. If the gun is already pointed at you, why?

How did you wind up in this mess to begin with? What led up to the encounter? Does the gunman have a personal beef against you or is this a random meeting? Is he under the influence of drugs or alcohol? Is he or she calm or angry? All these factors play a pivotal role in the outcome, and more importantly, in what your best response might be. Other than pointing a gun at you, **what is the threat doing at this moment**? For example, is he or she:

- **In the process of pulling the trigger**?
- **Demanding your money**?
- **Telling you to get on the floor**?
- **Screaming at you to leave**?
- **Insisting that you to come along quietly**?

The preceding are but a few examples of what might be taking place, but as you can see each could indicate a very different motivation on the gunman's part, hence require different tactics to diffuse appropriately. If the threat really is actively trying to kill you, the pulling the trigger scenario above, **why didn't you act before he cleared leather** (or Kydex® or whatever the holster is made of) or immediately thereafter so that the weapon was not actually pointed at you in the first place? By the time the weapon is aimed at your heart or head it's often too late. Since action beats reaction, you'll likely be shot before you can act. This doesn't necessarily mean that you cannot still defend yourself, or even take him out with you, but **it's a hell of a lot easier to win a fight if you don't have to contend with bullet wounds, blood loss, and shock** in addition to whatever else the other guy is trying to do to you.

If the threat is demanding money and you give it to him that very well might mean the end of the encounter. He either leaves or chases you away, and unless you pop off and say something stupid that's the end of things. **Violence is unnecessary.** If he manages to obtain your car keys and identification, on the other hand, that's another story, which is a very good reason for carrying your cash separate from your ID. Nevertheless, the point is that it's not likely to be a lethal encounter unless you turn it into one. Conversely, if he's telling you to get on the floor that could turn into a hostage scenario (which we cover in Chapter 19) or may be part of a home invasion (Chapter 29). Either of these situations can be horrifically dangerous and must be treated accordingly.

In a scenario where the threat is screaming for you to get away from him you are likely facing a threat display, not an attack, and a fear-induced one at that. **Disengaging is often the safest course.** The encounter came with instructions: Leave and you won't be hurt. Moving in to attempt a disarm under this scenario will usually make the gunman feel trapped, hence open fire. He's already demonstrated that he's scared of you, yet you are closing distance toward him?! Even if you succeed in taking the weapon away but injure or kill the other guy in the process during this type of encounter your actions would be horrifically difficult to justify in court (assuming video evidence or eyewitness testimony which happens more often than you might think). Worse, if you don't succeed you would be needlessly maimed or killed when **all you had to do in order to remain safe was walk away**.

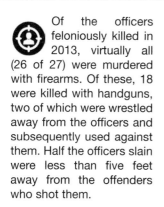

Of the officers feloniously killed in 2013, virtually all (26 of 27) were murdered with firearms. Of these, 18 were killed with handguns, two of which were wrestled away from the officers and subsequently used against them. Half the officers slain were less than five feet away from the offenders who shot them.

If the other guy insists that you come along quietly, well that's more than likely a prelude to predatory violence. **You will most likely need to run or fight back**. There may be an issue of timing, depending on the specifics of the situation, but attempting a disarm in this type of scenario might very well be prudent. Similarly if you encounter the gunmen in your own home or some other isolated location where he has the privacy to work you over at his leisure it may very well be go time. You'll need to fight to survive.

As you can see, each situation is distinctive and must be considered uniquely in order to determine the best thing to do.

Scenarios aside, let's talk about positioning for a moment. Disarms must be performed up close and personal, both to reach the gun as well as to have optimal leverage, yet the farther away from the gunman you are the safer you'll be in most circumstances. If the proxemics don't work in your favor, **you may actually be better off running to cover instead of fighting in close where you are easier to hit**. Even highly trained professionals have a hard time hitting a moving target with a handgun.

Most gunfights take place at a distance of less than ten feet. According to FBI statistics, 95 percent of officer involved shootings occur at less than 21 feet, with approximately 75 percent taking place at less than 10 feet and a little over half at closer than five feet. And, combatants miss far more often than they hit. For example, in Los Angeles, which has 9,699 law enforcement officers, the police fired 283 rounds in 2006, yet managed to hit their intended target a mere 77 times for **a hit ratio of just 27 percent**. That means that officers, whose training and experience far exceeds that of the typical criminal or civilian, **missed their intended target 73 percent of the time**! Shocked? You shouldn't be. That's very similar to the New York Police Department which managed a 34 percent hit rate over the eleven year period from 1996 through 2006.

Every situation is different, yet all too many martial artists treat them all the same in training, which leads to significant disadvantages in real life. **Context is king**... Get it wrong and you're in a whole lot of trouble.

Disarms are horrifically dangerous and should **only be attempted as a last resort**. Sadly all too many martial artists see every situation through the lens of applying their art. See the threat; hit the threat. Or, grapple with the threat (or whatever they've been training for) even when that's the worst possible response to a given situation. It's not just in the *dojo*. We have seen folks move into danger by attempting a disarm during a threat display where the practitioner would have remained unharmed if he'd only buggered off instead... such things often end tragically

Just like you can't use a hammer to turn a screw, you cannot use a disarm for the wrong purpose. Well, you can, but the odds are high that it won't end well. Don't get us wrong, disarms are occasionally necessary and may just save your life, so they are worth knowing. And practicing. The question is when and under what circumstances to use them.

Now, let's discuss the surrender position from which many disarms are taught, that is standing with your arms up and to the sides. Here's the rub, in those last ditch instances where you truly need to attempt one, **the disarm has a better chance of success if performed as your hands rise up, not starting from the surrender position with your arms moving down** as they are commonly taught. With the former your movement is expected, oftentimes mistaken for compliance, hence you can gain a couple of microseconds in the other guy's OODA loop.[23] Downward movement, on the other hand, is virtually always perceived as an attack which more often than not **gets you shot**! This is because **there's no legitimate reason to suddenly move your hands back downward once you've already surrendered**.

In fairness, there is another alternative to this that does not rely on downward movements yet begins in the classic disarm position. In this variation you twist your body out of the line of fire while simultaneously striking the assailant's gun arm with your forearm and then move in for the

---

23 The OODA loop, oftentimes referred to as Boyd's law for military strategist Colonel John R. Boyd who codified it, stands for Observe, Orient, Decide, Act. It is a way of quantifying reaction times in combat.

disarm. In this manner it is possible to make things work if your arms are already up. Having said that, the challenge is that it's much harder to be successful this way since you must rely on a complex series of movements executed with precise timing and perform them flawlessly while adrenalized. And, there's a pretty good chance the other guy will get a shot off while you're doing it (if you do things right the bullet will miss you, but you still need to avoid freezing or flinching from the noise and shockwave).

So, **if you're going to practice disarms, do them the smart way.** Use realistic scenarios based on how things actually go down on the street. If you're a civilian, practice for a civilian context. If you're in the military the things you are likely to encounter will be different. The same thing goes for law enforcement personnel. Different scenarios are common and different rules of engagement may apply. Further, whether you or the threat has a rifle, pistol, or both, any secondary weapons (e.g., knives, batons, Tasers®, or backup guns) that might come into play, whether you or the other guy is carrying a weapon open or concealed, and whether or not there's a holster... these factors all make an important difference.

If you are going to practice disarms with a handgun, or any firearm for that matter, **do not use a loaded weapon. Use a training gun and remove the trigger guard if possible** before trying things out so that you don't inadvertently break your training partner's finger in the process. Or, have him or her keep their finger alongside the trigger guard instead of inside it. Busted fingers are a very common, painful, and unnecessary *dojo* injury that can result from this type of training (and, a nice side benefit if you do this successfully on the street).

For best results with disarms, we suggest the following:

- **Check your mindset.** Just because you *can* perform a disarm doesn't mean that you *should* attempt to do so. Create scenarios that test principles around **when to engage, when to retreat, when to talk your way out, when to act, and how to run** such as those we laid out earlier in this chapter. Don't let yourself get locked into blindly following the drill and forgetting the context of why you're doing it. In fact, drills that force you to do a reality check and discuss what happened afterward are some of the best training you can get, especially when done on camera so you can debrief the video afterward.

- **Build realistic scenarios.** Training should be set up to mirror real-life events to the extent possible. Rarely does one begin in the classical disarm position. You might be grappling, for example, when suddenly a weapon is brought into play. Attempting a disarm when you are already struggling on the ground is a whole different kettle of fish than when both combatants are disengaged and standing up at arm's length apart. Practice with the "bad guy" starting in front, behind, to the side, and at various distances both with the weapon in the holster (or waistband) and at various stages of being drawn and deployed.

- **Practice in a variety of locations**. Where you can safely and securely do so, vary your training locations too. Performing techniques while wearing civilian clothes within the confines of a vehicle or a bathroom stall, in a debris-strewn back alley, or in a crowded barroom is quite different than doing the exact same things while wearing a *dogi* (traditional martial arts uniform) on a pristine training floor. We have rented various facilities from time to time in order to get the touch of realism they can bring. Wherever you practice, don't freak the mundanes or get arrested in the process however.

- **Introduce pain and fear**. Use Simmunition® non-lethal training ammunition (under appropriate supervision, with protective gear of course) when conducting these exercises whenever possible. They are not real bullets, but they're as close to the real thing as you can get with relative safety and it hurts like a son-of-a-bitch when you get hit by them. **Adrenaline and pain are fabulous tools for learning** to do things effectively. The tried-and-true rubber gun approach simply doesn't have the same affect. It's not horrible, but it's also not horribly realistic either. With rubber weapons the fear and pain factors simply aren't there. Similarly if you want to practice knife disarms, use a Shocknife™ or similar device whenever you can. These tools are expensive but worth it.

- **Practice running to cover and concealment**. Cover can stop a bullet whereas concealment makes you hard to see (hence hard to hit). You can use paintball guns (with appropriate supervision and protective gear) to practice under pressure and obtain immediate results. All too often martial artists practice how to engage without considering how to safely disengage and retreat. It's an acquired mindset and skill, especially for martial artists, but the "Brave Sir Robin defense" can easily save your life.

- **Excel at maintaining control of your weapon**. If you carry a weapon, work primarily on handgun *retention* techniques. It's far more likely that you'll have to keep someone else from getting a hold of your gun than it is that you'll need to take a gun away from the other guy. Work on maintaining control at all stages of the draw and deployment process, learning how to use leverage, body positioning, and such to maintain possession of your handgun and utilize the weapon effectively. Even if you don't carry, starting from this perspective makes learning how to take a gun away from somebody else more realistic.

- **Become proficient at keeping the other guy from pulling his gun**. Spend at least as much if not more time practicing keeping the other guy from drawing his weapon as you do trying to control it once it's cleared the holster or waistband. That's the safest stage of the process in which to engage. If you spot the cues early enough, it's not too tough to keep someone from accessing a shoulder or fanny pack holster, at least momentarily, whereas hip holsters can be a much greater challenge. Work on timing, moving in, preventing the draw, and applying countervailing force (e.g., kicking, stomping, head-butting, etc.) while keeping the other guy's gun in his holster and/or the muzzle off line.

- **Don't make it too easy**. Honor your training partner's technique, but don't make it easy. Oftentimes we make it too easy on each other when we practice, which isn't always a bad thing, but it can lead us to think we're better at applying various applications than we truly are. You really don't want to find out the hard way that you're not as good as you expected when struggling over a deadly weapon. Once you have mastered the fundamentals, make it a game, say 100 pushups every time you get "shot." That tends to bring a touch more realism into the equation even if you can't use Simmunition® or the like.

Never forget that what gets trained gets done. This is monumentally important when practicing with weapons. In his book *On Combat*, Loren Christensen described what can happen when you bake in bad habits through repeated, unrealistic practice:

> "One police officer gave another example of learning to do the wrong thing. He took it upon himself to practice disarming an attacker. At every opportunity, he would have his wife, a friend or a partner hold a pistol on him so he could practice snatching it away. He would snatch the gun, hand it back and repeat several more times. One day he and his partner responded to an unwanted man in a convenience store. He went down one aisle, while his partner went down another. At the end of the first aisle, he was taken by surprise when the suspect stepped around the corner and pointed a revolver at him. In the blink of an eye, the officer snatched the gun away, shocking the gunman with his speed and finesse. No doubt this criminal was surprised and confused even more when the officer handed the gun right back to him, just as he had practiced hundreds of times before. Fortunately for this officer, his partner came around the corner and shot the subject.
>
> "Whatever is drilled in during training comes out the other end in combat. In one West Coast city, officers training in defensive tactics used to practice an exercise in such a manner that it could have eventually been disastrous in a real life-and-death situation. The trainee playing the arresting officer would simulate a gun by pointing his finger at the trainee playing the suspect, and give him verbal commands to turn around, place his hands on top of his head, and so on. This came to a screeching halt when officers began reporting to the

training unit that they had pointed with their fingers in real arrest situations. They must have pantomimed their firearms with convincing authority because every suspect had obeyed their commands. Not wanting to push their luck, the training unit immediately ceased having officers simulate weapons with their fingers and ordered red-handled dummy guns to be used in training."

As you can see by the preceding examples, it's very **easy to train yourself physically or mentally to self-destruct**. Visualization exercises can be an important aspect of your training. As with any hands-on practice, you need to conduct your mental exercises realistically and with solid forethought. **Plan to succeed by setting yourself up for success**. Should you attempt this sort of thing in real life you will need to account for adrenaline, muzzle blast, fear sweat, environmental hazards, and a host of other factors that are challenging if not impossible to cover in training. It might seem easy in the *dojo*, but that doesn't mean it will be on the street. Learn both **how** *and* **when** to attempt disarms before you ever consider actually doing them in real life.

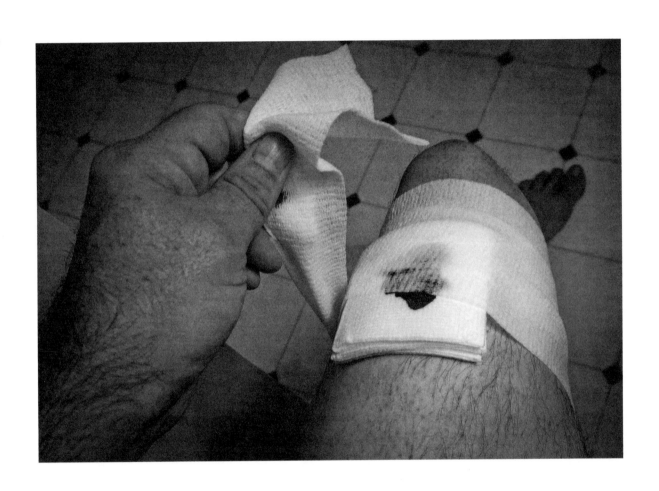

CHAPTER 17

WHY NOT JUST SHOOT 'EM IN THE LEG?

"I never cease being dumbfounded by the unbelievable things people believe."

– Leo Rosten

On Friday December 26, 2014 a Los Angeles police officer shot a woman in the leg at a Hollywood parking structure after she fought with another woman and then pointed a gun at the responding officer. This incident occurred at the Hollywood & Highland Center, which hosts the Academy Awards in its Dolby Theatre. The 47-year-old suspect, Diamond Vargas, was reported in stable condition at a nearby hospital. She was booked for assault with a deadly weapon against a police officer.

Upon reading of this incident many will think it was a "textbook shoot." After all, the threat was neutralized with a bullet to the leg. No one died. That's a good thing, right? In fact, why not shoot the bad guys in the leg all the time? It's the humane way to resolve force incidents, isn't it?

Actually, it's not. In fact, **it's downright stupid**.

Here's the deal, only a deadly threat may be met with deadly force, not just legally, but morally and ethically as well. Clearly a firearm represents a deadly threat, one that often warrants an armed response, but **shooting the bad guy in the leg is a very poor, extraordinarily risky tactic**. Here are three reasons why it's such a bad idea:

1. **Limbs are easy to miss**. One of the first things you learn when training with firearms is, "your bullet, your responsibility." If you fire at a threat in a populated area and miss you risk hitting someone else. That can be incredibly tough to live with (ignoring that whole jail and lawsuit thing), especially if it's a friend, relative, or child. Adrenaline can degrade a person's aim so badly that even highly trained police officers miss close to two thirds of their shots—which is pretty scary considering that the average gunfight takes place at a range of five feet or less—one of many reasons folks are taught to aim center mass. In fact, chances are good that in the incident described above the officer was actually aiming for Vargas' chest but struck her in the leg accidentally.

2. **A leg wound may not stop the threat**. While a leg wound can easily cause the victim to bleed out, exsanguination takes several minutes. Leg wounds rarely stop a determined adversary right away. In fact, Lawrence's next door neighbor in the house where he grew up had both legs blown off on the battlefield during the Korean War and didn't even notice until after the firefight ended when he tried to stand back up. While he was awarded a Distinguished Service Medal for heroism for that incident, he was far from unique in continuing to fight even after being severely wounded. In fact, mortally wounded attackers can continue fighting for ten seconds or more (which is where the term "dead man's ten" came from) unless they've been hit in the brain stem.

> In 2013, 19 of the 27 officers feloniously killed were wearing body armor at the time of their deaths. Fatal wounds included the side of the head (5), the front upper torso/chest (5), the front of the head (4), the neck/throat (3), and the rear lower torso/back (1). Half the fatal events took place between 12:01 AM and noon, and the other half between 12:01 PM and midnight.

3. **Limbs shots tend to over-penetrate**. Most folks use hollow point rounds to avoid over-penetration, but they are not legal everywhere. And, even if you use one and hit to the threat's arm or leg your bullet may very well travel through the threat and hit someone beyond them, even if it strikes bone (in many of the real-life examples described in this book a combatant was hit in the arm yet the bullet continued to travel until it stopped in their torso). Not only are there a lot more vital areas in the head and torso, meaning more chances to stop the threat, but there is also more mass to catch the bullet and retain it inside the threat. This transfers more energy, increases the odds of stopping the assailant, and decreases the chance of hitting an innocent as well.

While intentionally shooting someone in the leg seems like a good idea, the more you know about firearms, self-defense law, and tactics the less likely you are to try doing it. **If it's legally, ethically, and morally appropriate to shoot someone it is legally, ethically, and morally appropriate**

to kill them. And, it's imperative to do so instantaneously. In certain circumstances the leg may be the only target available, but it should never be the primary target of choice. Aiming anywhere other than center mass (or head if you're really, really skilled) when you have to fire your gun at a threat risks harm to yourself and others.

Thus endeth the rant…

photo courtesy of Rory Miller

CHAPTER 18

ONLY THREE DAYS?

"I'd rather be a pessimist because then I can only be pleasantly surprised."

– Benjamin Franklin

In 1822, The United States of America and Canada were establishing part of the border between their countries along the eastern states and provinces. Hugh Glass was a frontiersman who explored the upper watershed of the Missouri River during that time. He spent his time trapping, fishing, and exploring the areas that would eventually become North and South Dakota as well as Montana. Glass was adept in all aspects of survival, from hunting and gathering to using makeshift shelters. He had every skill necessary needed to survive in the wild, able to compete with virtually anything he would come across in order to survive. He was prepared, resourceful, intelligent and very, very clever. In fact, although he didn't know it at the time, that year Hugh Glass would demonstrate one of the greatest acts of grit, resilience, and resourcefulness ever recorded.

On the eventual border of North and South Dakota in what would become Perkins County, Glass was scouting ahead of his group looking for food when he surprised a grizzly sow with her two bear cubs. He knew instantly that he had stumbled into a life-or-death situation: Brown bears are very aggressive, but if you run across a well-fed male and if you're careful and have a little distance in your favor, you very well may get a chance to walk away. Get between a sow and her cubs, however, and you're dead meat… Glass drew his gun, but before he could fire the sow closed the gap. Knowing that there was no way he could outrun a charging bear, Glass drew his knife and the mauling was on.

Three-inch claws tore into him leaving horrific rends in his flesh. His arm and leg were broken, his back laid open, yet the combination of slashes from his knife and gunshots from his associates in the scouting party who arrived during the fight was eventually able to overcome and kill all three bears.

The scouts bound Glass's wounds with what few supplies they had, knowing that in all likelihood he would not survive the night. They camped at the water's edge and quietly waited out the night for him to die. In the morning, however, Glass still lived. This was both good and bad news for his compatriots. The party needed to move on as they were in hostile territory; any of three or four Native American tribes would gladly separate them from their lives if caught. They talked amongst themselves and made the decision to abandon the camp and move on. However, two men volunteered (for an increase in pay), to stay behind with Glass and give him a decent burial when he finally passed on. When he didn't die quickly, they got nervous. You see, they reasoned that Hugh Glass was a dead man, but he was taking way, way too much time to die. Waiting around any longer would get them killed too, so in short order they took all the supplies and left him to his fate.

Abandoned, Glass lay under a tree on a bear skin 250 hundred miles from the nearest fort, which unbeknownst to him lay empty and abandoned. He was by all accounts as good as dead. Miraculously, however, he survived. Here's a summary of what happened:

- He wrapped himself in the bearskin upon which his comrades had been left to die. This provided shelter from the elements, keeping him warm and dry.
- He set his own broken leg (Glass was a tough, tough man).
- He pulled berries from nearby bushes, crushed them in his hand, and blended them with water from the nearby stream to make a fruit paste that he could swallow. This paste provided the vitamins and simple sugars he needed to regain his strength.
- When a snake slithered near where Glass lay he was able to kill it with a rock. He skinned the snake and cut the meat into tiny pieces that he was able swallow. From the snake meat he found a source of protein.
- Knowing that his rotting flesh needed to be removed to prevent infection from setting in and killing him, yet unable to reach the wounds on his back with only one functioning arm, he deliberately rolled in maggots to have them eat away the infected skin. This kept him infection free.
- Once he had the strength to travel, Glass foraged bison carcasses for bones, smashing them open and eating the nutrient rich marrow while making his way to Fort Henry.
- A little stronger, Glass watched a pack of wolves bring down a buffalo. He waited until they had eaten a bit and then scared them off so he could take their kill for his own.

He ate the buffalo's remaining liver first. It was high in iron, copper, and vitamin A, all vital nutrients for his survival.

- He dug for edible roots, finding simple sugars and starches and robbed bird's nests for eggs which provided protein and vitamin D.

By the time he walked into the stockade at the mouth of the Bighorn River, the nearest source of civilization, he looked like a shambling corpse. But, he was still alive! He made it because he was resourceful, resilient, driven by desire to take vengeance on those who had left him behind, and, by all accounts, more than a little lucky. His experience allowed him to make the most of that luck.

Being prepared for *any* situation is unreasonable and, frankly, impractical, but being resourceful is by any stretch of the imagination not unreasonable. In fact it is a key to survival in life-threatening situations. The goal of this chapter is to make you think about disaster preparedness in terms of guarding yourself against potential violence, not just in terms of resource management.

The odyssey of Hugh Glass has much more to it and we encourage anybody who has an interest to spend a little bit of time researching this incredible man and his adventures. For our purposes, however, we need to focus on the three critical things that he had available and took advantage of in order to survive. These vital ingredients were (1) water, (2) shelter, and (3) food. The order of these three essential elements for survival can change with the circumstances you find yourself in as well as the season of the year, but in most instances water is preeminent. Here's how Glass made use of these elements for his survival:

- **Water**: A running creek next to where Glass had been placed by his cohorts served as a ready supply of fresh, potable water. Thankfully he could stretch out and reach it without traveling very far.
- **Food**: The berries that Glass was able to eat by forming a fruit paste using the stream served as an easily assessable, vitamin-laden food source. Once again he was lucky enough to be there when the berries were ripe as well as to have them in arm's reach.
- **Shelter**: Glass was attacked by the bear during the summer, so shelter was necessary to control his body heat, not to avoid hypothermia. Being able to wrap himself in the bearskin served, in conjunction with the surrounding trees, as his shelter. The shade and the bear skin allowed him to regulate his body temperature.

As a general rule drinkable water is number one on the survival necessity list, with shelter and food following in close order. Glass's situation was front-loaded in his favor for survival. The summer months made shelter keeps its place on the list at number two. Water, the most critical resource on the list, was already present. Food was quickly found in the berries growing next to that water. Glass was (and we hesitate to say this) in a really good place for a man mauled by a bear and left to die. He was plunked down into an area that gave him all the resources he needed to survive.

If Hugh Glass were present in our world after a natural disaster, say an earthquake, tornado, tsunami, or hurricane, he might notice the devastation left behind but simultaneously he would **immediately spot a veritable cornucopia of opportunity**. We must all train ourselves to see those things around us that can help us survive too. We are not suggesting that in the course of any given natural disaster civilization is going to give way to some dystopian Mad Max world, yet the events in recent years have brought to light human character, both good and bad. A natural disaster is violent, it changes the rules, but the event does not change who people are. A natural disaster in a community bound by common experiences and knowledge of each other is not a fertile ground for disaster-based violence. For those who never followed the rules, however, it becomes an opportunity for looting or worse. In other words, for those inclined to lawlessness, **anything that puts dampers on the natural order of things is a game on**.

Actress Brook Shields once said, "Someone said adversity builds character, but someone else said adversity reveals character." We agree with the latter. Disaster does not create character but rather reveals it. Every year a power outage affects major population centers. In some regions of the world that's commonplace, indication of a weak or underdeveloped infrastructure, whereas in others it takes a significant snowstorm, windstorm, or catastrophic lightning strike to knock out the power. In those circumstances chances are good that the local television and radio stations will immediately jump into a "How are we dealing with this?" segment. Without exception, they show people who have their Weber grill fired up on the back porch and a Coleman lantern blazing away. These people when interviewed say something like, "Aw, we just got out some steaks, fired up the generator…" This is where the authors blink slowly and shake our collective heads thinking, "No, no, no." We know that is a poor use of resources. It is not a New Year's party, but rather a situation of unknown duration and breadth. The power could be out for a few hours, days, weeks, or even months. It requires prudent resource management.

Kris was in the lobby of a hotel in South Dakota in 2015, and not too far from where Hugh Glass had his epic survival adventure. He struck up a conversation with a man who worked as a crop adjuster, assessing damage for insurance claims. Within one minute of the conversation, the man was talking about the ice storm of 2013. That storm left 90,000 people without power in cities and towns throughout the state, the countryside frozen solid from the cold. A local college student brought up the ice storm of 2013 without any prompting too. Clearly it was a deeply powerful event, even two years later, a time span which relegates most events into ancient memory.

We can guarantee that in South Dakota in the spring of 2013 it was all about resource management and absolutely nothing to do with posturing around the Weber grill. The ice storm was real, a life-threatening challenge on a massive scale. Among other things the cold killed 75,000 head of cattle. If the power is only going out for a day, a grill and a generator is fine. But, what does day five look like? Day ten? How far behind the curve are you in your resource use then?

What about a power outage as the result of a 7.5 earthquake? Utility repairs are going to take a very long time. After a week or so, resources will become scarce. **For those who use violence as a way of life prior to the natural disaster, violence becomes a very powerful tool afterward.** Unchecked and only restricted by the desires of the perpetrator, things can get very ugly. Consider all the violence that swept through New Orleans after Hurricane Katrina. Speaking of which, we offer a tip of the cap to South Dakota for the way they conducted business after the ice storm. There was virtually no violence then, the community came together and dealt with things in a gentile and responsible manner.

Remember, when people are operating at the bottom of Maslow's hierarchy, when water, shelter, and food are hard to find, things get ugly. Food may be third on the list of survival necessities, but that's only there because you tend to die faster without water or shelter than you do without food. In these instances we introduce the "Bad Chicken" rule:

> When food becomes scarce, it most often happens outside the spoilage window. For example, depending on the weather a chicken will spoil in about three days. This means that after the initial run on food, **you will have a three-day window of little or no food scarcity.** Consequently the Bad Chicken rule says after three days foods will begin to become scarce. **As the spoilage rates increase, crime increases proportionally.**

It's not just natural disasters. Food can become scarce due to droughts, poor harvests, improper storage or transportation, hoarding, contamination, pestilence, disease, or rapid inflation/price increases. Here are a couple of examples of what food or the scarcity of food can do to people:

- In 1977 in Egypt there was an insurrection, an uprising involving hundreds of thousands of people in the major population centers across the country. The cost of food had skyrocketed with the removal of state subsidies. The result was the deployment of the army, some 70 people dead and over 500 injured. Oh, and order was restored only after government subsidies were put back into place so that the vast majority of people could afford to eat.

- India 2007, in West Bengal, a political rally quickly turned into a crowd shouting for grain instead of political ideology… and the event quickly got out of hand. Flags got burned and people beaten. The police were brought in and quickly opened fire to suppress the mob. As the word of the events spread, people began to raid the shops that rationed food. Before the West Bengal Food Riots were over, three people lay dead at the hands police gunfire and 300 civilians were injured. The government took subsequent actions that removed corrupt shopkeepers.

There are many, many other examples of food riots in history, but we chose these two to demonstrate that it is not a thing of the past, that **violence around scarcity is a very real possibility**. Under the right (or perhaps we should say wrong) circumstances, say an earthquake, a hurricane, or a prolonged period of social unrest, the environment in which you live can go sideways, slipping very quickly into chaos as starving people will do just about anything in order to be able eat. Let's take a moment and strip these kinds of events down to their bare elements:

- **Scarcity of food**. Hungry people will do extreme things in order to survive.
- **Mob mentality/groupthink**. When others are rioting it's easier to join in.
- **Violence toward authority**. The perpetrators of injustice, or perceived perpetrators of injustice, must be punished for their actions which led to the lack of needed food.

These three elements are easily found, in various levels of intensity, in almost all situations of scarcity. We've talked about food, but things become even more severe where potable water is at stake. Looking at the longstanding drought in California where rationing has been put into place, for example, ought to make you nervous. It doesn't matter what the causes are, temporary shifts in weather patterns, global warming, or disruptions to infrastructure—to name a few—but water scarcity can be very, very scary.

Alchemists have tried and failed throughout history to turn lead into gold, yet if systems collapse water transforms into gold all by itself. When clean, readily available drinking water becomes scarce, **it quickly becomes like gold.** Don't forget that **even in normal times people will kill each other for gold**. So, potable water is like gold in a disaster situation and should be treated that way. You need to make a dramatic shift in how water is treated instantly and guard it as if it were the most precious thing in the world… because it probably will be. If you have time to prepare for an approachable disaster make the mind shift now, to the gold standard for water because during a disruption of the water supply you will have to shift to that gold standard in an instant.

So, if a disaster does happen, what should you do? We're talking something potentially cataclysmic here, like a Hurricane Katrina-style event, not a few inches of snow or other minor thing. Some folks are able to bug out, disappearing into the mountains or woods to wait things out in a well-stocked wilderness cabin. We're not those guys and likely you aren't either. Nevertheless, the tactic of disappearing is a pretty good one in many circumstances. You can burn up a lot of resources (e.g., fuel, food, water) trying to escape only to be caught in traffic, riots, or locked in place due to the natural disaster (such as a significant snow or ice storm). Clearly individual circumstances will dictate your approach, but **unless it's more dangerous to stay where you are, that's oftentimes your best bet**. Dig in and wait things out. Restrict movement to a minimum because:

- **Movement uses resources**.
- **Movement can give you away**.
- **Movement after dark is for predators**, not you.

If you do stay in place, however, you can become a target of rioters, looters, or roving gangs who are out looking for resources. If bad guys band together they can become a real challenge no matter how prepared (or armed) you are. Consequently **display nothing**. Cover up windows, lock doors, and give no indication that you are there. Show nothing of your resources. This includes light, fire (smoke), music, and other things that will attract undue attention. If you have family, relatives, or close friends nearby, band together for mutual support and comfort (this is a good reason to befriend neighbors too, by the way).

The government often promulgates a three-day rule; that is having enough supplies to last you three days in an emergency. It's important to have emergency supplies, of course, but in our book **three days' worth is nowhere near enough**. We suggest keeping a bug-out bag stocked with essentials such as water (and/or a water purifier), food, cash, clothing, medicine, and medical supplies, along with a flashlight, multi tool (knife), duct tape and the like in a place where you can grab it and go with a few seconds' notice. It needs to be light and small enough to lug around easily, the size of a daypack or smaller, so don't get carried away. Stick to the essentials that you truly can't live without for a week or more. Also keep a cabinet or closet with enough supplies to last everyone in your family for at least a week somewhere in your home. This means plenty of foods that won't spoil easily, but be sure to check and rotate through it every so often so that canned goods don't go past their pull date. Eating or drinking anything too old risks food poisoning, which is among the last things you'll want to suffer through in a dire emergency.

If you're on your own for any length of time and become injured that can turn into a life-threatening emergency very quickly. We recommend that you purchase a good first aid manual and pick up (and learn how to use) a haemostatic agent, such as QuikClot or Celox, that can be used to treat severe bleeding from gunshots, stabbings, shrapnel, and similarly critical wounds. Sanitary napkins and duct tape make good emergency bandages too, but the point is that it is vital to have a way to stop hemorrhaging, triage wounds, etc. when needed, especially when emergency services are hours or days away.

The following is a short checklist of suggested supplies, most of which you'll need to take with you if you have to bug out, but that can be used in or around your home or camp too. Be sure to adjust quantities for the size of your family and others in your care (for example, losing as little as one percent of your body's weight in water can cause fatigue and affect your ability to regulate temperature and heart rate, so it's best to plan for roughly nine to 13 cups of water per person per day):

- **Water**. Drinking water, water purification system (or tablets), and a water bottle or canteen.
- **Food**. Anything that is long lasting, lightweight, and nutritious such as protein bars, dehydrated meals, MREs[24], certain canned goods, rice, and beans.
- **Clothing**. Assure it's appropriate to a wide range of temperatures and environments, including gloves, raingear, and multiple layers that can be taken on or off as needed.
- **Shelter**. This may include a tarp or tent, sleeping bag or survival blanket, and ground pad or yoga mat. A camper or trailer is a fantastic, portable shelter, with many of the comforts of home. If you own one keep it stocked with supplies to facilitate leaving in a hurry, as it can take several hours load up and move out if you're not ready. In certain circumstances that might mean having to leave it behind.
- **Heat source**. Lighter or other reliable ignition source (e.g., magnesium striker), tinder, and waterproof storage. Include a rocket stove or biomass burner if possible, they're inexpensive, take very little fuel, and incredibly useful in an emergency.
- **Self-defense/hunting gear**. Firearm(s) and ammunition, fishing gear, multi-tool/knife, maps, and compass, and GPS (it's not a good idea to rely solely on a GPS as you may find yourself operating without a battery or charger).
- **First aid**. First aid kit, first aid book, insect repellant, suntan lotion, and any needed medicines you have been prescribed. If possible add potassium iodide (for radiation emergencies) and antibiotics (for bio attacks) to your kit.

---

24 MREs, or Meals Ready to Eat, are prepackaged meals that the US military uses in the field. Packed full of calories and nutrients, and with a shelf-life of about five years, these meals are useful for emergencies.

- **Hygiene**. Hand soap, sanitizer, toilet paper, towel, toothbrush, toothpaste, dental floss, and garbage bags.
- **Tools**. Hatchet (preferably) or machete, can opener, cooking tools (e.g., portable stove, pot, frying pan, utensils, and fuel), rope, duct tape, sunglasses, rubber tubing, and sewing kit.
- **Lighting and communications**. LED headlamp, glow sticks, candles, cell phone, charger (preferably hand crank or solar), emergency radio (preferably with hand crank that covers AM, FM, and Marine frequencies) and extra batteries, writing implements, and paper.
- **Cash or barter**. You never know how long an emergency will last. Extensive power outages mean no cash machines, so keep a few hundred dollars in small bills, gold or silver coins, or other valuables on hand.

Communication can be a real problem in an emergency. As we saw with the last California earthquake, cell capacity can quickly be overrun as panicked relatives compete with 911 calls and the like. Taking a cell phone, battery, and charger along is great but service may very well be down for a while as systems are tied up. To save power, turn on your phone only when you need to use it, but leave a message saying something along the lines of:

> "This is _____, we are all okay. We are safe, warm, and have plenty of food and water. We have turned off our phones to conserve power but will check messages from time to time. Again we are all okay."

Mindset is vital in any critical incident, but especially in navigating longstanding hazards like the aftermath of a massive social upheaval or natural disaster. It's very challenging to remain vigilant and mentally sharp for more than 20 to 30 days without the opportunity to decompress in a location of safety and comfort. Lack of sleep, physical discomfort, and shortages of water or food exacerbate the problems. Hugh Glass made it through his ordeal in part in order to seek vengeance on those who'd abandoned him to die. We can often do the same thing by thinking of loved ones and those who rely on us.

Elite operators show lower levels of cortisol (an indicator of physical stress), have lower heart rates when adrenalized, and get more restful sleep after stressful situations than ordinary people. They suffer less ill-effects post trauma too. Post-Traumatic Stress Disorder (PTSD), for instance, is more common for those who feel victimized or out of control than for those who felt able to determine their fate during a critical incident. Some mental tools taught in the military to help prepare soldiers for combat include:

- **Focusing on the immediate**. Long term planning is important, as is learning from the past, but during a critical incident it's vital to pay attention to what's going on in the existing situation and what you will need to do in the near term, say the next 15 or 20 minutes to extricate yourself from peril. Have a strategy, but focus on the tactics when under fire, either literally or figuratively.
- **Visualizing success**. Don't get trapped by the "what if" monkeys. It is important to visualize yourself succeeding, doing whatever is necessary in the moment. It's a game of all-in where failure is not an option, at least in your mind. There's an old saying, "A samurai never fears death," indicating the mindset that helped the elite feudal warriors engage in battle knowing that if they were not willing to die for their cause they had already lost. If fear is removed from the equation, success becomes far easier to achieve.
- **Concentrating on the positive**. Use only positive self-talk. It is easy to beat yourself up or second guess yourself if something goes wrong, but that's highly dysfunctional and self-destructive. We all know that plans never survive first contact with the enemy, so what really matters is flexibility and agile thinking. Focus on what just worked, what's working now, and the next positive thing that you believe will happen.
- **Avoiding panic**. If you aren't used to extreme stress your body oftentimes controls you rather than the other way around. Nevertheless, oxygen helps you think more clearly and respond most appropriately to whatever is going on. So-called "combat breathing" is the key to doing this. Here's how it works: Breathe in through your nose and out through the mouth, inhaling for four-counts (silently counting to four in your head), holding for four-counts, exhaling for four-counts, and holding once again before restarting the cycle. By focusing on breath control you not only bring in vital oxygen but also keep your mind focused on the task at hand which can reduce fear and panic.

Few of us are as tough or prepared as Hugh Glass, nor do we need to be short of a catastrophic event or zombie apocalypse. But, that's no excuse for not having a few vital supplies and a solid plan just in case something knocks us off the grid for a few days or weeks. If you have food, water, and shelter covered you can be self-sustaining, oftentimes waiting things out in relative comfort until order is restored and the lights come back on. For those who are unprepared, not so much...

One of the worst choices you'll ever have to make is **whether or not to turn predator in order to survive. Don't put yourself in the unfortunate position of having hurt or kill others or face starvation or dehydration or death because you were too lazy to prepare** ahead of time for what you'll need in an emergency. No matter where you live odds are good that the possibility of natural disaster looms in your future be it from an earthquake, storm, freeze, or heat wave. Further, social unrest and other conditions may be on the horizon as well. Hopefully these events will never come to pass, and your preparation will not be needed, but we wouldn't bet on it and neither should you.

CHAPTER 19

TAKING CONTROL IF YOU'VE BEEN TAKEN

"You gain strength, courage and confidence by every experience in which you really stop to look fear in the face. You are able to say to yourself, 'I have lived through this horror. I can take the next thing that comes along.' You must do the thing you think you cannot do."

– Eleanor Roosevelt

The videotaped beheading of American reporter James Foley by Islamic State terrorists in August 2014 made headline news around the globe. This event took place five months after reporter Javier Espinosa and photographer Ricardo Garcia Vilanova were freed by that same group. According to published accounts of his captivity, Espinosa reported that Foley and another hostage, John Cantlie, made two attempts to escape.

"The first time was a resounding failure before it even started," Espinosa wrote, "The second time the US journalist (Foley) demonstrated his enormous human depth. After managing to escape from the room where we were held prisoner, clutching onto a blanket, he had to wait for Cantlie. Foley could have tried to flee on his own but he prepared to turn himself in. 'I could not leave John on his own,' he said."

Clearly Foley might have made it to safety on the second try, but gave up the attempt so as not to abandon his friend. Sadly, this cost him his life.

On June 11, 2015 two Illinois men, 36-year old Firas Yasin and 38-year old Eyad Abdel Jalil, were arrested for beating a 21-year-old employee and holding him hostage in a small box at a Madison, Wisconsin retail store after accusing the victim of stealing from their company, (ironically named) Freedom Wireless Partners. Madison police spokesperson Joel DeSpain told reporters that the men punched and choked their employee and then placed him in a toolbox where he was forced to lay the fetal position for several hours, escaping when his captors left the box unlocked at one point. DeSpain related that Yasin and Jalil maintain that the victim stole from their company, yet assert they did not harm the employee despite physical evidence to the contrary.

On June 17, 2015 a 37-year-old woman escaped captivity and made her way to a Salisbury, Maryland police station, telling detectives there that she had been captured, restrained, and physically and sexually assaulted for four days before breaking free. Shortly after her report, 59-year-old Harry S. Jones was arrested on multiple charges including kidnapping and rape. Investigators reported that evidence recovered from Jones' home supports the woman's accusations.

On July 6, 2015 two masked thugs armed with handguns and a rifle burst into bank executive Tanner Harris's home, capturing him, his wife Abbey, and the couple's 5-month-old son. After blindfolding and handcuffing the adults, the gunmen herded the family into their car, drove to SmartBank in Knoxville, Tennessee where Harris works, and then forced him to rob the bank while his family was held at gunpoint. When Harris handed the money he had stolen to the gunmen they abandoned him in the bank's parking lot, driving off with his wife and infant still inside the car. Fortunately the woman and child were taken to a remote dirt road in West Knox County and left unharmed in their vehicle. Abbey subsequently drove to a construction site where she was able to borrow a phone and call the authorities for help.

Ed Reinhold, the FBI special agent in charge of the Knoxville office, told reporters that the case appeared to be related to a similar incident where a credit union CEO's family was kidnapped three months earlier. "There are very strong similarities between the two robberies," Reinhold said. "We haven't determined that positively, but it is a good possibility."

Despite dorky movies to the contrary, becoming a hostage is very, very serious thing. It's not something to volunteer for. In fact, it's worth reiterating that if you're tied up by a predator and transported to a secondary location, someplace where the bad guy has time and privacy on his side, it rarely ends well. He will do horrific things to you, stuff like rape, torture, or murder. In fact, such situations rarely end with you remaining alive to talk about them afterward unless someone intervenes quickly or the kidnappers get sloppy and you find a way to escape. But, thankfully, there's more than one kind of hostage situation… Law enforcement professionals categorize hostage takers' motivations to help determine their most appropriate course of action. In essence, there are three types of hostage takers: (1) psychological, (2) criminal, and (3) political:

- **Psychological**. These hostage takers include suicidal personalities, vengeance seekers, and disturbed individuals (e.g., paranoid schizophrenics, manic-depressives). Vengeance seekers can be suicidal too, a double whammy.
- **Criminal**. These hostage takers include extortionists, aggrieved inmates, and cornered perpetrators. While the first two intend to take a hostage as part of their crime, cornered perpetrators wind up taking hostages in the process of failing in some other crime such as a bank robbery.
- **Political**. These hostage takers include social protesters, fanatics, and terrorist extremists. Their purpose is to affect social or political change through violent acts.

> Three quarters of stalking victims know the perpetrator to some extent. The risk is highest for individuals who are divorced or separated. Victims fear for their safety or that of a family member or pet. More than half of stalking victims suffer emotional distress and lose 5 or more days of work due to the crime.

For clarity, a hostage situation is a different from an active shooter scenario. In the former, there is typically time for negotiation, police intervention, escape, or some other non-violent response on the part of the hostage, whereas in the latter, you are in imminent danger and must act immediately to save yourself, either by escaping or counterattacking. Hostage situations can end with the bad guy surrendering/being taken into custody or (rarely) escaping, but they can also end with him or her killing hostages and committing suicide. This dynamic makes them **extremely volatile and dangerous**.

So what should you do if you are taken hostage? Obviously the first and best option is not to be taken in the first place, but it is good to consider what actions you might take ahead of time since hostage crises incidents are tense, dynamic, and hazardous. Every situation is different, but it is, nevertheless, important to consider that oftentimes when a hostage taker feels the loss of power or control he (or very rarely she) may become more willing to resort to violence. Additionally, a hostage taker who makes no substantive demands may be contemplating a homicide/suicide scenario, especially if he or she expresses irrational anger at their hostage(s).

Oftentimes it is better to wait for events to play themselves out but sometimes it is preferable to proactively try to resolve the situation yourself, typically through violence. In choosing whether or not to act, it is important to **ask yourself the following questions**:

- **Is action necessary?** The first 15 to 20 minutes of a hostage crisis are typically the most dangerous. Should you act immediately or can you wait and hope for non-violent resolution of the situation? You may have a different answer when faced with a mentally disturbed individual or a cornered perpetrator as opposed to a terrorist. Your race, religion, or sexual orientation may play a factor as well, such as when Islamic terrorists have asked those they captured to recite Muslim prayers and shot those who could not do so.
- **Is the action risk effective?** If you act now, will the potential consequences outweigh the end results of not acting? It's a risk/reward equation. Once the use of force has been attempted by you (or by law enforcement personnel), negotiation almost always ceases to be a viable option. In other words, **you only get one chance so you can't screw it up**.
- **Is the action acceptable?** Is it morally, ethically, and legally acceptable for you to act? For example, if other hostages are also involved, your action or lack thereof may affect them as well. This is **a tough moral dilemma**. If, for instance, law enforcement is not aware of the situation it is often better to escape and run for help even if you have to leave family members behind. The longer a perpetrator has privacy in which to conduct his/her crime, the worse off you or your loved ones may ultimately be. Regardless, you'll have to live with the consequences of your decision.

If you are convinced that your captor is going to kill you, try to escape at an opportune moment, or possibly even immediately. If law enforcement has already intervened, say a bank robber caught in the act who takes hostages in response to a police presence outside, it is typically better to do nothing offensive, letting professional negotiators handle the situation. Unless you feel your life is immediately on the line, **you may choose to sit tight while attempting to gather intelligence** that may aid law enforcement personnel upon your release. Should you choose this strategy, it is important not to glare, stare, make suggestions, argue, moralize, threaten, negotiate, conspire, or otherwise attempt to draw undue attention to yourself or play the hero.

Do not speak unless spoken to; then be polite, calm, and friendly to the extent possible. **Unless you are a professional hostage negotiator, amateur hour can easily lead to your demise**. Hostage takers tend to be a bit unhinged in the first place hence can take umbrage over the slightest thing quite easily. Try to let your captor do most of the talking. People generally feel better about conversations in which they do the majority of the talking while the other person listens attentively anyway. If possible try to establish common bonds, helping the perpetrator see you as an individual. In this fashion you become somewhat harder to murder in cold blood, emotionally speaking.

If you are disobedient or uncooperative and your captor decides to gag and blindfold you, your peril will significantly increase as you become easier to eliminate and will have less opportunities to escape if your captor gets sloppy. Similarly, try not to turn your back on a hostage taker as **it is psychologically much easier to murder someone who is not looking at you then it is to kill someone who is**. This is why victims are oftentimes shot in the back of the head (plus that's a pretty effective target for a one-shot kill too). **Always look for avenues of escape but do not attempt to utilize them unless you are absolutely convinced of success or certain that you will be killed if you do not attempt to escape**. In most instances you will **only get one chance**.

Once police arrive, most hostage situations are resolved through negotiations rather than through armed rescues. In fact, roughly 80 percent of hostages killed during a hostage situation are killed by the hostage takers or by the police during a rescue attempt so officers will do everything they can to end the situation peacefully before resorting to force. If any hostage is killed by the kidnapper(s), however, the dynamic immediately changes. A counterattack at that point is almost certain. **In the event of a police assault, immediately hit the floor, cover your head, and stay where you are until commanded by the police to do otherwise**. If you are mistaken for a hostage taker, you will likely be injured or killed by the officers who are there to save you.

It takes time to set things up, but if you spot police barricades as you are being led past a window or out onto a sidewalk, you can be reasonably certain that your captor is in the crosshairs of tactical team sniper's rifle. If you are convinced of your imminent demise this might be a good time to wrench free and drop to the floor. Hopefully you will hear a loud noise followed by the impact of your captor's corpse landing on you.

If you witness a hostage-taking and are subsequently released or able to escape there is some important information that the police will want to know. This includes:

- What occurred (and why if you know)?
- What is the location(s) of the suspect(s) and hostage(s)?
- What is the number and identity of the suspects (accurate descriptions and clothing are important, especially if hostages and suspects may have traded clothing)?
- What is the number and identity of the hostages (accurate descriptions and clothing are important, especially if hostages and suspects have traded clothing)?
- Has anyone been killed?
- Is anyone seriously injured or bleeding?
- Why did the incident occur at this time?
- Did anyone see, hear, or threaten the use of weapons?
- What are the medical, mental, and criminal histories of the suspect(s) and hostage(s)?
- Are drugs, alcohol, or other intoxication suspected?

Most of us will never be taken hostage, but in an increasingly dangerous world there is a possibility, one that's best to prepare for ahead of time. Scenario training can be very useful here too, assuming it's conducted by folks with the requisite knowledge and training to do the topic justice. This gives you a leg up in successfully navigating the aftermath.

Additionally, it is incredibly valuable to identify escape routes wherever you are. Sometimes they are obvious, such as doors or windows, but other times they may require creativity such as breaking through drywall or utilizing a crawlspace. If you are captured and find a way to break free you won't want to waste time figuring out how to escape.

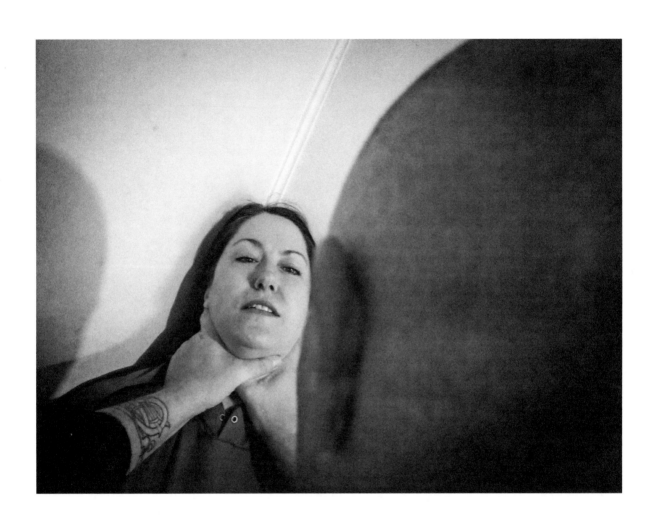

Chapter 20

Women's Self-Defense is Bullshit

"Live reality on realities terms."

– Dr. Drew Pinsky

In an assault in a Washington DC nightclub's parking garage, two Brazilian jiu-jitsu practitioners, Matthew Maldonado, 26, and Nicholas Shultz, 21, allegedly raped one of their one of their female teammates after a New Year's Eve party in 2012. According to court documents, the woman whose name was not released felt too drunk to drive home after the party so she left with her colleagues because they told her they would get her to a friend's house where she could sleep safely. Instead of driving her home, however, they reportedly knocked her to the ground, struck her in the head several times, and raped her. She was discovered unconscious in the garage afterward by a stranger.

Both men were charged with multiple counts of kidnapping as well as first and second degree sexual abuse. The victim testified that Shultz forced her to give him oral sex, raped her, and then said, "I'm sorry, I'm a sick bastard," before abandoning her. Nevertheless, both Maldonado and Schultz were acquitted in court in October, 2013. While the incident had been caught on video surveillance, the poor quality images made it difficult tell whether what took place was consensual as the defense stated or had been forced as the prosecution avowed. One juror told reporters afterward that he had watched the surveillance video of the incident a hundred times but, "Blurry images … you really couldn't tell heads or tails what was going on so it made it very difficult."

Women's self-defense is bullshit… at least **the way it is taught the majority of the time**.

Don't believe us? We'll explain: To begin let's start with professional sports. There is a reason that NFL defensive lineman are not allowed to hit the opposing team's quarterback in certain ways. The size, strength, and mass mismatches virtually guarantee an injury, potentially a career-ending one, for the quarterback despite the padding and helmet that he is required to wear. A heavyweight boxer is simply too much for a middleweight boxer, not due to skill, they might both be champions operating at the top of their respective games, but **because of size, strength, and mass**. In mixed-doubles tennis competitions both male and female players regularly try to drive the ball toward the female of the pair because she is virtually always the weakest link. This is because **even at the highest skill levels** of physical competition **bigger, stronger players tend to overwhelm smaller ones**, even if the littler one is faster. Sure, exceptions exist, such as 5 foot 6 inch tall running back Darren Sproles (who incidentally weighs 190 pounds), but they are rare and we think it's a safe bet that you are not the exception that proves the rule.

Due to these size, strength, and mass mismatches virtually all athletic competition is segregated, with athletes grouped by age, weight, experience, and gender. In this fashion players contend only against others in the same category to assure fair competition and minimize the chance of injuries.

A greater percentage of female than male victims experience socio-emotional problems, regardless of the type of violence or the victim–offender relationship. The majority (91%) of violent crime victims experience emotional symptoms for a month or more and most (61%) experience physical symptoms for a month or longer too.

One of the reasons for this is that the older you get, the longer it takes to heal. The weaker your body becomes from use and abuse, the higher the odds that you will find that you just can't move like you once did any longer. In professional parlance, this is known as "losing a step." Injury is also an issue. It is like buying a car. We all prefer the new car as it has no wear and tear on it and has not been abused by somebody else's bad driving. The used car can be a risk, something is not going to function as well as it once did. Weight mismatches amongst competitors make a difference that is indisputable. Ranks and skill levels are also used in leveling the playing field to assure that the contest is more competitive for athletes and simultaneously more interesting for fans.

You get the point, right? **Any competition where skill, size, strength, and mass are not comparable is unfair**. And, in most instances, women are smaller and physically weaker than men.

Now we are going to delve a little deeper and point directly to the physical and mental differences between men and women. Clearly we're talking norms and averages, not exceptions, so we really don't want to hear about the anomalies that you might put forth to disprove the norm. Yes, there are weak men and there are strong women, but as a general rule men are stronger than women. They are taller and have more mass in most instances too. And, more often than not, they're faster and more athletic. Anecdotally there is some evidence that women tolerate pain better than men, but scientific evidence has not concluded that definitively yet. For whatever it's worth, a study published in the December 2009 issue of *Neuroscience Letters* showed that women were more sensitive to pain than men; but women and men were equal in their ability tolerate pain intensity. Women do have an advantage in their adrenal curve in that it kicks in slower and lasts longer which gives them a chance to think and plan more clearly in the early stages of conflict, but without a more significant equalizer (e.g., knife, gun) they are at **a significant disadvantage if they are forced to engage in hand-to-hand combat with a man**.

So, women in general are smaller, and not a physically strong, as men. With the previous knowledge in place and observed through the light of logic, **teaching women to fight like a man is ridiculous**. This pattern of teaching is as silly as Napoleon Dynamite's brother training to become a cage-fighter.

Kris had a woman, a mom of one of his students, ask about a women's self-defense course. She suggested that she had a few women in mind who wanted to do such a thing would he be interested having Kris teach them. He was happy to oblige, explaining that he had already put something together which he had taught several times before that should fit their needs. What he wanted to teach didn't take all day and, although there was some fairly intense work for a few minutes, it was not a punch here, grab that, strike there type of event. The mom took interest and asked more about what was involved. As they got deeper into the conversation, she asked why the class didn't focus all that much on the physical aspects of self-defense.

> Kris was blunt, saying, "Look if I wanted to attack you there is literally nothing you can do to stop me, you need to stop me before I start."
> The mom, without missing a beat said, "I wouldn't be so sure about that."
> Kris just smiled and suggested a date for the class.

Let's take a moment and break this interchange down. This is a woman who was speaking with the person she had entrusted to teach her child the basics of self-defense, effective karate techniques, and mental discipline and suddenly she suggested that his skill and experience might not be all that. Even though she has likely read his bio on the West Seattle Karate Academy website, hence knows that Kris had some 35 years of karate and 15 of judo competition under his belt, she tried to dictate what she thought the course might look like, the elements that she saw as important. Enter the Dunning-Kruger effect…

The Dunning-Kruger effect was codified by David Dunning and Justin Kruger of Cornell University. The effect is this: **a deliberate and thoughtful bias in judgment that is illogical.**

The person creates their own reality based on their perceptions and assumptions. An essential part of the Dunning-Kruger effect is the person who has come to the illogical conclusion simply cannot see their own incompetence or ineptitude. They are unable to realize that they are wrong. This moment with the mother of one of Kris's students was the Dunning Krueger effect in spades.

Sadly, we submit **the majority of women's self-defense classes mindlessly dance the Dunning-Kruger jig**. It looks like something like this:

- **False perceptions**. What the client wants is based on their perception of what they believe that they need, which are "real" fighting skills. What they don't realize is that self-defense is actually about not being there when the other guy wants to fight, or talking your way out of physical violence, rather than being about fighting which is what you do when you've screwed up your self-defense. In other words, **they falsely equate fighting with self-protection**. Let's face it, not fighting is far superior, especially if you are smaller, physically weaker, and have less mass than your adversary.

- **Well-meaning instructors**. This leads clients to find somebody (a martial arts instructor) who is trained in fighting and have that person teach them how to fight. The instructors give what their clients want, lessons on how to fight, which is invariably taught the way the instructor (more than likely male) has had success in fighting. Typically there is little or no focus on awareness, avoidance, or de-escalation skills. Lessons on the legal aspects of self-defense, "will" drills (that help you build mental strength/fighting spirit), how criminals think, impromptu weapons, and many other vital elements of holistic training are left out in favor of sparring, *kata* (forms), and the like. It's not that these classes have no value, just that **they are dangerously incomplete**. And, they are **rarely tailored for a woman's needs**. Even when the instructor is female she was often taught by a male who had little if any expertise in teaching to women's unique needs. Of the thousands of books published on martial arts, for example, only a handful specifically address how to tailor teaching to meet a woman's unique needs, abilities, and body types.

- **Flawed training**. End result, women who believe they have developed skills, when in fact they have learned to mimic a man. Sadly this tends to end badly if the need to test these skills on the street because they don't have the size, strength, mass, or instincts to pull off what they have learned on an unwilling partner. For example, even though eye gouges can be highly effective, most women are unable to intentionally shove their fingers into another human being's eye with the intent of displacing it. It takes concerted training, **both mental *and* physical**, to be able to pull something like that off in real life. So, even if she has learned techniques, that training alone is not enough to assure the ability to use them. And, of course, not every technique is viable for the physically smaller, weaker combatant.

What today's world tells women is that they are strong, fierce, have girl-power, etc., all of which is valuable in most aspects of a person's life. But, let's put the physical aspects of fighting into perspective. Simply put, there is a reason the men and women Ultimate Fighting Championship (UFC) champions don't compete against each other. It wouldn't be a contest. The two champion's skills and speed might be comparable, but their physicality does not match-up in a fair or sporting manner. That's competition. Now, let's talk combat. **A physical attack is not about the sport**, weight classes, aerobic conditioning, or a sense of how tough you are, **it is about fast, brutal violence**. Mass and explosive strength make all the difference in such circumstances. Even aerobic conditioning has little effect as street fights don't last very long, mere seconds most of the time if combatants are really trying to kill or maim each other. In fact, one of the ways to differentiate between social and asocial/predatory violence is the length of the fight and the type and extent of damage sustained by the combatants. **No amount of the Dunning-Kruger effect is going to reverse the immutable laws of violence**.

Another challenge is that a whole lot of women's self-defense training is taught as weekend seminars or even one-day classes. In part this is a commercial response to our short-attention-span, want it now culture. **Few people want to put in the time, discipline, and effort necessary to learn martial arts deeply**, which is why so many drop out in the early ranks. Similarly, few people want to spend a ton of time learning to defend themselves either. They see it as an insurance policy sort of thing, something that is nice to have, important perhaps, but simultaneously **something that they really never plan on using**, hence don't truly need. This is not a good thing. Mail order or one-day courses that offer a degree in virtually any subject are looked upon with suspicion, disdain, and distrust, yet for some reason this doesn't stop tens of thousands of people from attending short duration self-defense workshops. You would call a doctor with a mail-order degree a quack, right? So, why not take the long view when looking for something as important as protecting your health and welfare?

We wholeheartedly encourage women to get involved in martial arts classes, boxing, karate, gung-fu, judo, or whatever turns their crank. **Extended training is the best method of understanding the sensations of being hit, hitting, choking, and wrestling**. There is no substitution for experience. And, the more you understand aggression as well as techniques that work on stronger, faster, heavier opponents the better your chances of successfully putting what you have learned into play if you are forced to do so in self-defense. Sparring and violence aren't the same, of course, but if the first time you feel solid contact is out on the street you have a far better chance of freezing in fear than if you're used to it, viscerally know you can take a hit, and can therefore shrug off the pain and focus on fighting back.

Obviously we're assuming that you are simultaneously training for the non-physical side, building awareness, avoidance, and de-escalation skills too. This is because if a women is fighting against a man in a self-defense situation that means that something failed on the women's end of self-defense… or that she has met up with a skilled predator. An example occurred on April 14, 2015 when a man hid in a women's bathroom stall at a Manhattan sports bar and, when a victim came in to use the restroom, attacked and raped her. **This predator used an isolated area where the woman let her guard down to gain the privacy he needed and take advantage**. A skilled predator such as the bathroom rapist (or serial killer Ted Bundy for that matter) is difficult to predict or deal with. Their victims were not engaged in high-risk behaviors like prostitution or drug usage. It's not possible to live your life rolled up in bubble-wrap for safety, but it is possible to pay attention to your surroundings and make smart decisions.

Here's another example to consider:

> Carol DaRonch, one of Bundy's intended victims, narrowly escaped being abducted in Salt Lake City, Utah on November 8, 1974. She had been shopping at a mall when a man claiming to be a police detective approached and told her that there had been an attempted theft of her car and that she needed to file a police report. **He gave off a strange vibe but despite her misgivings DaRonch accompanied the man, who authorities later confirmed was Ted Bundy, to his Volkswagen and got into the car**. Once inside, he placed a handcuff on her wrist and attempted to hit her with a crowbar, but she fought back, jumped out of the car, and ran to safety. DaRonch wasn't a martial artist, she didn't have any special training, but her ferocity and unwillingness to become a victim held her in good stead. Barely. **However, if she had listened to her instincts she would not have been in danger in the first place**.

The DaRonch/Bundy incident is a great example of how fighting is what you do once you've screwed up your self-defense, not self-defense itself. And, of course, another proof point that any women's self-defense class that focuses solely on fighting is missing vital elements of keeping yourself safe.

While both men and women train, martial arts instructors are predominantly men. As men we don't see the world through the eyes of a woman. As a result when we try to teach a woman to fight, **we inadvertently teach her to fight like a man**. Yeah, it's that simple. And it's true most of the time. Remember the comments earlier about how women see self-defense, they allow the dominant vision of violence to dictate how they should defend themselves? Well-meaning instructors propagate this mistake. It is the instructor's duty to **break this circle of falsehood**.

Men, instructors, you don't see the world as women. Below are a few comments from women on how the world looks to them. The world that women see is as different from the one men see as observing what is around us through the x-ray spectrum in addition to the visible light spectrum that everyone can perceive. Reality isn't any different, but we tend to miss stuff because it is invisible to our eyes... Comments follow:

> "Martial arts *dojos* have diagrams of a human body (usually a big beefy guy) that show all the vulnerable points. It's scary. Translate that to a one-hundred-pound woman and it becomes terrifying."
>
> – Dianna G.

> "If my friend and I see a sketchy guy on the other side of the street, we leave. The boys probably would make fun of him."
>
> – Stephanie S.

> "I have to say that I really feel different and a little vulnerable when I wear a dress and heels. I usually am in blue jeans and a jacket. It is kind of spooky how dressing up changes your sense of self." – Emma M.
>
> "If I am uncomfortable in a place, I leave period. I'm not hanging around."
>
> – Denise D.

> "I could never do that. I mean I like sparring and rolling on the mat, but I cannot imagine actually doing that [intentionally hurting another human being]. I'm more evolved."
>
> – Cheryl B.

So, if you're a man, especially a male martial arts instructor, what can you do to break the circle of falsehood? Begin by educating yourself about what violence looks like to women. We suggest:

- *The Gift of Fear and Other Survival Signals that Protect Us from Violence*, by Gavin de Becker. De Becker has done a great service in breaking down the predatory methods and illustrating their use. The first half of his book is a fantastic primer on situational awareness that applies for everyone but is especially pertinent for women.
- *Unmasking Sexual Con Games: A Teen's Guide to Avoiding Emotional Grooming and Dating Violence* by Kathleen M. McGee and Laura J. Buddenberg. A small book that is

designed for teenagers as the title suggests, but has some very solid information such as how to distinguish sweet talk from lies, recognize when you're being played, and how to set healthy boundaries for friendship and dating.

- *In Search of the Warrior Spirit*, by Richard Strozzi-Heckler. The author works with the military to help create better focus for people who may be asked to kill. A fascinating examination of hard people opening up to a different vision. There is much to learn in this book.
- *On Combat: The Psychology and Physiology of Deadly Conflict in War and in Peace* by Lt. Col. Dave Grossman and Loren W. Christensen. This book examines how the human body and mind are influenced by the stresses of combat. Understanding what happens to the nervous system, heart, breathing, visual and auditory perception, and memory under extreme stress helps you train accordingly. There's a great chapter on the moral and ethical aspects of fighting, something that is insightful to anyone but resonates especially well with most women too.
- *Fight Back: A Woman's Guide to Self-defense that Works* by Lisa Place (Christensen) and Loren W. Christensen. This book provides psychological, technical, and tactical knowledge necessary for women to make physical techniques work. The authors emphasize the importance of alertness, attitude, and mental strength in addition to outlining a variety of highly effective techniques.
- *Combat Fitness for the Elite Female Martial Artist* by Martina Sprague. This wonderful book explains how women can gain respect in a typically male-dominated *dojo* environment. It prepares women to participate in tournaments as well as to prevail in real-life self-defense scenarios, assuring that they won't train themselves into a false sense of security that doesn't account for the physical strength, mental tenacity, aggressiveness, and intent necessary to apply what they have learned.

If you are a woman, here are a few tips:

- **Learn as much as you can**. Begin by educating yourself. If you're serious about self-defense take a look at the reading list above. While you cannot learn to fight from a book, you can certainly learn the mindset and fundamental strategies that can keep you safe.
- **Be selective about who you learn from**. Take a self-defense course, but when you do be critical. Push the instructor with questions (politely of course). If he can't answer the questions you ask, well, get what you can from that class and move on. As a side

note, while we didn't make a big deal out of it, both authors have quietly walked out of classes that failed to make the cut, both martial arts seminars as well as university classes. There's only so much time in the day. If you're not getting what you're paying for you've already wasted your money so there's no point in wasting your time too. You should be just as certain about what you want as you are about what you don't want.

- **Carry a weapon… or, get fat.** Seriously, killers don't like moving or dismembering large bodies. Rapists tend to avoid obese victims too. Sure it is a flip statement, but there is a fundamental truth in it. And, **it demands thought about what self-protection really means to you**. If you must fight for your life against a male predator and you are not carrying a weapon the odds are good that you'll lose. Think carefully on that and plan accordingly.

- **If you have to fight, fight dirty**. If you are fighting you failed the first test, but sometimes the über-predator is just that good. Physical skills such as karate are a last ditch effort, something to help you extricate yourself from a truly bad situation. Learn the weak points of the human body, areas that can be broken by someone who is at a size, strength, and mass disadvantage like the eyes, ears, cervical spine, solar plexus, groin, elbows, knees, and ankles. And, learn how to attack them properly. For example, it's very hard to kick a guy in the groin, even untrained fighters instinctively cover that area well, but there are angles of attack that exploit the region. And, methods that are far superior to a kick (like the lawnmower pull, which has you swat, grab, twist, and pull). When physically overmatched, deception, distraction, and disruption are your friends.

The great military strategist Sun Tzu wrote, "Battles are won or lost before they are fought." When you are the physically weaker combatant you need every skill you can use, mainly to create distance and escape, but also to break your adversary at times too. Woman's self-defense as often taught may be bullshit, but with the right instructor, holistic training, and a little discipline it can hold you in good stead.

Let's go back to the parking lot rape accusations against two Brazilian jiu-jitsu practitioners that were described in the introduction to this chapter… Whatever did or did not actually happen that night has already been adjudicated in court, **the accused were both declared innocent**, but let's take the larger lesson instead of the specifics of that introductory story in order to wrap things up. Let's say we have two street-fighter/rapists going after a woman, any woman. **If the potential victim was sober**, rather than falling down drunk, **would she have had a chance against two trained fighters in peak physical condition? Probably not**. But, and herein lies the vital lesson,

if she was able to make it painful enough for them to succeed by fighting back they may have given up. Or, she may have either been able to cause enough of a ruckus to attract help or make them so worried about getting caught that they would have run away. Either way, perhaps **she would not have been raped**.

For example, in a similar incident 25-year-old Svetlana Serafina was attacked by serial rapist Dmitry Zubarev on August 1, 2012. **When he shoved his penis into her mouth she bit it off**.[25] According to news reports the last thing she remembered was the man running out of the store screaming before she passed out. The unconscious woman was found by another customer with the severed penis on the ground next to her and blood splattered all over the place. Police spokesman Vladislav Arsibekov told the court that the missing penis was deemed impossible to reattach thus had been placed in a box and kept at police headquarters as evidence until the trial where Zubarev was found guilty of the attempted rape. Due to previous convictions for sex attacks **he was jailed for life**.

The woman who the two Brazilian jiu-jitsu practitioners were accused of attacking was drunk out of her mind. Let's ignore the stupidity of performing or engaging in a public sex act, even a consensual one, in a parking garage (which is far from the most romantic of locations). And let's, just for a moment, pretend that it really was a rape even though the court found that the accused were innocent. Despite her martial arts training, the alleged victim **did not have the wherewithal to fight** back as Serafina (who had no martial arts training) did. While it was two perpetrators versus one, **many of the details of the incidents, such as forced oral sex, were exactly the same. The major difference was that the alleged victim was inebriated**.

Never forget the impact of your everyday routine on your safety. If you are into the club scene, for example, traveling in a group with other women is far safer than going by yourself. Certain choices in clothing will garner more attention from guys (or gals) you may wish to meet, but in the wrong area it may very well be the wrong sort of attention, so choose both your wardrobe and location well. Maintaining contact with and observation over your drink at all times is common sense, as is not over-imbibing as well. With a designated driver and responsible friends it may be safer to get drunk in public, but it's really **never wise to lose the ability to think clearly and make good decisions**.

We conclude this chapter with the wisdom of Lisa A. Christensen,[26] co-author of *Fight Back: A Woman's Guide to Self-Defense That Works*:

---

25 It should be noted that rape is often more about having power over a victim than it is about sexual gratification. Forced oral sex is a common part of this dominance dynamic… and potentially an opportunity to fight back.

26 Lisa A. Christensen began training in the martial arts in the mid-1990s, earning belts in taekwondo, kenpo, American freestyle, kickboxing, jujitsu, and arnis. She has extensive teaching experience in the martial arts working with adults and children. She began training with her husband, Loren W. Christensen, in 2003 and has appeared in several of his books and DVDs. She has been the principal photographer for numerous martial arts books and magazine articles as well, and is the co-author of *Fight Back: A Woman's Guide to Self-Defense That Works*.

Understand this: A threat (it can be male or female) will attack a woman because she appears vulnerable by her bearing, and because of where she walks, jogs, socializes, eats, drinks and shops. The threat is convinced she won't resist and she will crumble under his assault. In short, she is attacked because **the threat believes he or she will be successful**.

An abusive male partner usually begins by being controlling and possessive. Where were you at noon? Why didn't you answer your cell? Who were you with? How long were you there? Soon he begins telling her what clothes to wear and discouraging her from seeing her family. The more he controls her the more she becomes dependent on him. Physical abuse and forced sex comes next. Although he might give a myriad excuses why he controls and beats her, they're meaningless. The real truth is that **he does it is because he believes he can**.

Your authors quote the military strategist, Sun Tzu: "Battles are won or lost before they are fought." This is absolutely true, and never is this more important than when contemplating women's self-defense. One of your objectives in training for self-defense—and there are many important reasons to do so—is to develop a confident mental attitude, hone an effective physical skill set, and recognize that self-defense begins with how you conduct your daily routine. Let's look at these three qualities a little closer.

- **Mental attitude**: You want to develop a powerful mindset that there is no way in hell you're going to be a victim. You do this by thinking defensively as well as offensively. The concept of offense refers to your physical skills, your confident demeanor, and your constant alertness and awareness of your surroundings.
- **Physical skill set**: When the confrontation has deteriorated to a place that requires a physical response, your technique—based on the reasons your authors discuss in this chapter—need to be delivered with a mental and physical intensity developed from your training and understanding of true self-defense. Know this, your weapons are a combination of realistic physical techniques, a powerful mental intent, and a heart that not only pumps blood to your muscles, but **fills you with love, courage, and determination to do what needs to be done** to protect yourself and your loved ones.

- **Daily routine**: My husband is a retired police officer. While he is no longer on the job, his eyes still are. When we're out, he is constantly looking, watching, assessing, giving something extra attention, or dismissing something. I've seen him do this for so many years that I know he isn't even aware he is doing it. He says he learned it his first day on the job and it quickly became his routine, one that kept him safe for 29 years. It's also a daily routine you need to do as well. Some women argue that this is being paranoid. To them I say this: Of all the approaches you might take to enhance your safety and the safety of your loved ones, **do you really think obliviousness of your surroundings is an effective one**? Here's the good news about training yourself to be alert and aware. Make a conscious effort to do it for two weeks and it will be a habit, part of your daily routine, by day fourteen. Maybe sooner. The only time you'll know you're doing it is when something out of the norm catches your eye.

Stay safe out there.

As you can see self-defense is not just a narrow set of fighting skills; it's a lifestyle choice, a more enlightened way of looking at and moving through the world. Day by day **the choices you make and actions you take will increase or decrease the odds violence being used against you** as well as whether or not you will be adequately prepared to cope with and overcome it. You can never know for certain when something bad might happen, so it's important to keep your wits about you at all times, calmly and rationally appraising situations so you can do the smart thing and extricate yourself from danger. Obviously this counsel applies for both genders, but because of all the factors we've discussed previously it is absolutely imperative for women.

CHAPTER 21

PLANES, TRAINS, AND AUTOMOBILES, OH MY

"A number of years ago the NYC Transit Police asked the NYPD to assist them by assigning officers to 'turnstile duty.' The city was losing money because many people were jumping the subway turnstiles without paying fares. At first the NYPD officers resisted because it was considered beneath their dignity. However, in time it became a choice assignment. Why? Because officers who took this duty quickly developed the highest number of felony arrests in the department. You see individuals who engage in criminal behavior very seldom limit themselves to only one kind of crime. When someone jumped a turnstile, the officers would run background checks. The officers often discovered that there were warrants out for the individual. Viola! Instant arrest."

– Marc "Animal" MacYoung

On March 24, 2015 Germanwings copilot Andreas Lubitz waited until captain Patrick Sondenheimer stepped out of the cockpit to use the lavatory before locking the hijack-proof door and intentionally flying an Airbus A320 into the French Alps killing all 150 people on board, including himself. According to police reports the 27-year-old had hidden medical records from his employer and researched suicide methods and cockpit door security shortly before the incident. He may have spiked the pilot's coffee too. He had reportedly battled depression for several years and was seeing five or six doctors for various health issues at the time. Ironically the auto-lock feature that helped Lubitz take control of the plane was introduced in order to improve flight safety in the wake of the 9/11 hijackings. In voice recordings recovered after the crash Sondenheimer could be heard knocking, attempting to use the keypad to gain entry, pleading with Lubitz, and eventually attempting to break into the cockpit with an axe. Sadly he was unable to get through the armored door due to the emergency access lockout feature that his suicidal copilot had enabled.

The Germanwings incident isn't the first time a pilot has intentionally crashed a commercial airplane. Investigators believe that the November 29, 2013 crash of a Mozambique Airways Embraer 190 jet was due to a virtually identical incident, though the roles were reversed. That jet's captain, Herminio dos Santos Fernandes, waited until his copilot took a restroom break before locking the cockpit door, flying the plane into the ground, and killing everyone on board. Like Lubitz, Fernandes also pushed the jet's throttles to their maximum operating speed before the crash and, similarly, he was believed to be experiencing personal problems at the time of his suicide. Unlike FAA regulations that require two crewmembers in the cockpit at all times, it was permissible under European aviation regulations at the time of the incident to have just one person alone in the cockpit when these crashes occurred.

On December 22, 2001 Richard C. Reid (aka Tariq Raja, aka Abdel Rahim), an Al Qaeda terrorist, tried to blow up American Airlines Flight 63 over the Atlantic by igniting a bomb built into his shoes. The routine flight from Charles De Gaulle International Airport (near Paris, France) to Miami International Airport was interrupted when a flight attendant saw Reid attempting to light a match on the tongue of his tennis shoe. She tried grabbing his shoes, but was thrown to the floor where she began screaming for help. When another flight attendant joined in the struggle to stop Reid, he bit her on the thumb and threw her aside as well. After a long struggle, the 6 foot 4 inch tall terrorist was eventually subdued by a group of passengers.

Federal law enforcement authorities later found plastic explosives with a triacetone triperoxide detonator, hidden in the lining of his shoes. On January 30, 2003, he was found guilty of terrorism charges at a federal court in Boston, Massachusetts and sentenced to life in prison. During the sentencing hearing, he openly stated that he was an Islamic fundamentalist and declared himself an enemy of the United States of America.

On March 2, 2005, Cumberland City (Tennessee) school bus driver Joyce Gregory was shot to death with a .45 caliber handgun as she drove along her route. The alleged perpetrator was a 14-year old male student whose name was not released because he was a minor. The bus, which was carrying twenty students at the time, crashed into a utility pole. Two weeks before the incident Gregory told family members that she was having trouble with students chewing tobacco on the bus. After several warnings, she reported them to school administrators. The suspect was one of those students. Luckily, the bus was moving slowly along a residential street at the time of the shooting and no one else was seriously hurt by the crash.

On November 26, 1998, as a 60-foot-long Metro bus crossed the Aurora Bridge in Seattle Washington, a mentally disturbed passenger, Silas Cool, stood and pulled out a pistol. Without saying a word, he shot the driver Mark McLaughlin in the torso and then shot himself in the head. Fatally wounded, McLaughlin lost control of his vehicle. It burst through a guardrail, plunged 40 feet, tore through several evergreen trees, and then glanced off an apartment building. A 69-year-old passenger, Herman Liebelt, died in the crash. All 32 other passengers were injured, some severely, yet everyone but Liebelt, McLaughlin, and Cool recovered. Fortunately the incident occurred near the end of the bridge; if the bus had gone through the rail at the center of the bridge the fall would have been a most likely un-survivable 197 feet.

Public transportation presents a unique set of self-defense challenges. Beyond depending on the actions of the driver, engineer, or pilot to assure your safety, your environment will be different than you would find in virtually any other venue if you have to fight in a taxicab, bus, plane, or train. Two factors make all the difference; these locations are both (1) captive and (2) mobility impairing:

- **Captive**. You cannot always get off when and where you want to. This means that leaving to escape a confrontation may not be an option. It also eliminates the need to prove preclusion in order to show the need to use countervailing force in most instances as well.
- **Mobility impairing**. You cannot move around much during combat should things escalate to that point. Narrow aisles and low ceilings limit what you can do as well as how you can do them. Airplane aisles, for example, are only 17 inches wide on most models, with ceiling heights typically a little less than seven feet on commercial jetliners and about a foot lower on regional models. Clearly the repertoire of martial applications that can be performed in narrow spaces like this is limited.

In this chapter we will address how to prepare for self-defense on public transportation, starting with airplanes. Despite highly publicized crashes, a handful of which were intentional, air travel is still far, far safer than walking across the street. In fact, statistically-speaking, **if you were born**

on a US domestic airliner and you never got off, you would be over 2,000 years old before you encountered your first fatal accident and a fifty percent chance of living through it.[27] Nevertheless, it is good to prepare in case something untoward happens during your flight. Due to the hijack-proof cockpit doors that were promulgated post 9/11, there's not much you can do if the pilot(s) decides to ditch the plane, something which has **only happened five times in the history of commercial aviation** (though two of the five crashes were not definitively proven to be pilot suicide during post incident investigations). Fortunately there are a variety of safety measures that have been put in place by the regulatory authorities such as psychological screenings, requiring at least two crew members in the cockpit at all times, arming certain carefully-screened pilots, federal air marshals, and the like.

Our point is this: **Don't worry about the pilots**, there's really nothing you can do about them anyway. **Pay attention to your fellow passengers instead.**

Handguns account for the majority of both fatal and nonfatal firearm violence. There were 11,101 firearm-related homicides in the United States in 2011, down 39% from a high of 18,253 in 1993. Less than 2% of criminals buy their firearms at a flea market or gun show whereas 40% obtain them from an illegal source.

Your best defense, as always, is awareness. Pay attention to your fellow passengers, observing anything unusual or suspicious. Pay attention to impromptu weapons at your disposal such as flashlights, fire extinguishers, soft drink cans or bottles, belts, books, briefcases, or laptop computers, to name a few (the axe that Sondenheimer used is hidden in a secret location only known to crewmembers). Your seat cushions not only work as a floatation device in the event of a water landing but also as a shield that can trap an adversary or block an attacker's weapon. Choose an aisle seat if you can and be prepared to act if something untoward actually occurs.

All in all, the odds of another 9/11 style terrorist incident on an airplane are pretty remote since other targets are easier to access and much less well defended, yet certain terrorist groups such as Al Qaeda appear to be obsessed with taking down airplanes. Nevertheless, fellow passengers are unlikely to remain passive to any future hijacking attempts or other threats, so banding together as was done to thwart the infamous shoe bomber (Reid) or underwear bomber (Abdulmutallab) is a great tactic. You can facilitate this by getting to know passengers around you, at least a little, such that you may be able to act in concert to increase your odds of success and survival. This tactic works on other forms of public transportation such as busses, trains, and trolleys too.

---

27 This statistic comes from former Flight Safety Foundation Fellow and retired Boeing Chief Engineer Earl Weener, who is adept at explaining highly-complex, technical matters in everyday English. Weener currently works for the US National Transportation Safety Board.

Speaking of busses and trolleys, they are a convenient way to get around, especially in large cities, but they also present somewhat unique hazards. Unlike airplanes, other passengers most likely **have not gone through security screenings**, hence could easily be intoxicated, disorderly, or armed, hence dangerous. The good news is that many urban transit agencies have their own police force, so there may be undercover officers riding along in much the same way that federal air marshals patrol commercial aircraft. Nevertheless, unlike planes you do not often wait for busses in secure, well-lit, and carefully patrolled areas. Waiting for a bus in the wrong area could be problematic. Routes matter too. Use a bus stop you know is usually busy and well-lit, preferably in a good neighborhood. **Pay attention to not only where you get on and off the bus, but where it will travel in between as well**. There may be several options from which to choose; be familiar with the route and comfortable with the areas through which you must travel. Know the departure and arrival times and try to let someone at the other end know which bus you plan to catch.

Sit as close to the driver as you can. This not only places you in a position to guard him or her against attack, which happens far more often than you might think, but also allows you to respond should the driver have a medical emergency on the road. There is no sense in being paranoid, but you will always be dependent in large part upon the driver for your safety so you might as well position yourself to be able to act as appropriate if something untoward happens to him or her.

Pay attention to and report any suspicious items left unattended on the bus. Anything that exudes a liquid or vapor, makes you feel nauseated, has unusual wires, or produces an unexplained sound or odor should be reported immediately. Standard procedure is to isolate the object, evacuate the vehicle, and get help. The driver can stop the bus, order an evacuation, and radio for assistance as necessary.

Be conscious of unusual passenger behaviors. Beyond the normal interpersonal confrontations you can find anywhere, a common challenge on public transportation is the unlawful attempt to separate you from your possessions. If you are bumped or squeezed between people, be wary of pickpockets. Commotions or loud arguments may also be attempts to distract you and take your valuables. If someone starts up a conversation, be pleasant but do not give away any personal information like where you live or work. That friendly rider may be perfectly innocent yet he or she could have something nefarious in mind. It never hurts to safeguard your personal information.

In certain areas, suicide bombers are a significant concern as well. This tactic has been used by Abu Sayyaf, al Qaeda, Hamas, Islamic Jihad, Hezbollah, Islamic State, Kurdistan Workers' Party, and the Tamil Tigers, among other groups. The typical perpetrator is most often male, unmarried, in his late teens or early 20s, and fanatical about his beliefs. Surprisingly (at least to some readers, we suspect), he is often well educated, coming from a middle- or upper-class background too. Terrorists, by definition, wish to cause terror, hence are very conscious of media attention. This means that **they will time attacks carefully to achieve the highest possible level of public**

impact. After all, if no one knows about the incident they won't be terrified, whereas the higher the body count the more fear and horror is created. As mentioned in the previous chapter on behavioral profiling, no matter what the bomber looks like, his or her actions can give him away.

Trains and light rail are very similar to busses, though you have fewer options when it comes to choosing their route. Be sure to wait on a well-lit section of the platform, close to the exit or where there are other people around. Many transit stations have closed circuit television cameras and security staff who are trained to deal with emergencies that they observe on them, so they can sometimes be safer than bus stops. When you get on the train, try to sit in a busy compartment and keep any bags and personal possessions you have next to you. If you feel uncomfortable with those around you, switch seats or get off the train at the first opportunity and catch the next one. Only do this if the station where you are getting off is manned and busy in case someone begins to follow you though... Know where the emergency button or cord is situated on the train as well as any help points at the station. Identify the location of emergency exits and intercoms in stations and on trains. As always, pay attention to and report any unusual passenger behaviors.

Taxicabs, Uber, Lyft, and the like can create unique hazards from other forms of public transportation in that **the driver may not be who he or she appears to be**. It is uncommon but certainly not unheard of for criminals to rob, rape, or murder their passengers, sometimes using stolen cabs to set victims up. Consequently it is better to choose a specific company rather than selecting any available cab that just happens to drive by. There's an app for that, of course, virtually every major cab company offers one (at least in most developed countries anyway). If you're old school, then carry the company's phone number with you. Either way, most drivers are required to post their license and photo identification so you can compare the person in the driver's seat with his/her photo to help validate their legitimacy. Uber and Lyft applications have the ability to send their drivers' pictures to your phone.

If you have to book your taxi in a public place via the phone, do it quietly where people are unlikely to overhear your name and address. If you are dropping a friend off at a taxi, comment on the driver's name if you can see it or the taxi number so that he or she will know that you will remember them. Even if riding alone, it is a good idea to casually communicate that you recognize the driver and his or her vehicle. If you can, share a ride with a friend. Two people are far less likely to be mugged than one. If ever you feel uneasy in a taxi ask the driver to stop in a busy place that you know well and get out.

These modes of transportation present unique challenges, some of which you can train for if you are so inclined. We recommend that you practice "fighting" in captive, mobility impairing settings in order to build strategies and tactics that may prove effective if you ever need to do that in real life. This can be accomplished in several ways:

- **Bear pit drill**. Make a circle on the floor and conduct sumo-like bouts where you win by shoving the other person out of the ring or by making him or her submit. This helps you find innovative ways if moving around and defending yourself in small spaces. You can make it a contest to see who can hold the middle longest, inserting a little fun into the mix too.
- **Aisle drill**. Make a hallway similar to ones found in airplanes or busses with mats or pads and practice sparring there. In most airplanes, you only have 17 inches from side-to-side to work in, which is very constraining. It's important to go slow, at least at first, so that you can adjust techniques to the circumstances.
- **Stuck in the chair drill**. It is one thing to fight when you can move around and quite another to do the same when you can't. Sit in a padded chair, run your belt through chair legs across your waist like a seatbelt, and then try sparring. The first few times you try it tend to prove enlightening.
- **Impromptu weapons drill**. Practice the drills above with a variety of impromptu "weapons" as well, using rubber or foam implements that won't injure you or your training partners. This is one of many ways to overcome mobility impaired situations, as well as why the authors tend to carry stout pens, flashlights, and other "legal" objects that could be repurposed into weapons when they fly.

Staying safe on public transportation can be a challenge, but it's one that is overcome by good situational awareness, pre-planning, and a little practice. In addition to the drills above, think about how you would go about hijacking an airplane, bus, or train, or carjacking a taxicab… or assassinating someone in one of those places if you didn't care whether or not you got caught. By thinking like a bad guy **you give yourself a leg up in spotting unlawful behaviors early enough to intervene**. Another scenario to consider: If you thought there was an air marshal on board a plane, or undercover cop on a bus or train, what actions could you take to identify him and get a hold of his weapon without his partner interfering? Sometimes seeing things through the bad guy's eyes can prove illuminating and help you prepare for the worst.

photo courtesy of Anthony Marshall

CHAPTER 22

COPS, RENT-A-COPS, AND POST INCIDENT INTERACTIONS

"The person in custody must, prior to interrogation, be clearly informed that he has the right to remain silent, and that anything he says will be used against him in court; he must be clearly informed that he has the right to consult with an attorney and to have that attorney present during interrogation, and that, if he is indigent, an attorney will be provided at no cost to represent him."

– United States Supreme Court (Miranda vs. Arizona)

On April 28, 2015 a park ranger used a Taser on 35-year-old Travis Ray Sanders who was flying a drone over a Hawaiian lava lake to capture video images of volcanoes at a national park in Honolulu, Hawaii. Sanders was stunned, knocked to the ground, and handcuffed in front of several startled bystanders, including family members, and cited with interfering with agency functions as well as operating an aircraft over undesignated land. He was taken to a Hawaii County police station where he was forced to spend the night in captivity and was subsequently released the next morning on $500.00 bond.

According to published reports, Sanders did not realize that the man yelling at him to bring the drone down was a ranger. "He sounded very angry, confrontational like he wanted to fight, and I didn't really want to stick around for it so I just told him, I don't have ID and I'm leaving," he said.

Another park visitor, Randy Horne, was setting up his camera and tripod at the overlook when he heard the commotion. He told reporters that he heard someone yell stop and when he turned around, he saw a man holding a stun gun with the weapon's "sparkly, glowing blue" wires attached to another man who was lying on the ground twitching. He watched as Sanders was handcuffed, checked by paramedics, and then put into a police vehicle, saying afterward, "I really didn't see there was any severe threat going on. In my opinion, I thought it was a severe overreaction."

Parks Department spokeswoman Jessica Ferracane offered a different view of events. She told reporters, "He [Sanders] was described as being very unpredictable, belligerent. The ranger felt he needed to be stopped for the safety of himself and others. Because the suspect fled and was near the edge of the caldera rim, where there's a 500-foot drop, the ranger deployed a Taser."

Tony Arambula and his wife Lesley heard two gunshots outside their Phoenix home shortly before an intruder came crashing through their front window and pointed a 9mm semi-automatic handgun at the couple and their two-year-old son Zachary. The gunman then took off down the hall into their 12-year-old son Matthew's bedroom. Arambula sent his wife and toddler outside the house to safety, then retrieved his own handgun, chased down, and cornered the intruder who surrendered and dropped his weapon which hit the floor and slid under the boy's bed. After calling for Matthew who had been hiding in his closet and sending the boy outside, Arambula dialed 911 while continuing to point his gun at the intruder. Lesley Arambula placed a second emergency call once both boys were safely outside their home.

Arambula waited in the bedroom holding the intruder at gunpoint until police arrived. When he got there, Officer Brian Lilly confused the homeowner for the intruder and shot him six times before realizing his mistake. The 911 call Arambula had made earlier was still recording when Lilly exclaimed, "We fucked up! I fucking shot this guy... fucked up." About six minutes into the call, on-scene supervisor, Sergeant Sean Coutts can be heard on tape saying, "Was the gun down here?" Lilly responded, "I don't know. I heard screaming and I opened fire." "Don't worry about it," Coutts replied, "I got your back."

Arambula, who survived but will be crippled for life from his injuries, alleged in a $5,750,000 lawsuit that not realizing that their conversation was being recorded Lilly and Coutts conspired to cover up their actions. He further asserted that even after the mistake was recognized he was treated roughly and dragged from the patio across the gravel in front of his house where his head banged against a fencepost. He was picked up again and, without receiving any medical treatment, placed on the hood of a hot squad car and driven for a time down the street before being transferred by ambulance to a hospital where he underwent surgery. His further claimed that his wife Lesley was interrogated for hours and kept in a police car with her children with no word on her husband's condition. At the hospital, Arambula was questioned by detectives immediately after coming out of surgery and told that the intruder would be cited and released because he was found to be unarmed, though the intruder's gun was found under Mathew's bed during a subsequent search.

Imagine for a moment that you are walking along minding your own business when suddenly you are ambushed by an attacker, some madman with a knife that looks like a sword as it gleams in the sunlight. "I'll give you money," you stammer, but he lunges anyway. Your hand rises up instinctively as you try to back away when you feel an intense burst of pain, something splatters across your face, and then your whole arm goes numb. The rest is a blur... You know that your training and skill kicked in, and a few seconds that felt like several lifetimes later the other guy is lying in a pool of blood, most of which appears to be his. You fumble with your phone using your offhand and call for help while staring in horror as rivulets of blood drip down your injured arm and splash onto the street.

You patch yourself up as best you can and as you start coming down off of the effects of adrenaline, tired, shaking, and hurting, an officer arrives on the scene. You begin to gratefully rush toward him when he draws his gun, points it at your heart, and screams at you to get on the ground...

What happens next?

Dealing with law enforcement after a critical incident can be tricky. It's a time when you may be injured, not thinking clearly, the first responder has little if any idea about what's going on, and you could easily be mistaken for a bad guy as Tony Arambula tragically was. Because of the trauma and confusion, it's also a time when many law-abiding citizens dig a hole, dive in, and keep on digging until they've all but convicted themselves of a crime that they likely have not actually committed.

In the example above, if you don't comply with the officer immediately you will very likely be shot dead in the next few seconds, or if you're truly lucky maybe Tased into oblivion, because you were covered with gore, standing over a corpse with a bloody knife lying at your feet, and then suddenly charged toward the officer. If, on the other hand, you proudly tell him that you followed your martial arts training, disarmed the threat (defanged the snake?), and then stabbed him seven times with his own blade you are likely to spend serious jail time for the homicide you just committed—and admitted to—even though you didn't provoke the incident. To make matters worse, oftentimes the first responder is a private security guard rather than, or possibly in addition to, a sworn police officer. That brings up further complications...

You're starting to see the dangers here, right?

Let's deal with who you may be talking to first, then we will delve into how to interact with them... Due to budget cuts, many smaller jurisdictions have needed to contract out substantial portions of their law enforcement work. Further, corporations often feel the need for an elevated level of security to safeguard their facilities, personnel, intellectual property, and other important data, hence hire or outsource such work. Many wealthy, gated communities hire private security patrols as a benefit to their clientele too. Due to these and other factors, the **number of private security personnel surpassed the number of sworn officers in the early 1980s** in the US. In fact, there were more than 2,000,000 private security workers on US payrolls in 2007, nearly **three times** the number of law enforcement personnel in the country that year. **While private security guards do not have police authority, they can carry both lethal and nonlethal weapons, wear tactical clothing and badges, and make citizen's arrests**. Security consultant Thomas Seamon, president of Hallcrest Systems, explained this dynamic to reporters:

> "You can see the public police becoming like the public health system. It's basically, the government provides a certain base level. If you want more than that, you pay for it yourself."

According to the Bureau of Labor Statistics, the number of private security personnel eclipsed the number of teachers nationwide in 2014, with **projected growth rates of 12 percent per annum** through 2022. This includes security guards, gaming surveillance officers, and other personnel who patrol and protect property against theft, vandalism, terrorism, and other illegal activities. Security guards received a median annual salary of about $24,000 per year in 2014, **less than half the average wage paid to sworn officers, detectives, or corrections personnel**. They work in a wide variety of places, including retail stores, office buildings, warehouses, private communities, banks, and casinos, oftentimes utilizing sophisticated audio and video surveillance equipment, providing physical deterrent, and delivering an armed response when necessary. Most of these jobs only require a high school diploma, though many states require private security personnel to register and obtain a license, especially when authorized to carry a firearm on the job.

Police officers, on the other hand, work directly for various governmental agencies. They protect lives and property, investigating crimes and arresting suspected lawbreakers to help assure public safety. Correctional officers are responsible for overseeing individuals who have been arrested by their fellow officers and are awaiting trial or who have been sentenced to serve time in a jail or prison. Education requirements range from a high school diploma to a college or postgraduate degree. Most police, corrections officers, and detectives must also graduate from their agency's training academy before completing an additional period of on-the-job training. Candidates must be US citizens, usually at least 21 years old, and able to meet rigorous physical, psychological, and personal qualifications. The median annual wage for law enforcement and corrections officers was about $57,000 in 2012, yet employment is **only forecast to grow by a mere five percent per annum** through 2022, a rate which is significantly slower than the average of most other occupations.

As you can see, private security guards typically have **less training and receive lower pay than police personnel**, but there are a whole **lot more of them**. This makes us **wonder about the wisdom of this trend toward the privatization of public safety**. Some experts assert that we all benefit from extra feet on the street whereas others say that private security officers are undertrained, underpaid, sparsely regulated, and constitute **a threat to our constitutional safeguards** relating to search and seizures because they are more likely than sworn officers to overstep their bounds.

Hard facts are extraordinarily difficult to come by as we cannot find an objective database of incidents (such as the Bureau of Justice Statistics), only a variety of agenda-driven websites that fall on both sides of the issue, but there is certainly plenty of anecdotal evidence that suggests a potential problem, including several incidents that Lawrence witnessed firsthand while working as a rent-a-cop at the stadium. For example, one of the event staff employees pulled out an ASP baton and began beating on students who took the field after the University of Washington Huskies won a football game against their cross-state rivals, the Washington State Cougars even though the policy at the time was for security personnel to back off, get out of the way, and let sworn officers deal with the situation. The offending security guard was promptly arrested, charged with multiple felony counts of assault and battery, and fired from his job.

Here's another example, one that made national headlines: On May 19, 2014 a security guard at a high school in Oakland, California was arrested and charged with a felony for an assault, child abuse, and other crimes for beating up a wheelchair-bound student in an incident that was caught on the school's video surveillance system. According to the letter that Principal Matin Abdel-Qawi sent home to parents, here's what happened:

> Francisco Martinez, who is confined to a wheelchair, was lingering in a hallway as security officers urged students to get to class. Martinez, who suffers from cerebral palsy, either didn't comply or was slow to do so. His delay prompted a school security officer, 23-year-old Marchell Mitchell, to push Martinez's chair handles in order to speed him up, but Martinez objected and slapped the guard's hands away. In response, Mitchell handcuffed Martinez and then attempted to roll him toward class once again, but Martinez objected more strenuously and spat in the guard's face. Outraged, Mitchell struck Martinez several times before dumping him from his wheelchair onto the floor, at which point another security officer intervened to restrain his partner. Martinez was taken to the hospital for his injuries but was expected to fully recover.
>
> "I'm shocked and deeply hurt by this behavior and apologize on behalf of the staff at Oakland High," Principal Abdel-Qawi said in the letter. "This incident is not reflective of the kind of culture we cherish at our school or how we treat

one another." The principal also wrote that the district's legal office and police department were reviewing policies, procedures, and training related to school security officers and their interaction with students.

Obviously the Mitchell-Martinez case isn't all that different from other alleged instances of police brutality, including infamous beatings such as what happened to Amadou Diallo, Rodney King, or Robert Davis, but when reading about these things it's important to put them in perspective. While millions of incidents are resolved peaceably, or lawfully when the use of force is required, **it is the handful of exceptions that make it to news reports**. Any miscarriage of justice is a horrific thing, of course, especially if you're the target, but most officers are professionals and operate in a manner that is above reproach. In other words, **if you handle yourself in a proper manner so will the responding officer**, regardless of your skin color, sexual orientation, religion, etc. Keep in mind that no matter how upset, injured, angry, insulted, or unsettled you are, **your words and demeanor can significantly affect the tone of the entire encounter** which in turn affects the eventual outcome of your case (e.g., whether or not you are charged with and/or convicted of a crime).

In 2013, 27 law enforcement officers died from injuries incurred in the line of duty. In these felonious assaults 6 officers were murdered during arrest situations, 5 were ambushed, 5 were investigating suspicious persons or circumstances, 4 were responding to disturbance calls, 4 were killed in tactical situations (e.g., barricaded offender, hostage taking, high-risk entry), 2 died during traffic pursuits or stops, and 1 was conducting investigative activities.

Officers, whether private or public, are there first and foremost to gain and maintain control of the situation. After all, until the scene is secure nothing else really matters all that much. Security guards can make citizen's arrests or call for law enforcement to back them up. Either way, if one points a weapon at you, **your best response is compliance. If you think that the officer overstepped the line, deal with it through your attorney later on**, not in the heat of the moment. Approach the responding officer(s) positively. They will be encountering an unknown, potentially hostile environment, where one or more combatants were, and possibly still are, armed. Like any sane person, they will be concerned, cautious, and likely scared. Since they do not know exactly what transpired they also do not know who the good guy is or who the bad guy is yet.

Once the immediate danger has passed, sworn officers should take over. It is their job to ascertain the truth, **gathering unbiased facts and evidence about what transpired**. If in their best judgment there is probable cause that you should be locked up because you committed a crime then that's exactly what will happen. Not exactly fair, but common enough nevertheless, especially if you used a weapon and there is not compelling evidence (e.g., witnesses, video) that you used it in self-defense. The way you interact with police officers when they arrive is critical to your continued wellbeing.

Whether or not you are arrested hinges on a concept known as "probable cause." Probable cause means that the responding officer has a **reasonable belief that a crime has been committed and that you are the perpetrator**. This belief can be based upon several factors including direct observation, professional expertise, circumstantial evidence, or factual information. Officers will make a decision based upon what, if anything, they saw during the incident, what they can infer about the incident based upon professional experience, physical evidence or other factors at the scene, statements from witnesses, victims, or suspects, available video surveillance, and other relevant data.

A confrontational attitude will do you no good and **may well guarantee that you will be arrested** or shot. Even undercover officers have been killed on occasion by their uniformed counterparts when they failed to immediately follow directions and/or did not identify themselves properly. **If you are training a weapon on a subdued attacker**, like Tony Arambula was doing in the example above, **follow the officer's instructions without any hesitation**. While the officer does not know whether or not you are the good guy, he/she knows with absolute certainty that **you are armed and dangerous**. It is advisable to warn the officer if the threat is still "on the fight," but it is far more dangerous to argue than to instantaneously comply with the officer's commands. Be respectful, courteous, obedient, and kind, **even if you believe that the officer is an arrogant son-of-a-bitch** who doesn't know his ass from a hole in the ground.

Responding officers may have extricated you from danger, perhaps saved your life, but it is important to remember nevertheless that the officer(s) is not your friend. He or she is **not your enemy, but not your friend either**. The officer's job is to **secure the environment, provide for aid, gather facts, and enforce the law**. Consequently he or she will not necessarily be on your side no matter how prudently you acted, at least not until all the facts are known. You may not be arrested, but if you are **do not resist for any reason**. Similarly, do not interfere with an attempt to arrest anyone who is with you at the time. **Attempting to flee, evade, or elude responding officers is almost certainly going to make you look guilty** and result in a chase and subsequent detention. No matter how fast you are, you cannot outrun a coordinated search backed up by helicopter or drone surveillance. The odds are good that you won't get away, so don't even try.

Control your emotions to the extent possible. Carefully and calmly explain just enough of what happened so that the responding officer(s) will know that you are the good guy. Retain your composure and conduct yourself in a mature manner at all times, **avoiding any words or actions that may appear threatening or volatile**. Never forget that **police are trained interrogators**. They will note your body language, speech patterns, and eye movements to help ascertain your probable guilt or innocence when deciding whether or not to make an arrest.

Say as little as possible. Here is an example of something you might say based on the example of being ambushed by a guy with a knife and surviving the assault that should be relatively well received:

> "I was walking along minding my own business when this guy jumped out and threatened me with a knife. I tried to reason with him. I tried to get away. It didn't work. When he attacked I defended myself. This was very traumatic experience. I think I'm in shock. I don't think I should say anything else until I'm calmer. Can I please call [your attorney or contact person]?"

Do not, under any circumstances, make any incriminating statements that may be used against you at a later time. **Do not confess to any crime, even if you think you exercised poor judgment** or are actually guilty. While there may be a fine balance between implying guilt through silence and being overly talkative, if you are going to err, err on the side of caution. **You really do not have to say anything at all without an attorney present** though it is generally prudent to identify yourself, warn the officer about any threats that may still be in the area, and state that the other person attacked you. You may wish to tell the officer that you were in imminent and unavoidable danger, fearing for your life. You may even wish to explain why you could not simply run away. If you used a weapon and have a concealed weapons permit, it is generally a good idea to let the officers know that as well.

The Fourth Amendment generally prohibits seizure of persons without a warrant. However, in some instances a warrant may not be required. These instances can include felonies, misdemeanors, danger to the public and violent crimes. A fight probably qualifies for warrantless arrest under any of these conditions. If you are arrested and taken into custody **be sure to understand why**. You should always carry the phone number of an attorney you trust and of a person who can contact an attorney for you if your lawyer is not immediately available. Have these contacts programmed into your phone and also written on a card in your wallet in case your phone is damaged during the encounter.

Ask permission to telephone your attorney or contact person immediately after being booked into jail. **Be polite and respectful** to the jail guards. They can deny you phone access and generally make your life even more miserable if you act out inappropriately. In most jurisdictions you must be taken before an officer of the court (e.g., judge, magistrate) within 24 hours of your arrest. You should always secure counsel and have legal representation before this initial court appearance. If you cannot afford an attorney you can be represented by a public defender though as stated earlier that is not preferable.

Despite Miranda requirements, your fundamental rights and responsibilities may not always be clearly spelled out by the responding officers, especially if they are contract security personnel.

You should keep in mind that **conversations that precede an arrest and spontaneous statements are usually admissible in court**. Remember that you have a Fifth Amendment right against self-incrimination and that it is prudent to have an attorney present during any questioning. It is a good idea to consult with an attorney before any incident happens to get professional advice about what you should do or not do as an insurance policy against what might eventually occur too. The bottom line is that your priority should be to alleviate or minimize any potential charges against you, so **be enormously cautious about what you say** and do **before you have a chance to talk to your attorney**.

Never forget that anything you say can be used against you later on. While the Miranda rights must be given once you are placed in custody and questioned in the US, they always apply.[28] Custody begins when a reasonable person feels they are not free to leave. Rightly assume that **once the police arrive at the fight scene you are not free to leave unless specifically told so** by the responding officer(s). A court will generally give more weight to statements made during or soon after an incident, because events are very fresh in everyone's mind. The assumption is that those involved are still in the grip of the moment and generally have not had time to create a false story, even though memory studies show that you actually have a better chance of accurately recalling what took place during a critical incident after a full night's restful sleep.

As mentioned previously in the section on creating witnesses in Chapter 14, the mind fills in any holes of missing data. Filling in these gaps is a process of trial and error conducted by the mind until it finds a reasonable explanation given your past experience. What holds true for witnesses also happens for victims. You only know portions of what happened, seen through eyes otherwise busy calculating threats and defenses as we tried to demonstrate in the opening to this chapter. Soon after the event, the effects of adrenaline and injury interfere with the process of distilling what happened. **When forced to talk shortly after an incident your mind simply runs the trial-and-error process out loud. The result is frequently disjointed and may lead to contradictory statements that will be given great weight later on**, even when you were trying to be completely truthful in the first place. That is what happened to Helen Weathers, whose story we relayed in the introduction to this book, and it is a big part of the reason why her assailant was not convicted of a crime.

The real trick is to feel comfortable with not having everything make perfect sense. There is no need to create a complete story. **Be honest. Be brief.** Using the prior example, "I was walking along minding my own business when this guy jumped out and threatened me with a knife. I tried to reason with him. I tried to get away. It didn't work. When he attacked I defended myself."

---

28   If the officer is not interrogating you he/she does not have to Mirandize you. Nevertheless, once you are taken into custody and brought to the police station you will be read your rights and (usually) asked to sign off that you understand them.

That's it. Repeat it over and over to all the questions and do not try to be more specific. You most likely will **not be able to remember everything you said or did let alone everything the other guy said or did**, at least not until after getting a good night's sleep. You also **cannot know what was in bad guy's mind** at the time of the incident. **Never guess about such things**. Be factual and pithy.

In any encounter there is always a metaphorical "his truth," "her truth" and the "real truth" somewhere in between. In the eyes of the law, it really does not matter what actually was. **It only matters what can be proven**. If you exercise your constitutional right against self-incrimination, the fact that you did not speak cannot be used against you. It is almost always better to keep your mouth shut and be thought a liar than to open it and have to explain in court later on why you were not a liar. If, based upon the facts of the situation, the responding officer(s) believe that there is probable cause to make an arrest **you are not likely to talk yourself out of a trip to jail simply by telling a good story**. Waxing long will only postpone your trip long enough for the officer at the scene to write down everything you say so that it can be used against you later on. Seriously, **do not talk too much**. And, never try to make anything up to bolster your case or fill in blanks that you do not clearly remember.

Simply act like what you are—a scared citizen who has just been in and survived a horrible situation. If you are going to talk at all, be honest, be contrite, and be brief. **Think about what you are going to say before speaking**. Rehearse it in your head. Know that everything you say is absolutely correct before you say it aloud, and then remember what you said. Set things up such that you cannot easily contradict yourself later on.

It's natural to want to talk about a critical incident to help yourself decompress afterward. **Don't do it!** No one at the scene, no one in jail, and no one other than your attorney is your friend when it comes to a violent encounter. Not even the responding officer(s). That's because **everyone other than your attorney can be called to testify against you** in a court of law. Other than your initial statement to police at the scene, **do not talk about the incident without counsel**.

In summary:

- **Follow orders**. If a guy or gal with a gun and badge tells you to do something, do it. Simple as that. Attempting to argue, run, or fight with a security guard or law enforcement officer may very well end in tragedy. Noncompliance emulates guilt. And, it's physically very dangerous.
- **Keep your temper in check**. If you think the officer overstepped his or her authority, treated you improperly, or did something illegal or unethical don't get your dander up and cause a scene at the time. You can, and often should, take action afterward. Follow departmental procedures, leverage a civilian oversight board, or file a lawsuit.

- **Don't convict yourself**. You have right to remain silent. In most instances you're far better off using it until or unless you have received counsel from your attorney. If and when you do speak, never confess, guess, or make things up.

Law enforcement is a very challenging profession. **Decisions made in microseconds during critical incidents are reviewed, second-guessed, and judged by oversight boards, the media and the court system for days, weeks, or even decades afterward**. Most folks who hold the thin blue line between us and the bad guys are well-meaning professionals who strive to do their absolute best every day. But, they've got a pretty shitty job too, a mostly thankless one that means that most of their interactions with civilians are unpleasant… giving you a ticket, making an arrest, rescuing you from a car wreck, or investigating something bad that happened to you.

While we've been speaking with a US-centric perspective, since that's what we know best, this absolutely isn't just a US thing. It's the same world-wide. Don't take our word for it, however, here's a first-hand perspective from a 30-year veteran of UK law enforcement:

> "In thirty years of working as an LEO I always tried to do the right thing, the right ways and to achieve the right outcome. It didn't always come out that way, usually because I made a decision to act which was based on too little information. But that was usually due to my perception at the time, of a need to act decisively in order to keep someone from getting hurt. In the cold light of day and when all the facts were out, my decisions appeared erroneous and at times, it may have appeared that I used excessive force, or even detained the wrong person. In my experience that happens occasionally and any decent, diligent officer can fall foul of it.
>
> General Patton was quoted as saying, "a good solution, applied with vigour now, is better than a perfect solution ten minutes later." Guess what, that's what Law Enforcement officers do much of the time. They work off a message from the dispatcher which is based on the biases of the caller, the so called 'victim,' so they don't have all the facts. Regardless, on arrival often they have to start making decisions straight away.
>
> "Despite what some people believe, not every cop is a lying, violent, right-wing, fascist, who is out to ruin your day just for the heck of it. The vast majority of officers—virtually all of them to be true—simply want the incident that you have become involved in sorted out with the least amount of fuss so that they can get to the next job on their kilometre long of 'jobs to do' list—those jobs which must be completed before they end the shift. At times, because the officer is trying 'rush' through his or her list, they may appear

distant, their mind occupied with stuff not relevant to your problem. That is a hint of ineffective communication skills, but that is all it is. There is a juggling match going on in his head, as he prioritizes how he or she utilizes time. Members of the public, especially those pulled over to the side of the road for no apparent reason (in their eyes) may read the officer's body language and behaviour wrong. That can make the driver respond to the officer in a way which is only ever going to end up badly.

"There is, however, a little known phenomenon out there which tends to be known about only by people who deal with the public on a daily basis. All contact professionals (those who deal with you on a professional level) know it and many use it. It's never going away—not while there are people who deal with the public. It is especially relevant to the emergency services – those professionals who deal with members of the public who are in trouble. It is called the 'Attitude Test,' and if you fail it your day can suddenly become full of obstacles.

"The Attitude Test is widely known, especially by LEOs, worldwide. I know because I work with cops from around the globe. However I also know that the same test is utilized by paramedics and fire fighters too. The one thing in common with all three groups is that they are all there to protect and save the public. They do it day in and day out and they enjoy their jobs. They choose to help the public. They choose to be the one to get covered in other people's blood, to pull people out of burning buildings, and to make right the horrendous injuries caused by violence and car wrecks. So the one thing which really can get on an officer/fire fighter/paramedic's goat is when the behaviour of a member of the public gets in the way of them doing their job.

"In the UK, people are cautioned by an officer when they have committed an offence, just like in the US. 'You are not obliged to say anything, but it may harm your defence if you don't mention now, something which you later rely on in court. Anything you do say may be used against you in court...' In essence it's the Miranda, or the 'right to remain silent,' but with the rider that the court might suspect that you are telling lies or hiding something if you first mention it after you have had time and advice from counsel.

"For example, if an officer is checking a driving licence, asks the driver to pronounce his surname and got the surly reply, 'it's on the license,' or 'I don't answer questions,' or some similar response, chances are good that officer may suspect that the driver is being unhelpful. The officer may have the licence in hand, but for some reason feels a need to investigate further. Maybe he or she needs the spelling confirmed. Maybe the writing is worn from sitting in a wallet for a while or the document is old and hard to read. Or maybe he believes that the licence or the suspect's vehicle is stolen. Maybe he just wants to pronounce your name right. Or, maybe he just wants to get this particular job out of the way, so he can get onto the next on his list…

"An uncooperative attitude may very well get your vehicle:

- Searched for drugs and/or contraband (by a search team who don't start their shift for an hour), or
- Impounded, because we cannot establish the true owner ('but Sarge, the driver told me that he doesn't answer questions and so I was scared that he might think I'm infringing his civil liberties... so we thought it better to arrest him and then run his ID though the computer.')

"There are many ways that the Attitude failure can come back and bite you— all because you failed the Attitude Test. At minimum a bad attitude will get you stuck at the scene for a very long time, while the officer writes everything up. I mean, you wouldn't answer anything and, as you were soooo unhelpful, it took ages. So very sorry and all that...

"Don't fail the Attitude Test when dealing with an experienced cop. It causes a world of (legal) hurt. But don't forget that all emergency services personnel know about and utilize the Attitude Test. I've seen drunks start arguing with an ambulance crew, instead of shutting up and letting them deal with whatever injury has befallen him. And trust me; paramedics can cause some serious pain in some awful places. Would you start smart mouthing your dentist, just as he starts drilling a tooth?!

"Next time you think a cop is taking a liberty with you and your rights try and remember that he or she is a hardworking parent, just like you and he really is doing his job—just like you would do. It will put a different complexion on things. And you will be assisting the law, by helping the officer to get to the next job on the list—a job that might really require the skills of the police.[29]"

To sum things up: If you encounter an officer in the course of your day don't make his or her job any harder than it already is. **You're the good guy** (or gal). **Act like it**.

---

29 Martin Cooper served thirty years in a UK police force, 18 of which were as part of a specialist firearms team. Since retirement, Martin has spent the last ten years as a private contractor, serving clients in the private sector, as well as Law Enforcement and the Military. He is the chairperson of the International Police Association's Defensive Tactics Group, an international body of professionals to donate their own time in order to research better and safer practices for Law Enforcement throughout the world.

CHAPTER 23

PREDICTING VIOLENCE VIA THE HOLMES-RAHE STRESS SCALE

"Over the years your bodies become walking autobiographies, telling friends and strangers alike of the minor and major stresses of your lives."

– Marilyn Ferguson

On October 28, 2012, John L. McKay went on a shooting rampage in Renton and Issaquah Washington. The 48-year-old suspect had earlier pled guilty to harassment and domestic-violence charges and was embroiled in a lawsuit with a bank over his used-car business. His estranged wife, Tina, had no-contact orders and warned neighbors to alert police if they ever saw him near her home. Here's the timeline of what is reported to have happened before that fateful day:

- In May a restraining order was issued against McKay after his wife reported that he had threatened to kill her, her children, and the rest of her family. "He told me to go ahead and get a restraining order," she wrote. "It can't stop a bullet."
- In June McKay pled guilty to felony harassment and domestic violence.
- In September, he pled guilty to malicious mischief. In both this case and the prior one in June the court issued no-contact orders and banned him from possessing firearms.
- Simultaneously, McKay was embroiled in a lawsuit over a used-car dealership he operated. The bank claimed he and his partners owed more than $163,000. A judge granted a temporary restraining order which prevented him from selling his inventory.

Tina McKay was terrified of her estranged husband, but thought that he did not know where she had moved to and was living. Nevertheless John found her house, broke in, pistol-whipped two people inside (Tina's daughter and her daughter's boyfriend), and shot a third (Tina's boyfriend). He then drove to his former mother-in-law Linda Ryan's home, some 15 minutes away, broke in, chased her into the backyard, and shot her several times. Both shooting victims were hospitalized but expected to survive. At the end of the day police found him dead in a rental car of what appeared to be a self-inflicted gunshot wound.

Thirty percent of female murder victims in the United States are killed by their husbands or boyfriends, a remarkable number considering that less than ten percent of male victims are killed by their significant others. Nevertheless, more than 100,000 men are violently assaulted by their wives or girlfriends each year. It is not always as newsworthy as having one's penis cut off thrown out the window of a moving car (Lorena Bobbitt, 1993) or flushed down the toilet (Kim Tran, 2005), or having a testicle torn off by someone who subsequently tries to eat it (Amanda Monti, 2007), but being on the receiving end of such violence is never a good thing. Although it flows both ways, male-on-female violence rates are roughly six times higher than the other way around.

Rates of domestic violence are highest for those in the 18- to 24-year-old age group. A weapon is involved in a larger percentage of violence committed by other relatives (26%) than intimate partners (19%) or immediate family members (19%). Three quarters of these incidents occur at or near the victim's home.

Any way you slice it, domestic violence is a serious crime, one that affects men, women, and children, even pets. It often stems from learned behavior, which means that children who grow up in dysfunctional households are much more likely to become abusers themselves. The danger can occur on multiple levels, everything from controlling behaviors to stalking, physical or sexual assault, or murder. And, these situations tend to escalate, with multiple minor incidents preceding more dramatic ones. Consequently it is vital to understand threat behaviors before it becomes too late to do anything about them.

As an old karate *sensei* used to say, "When stress goes up, intelligence goes down." Abso-damn-lutely! Let's say a man goes off, killing former co-workers or loved ones. Pretty common, right? It used to be that the back story was, "He was a nice enough guy, kept to himself, we really had no idea it was coming." That sort of thing... But Americans have become more sophisticated in recent years. Background stories, at least after the initial news cycle, are much more accurate in painting a picture of these shooters. Reporters are more aware of what to ask and how to ask it. Court records are far more accessible than in the past too, so more pertinent information can now be obtained more easily.

This leads us to the Holmes-Rahe Stress Scale. Developed by Holmes and Rahe, for whom the test was named, the stress scale rates life events and aggregates them to create an overall life stress score. Their goal was to find a link between life stress and illness. There are two versions available, one for children and another for adults, but we are only going to use only the adult chart here. Here's how it works, place a checkmark next to each life event that have taken place in the last year. Total the corresponding numbers in the right-hand column for a rough estimate of how much stress is in the subject's life:

Life Event	Life Change Units
Death of a spouse	100
Divorce	73
Marital separation	65
Imprisonment	63
Death of a close family member	63
Personal injury or illness	53
Marriage	50
Dismissal from work	47
Marital reconciliation	45
Retirement	45
Change in health of family member	44
Pregnancy	40
Sexual difficulties	39
Gain a new family member	39
Business readjustment	39
Change in financial state	38
Death of a close friend	37
Change to different line of work	36
Change in frequency of arguments	35
Major mortgage	32
Foreclosure of mortgage or loan	30
Change in responsibilities at work	29
Child leaving home	29
Trouble with in-laws	29
Outstanding personal achievement	28
Spouse starts or stops work	26
Begin or end school	26
Change in living conditions	25
Revision of personal habits	24
Trouble with boss	23
Change in working hours or conditions	20
Change in residence	20
Change in schools	20
Change in recreation	19
Change in church activities	19
Change in social activities	18
Minor mortgage or loan	17
Change in sleeping habits	16
Change in number of family reunions	15
Change in eating habits	15
Vacation	13
Christmas	12
Minor violation of law	11

"You can't stop a bullet." As noted in the introduction to this chapter, this is what John McKay told his wife when she threatened to get a restraining order against him. A suspended drivers' license does not stop scofflaws from driving, it only stops law abiding citizens. Similarly, **restraining orders do keep those who intend violence from carrying out mayhem**. For all their legal weight, at the end of the day they are just pieces of paper. Tina McKay told her neighbors that she feared for her life. In retrospect she was absolutely right to do so. Using the scale above, let's look at the long list of warning flairs in the McKay case:

Warning Flair #1 – Divorce

As we pointed out McKay had already been convicted, having pled guilty to domestic violence. His relationship with his wife was over and unlikely to be repaired. His wife Tina was scared enough that she asked the neighbors to watch out for her estranged husband and call the police if they saw him in the neighborhood. If they were not already divorced, they certainly were physically separated with a divorce looming in the not too distant future. So, with all signs pointing to "yes" on the divorce life event, McKay gets a quick 73 points. That's the second largest value, right under death of a spouse.

- Divorce = 73

Warning Flair #2 – Money Troubles

When it came to money troubles, McKay had them in spades. His used car dealership was in arrears $163,000 to the bank which got the courts to put a freeze on his ability to sell cars. While this undoubtedly secured collateral for some of what the bank was owed, it created a proverbial Catch-22. Unless he had another source of income not obvious form the news article, he was unable to generate revenue to cover living expenses, let alone to pay even the interest on his debt. This ticks off three more high-level stressors:

- Business readjustment = 39
- Change in financial Status = 38
- Foreclosure = 30

Warning Flair #3 – Trouble with In-Laws

We don't know exactly what issues McKay had with his Mother-in-Law, Linda Ryan, but it was obviously serious. After all, he tried to kill her... He kicked in the front door, fired several shots at her as she fled the house, chased her into the back yard, and shot her several times. Reports did not describe the caliber of the gun, exactly how many times he shot her, or where his bullets struck, but all that really does not matter. McKay undoubtedly believed that he had achieved his goal, leaving her dead or dying as he drove away.

- Trouble with in-laws = 29

Warning Flair #4 – Changes in Work Conditions

We already touched on the financial issues that McKay was facing regarding his business, so a change in work conditions requires little processing. He had a business that was unable to generate income, so going to work must have thrown his failure in his face, whereas not going to work most likely fed the flames of personal inadequacy. At this point there is nothing positive coming from this aspect of his life.

- Change in work conditions 20

Warning Flair #5 – Change in Residence

McKay had a no-contact order placed against him after the conviction for domestic violence. It is somewhat unclear what his living situation was, but he certainly was not living with his wife. According to reports she believed that he did not know where she lived. So, more points added to an already mounting total.

- Change in residence 20

Warning Flair #6 – Minor Violations of the Law

The Holmes-Rahe scale has no place for felony convictions; it was designed for the average person going through a normal life. Nevertheless, we had to place felony harassment and domestic violence somewhere. Furthermore, a mere ninety days after those convictions he pled guilty to malicious mischief, damaging of another person's property. Breaking other people's things is often a surrogate. Sort of like a voodoo doll in reverse, it transfers ill intent toward the victim onto his stuff. Damage to property and pets is very common with domestic violence. Although quite serious in the psychological realm of behavior, our scale just adds a few more points on the way out the door.

- Minor violation of the law 11

It is important to note that in all of these cases, McKay plead guilty, never fought one of them. It could be that he could not afford a good attorney, or that he had a public defender who recommended this tactic in hopes of a lighter sentence, or it may even be that he had chosen to defend himself and didn't know any better. Or, worse yet, perhaps he had already decided to go out in a proverbial blaze of glory so it really did not matter what the courts said. After all, this was **a guy with 260 life change units pushing against his psyche**.

While the McKay case may be an extreme example, it's by no means unique. Stuff like this happens so often that only the most egregious cases make the headlines. But, while most domestic violence does not end in murder, it can seriously mess up your life nevertheless. While it's not a perfect predictor, the Holmes-Rahe Stress Scale can give you **good indicators of when it's appropriate to pay very close attention to your significant other**. Even if he or she is not about to become violent, these life changes are times when **reassurance and understanding are both needed and appreciated**. If (or when) the Holmes-Rahe Stress Scale tells you to pay close attention, here are some of the things you should be looking for:

- **You fear your partner's temper**. Your partner frequently yells at you, reprimands you, or demeans you in public. You have cause to fear his/her temper or are concerned about what kind of mood he or she is in on a regular basis.
- **Your partner isolates you**. He or she prevents you from getting or keeping a job, keeps you from seeing friends or family, or otherwise alienates your friends or family so that they feel uncomfortable being around that person. This is a method of cutting you from the herd, eliminating your support group.
- **Your partner exhibits extreme jealously**. He or she checks in on you frequently, follows you around or hires someone else to do so, goes through your mail, or installs monitoring programs on your computer. He or she becomes angry when you talk to or look at people of the opposite gender even when you have a legitimate reason for doing so.
- **Your partner controls your movements**. Your partner keeps you from leaving your house or apartment from time to time, or conversely, occasionally locks you out of your home. Controlling behaviors are never a good sign.
- **Your partner makes threats**. He or she threatens to hurt or kill you, your children, your family, your friends, or your pets. Or, he/she expresses suicidal thoughts. All such threats, even ones given in jest, should be taken seriously.
- **You suffer physical violence**. Your partner hits, slaps, pushes, or shoves you, pulls your hair, or inflicts unwanted physical injury on you in any way, even during sex. The first time your significant other strikes, you should be the last. Screaming and yelling might be tolerated on occasion but physical abuse never should be.

Faced with clear and present danger signals, you will need to make a plan. Individual circumstances will indicate if it is it time to leave, get counseling, take legal action, or whatever, but **you cannot sit idly by and do nothing**. Temper, isolation, jealousy, controlling behaviors, and threats are very serious signs that your relationship has gone wrong. Physical violence proves it. **You cannot afford to ignore these signs**. Prudent, prompt action can help keep you safe.

If you want to get out of a bad relationship and fear that your partner will try to stop you there are support agencies and legal avenues that might help. One of the most common actions is to obtain a restraining order, which can be issued by a judge to help protect those who fear for their safety due to overt actions by an abusive partner. They are by no means a silver bullet, obviously, but can be an important part making the situation better in certain instances. This is because restraining orders prohibit an individual from taking actions that are likely to cause harm. This usually means preventing any contact or communication between two or more people. A restraining order differs from an injunction in that **it can be granted immediately, without a hearing and without any notice to the opposing party**. Restraining orders are temporary; they are intended to last only until a hearing can take place.

If you have been granted a restraining order due to a domestic violence situation, a copy of your restraining order should always be in your possession. A copy should also be on file with the police departments in whose jurisdictions you live and work, and filed with other counties where you regularly spend time. The court order may stave off further problems, but even if it doesn't **you'll have a paper trail that helps support your actions if you need to resort to countervailing force** in order to keep yourself safe. If the restraining order is violated, call 911 or your local emergency number and report the situation immediately. The violating party can (and generally will) be arrested and taken into custody.

Let your employer, neighbors, close friends, and family know about the restraining order. Ask that they contact the police if they see the other party near you or your home too. Be sure to protect your children as well by notifying school administration, teachers, childcare centers, babysitters, and neighbors of the restraining order and requesting that they contact police if they suspect the order is being violated.

Having said all that, a restraining order, no matter what its weight in court, is **really just a piece of paper**. If it is violated, there will be a time lag, no matter how small, between when the incident is reported and when law enforcement personnel arrive. It is important, therefore, to take additional steps to remain safe beyond that document. Suggestions include:

- **Harden your home**. Make it more challenging for the person who may be coming after you to break in. Change your locks, replace any exterior hollow-core doors as well as those leading to rooms you frequent with solid-core ones, and reinforce sliding glass doors by installing a lock and/or placing a piece of wood in the track so that they cannot easily be popped open without making a lot of noise. Add interior window locks so that windows cannot be opened or removed from their tracks from the outside of the house. Install motion-sensitive lighting to identify unwarranted movement outside your home. Consider installing a monitored security system as well. Finally, if you can afford it, a video surveillance system should also be on your list.
- **Plan an emergency escape route**. Know how to escape from all areas of your home, including upstairs, and make sure all family members are aware of the plan. Include family pets or other animals in your safety and escape plans. Animals are often targeted

by a batterer or stalker as a means of controlling, terrorizing, or punishing human victims. If it is not safe for you to remain at home, it is likely not safe for your animal(s), either.

- **Make it easy to call for help.** If you have small children, teach them how and when to call 911. Have them memorize your number and teach your children how to make a collect call to you (or family members) in case they are abducted by your estranged partner and do not have a cell phone available. Tell your children not to unlock the door if the threat tries to get into your home (it's hard not to open the door for mommy or daddy no matter how far off the deep end that person may have gone). Always keep your cell phone charged and carry it with you as you travel, even going from room to room within your residence, so that it will be immediately available if you or someone else needs to call for help.

- **Talk to your boss and coworkers**. If you work outside the home, consider informing your supervisor of the existence of the restraining order and of any concerns you may have for your safety at your place of employment. Park in well-lit areas or ones where there will be other people around and try to leave work in the company of at least one other co-worker. Many businesses employ private security, but whether or not that is available, have someone escort you to and from your vehicle to help keep you safe too.

- **Vary your routine**. Make yourself harder to detect and follow by using different grocery stores and shopping malls and regularly changing the hours you shop. Alter your route to and from your place of employment as well. Avoid walking in unlighted or isolated areas. If you are being followed while driving or riding in a vehicle, proceed to the nearest police station or look for a police officer near a hospital emergency room or other public location. Do not drive straight home.

- **Move if you have to**. We've already mentioned hardening your home, but no matter what you do there the threat still knows where you live and work, and may intuit how and when you'll travel back and forth. Sometimes it's better to leave and go somewhere else, either temporarily such as staying with a friend or relative (preferably one that your estranged partner doesn't know) or packing up and moving permanently to another part of the country. The latter can seem daunting, but there are plenty of resources to help. In most communities, there are both government and private agencies that can provide temporary housing, relocation assistance, help you find a new job, and do the heavy lifting necessary for you to see your decision through. It's a tough call, but sometimes a necessary one. There are counselors available in those same agencies who can objectively evaluate your case and give you advice on how to chart your best course.

- **Learn advanced defensive driving**. We're not referring to run-of-the-mill driving school stuff here, but rather unconventional techniques that bodyguards and law enforcement officers learn. It's not cheap, but having the skill to maneuver, evade, and shake off anyone trying to follow you can be lifesaving. Even if you never need to utilize advanced threat assessment, evasive driving, skid control, counter-ambush, or other skills, this type of training provides, it can help keep you safer and more secure in your daily routine on the highways and byways on which you travel.
- **Stay sober**. Much as you may be tempted to drown your sorrows (who wouldn't be) if you find yourself in a situation like this, it is vital to avoid alcohol or drugs as they can affect your ability to react quickly and make rational decisions. As we pointed out with the BJJ practitioner's alleged rape case, it's damnably hard to defend yourself if you are inebriated.

Obviously restraining orders and other defensive actions such as having neighbors and co-workers watching your back may work out fine, but as we pointed out in the McKay case above things can go south quickly if the threat resorts to violence. Consequently, in addition to the steps listed above, strongly consider purchasing a weapon for self-defense if you don't already own one. As mentioned previously, guns aren't for everyone, but in certain situations they are just about the only thing that can extricate you from harm. Domestic violence can certainly become one of those circumstances. Think carefully on that.

CHAPTER 24

CROWDS, MOBS, AND NOT GETTING CRUSHED TO DEATH

"When I got to the inside doors, people were stacked like cordwood. They were clear up to the top, the people. They just kept diving on each other trying to get out."

– Bruce Rath[30]

The Beverly Hills Supper Club in Southgate Kentucky was a sprawling, multiuse facility, one that frequently hosted banquets, concerts, and receptions simultaneously. On May 28, 1977 there were at least a thousand people crammed into a space built for about 600 when a fire broke out. Although busboy Walter Bailey stopped one of the shows to make an announcement, many failed to take the threat seriously until flames reached the ballroom. Then the crowd panicked. As people fought with each other to reach the few safe exits 165 revelers were crushed, burned, or asphyxiated to death.

Six months later at the Cincinnati Riverfront Stadium in Ohio the rock band *The Who* was set to play for a crowd of some 18,000 fans, most of whom had purchased general admission tickets. The concert was set to begin at 8:00 PM, yet the doors to the venue weren't opened until fifteen minutes before the show. Hearing *The Who*'s warm up and mistaking it for their opening number

---

30 One of the first firefighters who arrived at the scene, Rath was interviewed by reporters shortly after the Beverly Hills Supper Club disaster on May 28, 1977. This quote is an excerpt from that conversation.

just as the doors began to open, the anxious crowd surged forward past the 25 uniformed officers who were assigned the unenviable task of crowd control. Caught in the melee, 11 people were crushed to death before the show even started.

———————————

Fast forward a quarter century to the Station Nightclub in West Warwick, Rhode Island. On February 20, 2003 overcapacity crowds were rocking out to *Great White* when the band's pyrotechnics accidentally set the venue's insulation ablaze. By the time the audience realized that the flames weren't part of the show it was too late. Caught in the mass exodus, 100 people died from suffocation, smoke inhalation, or fire, while another 200 were seriously injured and rushed to the hospital. *Great White's* lead guitarist, Ty Longley, was one of those killed in the melee.

———————————

Riots are horrifically dangerous. It's not just overcrowded nightclubs or panicked partiers that cause harm. Violence can stem from almost anything from political conventions to concerts, sporting events, jury verdicts, traffic accidents, excessive force claims against law enforcement officers, government austerity programs, land disputes, or defamatory cartoons. Here's a small sampling of recent riots, ones that occurred during 2014:

- Protest riots in **Kiev, Ukraine** led to **106 deaths and 1,880 injuries**.
- Anti-austerity riots in **Madrid, Spain** led to **76 serious injuries**.
- Anti-austerity riots in **Brussels, Belgium** led to **27 serious injuries**.
- Riots at the Zaatari Refugee Camp in **Jordan** led to **one death and 32 serious injuries**.
- Riots in **Rio de Janeiro, Brazil** over the 2014 World Cup, led to **53 serious injuries**.
- Riots in **Vietnam** over a land dispute with China led to **seven deaths and 113 serious injuries**.
- Riots in **Istanbul, Turkey** over internet censorship led to **59 serious injuries**.

If pressed, most of us can think of at least a few riots that have taken place over the years, things like Kent State, Tiananmen Square, Seattle Mardi Gras, WTO, Watts, Ferguson, or the aftermath of the Rodney King incident. Crowds can turn into dangerous mobs if members feed off each other's fear, become indifferent to laws, choose to disregard authority, or take advantage of the perceived anonymity that a large group can provide and follow instigators into violent acts. These riots are frightening, fascinating, and shockingly widespread.

The crowd mindset of being one face among hundreds can be a very dangerous thing. It's quite easy to get caught up in the fray, not truly thinking about what is going on, particularly if law enforcement takes a hands-off approach and does not quickly clamp down on lawbreakers. It can even be a lot of fun for those involved, particularly when they don't consider the consequences. For some, **it's an adrenaline rush that rivals any amusement park ride**. Consequently, things can get out of hand pretty quickly. When they do, they are very difficult to stop, even once law enforcement officers move in to take control.

According to Loren W. Christensen, a retired law enforcement officer, high-ranking martial artist, and prolific author, there are five psychological influences that affect rioters, their targets, bystanders, and the police who try to break things up. These include:

- **Impersonality**. As mentioned previously, "groupthink" is an impersonalizing factor that makes it easier for people to follow the crowd and lash out violently. Rioters do not see their victims as individuals with families, hopes and dreams, but rather as objects on which to vent their rage. Impersonality makes it easier to attack victims because of their race, ethnicity, gender, sexual orientation, religion or any other factors that set them apart from the mob. Businesses are often targeted as they are seen as representing corporate greed and corruption, or just because they hold valuable things to steal.

- **Anonymity**. The large mass and short life of a mob tends to make many of its members feel anonymous and faceless, even when they know their actions are being recorded on video. Participants can more easily convince themselves to act without conscience, believing that the moral responsibility for their behavior belongs to the entire group. Consequently, in their own minds they are not responsible for their actions. Those already inclined to act out are given the perfect excuse to do so.

- **Suggestion/imitation**. The massiveness of a mob discourages many of its members to act as individuals, making them more susceptible to follow others like a bunch of lemmings diving over a cliff. There is a powerful instinct to follow the crowd. Only those with deeply ingrained convictions are strong enough to repulse this urge.

- **Emotional contagion**. The size of the mob and its activities generates a building emotion that can be felt by each member of the mob. It is a powerful influence. Often called "collective emotion," even bystanders can be caught up in this wave and soon find themselves involved with the mob as things spiral out of control.

- **Discharge of repressed emotions**. As a result of the other four influences listed above, certain individuals feel a sense of freedom to discharge any repressed emotions they harbor. Particularly if they see themselves as victims of systemic injustice, the crowd affords an opportunity to get even. They feel free to release pent-up rage, hate, revenge, or a need to destroy, acting out accordingly.

Fortunately these influences don't impact everyone. Unfortunately the minority who are affected can cause serious confusion, destruction and injury for everyone else. Because riots can be hard to predict and even harder to stop, it is prudent to pay careful attention to what is going on around you whenever you are part of a crowd. Even if you sense the mood change, catch a glimpse of the opening acts, and anticipate what's coming, it can be very hard to force your way through the press of bodies and escape to safety.

A panicked crowd is just as dangerous, if not more so, than a riotous mob as we pointed out in the vignettes at the beginning of this chapter. When someone believes that there is imminent danger and flees in panic, his or her actions can spark fear in others who act accordingly. This fear can be initiated by actions from others such as setting off a bomb or discharging a firearm, and may be exacerbated by environmental factors such as flooding, smoke, fire, or tear gas. It gets even worse if there are limited escape routes, blocked exits, or other factors that lead to desperation where **people begin fighting each other to clear a path so that they can get away**. Think about all the people who have been crushed to death at nightclubs, concerts, or sporting events when crowds got out of control.

One of the deadliest concert riots in the world took place in Buenos Aires, Argentina in 2004 at the Cromañón rock club. Approximately 3,000 revelers were crammed into the venue when a roman candle set off by a fan ignited a fire. Because emergency exits were fenced off to prevent people from sneaking in without paying a cover charge, 194 people became trapped and perished trying to escape.

While it is easy to plan a demonstration, it is somewhat harder to instigate a riot. Nevertheless, anarchists try to do so all the time. Even when they don't, irrational exuberance can turn darn near any large gathering into a riotous mob too, leading to situations where people overturn cars, set fire to buildings, damage property, assault law enforcement officers, and harm civilians. Alcohol and other intoxicants play a critical role as well.

Lieutenant Dan Marcou, crowd control trainer of the La Crosse Wisconsin Police Department, has codified various behaviors that are noteworthy in a crowd. It is possible to sense rabble-rousers, hooligans, and potential troublemakers by spotting these behaviors in the throng. In most cases, if leaders can be identified and neutralized quickly then followers can quickly be brought under control. This is one of the reasons that when law enforcement acts appropriately riots can be nipped in the bud.

- **Impulse-lawless.** These people can be found in any mob, and tend to be capable of criminal activity in any scenario. They are typically the leaders who instigate a riot. They are the ones you will find standing on overturned cars; very important to fueling the flames of a demonstration. Many show up at events such as demonstrations against alleged police brutality solely to attempt to start a riot.

- **Suggestible**. These people will do just about anything. They are followers who will easily get caught up in the emotion of the day and almost immediately join in illegal acts sparked by impulse-lawless individuals.

- **Cautious**. Like suggestibles, these people are also followers. As the name implies, however, they will only do so if they feel they will not get caught. A strong law enforcement presence or even an obvious CCTV or camera crew may limit their participation.

- **Yielders**. These people are followers, but they will be the last ones to join in the fray. They will eventually succumb to the will of the mob if events run uncontrolled for long enough however.

- **Supporters**. Supporters show up to watch. They are supporting the event rather than a particular cause. These people are likely to put themselves in a position to watch the show rather than participate in it.

- **Resisters**. These people are completely unpredictable. They may or may not participate. While resisters are not followers, they may use the occasion to espouse their own cause separate from the mob. This is where discharge or repressed emotions can come into play.

- **Psychopaths**. Like resisters, you have no idea what these folks will do. Watch out for these people as they have the ability to go off the deep end and cause very serious injury and/or damage, particularly if weapons come into play.

If you are a civilian concerned about self-defense then **your goal will be to escape to safety**, remaining as anonymous as possible and avoiding as much of the conflict as you can in the process. You will want to move away from the danger. Here are some general guidelines for self-protection and escape:

- **Recognize that riots can materialize unexpectedly**. Almost any incident involving people and emotion can trigger a violent disturbance, particularly when alcohol or other intoxicants are thrown into the mix. The situation may ignite suddenly with very little warning. Maintain a higher than normal level of situational awareness when navigating crowds, identifying and evading potential sources of trouble to the extent practicable. Diligent observation can protect you not only from violence but also from more mundane threats like pickpockets. Be constantly aware of cover, concealment, and potential escape routes as you move about in case you are forced to flee with little warning. When inside a crowded venue identify all the various ways in which you can escape the building if needed.[31] In night clubs, for example, windows are often blacked-out so they are easy to miss if you are not actively looking for them. Alternate exits may include even interior walls that you can break through to access another part of the building in an emergency.

- **Monitor warning signs**. Like a rock thrown into a pond, you may not spot the initial impact but you can readily detect the ripple effect that flows outward from the point of contact. Pay attention to the body language of people around you. They may be reacting to something important they noticed that you have missed. Any sudden change in the demeanor of the crowd, unforeseen gathering of onlookers, agitators overseen encouraging a confrontation, or people rapidly moving into your space may be warning signs of impending violence. Look and listen to what is going on around you. Shouting, screaming, or other loud commotions also constitute danger signals. If people suddenly begin running it's for a reason.

- **Watch everyone**. Be especially alert for the presence of weapons. If a weapon is fired the situation immediately escalates into a very serious tactical affair. You may be assaulted directly, caught in the cross-fire as law enforcement officers move to restore order, or trampled by terrified bystanders who are trying to get out of the way. Everyone can become a threat, even the good guys. In addition to monitoring the crowd, pay attention to unattended vehicles parked where they shouldn't be, packages left in high traffic areas, abandoned luggage or backpacks, or anything else that appears suspicious. The sooner you spot potential dangers the better your chances of reacting appropriately. It's always better to quietly fade away than to have to fight your way free of a panicked crowd.

- **Evaluate your options before you act**. Sometimes it's best to flee right away, but occasionally it may be more sensible to hunker down behind something and defend in place. Take a moment to evaluate your options and make a reasoned choice before embarking on any course of action. If you are inside a building move toward alternate exits, particularly in a panicked crowd scenario where the main exit will almost certainly be blocked by the sheer number of people trying to use them. Further, taking a moment to think things through helps separate you from the collective emotion of the crowd and assure that you will behave as rationally as possible when you act.

---

31 In many countries chaining and padlocking emergency exits is a common practice, even in the workplace, to prevent outsiders from getting in while simultaneously preventing egress for those inside. This is usually illegal but rarely enforced.

- **Don't enter an agitated crowd if other alternatives exist**. There is a huge difference between a highly-spirited crowd of shoppers, a restless throng teetering on the edge of violence, and a riotous mob, one that most anyone actively paying attention can sense even if you have not experienced such things before. As things begin to turn ugly, don't hang around to watch no matter how fascinating it might be. Leave as quickly and quietly as possible. Plan your exit route to minimize contact with others, even if that means taking the "long way" around the scene. Slip through gaps between others rather than shoving people out of your way to the extent practicable.
- **Don't fight unless you have no alternative**. If you are forced to fight you may attract undue attention and quickly find yourself facing multiple opponents who want to beat you down or law enforcement officers who don't realize that you are the good guy and come at you with the same intent. If you are knocked to the ground or stumble and fall you may very well be trampled. If you have to fight you will lose valuable time and there is no guarantee that you will survive the encounter, so rather than engaging opponents directly, attempt to deflect or redirect anyone who tries to slow your escape using open-hand techniques. This is sometimes called swimming through the crowd.

If you are a law enforcement officer or security professional, your goal will be to minimize injuries and prevent property damage by managing the crowd to the extent possible. We have freedom of association as well as freedom of expression in this country. Those who wish to gather and express their opinions must be given the right to do so, even if you don't like what they have to say. But, there's a difference between lawfully protesting and instigating a riot. When the worst occurs, your job requires that you move toward the danger. Here are some general guidelines for crowd management and control:

- **Know what you're facing**. If there is no immediate danger of death or grave bodily injury to you or to a member of the crowd, take whatever time is necessary to learn about the disturbance before you do anything active to suppress it. Know the who, what, why, and where of it. Information is important. All too often agitators are trying to evoke an excessive response that is not warranted by what has occurred. Protect people first and then worry about property.
- **Don't act alone**. The last thing you should do is enter a crowd alone. If you can, co-opt others, encouraging crowd members to break up disturbances within the mob rather than wading into the group by yourself. Assess the situation, wait for adequate backup, and don't do anything hasty. Rioters facing 200 uniformed officers may be emboldened whereas those facing 2,000 decked out in riot gear will often disburse on their own volition.

- **Don't get ambushed**. Disturbances or obvious violations just outside your reach may be attempts to separate you from your support, lure you into the crowd, and set you up for attack. Don't get drawn in. Maintain the perimeter and push back. Don't get pulled into the middle and surrounded. In addition to physical entrapment, beware of video surveillance as well. Just about everyone has a camera on their smartphone or cell phone these days. Control your emotions; don't get caught doing something stupid on film.

- **Beware of "cop baiting."** Members of the crowd often go to great lengths to make officers angry, hoping for an overreaction that will play to the media. That's not only bad public relations but also a lawsuit begging to happen. In some areas, anarchists actually teach classes on how to make police officers look bad on camera. You can easily find such information on-line as well... Baiting can be aimed at any authority figure though, so bouncers, ushers, and security personnel need to be cautious of this tactic too. Give verbal commands telling the crowd to leave. Fair warning will help legitimize the use of reasonable force later on if it comes to that.

- **Control contact with the crowd**. Make initial contact on safe turf, avoiding spots where obvious troublemakers are already at work. You should determine when and where to intervene, formulating a strategy with your compatriots. When you decide to act, do so decisively but with diligent restraint. When they see troublemakers being immediately arrested and carted away, suggestibles are less likely to join in.

- **If they're going on their own, let them leave**. Don't forget that more often than not the crowd outnumbers you. If members want to leave, let them. Your goal is to minimize injuries and prevent property damage to the extent possible. If the crowd begins to disperse at your command, or on their own, it makes your job easier. Don't slow the process of people leaving by detaining minor violators. Always leave them an escape route. If otherwise law abiding people feel trapped they are likely to panic and lash out violently.

- **Make noise**. It often makes sense to approach a scene loudly (e.g., using sirens and lights). While sometimes such actions can escalate a situation, oftentimes followers will flee when they see the authorities coming. In such cases you will only need to deal with the hardcore rioters, individuals who will try to cause things to escalate no matter what you do. Aggressive noises, such as synchronized pounding of riot shields with batons, can be very intimidating and cause many crowd members to disperse on their own. Play to the audience and the news cameras, creating witnesses and managing the image you wish to present whenever possible.

- **Rely on the right equipment**. Having the right equipment and knowing when and how to use it is essential. You can be needlessly injured or unnecessarily forced to hurt others if improperly equipped. Make certain your vehicles and equipment are not trapped where the crowd can attack them, steal weapons, or cut you off from needed supplies. Have plenty of water available when using full gear as it can cause you to overheat even in cool temperatures.

Crowds can be dangerous, mobs more so, but forearmed with knowledge and awareness it's possible to navigate the hazards and escape unharmed much of the time… assuming you don't take unnecessary chances. Pay attention to the mood of the people around you, especially if something has been building for a while.

For example, during the Ferguson protest in Missouri Chris Schaefer, a University of Missouri-St. Louis student, was chased by a half a dozen other protesters from the Greater St. Mark Missionary Church where a meeting was taking place and beaten severely enough to require hospitalization. It really doesn't matter why this attack took place, the motive was reportedly that the victim was videotaping the crowd with his smartphone when others took offense, but there may have been racial or other components too. What matters most is that **after weeks of violent clashes with police, emotions were running high**. That's not the time to draw undue attention to yourself.

Sometimes the tension is based on a significant event such as in Ferguson, but other times it's an annual occurrence. May Day riots in Seattle are much like the seasonal flu outbreak, you know they are coming every year but **you just don't know how bad they will be**. Mass protests, violence, property damage, clashes with police, and arrests happen virtually every time. Sometimes the crowds get ugly quickly, other times it's a slow burn, but either way you know that it's going to spin out of control eventually. Some examples:

- In 2015 three officers were injured, 25 vehicles damaged, and 16 protesters arrested, including one who was found carrying a soda bottle filled with green paint, a wrench, and a machete painted with the word "death."
- In 2014 there were ten arrests, including one where an illicit firearm was recovered.
- In 2013 it was 18 arrests, including one where a large, fixed blade knife was confiscated, and eight officers were injured in the melee.
- In 2012 there was widespread property damage, broken windows, looting, a firebombing, and more than 70 weapons confiscated. Dozens of arrests were made throughout the day and late into the night, and four protesters were brought to trial afterward.

You get the idea… The May Day worker's rights rally has been an annual recurrence for quite some time, one that often devolves into violence. While the number of arrests might seem low, law enforcement is held on a very short leash by the mayor and city council (in part due to a Federal consent decree). Only the most egregious rioters are arrested and even fewer lawbreakers are prosecuted for their crimes afterward. Consequently these arrest statistics understate the severity of lawlessness that takes place (primarily in downtown Seattle and on Capitol Hill) every year.

When you know something like this is coming you can **make an informed choice of whether or not to be there** when it happens. Perusing the news might not be your thing, but the media can be your early warning system in certain circumstances. If you think trouble might be brewing it's useful to tune in from time to time to find out what's going on and plan your day accordingly.

CHAPTER 25

WORKING IT GANGLAND STYLE

"People are more violently opposed to fur than leather because it's safer to harass rich women than motorcycle gangs."

– Unknown

On May 17, 2015 members of the Bandidos and Cossacks motorcycle gangs met at a Twin Peaks restaurant in Waco, Texas to settle disputes over territory and recruitment. The discussion didn't end well. According to police reports an argument started in a bathroom where a fistfight quickly escalated to include brass knuckles, knives, chains, clubs, and handguns. Shots were fired both inside and outside the restaurant and the melee quickly spilled out into the parking lot. By the time it was over the scene was littered with bullet casings, bodies, and blood. Nine bikers were killed, 18 injured, and 170 arrested. Law enforcement officers found 319 weapons (including 118 handguns, 157 knives, and an AK-47 rifle) at the scene, some hidden in sacks of tortilla chips, stuffed into seat cushions, dropped into a toilet, or ditched elsewhere around the venue so that the gang members would appear unarmed when taken into custody. Parts of downtown Waco as well as the nearby hospital where the injured were transported were placed on lockdown to quell further violence.

"Our citizens are safe. I will tell you that we have had threats against law enforcement officers throughout the night from various biker groups. We are very aware that some of them have come into our city and we have a contingency plan to deal with those individuals if they try to cause trouble here," Sergeant W. Patrick Swanton told reporters afterward. "This is probably one of the most gruesome crime scenes I've ever seen in my 34 years of law enforcement. Within 25 feet there were families eating dinner... I was amazed that we didn't have innocent civilians killed or injured."

In a 2014 gang threat assessment, the Texas Department of Public Safety classified the Bandidos as a Tier 2 threat. They were formed in the 1960s, and are reported to be heavily involved in drug trafficking, selling illicit substances such as cocaine, marijuana, and methamphetamines. Other gangs in the second highest tier included the Bloods, Crips, and Aryan Brotherhood of Texas. The Cossacks were not listed in that report.

Kent Washington (near Seattle), July 23, 2011: It was a free low-rider show sponsored by *Lokos Music*. Fifty classic cars gleamed in the sunlight as a boisterous crowd wandered through the exhibition, enjoying live music while they took in the displays. All in all it was a pretty good show, a free, family-friendly way to spend the day. But for those who were paying attention, it began to take on an ominous vibe early in the afternoon.

Partygoers got nervous as they noticed groups of young men "mugging" each other. They weren't stealing anything, that's not what mugging means in this instance, but rather glaring threateningly, putting on testosterone theatre. The astute observers faded away, unobtrusively leaving the area, but most folks simply ignored the teens. After all, kids will be kids, right? But staring soon escalated to threatening, shoving, and fist fighting. Then gunshots rang out.

In the span of a few horrifying seconds, twelve people were hit. Victims ranging in ages from 14 to 32 were rushed to Harborview Medical Center. Later that night, a 13th person was injured in what police determined to be a retaliatory shooting by matching shell casings found at both scenes.

Suddenly a full-fledged gang war had broken out.

It really doesn't matter where you live, gangs are everybody's problem. According to the FBI there are more than a million gang members nationwide. Less than half of all gang-related crimes are reported to the police, so it's challenging to know the exact level of mayhem they cause. Nevertheless, these thugs are responsible for as much as 80 percent of crime in some communities. The King County Sheriff's Office estimates that there are 140 criminal street gangs that collectively comprise more than 10,000 members in Seattle, a city of a little over 653,000 people which has never been known as a gang paradise. While the overall crime rate has been steadily decreasing across the United States in recent years, gang-related crime has increased 165 percent since 2005. And that's just what has been reported...

Gangs are involved in everything from drug trafficking and manufacture to robbery, auto theft, carjacking, burglary, assault, rape, murder, kidnapping, weapons trafficking, arson, prostitution, fraud, identity theft, vandalism, money laundering, extortion, and human trafficking. Bangers carry the marks of violence with pride, comparing knife scars, bullet wounds, burns, and various disfigurements to prove how tough they are and augment their reputations.

 Firearms are the weapon of choice in about 10% of all violent crimes, whereas approximately 6% are committed with a knife or other sharp object (e.g., scissors, ice pick, or broken bottle); 4% with blunt objects (e.g., brick, bat, rock, or pipe), and 5% are committed with other objects (e.g., ropes, chains, poison, or martial arts weapons).

Criminal gangs are defined as groups of people who share a group name and identity, interact among themselves to the exclusion of others, claim a territory, create a climate of fear and intimidation within their domain, communicate in a unique style, wear distinctive clothing, and **engage in antisocial activities on a regular basis**. Members frequently utilize tattoos, scars, or cigarette burns to announce their affiliation. These markings are usually obvious, seen on the arms, neck, or chest, but can also be discreet such as wearing a tattoo inside the lower lip. Even their vehicles may be distinctive, with lowered frames, neon, excessive chrome, or tinted windows.

Unlike what many have been led to believe, gang membership crosses all racial, ethnic, social, and economic lines. **It is not just a "ghetto thing."** There are Asian gangs, black gangs, white gangs, Hispanic gangs, skinhead gangs, outlaw motorcycle gangs, and so on... These gangs include both umbrella groups and associated sets. Both **male and female gang members instigate violence, carry weapons, participate in crimes, and take leadership roles** within the organizations. While some youths seek gang affiliation to make up for parental abuse or neglect at home, others simply crave the lifestyle which is popularized in music, videos, movies, and television shows. Sex, drugs, money, and weapons can be glamorous to young people, especially teenaged males. Some people simply grow up in the wrong neighborhood or spend a bit of prison time and are forced to join a gang in order to survive. Regardless of how they get involved, the group becomes the member's surrogate family.

No matter what their affiliation, gang members hold three things preeminent:

4. **Respect**.
5. **Reputation**.
6. **Revenge**.

If you cross a gang member things will get ugly. Simply looking at one with the wrong expression ("mugging" or "mean mugging" as it is often called) can get you killed. Imagine a gangbanger's reaction to a more obvious sign of disrespect such as a derogatory comment, push, kick, or punch. However much respect you might feel you want or deserve the average gang member craves it tenfold. Gangbangers do everything they can to disrespect outsiders. Graffiti, hand signs, verbal challenges, stare-downs, and physical assaults are common. While typically targeted at rivals, innocent civilians can easily become victims or get caught in the middle such as what happened at the car show.

New gang members must pass through some form of initiation, often a violent one such as being beaten by other members, in order to join. As mentioned previously, this process is called "getting jumped in." It instills a sense of toughness and pride by those who survive. Gang reputations are made through violent antisocial actions, so new members are frequently required to commit a violent crime such as an assault, rape, or murder to earn their colors. Reputation is so important that gang bangers will even brag to the police, admitting crimes (or even making them up on occasion) in order to boost their status. For example, when a 25-year-old gang member was arrested after a club fight where a 36-year-old victim was beaten to death, he told the responding officers, "I got good elbows. People don't know about my elbows." He later pled guilty to negligent homicide when it was determined that an elbow to the head had caused his victim's fatal trauma.

Because gangbangers often do not expect to have a long-term future, **they tend live in the moment, doing whatever they feel like without regard to consequences**. Many do not expect to live past the age of twenty-five. That can seem like a pretty long time if you get jumped into the gang at the age of thirteen or fourteen.

Revenge is a huge deal with gangs. If a gang member feels disrespected or thinks that his reputation has been harmed, retribution will certainly follow. If it does not, he'll get knocked down a peg or two, beaten, disgraced, or possibly even killed by his associates. Consequently, no assault or insult can be left unanswered, no matter how small. Wearing the wrong colors, traveling in the wrong area, or gazing with an unsuitable expression can bring same type of retribution such as a rape, murder, or physical assault. While this vengeance is often swift, that is not always the case. Asian gangs, for example, sometimes talk about the "100-year revenge," patiently waiting for the right opportunity to strike.

If it comes to a fight, however, individual gang members tend not to be all that much of a problem for skilled martial artists. There are exceptions, of course, but unless they're fresh out of prison gangbangers tend not to work out or train all that much, hence can be either meth-skinny or McDonald's-fat based on lifestyle factors. **But, if you think you are "bad" enough to take on a gang member, you are downright stupid**. The challenge isn't fighting the individual, but rather that if you get into an altercation with an individual in reality you've just taken on the whole group even though you may not know it yet. That doesn't end well. Nevertheless, there are a variety of things you can do to stay safe. Here are some tips:

- **Don't be there**. Nine out of ten dangers can be identified and avoided by exercising good situational awareness. Yeah, we keep saying that but it's that important. It's easy to get to know the normal vibe of areas where you live and work, so if something looks, feels, smells, or sounds "wrong," pay attention. If you sense danger or see others reacting to something hazardous you cannot see, leave. If you're not there when trouble starts, you cannot get hurt.

- **Blend into the background**. Don't draw attention to yourself. If you're a law abiding citizen the chances are reasonable that you will not have not have problems with gang members since you operate in different circles than they do, but don't forget that they have self-identified as operating beyond the law hence can be very dangerous. Don't make yourself an obvious target. If you see a fight starting, leave. If you spot a drug deal in progress, leave. If you see a group of guys dripping color or flashing gang signs, walk away. Avoid dangerous people, situations, and locations whenever possible.

- **Plan your day**. If you need to use an ATM, the one inside a crowded grocery store is much safer than a standalone kiosk, especially at night. If you need to get gas, doing so during rush hour makes a lot more sense than at 2:00 in the morning. As you travel, be cognizant of areas and times best avoided and plan your routes accordingly, even if it takes longer. A little common sense can save you a lot of grief.

- **Avoid public transportation, especially at night**. Yeah it's "green," but it's also damnably dangerous in many areas. Unless you know that the entire route you plan to take is safe, well patrolled, or both, use a car or take an Uber. As mentioned previously, if you're assaulted on a bus or train there's no place to escape to. Gang members often ride public transportation to airports where they steal cars from one of the long-term parking lots and drive away since they know folks are unlikely to notice for several days. These vehicles can then be used for drive-by shootings, strong arm robberies and the like. They have also been known to assault or rob folks on the train or bus, as well as those in the airport parking lot as targets of convenience (especially those leaving the airport as they are virtually never armed due to TSA security rules).

- **Learn how to make proper eye contact**. Locking eyes with someone can be perceived as challenging. This is not a good thing generally, but it can be especially bad when gang members are involved. Nevertheless, breaking eye contact can cause problems too. If you look up it is considered dismissive, a sign of arrogance. If you look down, it's weak, indicating you're a victim. Always break contact by looking sideways; it's the least threatening action.

Finally, **let the professionals handle it**. No matter what you see happening around you, if you do not need to get involved, don't. You can report crimes anonymously, of course, but don't physically interfere unless your life or that of a loved one is in danger. It's not that you can't handle the situation necessarily, but rather that if you do there may be long term repercussions for doing so. In most jurisdictions law enforcement has gang units specifically trained to deal with these crimes.

CHAPTER 26

WAR IS TERRORISM?

"War is Terrorism!"
    – Bumper sticker seen in downtown Seattle, WA.

Amine El Khalifi was carrying an automatic weapon and a suicide vest laced with explosives when he was arrested near the US Capitol in Washington, DC on February 17, 2012. The 29-year-old Moroccan-born illegal immigrant was stopped by law enforcement and taken into custody. News reports indicate that El Khalifi has been under investigation for over a year and had discussed a number of targets with undercover FBI agents, including military installations, US Army generals, a restaurant, and several synagogues before deciding to attack US Capitol. The arrest was the culmination of a lengthy and extensive undercover operation during which El Khalifi was closely monitored and his weapons clandestinely rendered inoperable. This was the 45th (publicly known) attempted terrorist attack against the United States since 9/11 and the sixth such attack targeting Washington, DC.

On April 25, 2015 Boko Haram terrorists raided the Nigerian settlement of Karamga Island, massacring soldiers who guarded the town before turning their guns on civilians. Residents fled for their lives, many jumping into Lake Chad to escape. Those who could not escape were shot or burned to death by the Islamists. Umar Yerima, a fisherman who lived on the island told reporters:

"The troops were caught off guard. After finishing with the soldiers, the terrorists turned their guns on residents. Some sought to escape by plunging into the lake but gunmen stood on the shore shooting them. They would aim their gun from the edge of the lake and shoot any head that emerged from the water, shouting *Allahu Akbar*. They burnt the entire village and went on a shooting spree. Many residents were burnt alive in their homes."

Yerima managed to stay out of sight by hiding in the long grass that lines the water's edge, where he witnessed the entire massacre. He also saw the Islamists kidnap a number of women and children before leaving the village with their hostages. The Boko Haram insurgency has led to the deaths of more than 13,000 people since 2009, mostly in northern Nigeria, though fighting has increasingly spread to neighboring states since 2013.

Is war is terrorism like the bumper sticker asserts? Seriously?! We hate to break it to you, but war is most definitely not terrorism. The two words have very different meanings. Those who wage war operate under very different rules of engagement and try to achieve very different aims than those who commit acts of terror. As much as it pains us we need to break these down, we feel that it's important to do so in order to help folks better prepare to defend themselves against a growing and ubiquitous threat.

At least fifty known terror attacks on the United States were thwarted between the successful September 11, 2001 attacks and the death of Osama bin Laden on May 2, 2011. While 3 of the 50 plots were foiled by luck or the quick action of the American public, the remaining 47 were thwarted due to the concerted efforts of the intelligence and law enforcement communities.

A simple and not totally inclusive way to look at war is as **an armed conflict between countries**. The main attribute of war is state-sanctioning of the conflict. In other words, there is necessary political component—you're fighting for a country, an administration, a policy, so you don't lose by being completely destroyed by the adversary but rather by losing the political will to continue. The Vietnam War was an example of that; despite having a significant advantage in technology, firepower, and personnel, the United States lost the will to continue fighting and abandoned the conflict.

Armed disputes between governments often lead to widespread destruction and enormous mortality rates, yet the so-called rules of war that most combatants follow such as the Geneva Convention outline what actions are on or off the table tactically. For example, since the end of World War I chemical and biological weapons have not been allowed to be brought into the fight (by signatories of the Geneva Convention, obviously). As technology progresses there are fewer and fewer unintended collateral impacts such as wanton destruction of civilians or property. Civilians *may* be killed in the conflict, of course, but attempts are made to **limit casualties exclusively to armed combatants**.

Terrorism, on the other hand, is the use of **violent acts to attempt to frighten people into compliance with** an individual or group's **religious, political, or social objective**.[32] Anything is on the table, including turning women and children into human weapons (e.g., suicide bombers), chemical, biological, radiological, and even nuclear weapons (if they can be obtained). Rather than (or in addition to) armed combatants, **civilians are often targeted directly**.

While war is based in part on the idea that one country has the horsepower to pound the other back into the Stone Age, terrorism doesn't even have a pony let alone a horse. But, it doesn't need one. Superior equipment and personnel are unnecessary because **terrorism can be carried out by a handful of dedicated individuals who are willing to perform asynchronous actions against others**. Since terrorists are often ideologically driven, killing or capturing leaders of the cause does not necessarily mean victory. In fact, in certain circumstances martyrs benefit the cause more than their deaths impair it.

War is full out, power slamming against power, the magnitude of the effort is almost beyond measure when it moves from nation against nation and erupts on a global scale. The bigger the conflict, the greater the opportunity for things to get truly ugly. The rules of war can fall by the wayside when troops on the battlefield choose to disregard them… As an example, it is suspected that in excess of some 200,000 Germans were raped by Soviet troops after the collapse of Berlin in 1945. Mayhem ruled and vengeance was on the menu, yet no one to our knowledge was prosecuted for this atrocity. It wasn't just the Soviets who lost their cool; when the US Troops seized the Nazi concentration camp in Dachau, Germany they were shocked to discover railway cars full of emaciated corpses and in their horror promptly turned their guns on the German guards after they had surrendered. The guards they killed were actually newly assigned Waffen-SS troops conscripted by the Nazi government to submit to the Allied forces. These conscripts weren't actually the ones who had committed the atrocities that took place in Dachau, yet nobody stood on charges for their murder.

Those incidents took place as the war was winding down, but let's talk about a few events that took place earlier on for a moment. For example, the World War II bombings of Dresden Germany and Tokyo Japan were some of the most horrific bombardments of civilian populations in the history of man, in part due to inaccuracy of the targeting technology of the day which led to mass or "carpet" bombing runs in order to help assure destruction of planned targets (and virtually everything around them). After bombing Germany it is reported that the Royal Air Force (RAF) bomber crews were eschewed by their fellow aviators because they smelled of burnt human

---

32 The US Code (18 U.S.C. § 2331) defines terrorism (both domestic and international) as involving violent acts or acts dangerous to human life that violate federal or state law that appear to be intended to intimidate or coerce a civilian population, to influence the policy of a government by intimidation or coercion, or to affect the conduct of a government by mass destruction, assassination, or kidnapping.

flesh. They flew low enough that the undersides of their aircraft became covered in human soot. If you've ever gotten a whiff of burning hair, multiply that by a thousand-fold and you'll have an inkling of what that must have smelled like.

Air Force Major General Curtis Lemay was the mastermind of incendiary bombings of Japan during the war. Japanese cities in those days were constructed almost exclusively of wood, so firebombing meant that the majority of civilians caught in the conflict were burned to death, one of the most horrific and painful ways to go we can imagine. The causality reports were collated by Robert McNamara, who later became the US Secretary of Defense. After looking at one of the reports from the previous night's bombing runs where some 30,000 Japanese died, legend states that Lemay turned to McNamara and stated, "You better hope we win this war or we are both going to be tried as war criminals." After the victory Lemay went on to enter politics as a Vice-Presidential Candidate in 1968.

Clearly modern conflicts have far less collateral impact, civilian deaths, and wanton destruction as those that took place during World Wars I and II. Advances in technology, smart bombs, missile guidance systems, forward observers, and the like allow many countries to target their foes with pinpoint accuracy. Everyone does not have that ability, of course, but many do. Even those that do not tend to pursue tactics that limit noncombatant deaths. As you can see, **war is sanctioned by the state and targets military personnel and infrastructure**. Regardless of what takes place on the battlefield, however, in most instances whoever wins gets to write the rules about what happens to the losers.

Terrorism is different.

In 1972, terrorism landed on the United States of America via then West Germany… and traveled into our homes via our television sets. At the height of the Cold War the Olympics were magic. As young kids we watched as America's best went head-to-head with the communists in athletic competition to prove who was better. Yeah, other countries participated too, of course, but it was the US and USSR who took center stage. Until terrorism struck. In the summer of 1972, **eleven Israeli Olympic team members were taken hostage by the Palestinian terror group Black September**. Black September demanded that 234 jailed Palestinians held in Israel be set free. When their demands were not met, the terrorists **killed every hostage** (along with a German police officer who got caught up in the fighting). As kids the geopolitical battle in the Middle East made no sense, none of it made any sense. We asked our parents, "Why would these people want to capture others in order to torture and kill them?"

Thirteen years later in 1985, four hijackers from the Palestine Liberation Front (PLF) boarded the cruise ship Achille Lauro off the coast of Egypt. Leo Klinghoffer, a 69-year-old retiree was celebrating his 36th wedding university with his wife Marilyn. The PLF took control of the cruise ship and demanded the release of 50 Palestinians who were being held in an Israeli prison. To demonstrate that they meant business they shot Klinghoffer as he sat helplessly in his wheelchair and then rolled his body into the sea.

Terrorism often attacks symbols. The Twin Towers in New York City symbolized the power of the United States on the stage of world commerce, which is why they were attacked on 9/11. The Israeli Olympians where the best and brightest that Israel had to offer and the Olympic Games provided the stage to demonstrate to the world that even the best can come under the thumb of terrorism. Klinghoffer's death was a demonstration that even the weak, the elderly are targets, that the terrorist's objectives knew no bounds. One of the terrorists who the PLF demanded be released from jail was Samir Kuntar, who had among other things killed a four-year-old girl by smashing her head with the butt of his rifle and a large rock.

The context of war is so massive that hundreds of thousands of people can die brutal and unfair deaths, or suffer many other atrocities. Despite this, the tactics that terrorism uses makes their actions even more horrific. **Terrorists are savages**, in some cases genocidal ones. Civilians are routinely targeted. Joyous and somber events alike, such as weddings and funerals, get shot-up or blown-up **in an effort to deliver mass casualties**. While war takes an enormous budget and has governmental checks, balances, and oversight, **terrorism takes very little resources and writes its own rules**. The planes that Al Qaeda flew into the World Trade Center and the Pentagon were hijacked by a few dedicated terrorists with box cutters.

United States General George Patton is supposed to have said this, or a variation of it, to inspire his troops:

> "I want you to remember that no bastard ever won a war by dying for his county. He won it by making the other poor, dumb bastard die for his."

Terrorists believe that dying for their cause if just fine and dandy. However it is important that the idea of dying for the cause applies to the lower ranks of the organizations. You never see the terrorist leaders strapping one on (so to speak) for the team. **We called terrorists savages but it's important to realize that they see us through the same eyes**. It's very difficult to wage war against someone you see as human, so terrorists must "other" those they wish to destroy in order to make it easier. In the case of Islamic radicals like Al Qaeda, Islamic State (ISIS/ISIL), Boko Haram, and their brethren, well their God tells them you must die. There is no higher calling than to destroy the infidel, it is nonnegotiable. It's not just radicalized Muslims who want to kill you though; terrorists come in all sizes, shapes, and flavors. A few examples include Euskadi Ta Askatasuna (ETA), Fuerzas Armadas Revolucionarias De Colombia (FARC), Kahane Chai, Real Irish Republican Army (RIRA), and Shining Path.

In some parts of the world terrorists have pretty much taken over, such as the Nigerian example with Boko Haram that we used above, or Islamic State who they have allied themselves with in much of the Middle East, but what about here? Why should we worry about what happens thousands of miles or half a world away?

Between 2001 and 2012 there were **more than 50 attempted terrorist attacks against the United States** (that we know of) **that were thwarted**. A few examples:

- **Richard Reid**. The "shoe bomber" attempted to blow up an airplane with explosives hidden in his shoes but was thwarted by fellow passengers. He was convicted and sentenced to life in prison.
- **Jose Padilla**. A disciple of Khalid Sheikh Mohammed, the mastermind of 9/11, who attempted to set off a dirty bomb (explosives laced with radioactive materials) in the United States. He was convicted and sentenced to 17 years and four months in prison.
- **Virginia Jihad Network**. Eleven men with connections to Al Qaeda and the Taliban were arrested on illegal weapons charges and convicted of plotting attacks in the United States. Their ring leader Ali al-Timimi was sentenced to life in prison while his co-conspirators were sentenced to terms ranging from three-years-and-10 months to 15 years in prison.
- **Dhiron Barot**. Barot and seven members of his terrorist cell were convicted of plotting an attack on the New York Stock Exchange and other financial institutions. He pled guilty and was sentenced to 30 years in prison. His co-conspirators were sentenced to terms ranging from 15 to 26 years in prison.
- **Michael C. Reynolds**. Reynolds was arrested for plotting to blow up a Wyoming natural gas refinery, the Transcontinental Pipeline, and a Standard Oil Refinery in New Jersey. He was convicted and sentenced to 30 years in prison.
- **The Fort Dix Six**. After a 16-month FBI operation that included infiltrating the group, six men were arrested and convicted of planning to assault and kill US soldiers with at Fort Dix with rifles and grenades. They received sentences ranging from 20 months to life-plus-30-years in jail.
- **Michel Finton**. Finton was arrested for planning to detonate a car bomb containing close to a ton of explosives outside the Paul Findley Federal Building and Courthouse in Springfield, Illinois. He pled guilty and was sentenced to 28 years in prison.
- **Umar Farouk Abdulmutallab**. The "underwear bomber" attempted to bring down an airplane with a bomb hidden in his skivvies but was subdued by other passengers. He was sentenced to life in prison.

Even if you don't remember hearing about these specific examples, it's easy to see that terrorism now lives on our flat-screen televisions, our car radios, and our smartphones whenever we choose to peruse the news. More recently on May 6, 2015 Islamic State took credit via social media postings for an attack on the "Draw the Prophet" contest in Garland, Texas the previous weekend where two men (Elton Simpson and Nadir Soofi) with rifles wounded a security guard but were quickly shot and killed by a nearby police officer. Here is an excerpt that gives you the gist of what the terrorist organization posted:

> "Two soldiers of the Caliphate attacked an exhibit in Garland in American Texas, and this exhibit was holding a contest for drawings offensive to the prophet Muhammad... The disbelievers who shot our brothers think that you killed someone untrained, nay, they gave you their bodies in plain view because we were watching. Out of the 71 trained soldiers 23 have signed up for missions like Sunday, we are increasing in number. Of the 15 states [with IS infiltrators], five we will name... Virginia, Maryland, Illinois, California, and Michigan... We tell America that what is coming will be even bigger and more bitter, and that you will see the soldiers of the Islamic State do terrible things."

Whether or not Islamic State ordered or inspired the violence, their posting is clearly a threat of future attacks, one we need to take seriously. This leads to the obvious question: **What do you need to do in order to be safe?**

Well first we all need to **acknowledge that the terror threat is real and not likely to go away anytime soon**. We do not intend to provide a breakdown of the sociological, moral, or theological reasons that terrorism exists, we'll leave that to others. We are also not here to tell the world how to defend against terrorists on a geopolitical scale either; there are policy professionals in government who have that job. We are, however, here to make it personal, to point out how you can **make a difference in your own personal safety** and that of your loved ones. Some things you can do:

- **Pay attention**. We have already covered behavioral profiling and situational awareness in other chapters, though clearly those principles apply here as well. Pay attention to what's going on around you, looking for pattern disruptions, unusual things that warrant closer attention. Retreat to a safe location and call authorities if you identify a threat or potential threat.
- **Carry a weapon**. Yeah, we keep saying that, but compare the *Charlie Hebdo* magazine attack in France (January 7, 2015) with the similar event in Texas (March 6, 2015). The

first was a massacre in which eight journalists, a caretaker, and a visitor were murdered because nobody was armed, hence could not fight back, whereas the second barely even got started before the perpetrators were shot and killed. You can't take on two guys carrying AK-47s without a weapon of your own and expect to prevail.

- **Travel safe**. Hits on the homeland are tougher to pull off than attacks on Westerners who travel abroad. You can find information from government websites such as the US State Department as well as private organizations such as Stratfor Global Intelligence which provide in-depth geopolitical analysis and insight into regions you may need to travel to for business or pleasure. Routinely read these briefings as you make your plans and you'll be far safer for it.

- **Keep a low profile**. Carrying a passport from a Western country (especially the US), using American money, and speaking American-accented English can make you a target overseas. Certain clothing or shoes that proclaim your country of origin can do that too. For example, most Europeans don't wear shorts or sneakers except when participating in athletic activities. Ball caps and sweatshirts advertising American sports teams can make you stand out in a dangerous way. Similarly, certain hotels are known hangouts for Westerners. If there is an elevated threat level and you cannot avoid a trip to a dangerous region consider carefully where to stay, how to dress, and how to act to keep as low a profile as possible.

- **Have both a shelter-in-place and a bailout plan**. The odds of being targeted directly are smaller than the odds of being hit by a collateral impact if the worst happens in your area, be it at home or abroad. Take a dirty bomb, for example. Anyone who survives the initial explosion will need to get away quickly to avoid fallout. Again, we already discussed this in more detail in Chapter 18, but it is vital to have plans and supplies in case you suddenly need to shelter in place or bail out due to a terrorist attack. Be sure to include pets in your plans as they're frequently not allowed in government run shelters or private hotels.

- **Establish a meeting place and communications plan**. In a dire emergency phone lines may be down and cell towers overloaded, so figure out where and how to meet members of your family if you cannot connect by phone. This is especially important if you have children in school or daycare in one area and work or live in another. You may need to choose both primary and secondary locations in case key infrastructure components such as bridges or tunnels are compromised or inaccessible. Once you are able to meet you can implement the shelter-in-place or bailout plan you have already created.

In addition to what we've written above, **always be prepared for evasion and escape**. Some terror attacks hit targets of opportunity, but others are well-funded, well-planned, and carefully coordinated efforts. If you suddenly hear or see gunfire, explosions, or other indications of a terror attack, you are almost always better off being somewhere else as quickly as possible unless you are so close to the action that attacking back keeps you safer. Most of us who practice martial arts want to be heroes, to use our skills for the greater good. We gave an example of a waiter stopping a lone suicide bomber earlier, but against a coordinated band of terrorists our odds of successfully intervening are very, very low. Keep that in mind when you decide how or if to act. Also know that a common terrorist tactic is to set off a bomb, be it in a vehicle or strapped on a person, and then follow up with another attack on first responders as they arrive. So, **just because an attack seems to be over doesn't mean that it truly is concluded**. In many instances you are far better off taking the better part of valor, getting the hell out of harm's way, alerting the authorities, and letting somebody better armed, armored, trained, and prepared deal with the situation.

While many folks watch the news from time to time, most of us are not political junkies. Unfortunately safety from terrorism includes **paying careful attention to the geopolitics in your area**. If the government begins breaking down and terrorists gain a foothold similar to what has taken place in Syria, Iraq, Nigeria, Yemen, and many other countries, your best bet is finding somewhere else to live. For example, Lawrence's grandfather and uncle escaped Russia just after Bolshevik Revolution, arrived penniless, and started new lives in America. Other relatives who could not or would not leave were murdered at the hands of the communists. **When the winds of change begin to blow the wrong way, it is vital to get out of Dodge**. If you recognize the threat too late… well, it'll often be too late to do anything about it.

We'll leave you with the words of Pastor Martin Niemöller (1892 – 1984), as displayed at The United States Holocaust Memorial Museum:

> "First they came for the Socialists, and I did not speak out because I was not a Socialist. Then they came for the Trade Unionists, and I did not speak out because I was not a Trade Unionist. Then they came for the Jews, and I did not speak out because I was not a Jew. Then they came for me… and there was no one left to speak for me."

Hopefully we'll never face a threat of that magnitude, but what has happened once can certainly happen again. As the old saying goes, those who fail to learn from history are doomed to repeat it. Pay close attention to what's going on and plan accordingly.

CHAPTER 27

Brave Sir Robin and Nike-do

"Brave Sir Robin ran away. Bravely ran away, away! When danger reared its ugly head, he bravely turned his tail and fled. Yes, brave Sir Robin turned about and gallantly he chickened out. Bravely taking to his feet, he beat a very brave retreat, bravest of the brave, Sir Robin!"

– Monty Python

On October 31, 2003 attorney Gerry Curry was walking in front of the Van Nuys courthouse in California when a stranger approached him.

"Are you Mr. Curry?" the man asked.

"Yes, who are you?" the attorney replied.

Suddenly Curry heard a loud pop and blood splattered across his face. He hadn't seen the other man's gun, but Curry immediately realized that he'd been shot. Luckily, the 55-year-old attorney was neither killed nor severely disabled by the initial attack and had the presence of mind to flee to the dubious shelter of a nearby tree, the only solid object close by. Wounded and bleeding, Curry frantically ducked and dodged, trying to keep the medium-sized tree between him and a continuing barrage of bullets. This quick thinking and use of cover ultimately saved his life. When his assailant finally ran out of ammunition, he was tackled and arrested by an off-duty sheriff's deputy.

A cameraman at the scene for another trial caught the whole incident on film where it made headline news across the country for weeks afterward. Footage of Curry frantically dodging around a tree as his distraught attacker, 64-year-old William Strier, chased after him firing shot after shot from a revolver not only captivated television audiences, but also poignantly pointed out the value of running for self-defense.

Afterward Curry discovered that his assailant was furious that the attorney was going to be paid from his trust fund for representing Evelyn Murphy, a trustee whom he claimed was withholding money he needed for medical care. The wounded lawyer was shot five times in his right arm, where doctors told him there was some muscle, tendon, and nerve damage. He also had a bullet lodged in the back of his neck which surprisingly turned out to be non-life-threatening. "Physically, I'm doing pretty good," Curry told the press from his hospital bed afterward.

It is important to always be prepared and able to escape, evade, or fight for your life. The Curry/Strier incident described above took place in a usually quiet neighborhood in the middle of the day. In front of a courthouse. This is not exactly the sort of location where one would normally expect shootings to occur. Preparation includes not only the obvious stuff like staying in shape and exercising good situational awareness, but also things many people do not think about like wearing clothing and footwear that allows you to run at full speed, knowing the areas you operate in so that you won't become trapped, and using the restroom in a timely manner so that you don't urinate or defecate all over yourself under adrenal stress. Not only is that embarrassing, but it can also slow you down or leave a trail for others to follow too.

The tactic of running from danger is a practical way of saving your ass when things get ugly, though all too many martial artists and tough guy wannabes have a hard time wrapping their heads around evasion and escape as a legitimate tactic. We consider the "Brave Sir Robin defense," sometimes known as "Nike-do," a valid and reliable option in violent encounters. Sometimes you do have to fight, at least long enough to deal with the immediate threat, but as soon as practicable **running like hell is a far better alternative to sticking around and slugging it out with a bad guy**, especially one who's highly skilled, armed, or brought friends to the fight.

Running can be good, but when you sense trouble brewing, subtlety is usually your best initial reaction. Fast or big movements **might draw unwanted attention** to you or ignite a smoldering situation. Running from an aggressive dog, for example, might cause him to chase you, while moving away calmly may allow you to escape. The same thing often goes for dealing with thugs on the street. What you do about it must match the tactical situation you find yourself in:

- **Take the better part of valor and leave**. Be aware and leave an area if trouble seems to be brewing.
- **Listen to your instincts**. Walk away normally if you only have a "feeling" that things are not right.
- **Evade when you can**. Evade potential or developing threats by crossing the street, turning and walking back the way you came from, turning down another street, or

otherwise moving toward a safer location. If you misinterpret the threat no biggie, but if trouble follows it will quickly become obvious.

- **Calmly slip away when you are able**. If actual trouble becomes apparent, move away from it quickly but calmly, heading for a safe place or source of assistance.
- **Run like hell if you must**. If the trouble starts after you, run away swiftly. We'll talk tactics of evasion and escape in a moment.

In addition to the steps above, it is oftentimes useful to call attention to your predicament by yelling for help. This tactic can be used for denying privacy to the bad guy, soliciting help from friendly bystanders, and creating witnesses who will realize who the good guy is if you need to go hands on. Shouting "he's got a knife[33]" or similar attention-getting phrases appropriate to your situation works much better than any generic cry for help. It demonstrates that you were under true peril and clarifies the danger, hence tells witnesses why you had to act. As mentioned previously, fighting with your voice is a very commonly overlooked and underappreciated tactic, but it can distract or disrupt an adversary, create witnesses who may be favorable to your cause, or set yourself up for success if you wind up in civil or criminal court for whatever you have to do in order to fight your way to safety.

Once you are prepared to react to a potentially violent encounter it is important to plan what you will do. Simply running is not good enough, **it must be done strategically**. There are two elements to this:

1. **Evasion**. This means avoiding or dealing with the immediate threat.
2. **Escape**. This gets you away to safety.

Marc MacYoung wrote:

> "Before you consider doing anything else, your first priority is to neutralize the threat! You do what you need to keep from getting hurt by the particular attack. This does not mean you immediately start pounding on someone until he is flat. Nor does it mean you immediately run like hell. It means, before you even consider anything else, you make sure your ass is safe from the specific attack!"

---

33 Interestingly, in studies conducted by the Force Sciences Institute witnesses often perceived a knife even when there wasn't actually one present because one party to the conflict yelled for help in a manner that pointed to a specific, albeit fabricated, peril.

As the quote above points out, **evasion deals with the immediate threat strategically**. If there is a weapon or multiple attackers involved you need to both move and counterattack in a way that simultaneously puts you in a stronger position and neutralizes the threat. Even one-on-one that's prudent. Once the immediate danger has passed, you have the choice of sticking around and continuing the fight or running away and escaping. In some cases escape may be your only viable option. Other times, such as if you find yourself having to defend someone very young, elderly, or disabled who cannot escape with you, it may not be an option at all.

If you decide to beat feet once the immediate threat has been dealt with, you not only need to get away but also must find a way to keep the bad guy(s) from deciding to chase you. If that doesn't work and they start to follow, you will need to keep him or her from catching up. If possible, you further want to discourage him from coming after you again. Sadly, **in self-defense it's rarely over when it's over**… The primary ways this is accomplished is by either disabling your adversaries or by distracting them long enough that you can get out of their line of sight or develop an insurmountable lead.

If you are part of a group and find yourselves in a hazardous situation, the best policy is that either you **all run at once or everyone stays to fight**. Running away together, even if you flee in opposite directions, leaves no one in a tight spot. If the person you were counting on to cover your back flees, on the other hand, you could be in a world of hurt. Similarly, you should not leave your friends to the wolves either. Whether you are in a group or working alone, you can use distraction, disruption, or destruction. For example, knocking one guy out with a single punch may well give the rest pause and keep them from going after you. Alternately, attacking the feet, ankles, or knees of an assailant in order to temporarily disable him will give you a head start for running away. No matter what you do, always use your highest percentage techniques, those things you are truly skilled at performing, which are most likely to disable the attacker and facilitate your escape.

Your number one goal must be not getting hurt. If there is more than one adversary you must do your best to avoid becoming entangled with any single attacker long enough that his/her buddies can join in the fray. Beyond that, the way in which you escape is dependent upon how many attackers there are, how badly they want to catch you, and the tactical situation you encounter (e.g., terrain, bystanders). If you encounter a couple of thugs looking to make a quick buck, they should be relatively easy to distract and escape from, especially if you throw something valuable their way before you run, which is why Lawrence always carries some bills in a money clip when he travels.[34]

---

34 A friend of ours who travels internationally regularly carries a second, throwaway wallet with expired membership cards, dumb credit cards (the fake ones that come with offers you get in the mail) and a few dollars. He also carries a pocket full of coins and small notes to get rid of street kids who pester Westerners in certain countries.

Thankfully, most thugs you encounter on the street are not motivated to chase you beyond a certain distance. Nevertheless, you need to get to a place of safety. It is vital to move in ways that keep as few adversaries as possible in striking distance. **If you get tied up by engaging in combat, others may have time to join in before you can end the battle**. The longer you keep out of their hands, the more likely they will be to give up, a great argument for regular aerobic conditioning as part of your normal workout routine.

Dragging stuff into pursuer's way, dodging around obstacles, over fences, or through hedges, or otherwise slowing them down is a good way to string your pursuers out, facilitating your ability to escape successfully. If you can get a big enough lead you may be able to lose your pursuers completely, find somewhere safe to hide, convince you're the bad guys to give up, or reach a place of safety where they dare not follow (e.g., police station, hospital, fire station, crowded public place with CCTV cameras). As you run, look for shops you can duck through, fences you can climb over, gaps in hedges you can worm through, and other bottlenecks where only a single person can slip through at a time. Be careful about climbing anything though. Unless your pursuers are a good distance behind you, slowing your forward progress long enough to overcome an obstacle may let them close too much of the gap you have created. After all, **in the time it takes you to scale a ten- to twelve-foot fence a pursuer can cover twenty to fifty feet** of territory, depending on how adept at scaling you are and how fast a runner he is. If he or she can grab your legs before you make it over the top, you are in a world of hurt. Not only have you been captured, but also you will undoubtedly be slammed onto the ground as you are dragged off the fence you were trying to climb, which can do significant damage.

If you know your neighborhood and are friendly with the local canine population, hopping fences can provide and extra level of safety, assuming the dogs will leave you alone and harass your pursuers, of course. If you have a choice, going over a fence at the corner where four yards meet is an excellent location. That way, if you choose unwisely and the dog or neighbor is not as friendly as you expected, it is just a short hop into a safer yard. In areas that are less familiar to you, you must be especially cautious about what is on the other side of a fence, however. If you cannot see through the fence, you may wish to choose an alternate route. After all, it would not do to hop over a fence only to discover an angry Rottweiler, land in an empty pool, become entangled in thorny rosebushes, or break your ankle from an unexpectedly long drop.

Crossing a busy street is another good way to escape pursuers. To be most successful, be sure to run parallel to traffic, choosing your best moment to act before crossing. If there are multiple lanes, you can implement this run parallel and then cross methodology for each lane. If you have ever played the video game "Frogger," the real-life strategy works similarly. Cars and trucks hit a whole lot harder than feet and fists so be cautious about your timing and angle of approach. It may even be useful to point where you intend to run to give oncoming drivers a heads-up, sort of like the hand signals that bicyclists and motorcyclists use. Don't worry about your pursuers spotting your signals; they'll figure out what you are planning anyway. If you time things right you'll still be safe and the oncoming traffic will slow your pursuers facilitating your ability to escape.

If someone is chasing you in a car, he or she can travel a whole lot faster than you can. He can also use it as a weapon to squash you. Be sure to cut ninety degrees at your first opportunity, bolting between parked cars, through any convenient business, housing complex, narrow alley, or other area that the pursuing vehicle cannot easily pass through. **Travel a couple of blocks then change directions again so that your pursuers cannot simple go around the block and catch sight of you all over again.** Be cautious if you see or hear some of your pursuers leaving the vehicle because they may be able to split into more than one search party. Knowing that they have done so will influence which directions will remain available for escape.

Once you have made your initial escape it may be time to hide. Hiding, as most of us learn during our childhood playing hide-and-seek is a bit of an art form. **Try not to hide anywhere that you cannot escape from quickly** if your pursuers stumble across you. People in general are good at spotting human-shaped forms regardless of the surrounding terrain and are extremely good at spotting other people's eyes. Ditches, rooftops, woods, vehicles, and a whole host of obstacles can make good temporary hiding places. Be cautious about your silhouette, however. Do your best to keep your arms and legs tucked in behind cover, hunch as necessary to disguise your profile, and be careful not to stare at pursuers if they get close. Odd as it may seem, **many folks can feel the weight of your gaze** and may notice you because of it.

Be sure to hide somewhere you can rapidly flee from if your pursuers ultimately do find you again. Hiding in a dumpster, under a vehicle, or in a blind alley can be dangerous. **While you might get away with it, these are fairly obvious hiding places**—ones that might attract attention and additional scrutiny if there is nowhere else to which you could logically have continued to run. Further, they are all places that **take time to extricate yourself from**. If your pursuers catch up to you and you cannot escape quickly enough, you are back to evading or fighting your way clear once again. Trying to fight your way out of a dumpster or from under a vehicle is problematic at best.

Running is a good idea virtually all the time, even if the bad guy has a gun. There aren't reliable statistics we could find, but anecdotal evidence and expert experiences state that **only two to four percent of people who run from gun-wielding assailants actually die.** This is both because **it's hard to hit a moving target** and because oftentimes what the assailant is really looking for is a compliant victim who he can take to a secondary crime scene. In such instances it is lower risk to let the person go than it is to pull the trigger and draw attention to himself in the process.

If you're going to run from a gunman, or anyone else for that matter, **it is imperative to run toward something or someplace safer**. Running at an angle to the shooter toward cover gets you to safety faster than zigzagging or otherwise dodging around. This advice is based on the theory that the farther from your attacker you can get the safer you will be, which is certainly statistically true, so distance is the most important attribute of safety. If the gunman attempts to chase you rather than standing his/her ground and firing, experience shows that it is nearly impossible to hit anything when both the shooter and the target are moving even for trained law enforcement officers who are generally better shots than most criminals or ordinary civilians. Unless the other guy is a trained sniper, in which case all bets are off…

Right-handed shooters are almost universally better at tracking and hitting moving targets that move from right to left rather than vice versa. Whether you do choose to zigzag or run straight toward your objective, your best bet would initially be to move from left to right if the attacker is right-handed and right to left if he or she is left-handed. Either way, **gaining distance and cover quickly or closing to counterattack immediately is vital**. Hesitation can get you killed since it's not that hard to hit a man-sized standing target at close range.

So, what are you running to? Concealment or cover? **Concealment hides you from an enemy's sight**, but offers little or no protection from projectile weapons (e.g., bullets, rocks) or other forms of attack. Oddly enough, the vast majority of untrained people will not try to shoot through many forms of concealment such as windows or drywall, though you probably do not want to count on that. **While concealment is good, cover is better because it simultaneously hides and protects you**. A secure hiding place with a solid, lockable door and alternate escape route may serve as cover from many forms of physical assault, yet drywall and residential framing is only concealment if an assailant has most any type of gun. Speaking of drywall, it can make a decent emergency exit if you find yourself in a situation where you cannot escape through a door or window. Standard construction is 17 inches on center, so there's plenty of room for most people to kick their way through. Always know how to escape any room you're in, even if you have to get creative in doing it.

It's also important to know how and where to hide. Indoor cover can include certain items of heavy furniture, as well as some walls, doors, stairwells, and alcoves. Hollow core doors found in most residential construction, on the other hand, will not even stop a determined fist let alone a bullet. Lawrence once punched through one with a *nukite*, or finger strike, on a bet. It didn't even hurt (except in the checkbook; he had to pay to replace the door). And yes, alcohol was involved.

Outdoor cover can include trees, vehicles, rocks, retaining walls, buildings, industrial garbage bins, and even metal mailboxes. Even though through some trick of psychology most folks won't shoot through a closed window, beware of glass from vehicle or building windows that could either fail to stop a projectile and/or become shrapnel causing additional damage to you.

All-in-all, running is a fabulous self-defense technique. But, there are a few exceptions:

- **Don't run if it creates greater peril**. Sometimes it's more dangerous to turn your back on a threat than it is to stand your ground and fight. Typically it's when the other guy has a weapon or you're facing multiple assailants. That doesn't mean you cannot run, of course, only that you must take countervailing action until you can flee safely.
- **Don't run from the cops**. If the other guy is a cop (in the United States), don't even consider running. Even if you're guiltless, fleeing from the police makes them think you're a lawbreaker. And, in most instances, it's illegal. So, even if there's been a case of mistaken identity, running from the cops is very likely to end in tragedy. Or a beat-down, arrest, and the filing of charges. Besides, no matter how fast you are, you can't outrun a radio and officers are likely to call for backup if you rabbit on them. Don't do it.

Like anything else, getting good at evasion and escape requires practice. Be sure to use drills and training partners to hone your skills in this vital aspect of self-defense. Parkour classes, obstacle courses, playgrounds, and paintball sports parks are good venues to practice in.

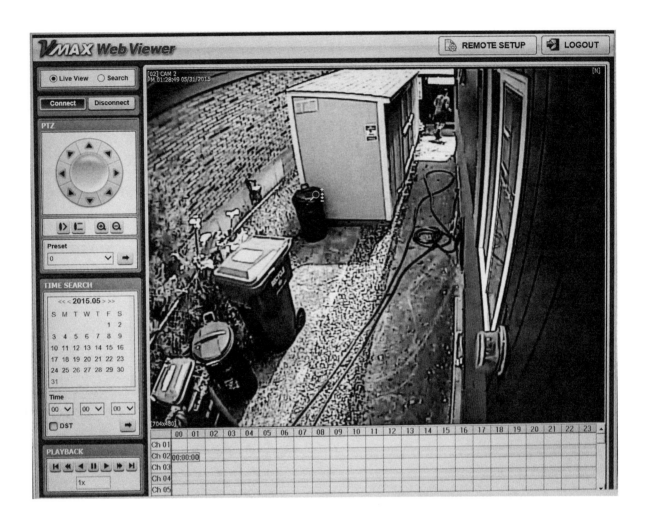

CHAPTER 28

KEEP YOUR EYE ON WHAT'S REALLY GOING ON

"The basic rule I have from carny [carnival workers] *is if you pick the person you are safe, if they pick you, you are completely fucked."*

– Penn Jillette

On March 18, 2005 Ronald Whitehead, a 61-year-old Boeing computer engineer, left for work for the last time. He never made it to the office. Less than three miles from his home, he was found shot to death, his body pulled from his black 2000 Mustang and left in the middle of an intersection by an apparent carjacker in what police characterized as a random crime. According to reports, Whitehead was shot four times, including once in the head, and three shell casings were found on the pavement near his body. Discussing the Whitehead murder, King County Sheriff's Sgt. John Urquhart told reporters, "It is pretty unusual for a carjacking to go this far wrong. They are always traumatic. They're always violent, but not to the point where someone dies."

While Lawrence only met him a couple of times in the cafeteria, Whitehead worked in the same building complex for the same part of the company so this case hit pretty close to home. It also didn't feel right... Carjacking is rarely associated with murder. In fact, while there are roughly 38,000 carjackings per year in the United States, victims are only killed about 15 times per annum, a mere 0.39 percent of such incidents. Well, it turns out that Lawrence's suspicions were correct. The initial story unraveled pretty quickly. Eventually Whitehead's wife, Velma Ogden-Whitehead, pled guilty and was sentenced to 22 years in prison for first-degree murder. The 50-year-old woman admitted helping her teenage son and his friend, who also faced murder trials, with a plan to steal her husband's car in retaliation for years of alleged abuse. She maintained that she did not expect him to be killed, but the judge didn't believe her.

"Domestic violence victims deserve our compassion and resources, but the domestic violence victim is not you," Judge Steven Gonzalez told the defendant in court. "Your claims of abuse and suffering, I must say, are hollow."

Sum Chai was a famous martial arts practitioner in the early 1980s who had great physical skill. An example of this prowess was his ability to leap up and kick the net of a basketball hoop, as well as perform many complicated martial arts moves smoothly and without flaw. Sum Chai founded the Institute of Shaolin Gung-Fu. Although he was an exceptional martial artist, he is best known for his ability to demonstrate telekinesis. Telekinesis is the magic of moving physical objects at a distance using only one's mind, real-life Jedi stuff. As you might imagine, as Sum Chai exhibited his skills before larger and larger audiences, his marital arts school grew in size exponentially.

Sum Chai learned his skills from a Chinese master of the ancient arts of gung-fu. He said that the skills that he had acquired were the results of "... background and through training with an ole' Chinese master." He also went to claim that:

"...everyone is born with it [telekinesis]; it is just a matter of development. Recognize yourself, your inner and outer self, to reach the fourth level of consciousness, matching the actions of the mind to the powers of the body."

Sum Chai wore silk Chinese gung-fu uniforms, clothing that was ornate, beautiful, and exotic. Appearing on television he would move pages of phonebooks using his hard-earned mental powers. Focusing intently, in conjunction with elaborate hand motions, Chai would move also would move pencils balanced on the edge of tables, sending them spinning to the ground. On the national television show, *That's Incredible*, host John Davidson accused Chai of blowing on the pencil in order to perform the trick. Chai was adamant that he had not done so, however, while Davidson was polite though equally unwavering that he had heard Chai blowing on the pencil. Chai offered to have Davidson cover his mouth, which Davidson did, and then seconds later the pencil went spinning to the ground sending the audience and hosts into awes and gasps.

Chai may have hoodwinked the television audience, but **he was in fact a charlatan**.

Sum Chai's real name was James Hydrick. He was a con artist who had already done a short stint in jail, and that was where his skills truly came from. Over time, and what did he have but time while languishing in the clink, he taught himself a magician's trick of using puffs of air to move small objects. Hydrick learned to move pencils that had been delicately perched on the edges of a tables or light objects such as the thin pages of phone books. **Con artists like Hydrick make their money through the art of deception**. There is often no violence involved yet this can serve as a fantastic laboratory to hone the skills of watching for what is really taking place. There are several kinds of cons, but we will focus on the "confidence game."

The confidence game is built around the simple premise of finding what the other person fears, and playing off that fear. Conmen and women take versions of their victim's concerns and insecurities, the fear of being alone, the fear of being hurt, and the fear of [insert your fear of choice]. This is half of the formula. The other half of the formula lies in the lack of conscience and the self-assurance exhibited by conman.

James Hydrick was eventually tested by the Amazing Randi, a magician and debunker of people claiming otherworldly powers such as telekinesis and telepathy (mind reading). Randi created a simple task for Hydrick to overcome. During the early eighties, Randi appeared on the television show *That's My Line*. Randi simply placed lightweight Styrofoam pellets around the phone book and then challenged Hydrick to move the pages with his mind as he had done many times before but this time without disturbing the Styrofoam. In front of a national audience and a panel of experts in physics, Hydrick was unable move the pages of the phone book. He claimed the static electricity generated from the studio lights and the Styrofoam was creating a charge making the pages adhere to each other. The board of experts, however, had none of it. They remained unconvinced and the event was a spectacular failure for Hydrick.

About 7% of citizens over the age of 16 in the US were victims of identity theft in 2012. While 85% of these incidents involved the fraudulent use of existing accounts (e.g., credit card, savings, checking), victims who had their information used to open new accounts or conduct other types of fraud were more likely to experience financial, credit, and relationship problems as well as undergo severe emotional distress.

Danny Korum, author of *Powers: Testing the Psychic and Supernatural*, also debunked Hydrick, but he did it in the simplest way possible: Korum was able to get a videotaped confession from Hydrick. On the video, Hydrick admitted that had developed the skill in jail and went on to explain the technique. It is important to note that **even in the confession, Hydrick was still in the con**. He claimed the whole thing was an elaborate ruse, "My whole idea behind this in the place to see how dumb America was, how dumb the world is." **Hydrick used a simple magician's trick** wrapped in the mysticism of gung-fu, a silk set of pajamas, and words that spoke to others' hopes of achieving some supernatural power beyond their daily lives. A pretty effective con, yet The Amazing Randi used his magician's skills to figure out what was going on, blow past the window-dressing, and make Hydrick fail in his ruse. Korum went at Hydrick like a cop in an interrogation and achieved the same results. **Both men saw Hydrick's play and both solved the problem in different ways**.

We are awash in information these days. There is data, the most basic of the continuum. Data represents something, but we have no context with which to assess it. Data simply is, but put that data in context by giving it something to be measured with and we now have information. What you do with that information can become wisdom... and there are many variations of wisdom.

Being awash in information is not a good thing in the sense that it is not the way the human brain was designed to function. The brain throws away great deals of both data and information on a moment-by-moment basis. The brain has to discard unneeded information because if we become overloaded we would cease to function, experiencing a true analysis paralysis.

Information can be difficult if not impossible to sort through if you don't have a method. Brian Billick, the former coach of the Super Bowl champion Baltimore Ravens football team, is fond of saying that American football is a simple game in many ways. He points to his method of analysis, and we paraphrase, "You need to have more men on their men, if you can't do that you need to have better angles. If you can't do that then you need better personnel." That's pretty much the strategy of American football in a nutshell, isn't it? Complicated, violent mayhem on the gridiron now becomes simple.

Billick created a simple means of breaking down the information and then he gets to apply his wisdom to the moment. That's the mark of someone who truly understands his profession, who is at the top of his game. He distilled a mind-bogglingly complex subject down into a few, simple sentences in everyday English that anyone with a rudimentary understanding of the game of American football can understand. That's the mark of genius.

The Amazing Randi doesn't believe in telekinesis, so he set out to debunk Hydrick's ruse. Korum thought he could get results using a police methodology, taking on a confidence man. In both instances these men were not blinded by the ruse. **They paid attention to what was really going on.** Unfortunately it's really difficult to do that and **it only works with focused attention and pattern recognition**. If you look at all three of these men, Randi, Korum, and Billick, you will see that they all focused on the task at hand and used methods of pattern recognition. Pattern recognition is believed to be linear, but we are here to tell you that it is actually based on intent and favorable conditions. In other words, when intent meets opportunity, stuff happens. It's oftentimes as simple as that. Here's an example:

> When Kris got home that evening he wasn't feeling well. He fell into bed where he would spend the next two days sick from the flu. Later on the third day he went out to get something from his van and discovered that it had been broken into... well truth be told in his sick state and desire to get to bed he had inadvertently left the vehicle unlocked. Kris went back to his surveillance system and watched two young men walk up to the other car in his driveway, look into the vehicle, and it appears that when they saw the flashing security light on the dashboard they walked away. No opportunity. A quick flashlight

pass on the adjacent van's interior with no indication of an alarm system and the door was tested. They discovered that it had been left open. Suddenly intent meets opportunity… They both climbed into the van and rifled it for a minute or two and then they walked away with little since Kris hadn't left much of value inside.

If you looked into the background of the two young men who broke into Kris' van, you would no doubt see a criminal record, most likely made up of petty crime. And the response to seeing their criminal records would be, "Of course they broke into your car, look at the record!" That is a linear view of the criminals however. A vertical perspective shows a different picture. The vertical says that when intent meets opportunity the crime occurs. In other words, the intent (looking for stuff to steal), the opportunity (an unlocked van), and the means (flashlight, knapsack) need to be present for the crime to occur. Sound familiar?

To extend our assertion, the night that Kris' van was broken into no other car in the neighborhood was hit. They were all locked and/or had security systems in place. In fact, these cars were all much more valuable than a decade-old van, but they were passed over nevertheless. The intent was in place, "Let's go rifle through some cars and see if we can find some good stuff." And the opportunity, "This van is unlocked." The rational mind says, "Why on earth would you break into a decade-old van, one with virtually nothing in it?" But, the criminal mind says, "We are stealing, open door."

We tend to look at the world as if it is linear when, in fact, a whole lot of crime is vertical. Most criminals are not lasers, they are billiard balls, bouncing from one crime to the next. The laser-focused criminal is the one that scares us the most because **he or she is intelligent, organized, and has many of the attributes of what we think are some of our own best characteristics**. The other criminal that scares us is on the other end of the spectrum, they are **random, violent, spontaneous, and out of control**. Few of us consider ourselves random and illogical, so when a criminal appears to be like us we are deeply threatened… and fascinated. When a criminal is not like us, we are terrified. As a society we enjoy the high profile studies of serial murderers and make movies about them, but the smash-and-grab of car break-ins is only a statistic that has little meaning, one that is ignored or quickly forgotten about.

When a crime is nestled in numbers, it is safe. Look at subprime mortgage crisis of 2009, companies were destroyed, banks closed, hardworking peoples' retirement accounts and life savings lost, and who was held accountable? Who went to jail? Can you list even one person? The United States Internal Revenue Service targeted conservative entities, a violation of the law regardless of political affiliation, and again who was held accountable? Who stood trial? **These are examples of crimes where people who paid attention saw it coming**. These crimes are in the soft statistical middle. They may be large, but they possess none of the attributes of either end of the criminal spectrum. **If the billions of dollars had been misappropriated through armed robbery**, on the other hand, **how long do you think that would top the headlines**?

Comedian Norm MacDonald was once asked what his style of comedy was and he replied, and we paraphrase here, "I just state the obvious in stark terms."

Think of the scene in the movie, *Kingpin*, the popular 1996 comedy. In one scene the protagonist, Roy Munson (played by Woody Harrelson) can't make the rent payment for his female slumlord. The slumlord extorts her tenant, he has a choice: Be evicted or perform a sex act. Munson chooses to perform sex and afterward the slumlord explicitly tells him that he had better be ready for more soon, and demonstrates what he will be responsible to perform on her. This, or some other form of sexual exploitation, happens every day and multiple times a day, though more often with males exploiting females than the other way around as occurred in the movie. **In the context of a comedy this makes us wince**, you could hear the audience groan in the theater. It was funny in that gross-out way that makes the genre amusing. **In the real world**, however, **it is horrific**. Nevertheless, **we saw somebody being bullied into abasing himself and laughed**... Now we are not suggesting that every comedy should be an exercise in seeing what is really going on, but we are suggesting that it is an excellent opportunity to **take a hard look and digest what we see**.

Use your eyes to recognize pattern disruption. A police officer once told Kris, "You know what my job is? **It is to investigate the unusual**." From a self-defense perspective **that's your job description too**. You are likely not a police officer. You are not likely a member of the military on deployment. If you are, you are rare. You are rarer than the ordinary citizen by far. As a law enforcement officer your job is to seek contact with the unusual. As a member of the military you seek out the enemy. However, the majority of people are everyday citizens and as such need to use their skills **investigate the unusual so as to avoid contact with the enemy, the criminal, the thug**. The investigation is the same, only the response is different.

The eyes are the standoff early warning system of the human anatomy. Think of your eyes as the radar system on a modern jetfighter. The aerial dogfight is a rarity now days, to a great extent a relic of the past. The radar systems that the modern jets possess allow for acquisition and destruction of the enemy before the enemy even knows they're there. Once the enemy is acquired an informed decision can be made as to what actions must follow. In blunt terms, the heroic dogfight of the past has turned into an assassination today. Like the pilots of these sophisticated, multi-million dollar fighters, **we want to see what's coming before the other guy takes notice, make our decisions, and slip away before the bad guys ever know we were there**.

Know this: the eyes can set the whole body in motion in an instant by igniting hundreds of muscles into action. Further, the eyes can control internal organs, like the adrenal glands or even the stomach (e.g., making you throw-up). Use the power of your eyes in the same way a jetfighter pilot uses his radar. Breaking the pattern reveals the code. In other words, to ascertain what's really going on look to see what's different, unexpected. Here are some tips on keeping your eyes on what is really going on:

- **When others start to lose attention, you take the extra look**.
- **Ask the difficult question, even if it's just in your own mind**.
- **When others feel safe, you double-check the metaphorical locks**.
- **When others walk on by you pause for a moment**.
- **When others hurry you slow down**.

Have you ever bought a car and then suddenly it seems that everybody else out there is driving the same make or model vehicle? The number of cars on the road has likely not increased, and certainly there hasn't been a massive run on the vehicle that you just bought, so what's different? Your mind now has a deeply etched pattern buried inside. You just spent several days or even months looking for the perfect vehicle and when you finally find it there is a pattern impressed in your brain. Also writing a check and making an obligation for payments doubles-down on that imprint. And then there is the excitement of the purchase. How can this pattern not be deeply etched into your brain? This is where the **pattern recognition kicks in**. You see somebody in the same car, maybe even the same color. Now you have an imprint of the other side of the emotional spectrum. It is virtually impossible to escape this recognition now. Everywhere and on every street your car (or one just like it) is waiting for you to notice.

Okay that's nice and all, it 'splains stuff, but it's the opposite of what we're actually looking for... Here's how you control this natural pattern recognition. The next time you go to the store preset your mind. Think, "I need red apples." and imagine a red apple in your mind. Then see how fast you discover the red apples in the store. As you are standing in front of the red apples. Look at either your left or right and notice the produce that is on either side. Take note of how inconsequential these fruits or vegetables are to your process. This is the way to set your visual acuity to aid you, in the same way, a fighter pilot's radar works.

With this experience you can start to set your intent to look for a pattern disruption. An example might be a cluster of people. Preset your brain to look for the unusual, the disruption in the pattern. It might be a coat or hat worn in warm weather. It doesn't matter for practicing, it's just the determination to **see what's different, to take notice and get used to taking notice**. You make the choice as to what to set yours pattern disruption trigger. After a few years of working at the stadium Lawrence has developed the ability to spot problems in just about any crowd. It's not that he has any special powers of observation, but rather that because he viscerally knows what's normal his mind automatically hones in on what's not. That's what you want to be able to do as well, naturally and instinctively notice anything that disrupts the normal pattern not just in crowds but wherever you are.

Here's how to make this work well in a defensive situation. We call it sweeping. Sweep your eyes left to right, approximately from shoulder to shoulder, looking a few feet in front of yourself and then shifting outward. You will move your head less and use your eyes more to sweep farther from your body than you will up front. By consciously keeping your eyes constantly moving and turning your head from time to time you make yourself notice things. You're looking for disruptions in the pattern. Things that are new or not normal. Once you have identified people and objects that belong, those you see on a regular basis, you can usually disregard them as potential threats and concentrate more on those who deserve further scrutiny because they are new to the environment. It doesn't matter what you see so much as that you identify whether or not it's worth paying additional attention to.

CHAPTER 29

HANDLING HOME INVASIONS

"A human being should be able to change a diaper, plan an invasion, butcher a hog, conn a ship, design a building, write a sonnet, balance accounts, build a wall, set a bone, comfort the dying, take orders, give orders, cooperate, act alone, solve equations, analyze a new problem, pitch manure, program a computer, cook a tasty meal, fight efficiently, die gallantly. Specialization is for insects."

– Robert A. Heinlein

On June 8, 2014 Oscar-winning actress Sandra Bullock locked herself in a safe room while a home invasion robber angrily pounded on the door. In the 911 call played at the trial of Joshua Corbett, the 39-year-old alleged robber, the jury could hear her terrified voice crying, "Someone has broken into my house. I'm hiding in the closet. I'm locked in my closet. I have a safe door in my bedroom, and I've locked it, and I'm locked in the closet right now. I hear… I hear them. I hear someone banging on the door…"

Corbett pled not guilty to several felony charges, including burglary, stalking, and possession of a machinegun, in addition to 19 other felony weapons charges. Police reported finding several illegal machineguns and other proscribed firearms at his home in Montrose, California after he was arrested for robbery in Bullock's upscale Beverly Hills-area neighborhood.

On May 22, 2012 three African American men described as being in their early 20s wearing hooded sweatshirts, jeans, gloves, and tennis shoes broke into the home of a Renton, Washington man who was identified in news reports only as "Bobby P." The 28-year-old victim told detectives he had just returned home when he heard glass breaking. When he went to investigate he was confronted by a gunman who threatened to shoot if Bobby did not comply with his orders. Two more men then entered through the shattered glass patio door. They took his shoes off, used his shoelaces to tie him up, and then put a blanket over his head.

"They tied my hands and feet and they covered me and I couldn't breathe," he told reporters. "It was very bad. I thought I was done." One of the thugs held a gun to his neck for about half an hour while the others ransacked the house before running off. The robbers used broken English when they spoke to the victim, but spoke fluent Spanish to each other. Bobby managed to hop out the front door and activate his home security system's panic alarm while he called out for help afterward. According to police reports the victim did not indicate that he knew his attackers.

"We believe this is totally random," said Sergeant Cindi West, a spokeswoman for the King County Sheriff's Office.

On February 23, 2014, a Madison, Wisconsin woman and her husband were awakened at 5:00 AM by three armed assailants who burst into their bedroom. "Someone's gonna die tonight!" one of the home invaders shouted. He then dragged the male victim from the bed and viciously began beating him. The female victim told her assailants that she was six months pregnant and let them know that they could take whatever they wanted if they would only leave her alone, but she was dragged into the hallway and raped by all three men, one of whom forced her to commit oral sex on him during the attack. The suspects stole the couple's credit cards, computer, cell phones, and wedding rings and then locked the battered and bloody victims in their laundry room before fleeing the scene.

"In my 27-plus years of policing in Madison, this is probably one of the most disturbing and heinous crimes I have ever seen," interim Madison police Chief Randy Gaber said in a press conference afterward.

In addition to the three men who broke into the home, three more conspirators were arrested for their roles in assisting the crime. According to media reports, the assailants had planned to rob a man who carried large sums of cash and lived in the same neighborhood, but went to a different address by mistake. Michon A. Thomas, Eric D. Bass, and Kristopher J. Hughes all face robbery and sexual assault charges for their roles in crime. DeAndrae L. Mayweathers Jr., alleged to be the getaway driver, was charged with conspiracy to commit armed robbery and two other men whose names were not in the news report were charged for their roles in helping to plan and facilitate the crime.

In a horrific event that not only shocked the nation but was subsequently turned into an HBO movie, one of the country's most infamous home invasion murders took place in Cheshire, Connecticut on July 23, 2007. Dr. William Petit was brutally beaten during the attack, but managed to escape before the two sociopathic invaders strangled his wife, raped her corpse, raped the couple's young daughter, poured gasoline on the two females, and set them and the house on fire.

Two years later, the Connecticut General Assembly voted to repeal the death penalty, which had been reinstated in 1973. The repeal was vetoed by Gov. Jodi Rell, in part because suspects Steven Hayes and Joshua Komisarjevsky had yet to be tried for the Petit family murders. Many in the state, including those who had previously opposed capital punishment, wanted to see the suspects sentenced to death for their heinous crimes. Hayes was convicted of the murders and sentenced to death in 2010, while his accomplice Komisarjevsky was found guilty in 2011.

Residential burglars tend to operate during the day when homeowners are off at work, whereas home invasion robbers most often work at night or on weekends when you're home. Automatically the danger goes up because **your home is the equivalent of a secondary location**. Intentionally conducting a crime in the presence of homeowner **indicates a more aggressive offender**. Professional criminals know that telling someone to move during the commission of a felony is kidnapping. **Kidnapping gets the same level of charges as murder—so really, why bother leaving you alive to testify afterward?** There is an automatic increase of danger and immediate threat with any home invasion. A friend of ours used to know a guy who would break into houses at night. He bragged about holding a gun aimed at the sleeping couple while his girlfriend looted the house and his willingness to pull the trigger if they woke up (fortunately he was blown away by someone he pissed off before he could murder anybody).

Home invaders tend to hit known drug dealers and others who deal primarily in cash and are unlikely to report the crime such as those who live in certain immigrant communities which distrust banks. Even if you don't fall into this demographic, they are often drawn to you through actions of your teenage or college-age children who may dabble on the dark side (e.g., drugs, stolen property) and unwittingly bring trouble home. Unfortunately home invaders also tend to select those who live alone (especially women), the elderly, and law abiding citizens with obvious wealth too.

Most home invaders are men. One of their biggest sources of information for targeting who they will hit is having a girlfriend inside a company who feeds them information about likely victims. Sometimes the bad guys themselves will spot you on the street, by the car you drive or the jewelry you wear, and follow you home. These follow-home robberies tend to start in your attached garage if you have one. Often what they do is pull up and rush in before the door closes behind your vehicle. Other times they use jobs that require access to your home, such as deliveries, repairs, installation, and the like to scout things out. Or, they'll spot your home as a target of opportunity as they move about their day.

Folks who perpetrate these crimes are armed far more often than not. Attacks tend to occur with extreme violence, especially during the initial stages where **the goal is to overwhelm, capture, and render you helpless to resist** (e.g., knock you out, tie you up). From there you risk being beaten, raped or murdered, or (if you're lucky) they might just keep you captive while they steal your valuables. At times they not only ransack your house but subsequently take you to a series of cash machines where they force you to empty your bank accounts.

All these options are on the table because you are home when they arrive. And, because their goal is to strike when you're there, they are less worried about alarm systems than residential burglars as they assume that you've switched any alarms you might have off.

Home invaders sometimes force their way in through the front, garage, patio, or back door. While kicking in a door or breaking a lock is not uncommon, attackers can operate with subterfuge too. They might simply knock on your front door and then rush in when you open it. Or, if they need more subtlety to initiate the ambush they might pretend to be a delivery driver bringing you a package or a stranded motorist who needs to use your phone, or perhaps they will tell you that they inadvertently sideswiped your car and wish to make an insurance report. Frequently it is a single perpetrator who does this; his accomplices lurk out of sight nearby. Regardless of the ploy, **the goal is tricking their way in through your door in order to initiate an attack**.

All in all, home invasions are one of the scariest forms of violence imaginable because **we all want to feel safe in our homes**. Anything that breaches our sense of peace and security in our residence is very hard to overcome psychologically. Much like rape, **it violates our sanctuary, our core, and the consequences can be long lasting and considerable**. And, since the bad guys are targeting you with overwhelming violence from the first moments they launch into the crime, you are unlikely to make it through the incident unscathed.

Fortunately there are several strategies you can put in place to reduce the chances of having to face home invaders. Begin by becoming knowledgeable. You can often have your local police department or a reputable security company, such as ADT, **do a perimeter walk and security check** for little or no cost. Even if you don't buy anything or hire the security company to install any equipment afterward you can learn a lot from a professional security analysis.

First and foremost, your defensive strategy should start by carefully choosing your neighborhood. Sure, crime can happen anywhere, even in Beverly Hills as Sandra Bullock discovered the hard way, but the odds of being targeted can vary significantly based on where you live. **Find the best**

neighborhood you can afford, and then strive for one of the lower priced, humblest houses on your block. This can be useful both for controlling property taxes as well as for not becoming a criminal's target. Then, get to know your neighbors, join or form a block watch, and pay close attention to anything that stands out from the norm to determine whether or not it's threatening.

Before buying or renting a home it is a very good idea to **look at crime statistics**. They're readily available online in many jurisdictions and can help you make prudent choices. For example, Lawrence looked at several areas before buying his house. At the time of his purchase the only reported crime in the last five years within a ten block radius of the house he selected had been a hit-and-run on a parked car that had been sideswiped. Another house he considered and very nearly placed a bid on was located in a well-kept, nice-looking, middle class neighborhood near a school yet he discovered two registered sex offenders living in the area and learned that dozens of reported crimes ranging from vandalism to armed robbery had been reported there in the preceding months. That's why he chose not to buy. Had he not done his homework he may have inadvertently settled in a high crime area. His real estate agent never mentioned any problems and there were no obvious issues that could be spotted by driving around. He never did figure out exactly why there were so many problems there, but it doesn't really matter. He chose someplace else and that proved to be a wise decision.

Crime can happen anywhere, but oftentimes it is predictable due to commonalities in incidents. Factors that affect target selection for home invaders and residential burglars can include:

- **Houses near criminal offenders**. Bad guys tend to target locations relatively close to where they live, work, and travel regularly, so houses near urban crime areas, transit stations, social service centers, and routes to and from these areas can be extra vulnerable to attack. Even upscale neighborhoods with drug dealers tend to attract trouble, for example, as rough clientele who frequent the dealer's location may spot valuables along the way that they covet and subsequently go after.

- **Houses that are secluded**. Landscaping that blocks a home from view of neighbors or passersby, poor external lighting, and homes that abut alleys, greenways, or parks that can be easily and discretely be placed under surveillance tend to make good targets because criminals can have access and egress unseen. Home invaders prefer enough distraction or distance between their target and surrounding houses that the neighbors won't notice and report their activities. Or they will plan their attack for a time when you are the only one in the area who is home.

- **Houses near major thoroughfares**. Heavy traffic areas, especially those on the outskirts of quiet neighborhoods or those near schools, malls, airports, or shopping centers where it can be difficult for residents to recognize strangers and nefarious activities due to all the movement and noise are at increased risk. Residential neighborhoods with ready access to highways make for excellent entry and escape points for criminals, hence often have a lot more crime. In fact **anything within a mile of a freeway is called a "robbery corridor"** because statistically most hold-ups happen within that area.

- **Houses in transient neighborhoods**. Neighborhoods with transitory populations, such as those near colleges or military bases, can have increased crime rates because it is difficult to tell who belongs there and moving trucks or cargo vans do not look out of place. Further, bad guys often use real estate listings to case a neighborhood. Consequently if you live near a home that has been placed on the market for a long period of time (or abandoned in some instances), the odds of criminals scoping you out increase.

- **Houses displaying obvious wealth**. In most instances the home invaders are looking for cash or jewelry, precious metals, electronics, and other items that are easily hocked for cash. Expensive vehicles, boats, RVs, high-end BBQs, and other signs of opulence can attract unwanted attention. This is why it's advisable to have the humblest house on your block in the nicest neighborhood you can afford and to store your stuff in a closed garage. If you don't park on the street nearby it makes it harder to tell whether or not you're home too.

Once you have settled on a location, **home defense should be like an onion, layers within layers, each reinforcing the other**. Start with your landscaping. Fencing, trees, and shrubs should not give potential invaders the privacy they need to do their dirty work. You will want something that looks nice but that doesn't make it easy to breach your doors or windows. In fact, roses, quince, and other thorny bushes have a desirable aesthetic but are very difficult to hide in, hence discourage nefarious activities. Planted under windows they make it not fun to break in that way, so consider placing prickly foliage under all the windows the security walkthrough identified as a likely break-in spots.

Further, you need to be able to **see everything that occurs on your property**. This means using motion sensing lights and (where possible) video surveillance so that you will always know what is going on outside. Signage indicating the presence of alarm systems can help too, as they incentivize burglars to move on to other locations where they are less likely to be caught and prosecuted, but home invaders typically count on your having turned them off, hence pay less attention to such things. With technology improvements of late these devices have become *really* cheap. For example video doorbells that let you see who's on the porch can cost as little as $50.00 or $60.00 when purchased online, with high-end models running around $200.00. That's a modest investment with a potentially large payback.

Moving inward from the yard to the house itself, solid core doors, deadbolt locks, reinforced door jambs, and double-paned windows make it much harder to break in without anyone noticing. And, these measures can delay entry to those who try to force their way in long enough for you to act. In most neighborhoods you won't need bars over your windows, but if you choose that option be sure that they can be opened from the inside so that you can escape in an emergency. You want to **keep the bad guys out, but not trap yourself or your family in**. Since most break-ins use entry points on the sides of the house (or in fenced backyards) where it is harder for neighbors to see, you may not need bars on all your windows. Nevertheless, they don't hurt over particularly vulnerable spots and some are decorative enough not to detract from your home's value. Many insurance companies provide discounts for physical security measures and alarm systems that help protect your home, a two-bird/one-stone opportunity.

If you're extremely concerned about your safety or live in a high risk location you might consider ballistic blankets or shields too, though in most instances those precautions are better for drive-by shootings than for home invasions. And, unless you're aware of someone actively hunting for you they are most likely overkill; you'd be better off spending your money on other precautions that have a better payback for your investment.

Despite any physical security you may have installed, it's amazing how often crime victims report that they either failed to lock their doors or windows or simply opened the front door to their home when somebody knocked, even late at night, and let the bad guy in. **Don't make it easy**. Turn on outside lights and **check what's out there via a security camera or peephole before ever considering opening your door** or letting someone in. And, if it's late at night and you don't recognize the individual think twice before letting him or her in, no matter what the other person says. That's good advice any time of the day, but especially at night when there are few legitimate reasons to be approaching your home.

If you have an alarm system, set it to "stay" mode so that it will beep if any doors or windows are opened while you are at home, keep a panic alarm handy, and don't forget to set the system whenever you are away. Pre-program emergency numbers into your phone so that you can easily call for help when adrenalized.

Some folks have specially-designed safe rooms installed in their homes. That can be a viable option, especially if you're really wealthy or handy with home improvements, but remember that they only work in limited circumstances. You not only have to have time to get there, but also if someone can break in once you've hidden inside you're dead meat since there's nowhere else to go. You're going to have to spend a pretty penny to build something that's proof against attack, contains the communication (and weaponry) you require, and is readily accessible if you need it. Whether or not the investment is worthwhile depends on your individual situation.

With or without a safe room, however, if you have more than one escape path you will have more options. Get together with your family or roommates and **make a plan for what you will do if the worst case occurs**. Like anything else self-defense related, you don't want to freeze because you have no idea what to do in the heat of the moment. You should **have both primary and secondary fallback locations, exit routes, and meeting points** identified so that you can check in on everyone after an evacuation. This works not only for a possible home invasion but also for a fire, earthquake, tornado, hurricane, tsunami, or other emergency as well. Don't forget that you may need rope ladders or other methods that facilitate getting out of any higher floors without hurting yourself if you cannot use your normal traffic path due to a critical incident.

Don't tempt the bad guys. Making an obvious or ostentatious display of wealth is never a good thing. In one of the examples at the beginning of this chapter the home invaders' target was supposed to be a man who regularly carried large amounts of cash. Similarly, leaving expensive vehicles in your yard rather than storing them in your garage might attract thieves, as can leaving drapes or shades opened so that passersby can observe large screen TVs, computers, and other valuables. **There's nothing wrong with wealth honestly earned, but showing it off can be asking for trouble**. This includes flashing cash or expensive jewelry too. If you hire a groundskeeper, handyman, plumber, electrician, real estate agent, or anyone else who may have a legitimate reason to go inside your home be cautious about what you leave lying around for them to observe while they're there. Home invaders oftentimes garner information from others and use it to select their targets. Also be sure to check out their company's reputation and validate their credentials before letting anyone inside.

If you have an alarm system you can usually safeguard your master code and give out separate codes to roommates or trusted confidants (like a live-in nanny) who you intend to employ for an extended period of time. Even if these folks return their house key, it is a good idea to rekey the locks once they move out though. Never give your alarm codes or house keys to a stranger unless it's your carefully vetted real estate agent because you are selling the place and moving out.

Don't pick fights. While some home invasion robberies are driven by greed, others **may be inspired by revenge or retribution**. Criminal activities aside, feuding with neighbors, belittling coworkers, driving aggressively, looking down your nose at people, and general douchery tends to attract trouble. Try your best to get along with people and you'll be much better and safer for it.

Consider owning a dog. Not only are these pets good company, but also a fiercely loyal hound will bark loudly enough at any stranger's arrival to warn most invaders away. Or, the dog may be able to help you defend your home if it is unable to scare potential invaders off. Burglars may breach an alarm system and home invaders might kick in a door, but more often than not **they are reluctant to tangle with a family dog**. Obviously pets aren't for everyone and not every animal will fight to protect its family. But, dogs are a tried-and-true, low cost alarm and defense system, one that has been used since the ancient times. There have been multiple studies of convicted felons in which they were asked what security measures were most likely to deter their crimes. Dogs virtually always show up at or near the top of that list. Reasons include:

- **Early warning**. Dogs tend to hear and warn homeowners of suspicious sounds earlier than any alarm or video surveillance system can. And, barking dogs may attract more attention. Concerned by the dog's behavior, homeowners (or neighbors) will often investigate or call law enforcement professionals who will do so.
- **Fear of being bitten**. Confronting a dog is more hazardous than dealing with any alarm system (and most homeowners). Dogs are rarely intimidated by criminals and many won't hesitate to attack if threatened (since, among other things, most don't understand hence are not scared of the knives or guns that home-invaders often carry).

Many jurisdictions have enacted "castle laws" which give homeowners (and even renters oftentimes) more leeway to defend themselves in their homes than they would ordinarily have on the street. The biggest difference is that in such cases preclusion may not apply. In other words, **you're not expected to automatically retreat if attacked in your own home**. Retreat may be **a good tactical decision**, regardless, but it doesn't always have to be a legal one. On the other hand, **do NOT go outside looking for trespassers or to try to trap a criminal in your yard**.

Five states have enacted "stand your ground" laws during the past decade. These include Kansas, Alabama, Mississippi, Montana, and West Virginia. During that time they reported no significant change in justifiable homicide rates. In Michigan, which passed its law in 2006, justifiable homicide rates decreased after the legislation was enacted.

Whether you choose to retreat or stand your ground, it's very challenging to defend yourself if you don't have a tool to do it with. There are a large variety of impromptu weapons that can be used in the home for defensive purposes, everything from cutlery to fire extinguishers, but this is another situation where a firearm can be extremely useful. A lot of self-defense experts suggest shotguns for home defense, but if you have a smaller residence and do not live alone they can be problematic since they are not as precise as rifles or pistols. Whatever you use, consider over-penetration, especially in urban neighborhoods where **a stray bullet might injure or kill a neighbor** close by. For this reason **we suggest hollow point or pre-fragmented rounds** (where legal) that can readily stop a bad guy but are less likely to travel through sheetrock than other types of ammunition if you miss. And, of course, **extensive training and practice can help you stay on target** and not miss the bad guy to begin with.

In a home invasion scenario **you will likely be facing one or more armed assailants**. You will rarely have enough time to go and get your gun, so you'll need to have it with you. Having your weapon under your direct control at all times is a good safety precaution too. Your gun should either be locked in a quick-release safe or biometric vault so that it will be readily available if needed, or strapped at your side where you have full control and instant access to it. If you don't carry it around, consider having more than one gun strategically placed (and safely stored) in locations where you spend most of your time (e.g., bedroom, living room).

One of the challenges with home invasion robberies is that they tend to happen at night with surprise and overwhelming force. But, if the bad guys can't find an unlocked door they may kick one in or break a window, either of which will alert you to their presence. If you hear a break-in it's vital to call for help and then carefully determine if or how you will investigate. If you're already in an upstairs bedroom and hear noises on the main floor, for example, **it's often advisable to arm yourself, call for help, stay in place, barricade the door, have an escape ladder ready, and loudly inform intruders that you have already dialed 911**. The most important goal is keeping you and your loved ones safe, not confronting or defeating the invader(s), so **don't leave a safe area *unless you have to***. Staying put in a defensive position strongly reinforces your claim that trouble came to you when have to defend yourself from legal repercussions later on too… and it's far safer. Police responses are relatively quick in most areas and simply setting off an alarm system or shouting that you're armed and have called the cops can resolve the situation without the need for any physical altercation much of the time.

But, if you have a child or children in another bedroom that's a whole different dynamic… You may have to go out and protect or bring a family member back to safety. While this is no doubt well-intentioned, clearing a house, even one you're intimately familiar with, on your own is problematic. **It's a good way to get shot or have your weapon taken away and used against you**. Or to make a tragic mistake. Don't do it unless you absolutely have to.

If you are moving about and think that you have spotted a threat it is vital to know your target and understand his or her intentions. **Never shoot blind!** Oftentimes this means having a light source or night vision device, even if your eyes have already adjusted to the dark. A "tactical" flashlight, one with a momentary on/off switch will do, but make sure it's not overpowered such that you'll blind yourself along with the bad guy when you switch it on. Anything over approximately 150 lumens can be problematic, especially if you live in a small home or have light colored or white walls. Strobe functions can be used to distract, lights can be used to blind, but either way if you're shining a light the other guy(s) knows where you are. Be cognizant of your surroundings and try not to silhouette yourself as you move around.

You don't accidentally want to kill a relative or family member or even a drunk person who stumbled into the wrong home (which happens more often than you might think), so it's usually a good idea to identify yourself, giving fair warning by shouting something like "**Leave NOW!**" or

"Freeze! Stop or I'll shoot!" before pulling the trigger. If the threat is compliant you may be able to get him or her to leave peacefully. **It is a bad idea to try to detain a threat unless you have had law enforcement tools and training**. You can get seriously hurt trying to make an arrest instead of barricading yourself in a safe location, bugging out, or chasing the threat away. And, you may be confused for the bad guy and killed by first responders when law enforcement arrives. Consider potential accomplices before acting as well. **Home invasions are one crime where the bad guys seldom act alone**.

If you're barricaded in a safe area, warning the threat that you're armed and will open fire if they attempt to breach the door can sometimes keep them on the other side where they'll leave you alone, quickly grab your stuff, and bug out before police arrive. Nevertheless, sometimes clearing the house is your only viable option, so here are a few tips to help you survive if you have to do that:

- **Start with a plan**. Before you do anything, develop a course of action. Even though breaking into your home will cause rage, fear, and other intense emotions, it doesn't matter if the bad guys are after your stuff, let them have it. Insurance should cover replacement costs. If they're after you or your family, on the other hand, all bets are off. If you have to move out to protect yourself or others you will need to be extraordinarily cautious. Military and law enforcement professionals clear houses using well-coordinated teams of highly trained individuals. That's not you. Sure, you can coordinate with a significant other, roommate, or child in the right circumstances, but even then without extensive training and practice you're asking for trouble. Don't rush in half-cocked; think things through carefully before you act.
- **Call for help**. 911 (or your local emergency number) is your friend in situations like this. The mere fact that law enforcement is on the way may cause the threat(s) to disengage and bail out. Or the sound of sirens might have the same affect. While it may take a while for them to arrive there's a certain psychological solace in knowing that the cops are on their way too. Nevertheless, be sure to describe yourself and any family members with you in sufficient detail (e.g., gender, hair color, skin pigmentation, clothing, visible tattoos, weapons, and any other obvious differentiating characteristics) to ensure that responding officers won't confuse you for the bad guy(s). You don't want to wind up getting shot by mistake like homeowner Tony Arambula was.
- **Arm yourself**. Bring a gun and a cell phone. Clearing a house with a baseball bat, knife, or some sort of impromptu weapon can work, but it's horrifically dangerous since most home invaders in the US are armed. The chances are good that the threat's weapon of

choice is a gun, so yours should be too. If you sleep naked put clothes on before leaving the bedroom if you can, it will boost your confidence psychologically. If possible, wear body armor too.

- **Maintain control of your weapon**. Move with your weapon close to your body until or unless you need to use it. If it sticks out too far it will not only give away your position but also enable someone to grapple for control more easily. Always be aware and in control of where your muzzle is pointing, especially if working with a partner. It's a really good idea to take a gun handling course that shows you how to do this sort of thing properly. They're often expensive but well worth it.

- **Beware the fatal funnel**. One of the most dangerous areas in any building is the doorways, oftentimes call "fatal funnels" by professionals. If possible approach doors from the handle side, using the wall for cover, turn the handle and swing the door as quickly as possible to expose the whole room, step back immediately, observe the room from a safe angle, and then move through at an angle as rapidly as possible. Don't pause or stand in the doorway! Check over your shoulder to the corner you couldn't see as you pass the doorway, then immediately clear the rest of the area. Leave no section unsearched before moving on. You don't want a surprise threat behind you as you exit who can shoot you in the back.

- **Slice the pie**. Like doorways, traversing corners is very dangerous too. Start close to the wall about an arm's length from the corner, then slowly "slice the pie" moving outward in a half circle pausing and scanning with each step. If you're proficient with both hands keep your weapon in whichever one keeps you most concealed. Never cross your feet or move into an unstable position as you may need to fire at any time during such maneuvers.

- **Methodically clear hallways**. Hallways are dangerous and dynamic as well, especially when approaching T-intersections so that you are, in essence, approaching two corners at once. Methodically clear every room in a hallway, moving along one side or the other but staying out of the middle. If you skip past one room to check another you may wind up with a surprise threat behind you. It takes longer but is safer to go with this disciplined, systematic approach.

- **Use caution on stairs**. Stairs should be treated much like hallways, though you'll need to check up or down additionally and watch your footing. You need to be able to move quickly at a moment's notice which is a real challenge in many stairwells. Watch for any exposed areas on the threat or yourself, you may see or expose head or feet as you move up or down. In some types of structures risers aren't covered or have a room beneath them, so beware of places like that where threats may hide in ambush.

Few things are as adrenalizing as fear for your life and that of your loved ones due to a sudden, violent, and overwhelming ambush in your home. Home invaders don't just bust in, more often than not they bust in violently—shooting, stabbing, clubbing, punching, or kicking. Such incidents are critical and fraught with danger, but **prevention and preparation can help you get through**. This is one of those things that you can get the gist of with a book but really, truly ought to **have professional, hands-on training** in order to give yourself the best chance to succeed. Buy a gun, learn to use it in scenarios like this, and practice, practice, and practice some more.

Conclusion

"A person may cause evil to others not only by his action but by his inaction, and in either case he is justly accountable to them for the injury."

– John Stuart Mill

We covered a lot of material in this book, some truly ugly subject matter, in an effort to get to the unvarnished truth. Some of what we have written even made *us* uncomfortable. It made us review what we knew to be true and how is squared with our beliefs about the world as we know it. We have made you think, question, and look through new eyes. And, hopefully we have also convinced you that **self-defense is not just a narrow set of fighting skills; it's a lifestyle choice**, a more enlightened way of looking at and moving through the world.

The bottom line is that we live in dangerous times nowadays. We could whine about that, but let's face it, there have been few moments in history when ordinary citizens have not been at risk of violence in one way or another. Weak-willed "sheeple" cower in fear, outsourcing their safety to others. Abdicating personal responsibility might be the easy way out, but this strategy does very little to actually safeguard your welfare. With the possible exception of your mother, **no one cares about you more than you do**, certainly not the government, your employer or school administrator, or the overworked and underappreciated police officer you may count on to save you some day. Take a pledge not to rely on others. Promise yourself that you will **become responsible and accountable for your wellbeing**. By reading this book (and its prequel) you are already more knowledgeable than most folks about the far-ranging, complex subject of violence. Now is the time to **implement what you have learned**. Exercise good situational awareness, be prepared to react responsibly to whatever dangers you may encounter, and don't be a douche.

As Patrick Swayze (as Dalton, in the movie *Roadhouse*) once said, "Be nice, until it is time not to be nice." Yeah, we quoted *Roadhouse*, not because we consider it the *Citizen Kane* of our time, but because what that character said is true. **Be nice... Until (or unless) you have to *not* be nice**.

Weapon use varies with the type of crime, with robberies the most likely to involve an armed assailant and sexual assaults the least likely. According to the Bureau of Justice Statistics, males, Blacks, Hispanics, and those between ages 15 and 24 are more vulnerable than their respective counterparts to violent crime committed by armed assailants.

So yeah, be nice. Live a happy life. Love, find joy in others, and make the best you can with what the world happens to let fall upon your head. The world simply doesn't care, but that doesn't mean that you shouldn't... If you happen to be in the wrong place, a bad place, at the right time there is simply nothing to be done except to deal with it.

Armed with the new knowledge you have gained here we encourage you to think, digest, and integrate what you have learned into your existence. However, we simultaneously want to make it clear that walking around cocked, locked, and loaded is a bad way to go through life. Life, organic organisms, are not designed for prolonged stress. It kills us from the inside out. Humans, like any animal, are designed to handle stress in short bursts. Fear, anxiety, hatred, loathing, and envy are all lower emotions; they come from deep down within your mind. We are well aware that what we have put forth can appeal to the lower emotions, hence we are cautioning you not to adopt a bad attitude. Nothing good can come from it.

There is an old account of a samurai who was sent by his *daimyo* (liege lord) to execute a prisoner. When the samurai arrived at the execution site the condemned man spat at him and slapped him in the face. Rather than carry out his task, the warrior turned around and left. As he walked away, the prisoner began to taunt the samurai saying that he was too weak, too cowardly to use his blade. Undaunted, the samurai replied that he was not in control of his emotions. He promised that he would return once his anger was properly held in check, because **killing the prisoner in a fit of rage over an insult would not be appropriate**. It was not the reason for which he had been sent to execute the other man.

There is a lot of wisdom in this tale. This is the attitude we encourage, to know why you do what you do when it comes to self-protection. **Do not act out of fear, but rather out of informed, thoughtful reason**. Hug when it is time to hug. Strike *only* when it is time to strike. Stay in touch with those you care about, be gentle, confident, and prepared... And, live a healthy life that others will honor when you have passed on.

Be safe... and be well.

APPENDIX A – TYPES OF VIOLENCE REFRESHER

"Most of them [criminals] are looking for victims, not challenges."

– Michael Janich

It's vital to understand what you're facing. Strategies that can de-escalate social violence can backfire and spark predatory violence. For those who have not read our previous works, here is a brief refresher on the various types of violence. Much of this was first codified by Rory Miller.

Social Violence

One key to social violence is the presence of witnesses, people who the other guy is playing to. He may be trying to establish status, deliver an educational beat-down, or even gang together with his friends to stake out territory. In most cases, however, there is an audience of his same social class to observe his actions. If he is going to win, he will want someone around to see it. Social violence can be roughly broken into the following categories:

- **The Monkey Dance**.
- **The Group Monkey Dance**.
- **The Educational Beat-Down**.
- **The Status-Seeking Show**.
- **The Territorial Defense**.

The Monkey Dance: Like animals in the wild, humans often delineate their social positions through violence. Rather than locking horns, however, these conflicts take the form of fistfights and other unarmed conflict. Monkey dances are almost always initiated with someone whom the aggressor sees as close to his social level. There is no status to be gained by a grown adult monkey-dancing with a child or elderly person. Similarly, regular people will not attempt to monkey dance with a very high-ranking individual. Mid-level people in everything from biker gangs to corporate management constantly jockey for position, but they do not do it with the folks in charge. It's too much of a leap. Challenging the group's senior leaders like that tends to be career limiting at best.

The Group Monkey Dance: The group monkey dance is about solidarity, as a way to establish territory or a method of discouraging outsiders from interfering with the group's business. Sometimes the victim is an insider who betrayed the group too. In these cases, the fight can become a contest of showing loyalty to the group by determining who can dish out the most damage to the victim. Unlike an individual monkey dance, the group monkey dance can easily end with a murder, even when killing the victim was not the initial goal, because of the group dynamics.

The Educational Beat-Down: In some places or elements of society, if you do something rude and inconsiderate, you could be socially excluded or ostracized. In others, you will have the crap beaten out of you. It's sort of a spanking between adults, an extreme show of displeasure designed to enforce the "rules." If the recipient did not do something horrific to initiate the attack and properly acknowledges the wrong, an educational beat-down can be over quickly and end without significant or lasting injury. Not understanding or conceding the wrongdoing or repeated behavior that is outside the group's rules, on the other hand, can lead to a beat-down that is designed to maim or kill.

The Status-Seeking Show: In certain segments of society, such as criminal subculture, a reputation for violence can be valuable, leading others to treat you with more respect or deference. The challenge is that for someone to be truly feared and respected, they may feel a need to do something crazy beyond the bounds of "normal" social violence, such as attacking a child, disabled individual, law enforcement officer, or elderly person. It's still social violence because it is designed to develop status for the aggressor, yet the outcome could easily be fatal for the victim.

The Territorial Defense: Defending one's territory against "other" members of different social groups is fairly common in certain aspects of society. Take gang culture, for instance, where it's an "us versus them" worldview that can easily lead to violence directed at people who look, act, or dress differently than the group. Territorial defense, which includes such things as driving others out or even killing them from straying onto your turf, is a bridge between social and asocial violence. While it is a defense of the group's turf or resources, it is often carried out in a manner that is profoundly asocial. This type of conflict is deliberately developed and maintained by the leaders of the involved group.

Asocial or Predatory Violence

Predatory violence is completely different than social disputes. Violence is either a means to an end or the goal itself. There are two basic types of predators: resource and process. The former is after your stuff while the latter is after you. Predators are often solitary because it is hard for antisocial people to band together for common purpose for any length of time. There are generally no witnesses to the attack, or the person is playing to someone of a different social class where his actions make no logical sense. The presence or absence of witnesses is one of the key methods of knowing what you face on the street.

Recidivism rates in the US are shockingly high. About two-thirds of prisoners are arrested for a new crime within 3 years of release, and three-quarters within 5 years. According to the Bureau of Justice Statistics, over 80% of property offenders are arrested for a new crime, compared to 76.9% of drug offenders, 73.6% of public order offenders, and 71.3% of violent offenders.

Resource predators: A resource predator wants something badly enough to take it from his victim by force. Examples include muggers, robbers, or carjackers. Such aggressors are often armed. If intimidation alone works, the resource predator may not hurt you, such as in a carjacking scenario where if the vehicle is surrendered quickly, the victim is almost always left behind uninjured. A ten-year Bureau of Justice Statistics study showed that while 74 percent of all carjackings were perpetrated by armed individuals, only 0.004 percent led to murder. Because auto-related abductions were thrown into the mix, the homicide rate from straight-up carjackings could potentially be even lower than that.

Process predators: Process predators act out in violent ways for the sake of the violent act itself. They are extraordinarily dangerous. Unless the process predator perceives that you are too costly to attack, it's going to get physical. You do not have to win, but you absolutely cannot afford to lose. The situation needs to end immediately. It may require you take a human life to come out as intact as possible. Rapists and serial killers are examples of process predators. A fight with a process predator frequently ends with someone in the hospital or morgue.

APPENDIX B – JUDICIOUS USE OF COUNTERVAILING FORCE REFRESHER

"Rambo isn't violent. I see Rambo as a philanthropist."
– Sylvester Stallone

Because claiming self-defense is an affirmative defense, the burden of proof shifts from the prosecutor to you if you're charged for a crime. The prosecution does not need to prove that someone was killed or maimed, or whatever, and that you did it. In pleading self-defense you just did the job for him or her, you've admitted to a crime but arguing that you should not be punished because it was justifiable under the circumstances. The challenge is that you must then prove that you had no choice but to do what you did.

There are two common principles for showing that you had to use countervailing force in self-defense, Ability, Opportunity, Jeopardy, and Preclusion (AOJP) or Intent, Means, Opportunity, and Preclusion (IMOP). Whichever version you use, all four of the criteria must be met before you have a good case for taking action or, conversely, if all four are not met you're in for a world of hurt. The presence of these may be sufficient for you to act in self-defense, but that may not be enough for you to prevail in court. You must also be able to explain how you personally knew that each element was present in a way that the judge and/or jury will believe.

IMOP

Intent, means, and opportunity are the desire, the ability, and the access to hurt you. You must be able to show all three to justify using force for self-defense. Here are some brief explanations:

- **Intent**. You must be able to show that the other guy wanted to do you harm and explain how you knew. Because people have chances to kill you all the time, judging intent is critical to claiming self-defense. For example, a waiter bringing you a steak knife has a deadly weapon and is well within range, yet no one attacks their server, nor do waiters live in fear, because we all understand that without intent there is no threat. We don't act.

- **Means**. All the intent in the world does not matter if the other guy couldn't hurt you. For example, a two-year-old throwing a temper tantrum has some of the purest intent in the world, but he or she lacks the size, strength, and coordination to do anything severe. You must be able to articulate exactly what led to your fear in a way that demonstrates it was legitimate.

- **Opportunity**. Intent and means do not matter if the threat cannot reach you. If someone is screaming he is going to kick your ass from across the room, he may be a threat but he is probably not an immediate threat unless he has a gun. Similarly, someone waving a knife at you from inside a vehicle while you are walking on the sidewalk is not an immediate threat either because you are out of reach. If he slams the accelerator and the car lurches toward you, that situation has changed significantly.

- **Preclusion**. Even if intent, means, and opportunity are clear, there is one other requirement (for civilians and in most states) to satisfy. You must be able to show that you had no safe alternatives other than physical force before engaging an opponent in combat. If you can retreat without further endangering yourself, this criterion has not been met. After all, it is impossible for the other guy to hurt you if you are not there. Could you have left? Could you have run without putting yourself in further danger? Did you in any way contribute to the situation getting out of hand? "Stand-your-ground" statutes or "castle laws" may reduce or eliminate the need to show preclusion in certain jurisdictions.

> Killing a felon during the commission of a violent felony is considered justifiable homicide. In 2013, a fairly representative snapshot of what has occurred over the last decade, private citizens killed 281 assailants in self-defense. During that same year, law enforcement officers killed 461 violent offenders while on the job. Collectively this is 742 justifiable homicides.

In addition to IMOP, above, you must use a level of force appropriate for the situation you face. In other words, would a reasonable person have seen a way out or seen a way that used less force? You must not only prove the threat was real and immediate, but that you had no other good options. Clearly you should never let fear of legal repercussions keep you from defending yourself when your life is on the line, but a broad understanding of the law as it relates to self-defense can help assure that you don't win the fight but lose the battle (as in go to jail, lose a lawsuit, etc.) afterward.

Disparity of Force

Another important aspect of self-defense is disparity of force. While there is no such thing as a fair fight in most instances, legally there is often an expectation of one. Equal-force doctrines in some jurisdictions require law-abiding citizens to respond to an attack with little or no more force than that which he or she perceives is being used against him or her. In some places, the law clearly specifies that equal force must be exactly equal. The attacked can respond with no more force than that by which he or she is threatened. Disparity of force exists if:

- The victim is being attacked by someone who is physically much stronger, fitter, or younger.
- The victim is being attacked by two or more assailants of similar or equal size.
- The victim is unarmed and facing one or more armed assailants.

Where disparity of force exists, you may legitimately be able to exert potentially lethal force to defend yourself. However, a person cannot legally respond to an assault of slight degree with deadly force. Such overreaction will land you in serious legal trouble.

Proportional Force

In practice, you will usually want to respond to an assault with a degree of force sufficiently, but not greatly, superior to that with which you are threatened. There are two advantages to this "slightly greater" degree of force doctrine:

- It places the defender in a more secure tactical position.
- It discourages the assailant from continuing to attack and escalating into a position where lethal force is required.

If you are found guilty in a jury trial, you will be spending time in prison. You may also suffer consequences with others in the community, facing challenges from family, friends, employers, and others you interact with. Consequently, while you should never let fear of legal consequences keep you from surviving a violent encounter, you must keep your wits about you at all times so that you do not overreact.

APPENDIX C – SITUATIONAL AWARENESS REFRESHER

"Fear without confirmation of danger is both paranoia and a self-fulfilling prophecy."
– Marc "Animal" MacYoung

Any time you are near others, especially strangers, it pays to be vigilant. Bad guys don't want to fight, they want to win. Consequently, tough, prepared targets are usually left alone in favor of easier prey. You cannot, however, walk around in a constant state of hyper-vigilance or paranoia. Self-defense experts often use a color code system to define appropriate levels of situational awareness that help you strike the right balance, paying attention to what's important, and keeping yourself safe.

Good situational awareness not only staves off trouble, letting you walk (or run) away from most dangers before they materialize, it also prepares you to react prudently in circumstances when trouble is unavoidable. Try watching a crowd at a mall, nightclub, or other public area with a predator mindset sometime; it can be an illuminating experience. Read other people's body language as they pass by you. Who looks like a victim and who does not? Whose pocket would you feel comfortable trying to pick? Who scares you? Why? Identifying body language and preparedness levels in others can help you find it within yourself.

The most commonly used approach for categorizing levels of awareness was codified by Colonel Jeff Cooper. His system was based in large part on the color alert system developed by the United States Marine Corps during World War II and later modified for civilian use. These color code conditions include White (oblivious), Yellow (aware), Orange (alert), Red (concerned), and Black (under attack). The colors themselves are far less important than the overall concept—different levels of awareness are appropriate for different situations.

While it is possible to move up and down the entire scale, clearly hitting each condition in turn, it is also possible to skip from one level to another very quickly. Consequently, while it is valuable to think of each condition as a distinct state along a continuum like rungs of a ladder, don't get too hung up on each level. The mindset and attitude of each condition are described below:

- **Condition White** (Oblivious). You are unaware of your surroundings, completely unprepared for trouble if it arrives. Drivers carrying on conversations with passengers, people talking on cell phones, joggers wearing headphones and jamming to their music, and other preoccupied individuals fall into this category. Folks who operate in this mode will often have their heads tilted downward toward the ground or fixed on a distant spot rather than scanning their environment. In this state they become easy marks for pickpockets, muggers, rapists, or other deviants they might stumble across. If you are attacked in Condition White, you are likely going to be hurt. If armed, you can easily become a danger to yourself or others. Even police officers, who have access to much better training than the average civilian, have been killed by their own weapons when they relaxed their vigilance at the wrong times or places.

- **Condition Yellow** (Aware). This is the baseline for situational awareness in public places because although you are not looking for or expecting trouble, if it comes up you will have a good chance to identify it in time to react. People in this condition are generally aware of their surroundings. You should be able to identify who and what is around you, spotting vehicles, people, building entrances, street corners, and areas that might provide concealment

> Hand-to-hand combat skills are used by soldiers deployed in war zones not only during close quarters combat, but also in crowd control situations as well as to maintain control over detainees and prisoners. Combatives training helps them develop the aggression and confidence necessary to close with an enemy in order to seize the initiative, dominate, disable, or kill.

and/or cover should something untoward happen. There is a natural feel to any area, something those who live and work there get to know and understand (which is why it's so hard for most folks to get a good night's sleep the first time they stay in a new hotel room; the sights, sounds, and smells are unfamiliar). Anything or anyone who breaks that normal pattern is not necessarily concerning, but the simple fact that something is unusual merits further scrutiny to assess the potential threat.

- **Condition Orange** (Alert). People in this state have become aware of some non-specific danger and need to ascertain whether there is a legitimate threat. You may have heard a nearby shout, the sound of glass breaking, or an unidentified sudden noise. You might also have seen another person or a group of people acting abnormally, someone whose demeanor makes you feel uncomfortable, or somebody whose behavior stands out from the norm. Scrutinize the situation while continuing to focus all around you since trouble may be starting in other places in addition to the one that has drawn your attention. Although it is premature to make any aggressive moves at this point, build a plan to evade, escape, or fight back as necessary. If things go south you'll have an easier time acting, yet if it turns out that trouble is not brewing you simply chalk things up to practice and abandon the plan.

- **Condition Red** (Concerned). People in this condition have been confronted by a potential adversary or are in close proximity to someone who is becoming aggressive and is near enough to confront them quickly. Because you have every reason to believe that the other guy(s) poses a clear and present danger, you must be prepared to fight, taking advantage of the plan you visualized in Condition Orange (assuming you had sufficient warning). Begin moving away toward escape routes, locations with strategic cover, or areas of concealment if you can do so. If the confrontation is immediate, it is often a good idea to try to move away from any weapons being brandished or distractions being made, while at the same time keeping well aware of them. If you are armed and the situation warrants a lethal response, this may be the point where you draw and ready your weapon or at least make its presence known. A verbal challenge at this point may prove useful if time permits. De-escalation may still be an option but it can also backfire so you must be prepared in case it does not work. Every reasonable attempt should still be made to avoid a fight yet you must resign yourself to the very real possibility that it will be unsuccessful. While a show of ability and readiness to resist with countervailing force may stop the confrontation in its tracks, it could also elevate it to the next level.

- **Condition Black** (Under Attack). People in Condition Black are actively being attacked. Although it is possible to skip nearly instantly from Condition Yellow all the way up to Condition Black, encounters generally escalate at a pace where you can adjust your level of awareness incrementally so long as you did not start off in Condition White. Once you have been assaulted, verbal challenges and de-escalation attempts are no longer useful. You must flee or fight back, using any appropriate distractions and/or weapons at your disposal. If armed and confronted by an armed attacker or multiple unarmed assailants, you may decide to use your weapon in self-defense. Be sure that you are legally, ethically, and morally entitled to do so before employing potentially lethal countervailing force. Your intent must be to stop the assault that is in progress so that you can escape to safety or otherwise remain safe until help arrives. Your goal is to be safe, not to kill your attacker or teach him a lesson.

Any time you are near others, especially strangers, it pays to be vigilant so as not to be caught unawares by sudden violence. If you appear to be a tough, prepared target, most predators, bullies, and thugs will likely look for their victims elsewhere. You cannot walk around in a constant state of hyper-vigilance, however. It's emotionally and physically untenable. A color code system, therefore, gives you a mental model that defines appropriate levels of situational awareness to help you strike the appropriate balance between obliviousness and paranoia. By constantly surveying and evaluating your environment, you achieve more control over what ultimately happens to you. It's not a guarantee of perfect safety, yet good situational awareness will help you predict and avoid most dangerous situations.

BIBLIOGRAPHY

Articles:

- Ayoob, Massad. "Alley Shootout: Death of the Garden Grove Rapist." *American Handgunner* (November/December, 1990).
- Ayoob, Massad. "An Urban Gunfighter: The Lessons of Lance Thomas." *American Handgunner* (March/April, 2002).
- Ayoob, Massad. "No One Ever Raped a .44 Magnum: The Helen Weathers Incident." *American Handgunner* (September/October, 1986).
- Ayoob, Massad. "The False Hope of Gun-Free Zones." *American Handgunner* (November/December, 2014).
- Ayoob, Massad. "Reflections on the Church Shooting." *Backwoods Home Magazine* (June 24, 2015).
- Ayoob, Massad. "'Safety Catch' Lessons from Real World Shootings." *American Handgunner* (March/April, 2011).
- Baker, Al. "11 Years of Police Gunfire, in Painstaking Detail." *The New York Times* (May 8, 2008).
- Connell, Katherine. "Man Arrested for Firing Warning Shots: 'I did what Joe Biden told me to do.'" *National Review* (July 18, 2013).
- Doughton, Sandi. "A History of Violence and 'No-Contact' Orders." Seattle Times (October 28, 2012).
- Duke, Alan, "'Mama said knock you out': LL Cool J broke burglary suspect's nose, jaw, ribs." *CNN News*. Atlanta Georgia (August 24, 2012).
- Football Italia staff. "Bonucci Punched Armed Mugger!" *Football Italia* (October 20 2012).

- Goldstein, Amy. "The Private Arm of the Law: Some Question the Granting of Police Power to Security Firms." *The Washington Post* (January 2, 2007).
- Lohr, David. "10 Most Notorious Criminals in American History." *Huffington Post* (September 12, 2013).
- Lott, Maxim. "Flintlock from 1700s could land elderly NJ man in prison." *Foxnews.com* (February 18, 2015).
- Millard, Stuart. "Fifteen-Minute Messiah – The James Hydrick Story." Goodreads.com.
- Netter, Sarah. "Family Suing After Phoenix Cop Shoots Homeowner Instead of Intruder." *ABC News* (October 6, 2009).
- Norris, Chuck. "Preventing More Church Shootings. World Net Daily (June 21, 2015).
- Peterson, Nancy M. "Hugh Glass: Legendary Trapper in America's Western Frontier." *Wild West Magazine* (June, 2006).
- Rossen, Jeff and Avni Patel. "Mistaken for a criminal: Eyewitness identifications are often wrong." *USA Today* (April 21, 2014).
- Stone, Dr. Michael H. "Men Who Kill Policemen." *Violence and Gender* (Volume 2, Number 1, 2015).
- Towns, Carimah, "Pennsylvania Teen Convicted of a Crime for Recording Bullies at School." ThinkProgress.com (April 15, 2014).
- Pow, Helen. "'Just get a Shotgun': Joe Biden tells Americans they don't need an AR-15 for home security." *UK Daily Mail* (February 20, 2013).

Books:

- Christensen, Loren and Dr. Alexis Artwohl. *Deadly Force Encounters: What Cops Need To Know To Mentally And Physically Prepare For And Survive A Gunfight.* Boulder, CO: Paladin Enterprises, Inc., 1997.
- Davidson, Thomas N. *To Preserve Life: Hostage-Crisis Management.* Indianapolis, IN: Crisis Incident Management Agency (CIMACOM), 2002.
- DeBecker, Gavin. *The Gift of Fear: Survival Signals That Protect Us From Violence.* New York, NY: Dell Publishing, 1998.
- Durose, Matthew R., and Alexia D. Cooper, Ph.D. and Howard N. Snyder, Ph.D., *Recidivism of Prisoners Released in 30 States in 2005: Patterns from 2005 to 2010,* Bureau of Justice Statistics, April, 2014.
- Grossman, David A. *On Killing: The Psychological Cost of Learning to Kill in War and Society.* New York, NY: Little, Brown, and Company, 1995.
- Grossman, David A. and Loren Christensen. *On Combat: The Psychology and Physiology*

of Deadly Conflict in War and Peace. Belleville, IL: PPCT Research Publications, 2004.

- Kane, Lawrence A. *Surviving Armed Assaults: A Martial Artists Guide to Weapons, Street Violence, and Countervailing Force*. Boston, MA: YMAA, 2006.
- Kane, Lawrence A. and Kris Wilder. *The Little Black Book of Violence: What Every Young Man Needs to Know About Fighting*. Wolfeboro, NH: YMAA, 2009.
- Kang-Brown, Jacob and Jennifer Trone, Jennifer Fratello, and Tarika Daftary-Kapur. *A Generation Later: What We've Learned about Zero Tolerance in Schools*. Vera Institute of Justice Center on Youth Justice (Issue Brief, December, 2013).
- Lott, Jr. John R. and William M. Landes. *Multiple Victim Public Shootings, Bombings, and Right-to-Carry Concealed Handgun Laws: Contrasting Private and Public Law Enforcement*. University of Chicago, 1999.
- MacYoung, Marc. *A Professional's Guide to Ending Violence Quickly*. Boulder, CO: Paladin Enterprises, Inc., 1993.
- MacYoung, Marc. *Street E & E: Evading, Escaping, and Other Ways to Save Your Ass When Things Get Ugly*. Boulder, CO: Paladin Enterprises, Inc., 1993.
- Miller, Rory. *Conflict Communication A New Paradigm in Conscious Communication*. Washougal, WA: Wyrd Goat Press, 2014.
- Miller, Rory. *Drills: Training for Sudden Violence (A Chiron Manual)*. Washougal, WA: Wyrd Goat Press, 2011.
- Miller, Rory and Lawrence A. Kane. *Scaling Force: Dynamic Decision Making Under Threat of Violence*. Wolfeboro, NH: YMAA Publication Center, 2012.
- Nance, Malcolm. *The Terrorist Recognition Handbook: A Manual for Predicting and Identifying Terrorist Activities*. Guilford, CT: The Lyons Press, 2003.
- Panné, Jean-Louis and Andrzej Paczkowski, Karel Bartosek, Jean-Louis Margolin, Nicolas Werth, Stéphane Courtois, Mark Kramer, and Jonathan Murphy. *The Black Book of Communism: Crimes, Terror, Repression*. Cambridge, MA: Harvard University Press, 1999.
- Quinn, Peyton. *Real Fighting: Adrenaline Stress Conditioning through Scenario-Based Training*. Boulder, CO: Paladin Enterprises, Inc., 1996.
- Rostker, Bernard D. and Lawrence M. Hanser, William M. Hix, Carl Jensen, Andrew R. Morral, Greg Ridgeway, and Terry L. Schell. *Evaluation of the New York City Police Department Firearm Training and Firearm-Discharge Review Process*. Santa Monica, CA: Rand Corporation, 2008.
- Sockut, Eugene. *Secrets of Street Survival – Israeli Style: Staying Alive in a Civilian War Zone*. Boulder, CO: Paladin Enterprises, Inc., 1995.
- Suarez, Gabe. *Tactical Pistol Marksmanship: How to Improve Your Combat Shooting*

Skills. Boulder, CO: Paladin Enterprises, Inc., 2001.

- Suarez, Gabe. *The Combative Perspective: The Thinking Man's Guide to Self-Defense*. Boulder, CO: Paladin Enterprises, Inc., 2003.
- Taubert, Robert K. *Rattenkrieg! The Art and Science of Close Quarters Battle Pistol*. North Reading, MA: Saber Press, July 1, 2012.

DVDs

- Caracci, C.J. *CQB Clearing Tactics for First Responders (Shotgun) / Patrol Tactics for 911 Officer (Pistol)*. Loti Group, 2006.
- Habermehl, Chuck. *High Risk Entry*. Loti Group, 2003.

Television Broadcasts:

- Takeo, Ryan, *KIPX Channel 5 News*. San Fransico, Califonia (January 9, 2014).
- "Officer Transforms Tragedy Into Action For Mentally Ill." *KOAT Channel 7 News*. Albuquerque, New Mexico (November 19, 2008).

Websites:

- Chris McGoey (www.crimedoctor.com).
- Force Science Institute (www.forcescience.org).
- Marc MacYoung (www.nononsenselfdefense.com).
- The Bureau of Justice Statistics (www.bjs.gov).
- The Federal Bureau of Investigation (www.fbi.gov).
- The New York Times (www.nytimes.com).
- The Seattle Times (www.seattletimes.com).
- Stratfor (www.stratfor.com).
- Unified Crime Reports (www.fbi.gov/about-us/cjis/ucr/ucr).
- United States Bureau of Labor Statistics (http://www.bls.gov).
- United States Department of State travel safe program (http://travel.state.gov/content/passports/english/alertswarnings.html).
- Yahoo News (www.news.yahoo.com).

Lawrence A. Kane, ECOP, CSP, CIAP

Lawrence was inducted into the Sourcing Industry Group (SIG) Sourcing Supernova Hall of Fame in 2018 for pioneering leadership in strategic sourcing, procurement, supplier innovation, and digital transformation. An Executive Certified Outsourcing Professional, Certified Sourcing Professional, and Certified Intelligent Automation Professional, he currently works as a senior leader at a Fortune® 50 corporation where he gets to play with billions of dollars of other people's money and make really important decisions.

A martial artist, judicious use-of-force expert, and the bestselling author of 19 books, he has won numerous awards including the 5th Annual Beverly Hills Book Award and Presidential Prize, the 13th Annual USA Best Book Awards winner, the 11th and 14th Annual National Indie Excellence Awards winner, a Next Generation Indie Book Awards winner, 3 ForeWord Magazine Book of the Year Award finalists, 5 USA Book News Best Books Award finalists, 3 Next Generation Indie Book Awards finalists, 2 Beverly Hills Book Awards finalists, and an eLit Book Awards Bronze prize.

Since 1970, Lawrence has studied and taught traditional Asian martial arts, medieval European combat, and modern close-quarter weapon techniques. Working stadium security part-time for 26 years he was involved in hundreds of violent altercations, but got paid to watch football. A founding technical consultant to University of New Mexico's Institute of Traditional Martial Arts, he has also written hundreds of articles on martial arts, self-defense, countervailing force, and related topics.

He has been interviewed numerous times on podcasts (e.g., Art of Procurement, Negotiations Ninja Podcast), nationally syndicated and local radio shows (e.g., Biz Talk Radio, The Jim Bohannon Show), and television programs (e.g., Fox Morning News) as well as by reporters from Computerworld, Le Matin, Practical Taekwondo, Forbes, Traditional Karate, and Police Magazine, among other publications. He was once interviewed in English by a reporter from a Swiss newspaper for an article that was published in French, and found that oddly amusing.

Lawrence lives in Seattle, Washington. You can contact him directly at lakane@ix.netcom.com or connect with him on LinkedIn (www.linkedin.com/in/lawrenceakane).

Kris Wilder, BBC

Kris Wilder is a Board-Certified Coach and internationally renowned martial arts expert who was inducted into the US Martial Arts Hall of Fame in 2018. He runs the West Seattle Karate Academy, a frequent destination for practitioners from around the world which also serves the local community. Sensei Wilder has earned black belt rankings in three styles, karate, judo, and taekwondo, and often travels to conduct seminars across the United States, Canada, and Europe.

A National Representative for the University of New Mexico's Institute of Traditional Martial Arts, Kris has also taught self-defense and lectured at Washington State University and Susquehanna University. He spent about 15 years in the political and public affairs arena, working for campaigns from the local to national level. During this consulting career, he was periodically on staff for elected officials. His work also involved lobbying and corporate affairs. And, he was also a member of The Order of St. Francis (OSF), one of many active Apostolic Christian Orders.

Kris is the bestselling author of 21 books, including a Beverly Hills Book Award and Presidential Prize winner, a USA Best Book Awards winner, a National Indie Excellence Awards winner, and a Next Generation Indie Book Awards winner. He has been interviewed on CNN, FOX, The Huffington Post, Thrillist, Nickelodeon, Howard Stern, and more.

Kris lives in Seattle, Washington. You can contact him directly at Kriswilder@kriswilder.com, follow him on Twitter (@kris_wilder), on Facebook (www.facebook.com/kris.wilder) or Instagram (https://www. instagram.com/thekriswilder/).

AMALGAMATED WORKS BY THE AUTHOR

Non-Fiction Books:

1. <u>Musashi's Dokkodo</u> (Kane/Wilder)

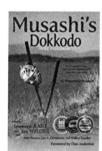

"The authors have made classic samurai wisdom accessible to the modern martial artist like never before" – **Goran Powell**, award winning author of *Chojun* and *A Sudden Dawn*

Shortly before he died, Miyamoto Musashi (1584 – 1645) wrote down his final thoughts about life for his favorite student Terao Magonojō to whom *Go Rin No Sho*, his famous *Book of Five Rings*, had also been dedicated. He called this treatise *Dokkodo*, which translates as *"The Way of Walking Alone."* This treatise contains Musashi's original 21 precepts of the *Dokkodo* along with five different interpretations of each passage written from the viewpoints of a monk, a warrior, a teacher, an insurance executive, and a businessman. In this fashion you are not just reading a simple translation of Musashi's writing, you are scrutinizing his final words for deeper meaning. In them are enduring lessons for how to lead a successful and meaningful life.

2. <u>The Little Black Book of Violence</u> (Kane/Wilder)

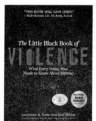

"This book will save lives!" – **Alain Burrese**, JD, former US Army 2nd Infantry Division Scout Sniper School instructor

Men commit 80% of all violent crimes and are twice as likely to become the victims of aggressive behavior. This book is primarily written for men ages 15 to 35, and contains more than mere self-defense techniques. You will learn crucial information about street survival that most martial arts instructors don't even know. Discover how to use awareness, avoidance, and de—escalation to help stave off violence, know when it's prudent to fight, and understand how to do so effectively when fighting is unavoidable.

3. Sh!t Sun Tzu Said (Kane/Wilder)

"If you had to choose one variant of Sun Tzu's collected work, this one should be at the top of the pile... I loved it!" – **Jeffrey-Peter Hauck**, MSc, JD, Police SGT (Ret.), LPI, CPT USA, Professor of Criminal Justice

Sun Tzu was a famous Chinese general whose mastery of strategy was so exceptional that he reportedly transformed 180 courtesans into skilled soldiers in a single training session. While that episode was likely exaggerated, historians agree that Sun Tzu defeated the Ch'u, Qi, and Chin states for King Ho-Lu, forging his empire. In 510 BC, Master Tzu recorded his winning strategies in Art of War, the earliest surviving and most revered tome of its kind. With methods so powerful they can conquer an adversary's spirit, you can use Master Tzu's strategies to overcome any challenge, from warfare to self-defense to business negotiations. This book starts with the classic 1910 translation of *Art of War*, adds modern and historical insight, and demonstrates how to put the master's timeless wisdom to use in your everyday life. In this fashion, the *Art of War* becomes accessible for the modern mind, simultaneously entertaining, enlightening, and practical.

4. The Big Bloody Book of Violence (Kane/Wilder)

"Implementing even a fraction of this book's suggestions will substantially increase your overall safety." – **Gila Hayes**, Armed Citizens' Legal Defense Network

All throughout history ordinary people have been at risk of violence in one way or another. Abdicating personal responsibility by outsourcing your safety to others might be the easy way out, but it does little to safeguard your welfare. In this book you'll discover what dangers you face and learn proven strategies to thwart them. Self-defense is far more than fighting skills; it's a lifestyle choice, a more enlightened way of looking at and moving through the world. Learn to make sense of "senseless" violence, overcome talisman thinking, escape riots, avert terrorism, circumvent gangs, defend against home invasions, safely interact with law enforcement, and conquer seemingly impossible odds.

5. Dude, The World's Gonna Punch You in the Face (Wilder/Kane)

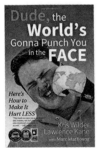

"As an emergency room physician, I see a lot of injuries. This book can save you a lot of pain and trauma, not just physical but also emotional and financial as well. Do yourself a favor, read it, and stay out of my Emergency Room." – **Jeff Cooper**, MD

We only get one shot at life. And, it's really easy to screw that up because the world wants to punch us all in the face. Hard! But, what if you knew when to duck? What if you were warned about the dangers—and possibilities—ahead of time? Here is how to man-up and take on whatever the world throws at you.

This powerful book arms young men with knowledge about love, wealth, education, faith, government, leadership, work, relationships, life, and violence. It won't prevent all mistakes, nothing will, but it can keep you from making the impactful ones that you'll regret the most. This book is quick knowledge, easy to read, and brutally frank, just the way the world gives it to you, except without the pain. Read on. Learn how to see the bad things coming and avoid them.

6. Sensei Mentor Teacher Coach (Wilder/Kane)

"Finally, a book that will actually move the needle in closing the leadership skills gap found in all aspects of our society." – **Dan Roberts**, CEO and President, Ouellette & Associates

Many books weave platitudes, promising the keys to success in leadership, secrets that will transform you into the great leader, the one. The fact of the matter is, however, that true leadership really isn't about you. It's about giving back, offering your best to others so that they can find the best in themselves. The methodologies in this book help you become the leader you were meant to be by bringing your goals and other peoples' needs together to create a powerful, combined vision. Learn how to access the deeper aspects of who you are, your unique qualities, and push them forward in actionable ways. Acquire this vital information and advance your leadership journey today.

7. Dirty Ground (Kane/Wilder)

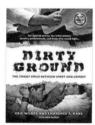

"Fills a void in martial arts training." – **Loren W. Christensen**, Martial Arts Masters Hall of Fame member

This book addresses a significant gap in most martial arts training, the tricky space that lies between sport and combat applications where you need to control a person without injuring him (or her). Techniques in this region are called "drunkle," named after the drunken uncle disrupting a family gathering. Understanding how to deal with combat, sport, and drunkle situations is vital because appropriate use of force is codified in law and actions that do not accommodate these regulations can have severe repercussions. Martial arts techniques must be adapted to best fit the situation you find yourself in. This book shows you how.

8. Scaling Force (Kane/Miller)

"If you're serious about learning how the application of physical force works—before, during and after the fact—I cannot recommend this book highly enough." – **Lt. Jon Lupo**, New York State Police

Conflict and violence cover a broad range of behaviors, from intimidation to murder, and require an equally broad range of responses. A kind word will not resolve all situations, nor will wristlocks, punches, or even a gun. This book introduces the full range of options, from skillfully doing nothing to employing deadly force. You will understand the limits of each type of force, when specific levels may be appropriate, the circumstances under which you may have to apply them, and the potential costs, legally and personally, of your decision. If you do not know how to succeed at all six levels covered in this book there are situations in which you will have no appropriate options. More often than not, that will end badly.

9. Surviving Armed Assaults (Kane)

"This book will be an invaluable resource for anyone walking the warrior's path, and anyone who is interested in this vital topic." – **Lt. Col. Dave Grossman**, Director, Warrior Science Group

A sad fact is that weapon-wielding thugs victimize 1,773,000 citizens every year in the United States alone. Even martial artists are not immune from this deadly threat. Consequently, self-defense training that does not consider the very real possibility of an armed attack is dangerously incomplete. You should be both mentally and physically prepared to deal with an unprovoked armed assault at any time. Preparation must be comprehensive enough to account for the plethora of pointy objects, blunt instruments, explosive devices, and deadly projectiles that someday could be used against you. This extensive book teaches proven survival skills that can keep you safe.

10. The 87—Fold Path to Being the Best Martial Artist (Kane/Wilder)

"The 87—Fold Path contains unexpected, concise blows to the head and heart… you don't have a chance, but to examine and retool your way of life." – **George Rohrer**, Executive and Purpose Coach, MBA, CPCC, PCC

Despite the fact that raw materials in feudal Japan were mediocre at best, bladesmiths used innovative techniques to forge some of the finest swords imaginable for their samurai overlords. The process of heating and folding the metal removed impurities, while shaping and strengthening the blades to perfection. The end result was strong yet supple, beautiful and deadly. As martial artists we utilize a similar process, forging our bodies through hard work, perseverance, and repetition. Knowing how to fight is important, clearly, yet if you do not find something larger than base violence attached your efforts it becomes unsustainable. *The 87-Fold Path* provides ideas for taking your training beyond the physical that are uniquely tailored for the elite martial artist.

11. How to Win a Fight (Kane/Wilder)

"It is the ultimate course in self-defense and will help you survive and get through just about any violent situation or attack." – **Jeff Rivera**, bestselling author

More than 3,000,000 Americans are involved in a violent physical encounter every year. Develop the fortitude to walk away when you can and prevail when you must. Defense begins by scanning your environment, recognizing hazards and escape routes, and using verbal de-escalation to defuse tense situations. If a fight is unavoidable, the authors offer clear guidance for being the victor, along with advice on legal implications, including how to handle a police interview after the altercation.

12. <u>Lessons from the Dojo Floor</u> (Wilder)

"Helps each reader, from white belt to black belt, look at and understand why he or she trains." – **Michael E. Odell**, Isshin-Ryu Northwest Okinawa Karate Association

In the vein of Dave Lowry, a thought-provoking collection of short vignettes that entertains while it educates. Packed with straightforward, easy, and quick to read sections that range from profound to insightful to just plain amusing, anyone with an affinity for martial arts can benefit from this material. This book educates, entertains, and ultimately challenges every martial artist from beginner to black belt.

13. <u>Martial Arts Instruction</u> (Kane)

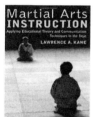

"Boeing trains hundreds of security officers, Kane's ideas will help us be more effective." – **Gregory A. Gwash**, Chief Security Officer, The Boeing Company

While the old adage, "those who can't do, teach," is not entirely true, all too often "those who can do" cannot teach effectively. This book is unique in that it offers a holistic approach to teaching martial arts; incorporating elements of educational theory and communication techniques typically overlooked in *budo* (warrior arts). Teachers will improve their abilities to motivate, educate, and retain students, while students interested in the martial arts will develop a better understanding of what instructional method best suits their needs.

14. <u>The Way of Kata</u> (Kane/Wilder)

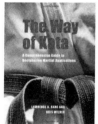

"This superb book is essential reading for all those who wish to understand the highly effective techniques, concepts, and strategies that the *kata* were created to record." – **Iain Abernethy**, British Combat Association Hall of Fame member

The ancient masters developed *kata*, or "formal exercises," as fault—tolerant methods to preserve their unique, combat-proven fighting systems. Unfortunately, they also deployed a two-track system of instruction where only the select inner circle that had gained a master's trust and respect would be taught the powerful hidden applications of *kata*. The theory of deciphering *kata* was once a great mystery revealed only to trusted disciples of the ancient masters in order to protect the secrets of their systems. Even today, while the basic movements of *kata* are widely known, the principles and rules for understanding *kata* applications are largely unknown. This groundbreaking book unveils these methods, not only teaching you how to analyze your *kata* to understand what it is trying to tell you, but also helping you to utilize your fighting techniques more effectively.

15. The Way of Martial Arts for Kids (Wilder)

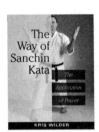

"Written in a personable, engaging style that will appeal to kids and adults alike." – **Laura Weller**, Guitarist, *The Green Pajamas*

Based on centuries of traditions, martial arts training can be a positive experience for kids. The book helps you and yours get the most out of every class. It shows how just about any child can become one of those few exemplary learners who excel in the training hall as well as in life. Written to children, it is also for parents as well. After all, while the martial arts instructor knows his art, no one knows his/her child better than the parent. Together you can help your child achieve just about anything... The advice provided is straightforward, easy to understand, and written with a child-reader in mind so that it can either be studied by the child and/or read together with the parent to assure solid results.

16. The Way of Sanchin Kata (Wilder)

"This book has been sorely needed for generations!" – **Philip Starr**, National Chairman, Yiliquan Martial Arts Association

When karate was first developed in Okinawa it was about using technique and extraordinary power to end a fight instantly. These old ways of generating remarkable power are still accessible, but they are purposefully hidden in *sanchin kata* for the truly dedicated to find. This book takes the practitioner to new depths of practice by breaking down the form piece-by-piece, body part by body part, so that the very foundation of the *kata* is revealed. Every chapter, concept, and application is accompanied by a "Test It" section, designed for you to explore and verify the *kata* for yourself. *Sanchin kata* really comes alive when you feel the thrill of having those hidden teachings speak to you across the ages through your body. Simply put, once you read this book and test what you have learned, your karate will never be the same.

17. Journey: The Martial Artist's Notebook (Kane/Wilder)

"Students who take notes progress faster and enjoy a deeper understanding than those who don't. Period." – **Loren W. Christensen**, Martial Arts Masters Hall of Fame inductee

As martial arts students progress through the lower ranks it is extraordinarily useful for them to keep a record of what they have learned. The mere process of writing things down facilitates deeper understanding. This concept is so successful, in fact, that many schools require advanced students to complete a thesis or research project concurrent with testing for black belt rank, advancing the knowledge base of the organization while simultaneously clarifying and adding depth to each practitioner's understanding of his or her art. Just as Bruce Lee's notes and essays became *Tao of Jeet Kune Do*, perhaps someday your training journal will be published for the masses, but first and foremost this notebook is by you, for you. This is where the deeper journey on your martial path toward mastery begins.

18. <u>The Way to Black Belt</u> (Kane/Wilder)

"It is so good I wish I had written it myself." – **Hanshi Patrick McCarthy**, Director, International Ryukyu Karate Research Society

Cut to the very core of what it means to be successful in the martial arts. Earning a black belt can be the most rewarding experience of a lifetime, but getting there takes considerable planning. Whether your interests are in the classical styles of Asia or in today's Mixed Martial Arts (MMA), this book prepares you to meet every challenge. Whatever your age, whatever your gender, you will benefit from the wisdom of master martial artists around the globe, including Iain Abernethy, Dan Anderson, Loren Christensen, Jeff Cooper, Wim Demeere, Aaron Fields, Rory Miller, Martina Sprague, Phillip Starr, and many more, who share more than 300 years of combined training experience. Benefit from their guidance during your development into a first-class black belt.

19. <u>Wolves in Street Clothing</u> (Wilder/ Hollingsworth)

"Teaches folks to rekindle tools that are already in us—already in our DNA—and have been there for thousands of years." – **Ron Jarvis**, Tracker, Outdoorsman, Self-Defense Instructor

This book gives you a new light in which to see human predatory behavior. As we move farther and farther from our roots insulating ourselves in technology and air-conditioned homes we get disconnected from the inherent and innate aspects of understanding the precursors to violent behavior. Violence is not always emotionally bound, often and in the animal kingdom is simply a tool to access a needed resource—or to protect an essential resource. Distance, encroachment, and signals are keys to avoiding a predator. Why would a cougar attack a man after a bike ride? Why would a bear attack a man in a hot tub? Why would a thug rob one person and not another? The predatory animal mind holds many of the keys to the answer to these questions. Learn drills that will help you tune your focus and move through life safer and more aware of your surroundings.

20. <u>70-Second Sensei</u> (Kane/Wilder)

"I'll let you in on a secret. The *70-Second Sensei* is a gateway drug. It's short, easy to read, and useful. It has stuff in it that will make you a better instructor. Even a better person." — **Rory Miller**, Chiron Training

Once you have mastered the physical aspects of your martial art, it is time to take it to the next level—to lead, to teach, to leave a legacy. This innovative book shows you how. Sensei is a Japanese word, commonly translated as "teacher," which literally means "one who has come before." This term is usually applied to martial arts instructors, yet it can signify anyone who has blazed a trail for others to follow. It applies to all those who have acquired valuable knowledge, skills, and experience and are willing to share their expertise with others while continuing to grow themselves. After all, setting an example that others wish to emulate is the very essence of leadership. Clearly you cannot magically become an exemplary martial arts instructor in a mere 70-seconds any more than a businessperson can transform his or her leadership style from spending 60-seconds perusing The One Minute Manager. You can, however, devote a few minutes a day to honing your craft. It is about giving back, offering your best to others so that they can find the best in themselves. And, with appreciation, they can pay it forward...

21. The Contract Professional's Playbook (Nyden/Kane)

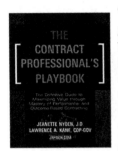

"While early career practitioners may understand the value of drafting, negotiating, and managing exceptional contracts, they often struggle to master the requisite skills. This comprehensive manual helps structure the negotiation process, thereby minimizing the perilous process of trial-and-error, expediting competency with leading practices and tools that can help reduce risk and speed outcomes for both buy-side and sell-side alike." — **Gregg Kirchhoefer**, P.C., IAOP Leadership Hall of Fame Member

Ever increasing demand for performance- and outcome-based agreements stems from pressure for enterprises to drive greater value from their strategic customer/supplier relationships. To achieve expected performance, contractual relationships are increasingly complex and interdependent, requiring more stakeholders be involved in the decision making. Unfortunately for contract professionals held accountable to these requirements there has been little in the way of resources that answer their "how to" questions about drafting, negotiating, and managing performance- and outcome-based agreements. Until now! *The Contract Professional's Playbook* (and corresponding eLearning program) walks subject matter experts who may be new to complex contracting step-by-step through all aspects of the contract life cycle. Invaluable competencies include identifying and managing risk, increasing influence with stakeholders, developing pricing models, negotiating complex deals, and governing customer-supplier relationships to avoid value leakage in the midst of constant change. It's an invaluable resource that raises the bar for buy-side and sell-side practitioners alike.

22. There are Angels in My Head! (Wilder)

"This is not a book on doctrine, dogma or collection of creeds to memorize in order to impress others with knowledge. This is a practical application of your participation in a new experience. Here you will find your questions answered even before they are asked." – **Br. Rich Atkinson**, Order of St. Francis

The unexplainable has happened. A prayer has been answered, a gift has been given, a communication has occurred... Is it the voice of God, or the voices in your head? Here's how to find out: In this groundbreaking book, you will discover the organization of the mystical experience. Based on the classic works of

G. B Scaramelli, an 18ᵗʰ Century Jesuit Priest, Wilder brings modern relevance to any person to apply to their journey as they seek the Divine. Using examples and principles from Christianity and other religions, Wilder demonstrates that mankind's profound mystical experience crosses all cultures and religions.

Fiction Books:

1. <u>Blinded by the Night</u> (Kane)

 "Kane's expertise in matters of mayhem shines throughout." – **Steve Perry**, bestselling author

Richard Hayes is a Seattle cop. After 25 years on the force he thinks he knows everything there is to know about predators. Rapists, murderers, gang bangers, and child molesters are just another day at the office, yet commonplace criminals become the least of his problems when he goes hunting for a serial killer and runs into a real monster. The creature not only attacks him, but merely gets pissed off when he shoots it. In the head. Twice! Surviving that fight is only the beginning. Richard discovers that the vampire he destroyed was the ruler of an eldritch realm he never dreamed existed. By some archaic rule, having defeated the monster's sovereign in battle, Richard becomes their new king. When it comes to human predators, Richard is a seasoned veteran, yet with paranormal ones he is but a rookie. He must navigate a web of intrigue and survive long enough to discover how a regular guy can tangle with supernatural creatures and prevail.

2. <u>Legends of the Masters</u> (Kane/Wilder)

 "It is a series of (very) short stories teaching life lessons. I'm going to bring it out when my nephews are over at family dinners for good discussion starters. A fun read!" – **Angela Palmore**

Storytelling is an ancient form of communication that still resonates today. An engaging story told and retold shares a meaningful message that can be passed down through the generations. Take fables such as *The Boy Who Cried Wolf* or *The Tortoise and the Hare*, who hasn't learned a thing or two from these ancient tales? This book retools Aesop's lesser-known fables, reimagining them to meet the needs and interests of modern martial artists. Reflecting upon the wisdom of yesteryear in this new light will surely bring value for practitioners of the arts today.

DVDs:

1. <u>121 Killer Appz</u> (Wilder/Kane)

"Quick and brutal, the way karate is meant to be." – **Eric Parsons**, Founder, Karate for Life Foundation

You know the *kata*, now it is time for the applications. *Gekisai (dai ni), Saifa, Seiyunchin, Seipai, Kururunfa, Suparinpei, Sanseiru, Shisochin,* and *Seisan kata* are covered. If you ever wondered what purpose a move from a *Goju Ryu* karate form was for, wonder no longer. This DVD contains no discussion, just a no-nonsense approach to one application after another. It illuminates your *kata* and stimulates deeper thought on determining your own applications from the *Goju Ryu* karate forms.

2. <u>Sanchin Kata: Three Battles Karate Kata</u> (Wilder)

"A cornucopia of martial arts knowledge." – **Shawn Kovacich**, endurance high—kicking world record holder (as certified by the Guinness Book of World Records)

A traditional training method for building karate power, *sanchin kata* is an ancient form. Some consider it the missing link between Chinese kung fu and Okinawan karate. This program breaks down the form piece by piece, body part by body part, so that the hidden details of the *kata* are revealed. This DVD complements the book *The Way of Sanchin Kata*, providing in-depth exploration of the form, with detailed instruction of the essential posture, linking the spine, generating power, and demonstration of the complete *kata*.

3. <u>Scaling Force</u> (Miller/Kane)

"Kane and Miller have been there, done that and have the t—shirt. And they're giving you their lessons learned without requiring you to pay the fee in blood they had to in order to learn them. That is priceless." – **M. Guthrie**, Federal Air Marshal

Conflict and violence cover a broad range of behaviors, from intimidation to murder, and they require an equally broad range of responses. A kind word will not resolve all situations, nor will wristlocks, punches, or even a gun. Miller and Kane explain and demonstrate the full range of options, from skillfully doing nothing to applying deadly force. You will learn to understand the limits of each type of force, when specific levels may be appropriate, the circumstances under which you may have to apply them, and the potential cost of your decision, legally and personally. If you do not know how to succeed at all six levels, there are situations in which you will have no appropriate options. That tends to end badly. This DVD complements the book *Scaling Force*.